THE MERTON ANNUAL

Studies in Culture, Spirituality, and Social Concerns

Volume 25	2012

Edited by

David Joseph Belcastro   Joseph Quinn Raab

THE MERTON ANNUAL
Studies in Culture, Spirituality, and Social Concerns

THE MERTON ANNUAL publishes articles about Thomas Merton and about related matters of major concern to his life and work. Its purpose is to enhance Merton's reputation as a writer and monk, to continue to develop his message for our times, and to provide a regular outlet for substantial Merton-related scholarship. *THE MERTON ANNUAL* includes as regular features reviews, review-essays, a bibliographic survey, interviews, and first appearances of unpublished or obscurely published Merton materials, photographs, and art. Essays about related literary and spiritual matters will also be considered. Manuscripts and books for review may be sent to the editors.

EDITORS

David J. Belcastro
Dept. of Religion and Philosophy
Capital University
Bexley, OH 43209
mertonannual@gmail.com

Joseph Quinn Raab
Religious Studies Department
Siena Heights University
Adrian, MI 49221
mertonannual@gmail.com

Grateful acknowledgement is expressed to The Merton Legacy Trust and the Thomas Merton Center at Bellarmine University for permission to print "Some Points from the Birmingham Non-Violence Movement" and the calligraphy by Thomas Merton for the cover artwork.

PUBLISHED BY:
Fons Vitae
49 Mockingbird Valley Drive
Louisville, KY 40207
502.897.3641
Fonsvitaeky@aol.com
http://www.fonsvitae.com

SPONSORED BY:
International Thomas Merton Society
Thomas Merton Center
Bellarmine University
2001 Newburg Road
Louisville, KY 40205
502.272.8187 or 8177
merton@bellarmine.edu
http://www.merton.org/ITMS/

Further details about membership and subscribing to *The Merton Seasonal* and *The Merton Annual* are available at http://www.merton.org/ITMS/membership.aspx or by contacting the Thomas Merton Center at the above address.

For members of the International Thomas Merton Society, available for $15.00, plus shipping and handling. Individual copies are available through bookstores and directly from the publisher for $19.95. Institutions $39.95. *Copyright:* All rights reserved.

ISBN 978-1891785-634   ISSN 0894-4857

Printed in Canada

The Merton Annual

Volume 25	2012

David Joseph Belcastro
Introduction: The Ineffable Desert and the City
or What We Call Home   7

Thomas Merton
Some Points from the Birmingham Non-Violence Movement   13

Martin E. Marty
An Interview about Thomas Merton
Conducted by *Vaughn Fayle, OFM*
Edited by *Joseph Quinn Raab*   23

Patrick F. O'Connell
Pilgrimage, the Prophet, Persecutions and Perfume:
East with Ibn Battūta and Thomas Merton   30

Malgorzata Poks
With Malinowski in the Postmodern Desert:
Merton, Anthropology and the Ethnopoetics
of *The Geography of Lograire*   49

Hans Gustafson
Place, Spiritual Anthropology and Sacramentality
in Thomas Merton's Later Years   74

Christopher Pramuk
"The Street Is for Celebration": Racial Consciousness
and the Eclipse of Childhood in America's Cities   91

David Joseph Belcastro
Voices from the Desert: Merton, Camus and Milosz   104

John P. Collins
Two Antiheroes: Meursault and Binx Bolling
Viewed through Thomas Merton's Literary Imagination   113

Fiona Gardner
You Are You: That Is the Most Important Thing –
Everything Is in It Somewhere: An Analysis of the
Correspondence from Thomas Merton to John Harris   124

Robert Weldon Whalen
Thomas Merton and Hannah Arendt:
Desert and City in Cold-War Culture   132

Hyeokil Kwon
Is Desert Spirituality Viable in the Twenty-First-Century City?
The Legacy of the Desert Fathers in Thomas Merton   144

Nass Cannon
Stand on Your Own Feet! Thomas Merton
and the Monk without Vows or Walls   154

Joshua Hollmann
Searching for *Sophia*: Nicholas of Cusa and Thomas Merton   169

Daniel P. Horan, OFM
No Spouse Is an Island: Thomas Merton's Contribution
toward a Contemporary Spirituality of Marriage   177

Mary Murray McDonald
The Soul-Rich Monk/Priest: Thomas Merton on *Lectio Divina*   197

Joseph Quinn Raab
2011 Bibliographic Review:
Pointing Fingers at the Calm Eye of the Storm   205

Reviews

Victor A. Kramer
A Silent Action: Engagements with Thomas Merton
by Rowan Williams   217

Daniel P. Horan, OFM
Thomas Merton: Twentieth-Century Wisdom
for Twenty-First-Century Living by Paul R. Dekar   221

Ian Bell
Thomas Merton: Contemplation and Political Action
by Mario I. Aguilar   225

Fiona Gardner
The Wounded Heart of Thomas Merton by Robert Waldron   228

David Joseph Belcastro
Silence Speaks: Teilhard de Chardin, Yves Congar, John
Courtney Murray, and Thomas Merton by Robert Nugent   233

Robert Grip
Thomas Merton: A Spiritual Guide for the Twenty-First
Century [CDs] by Anthony Ciorra & *A Retreat with Thomas*
Merton [CDs] by Donald Goergen, OP   236

Patrick F. O'Connell
Catholicism: A Journey to the Heart of Faith
[book and DVDs] by Robert Barron   237

Kevin Griffith
Afternoons with Emily by Paul Quenon
Belonging to Borders: A Sojourn in the Celtic Tradition
by Bonnie Thurston   243

Contributors   246

Index   251

Index to *The Merton Annual*, Volumes 17-25   258

The International Thomas Merton Society   294

Introduction: The Ineffable Desert and the City or What We Call Home

David Joseph Belcastro

Yi-Fu Tuan's *Space and Place: The Perspective of Experience*[1] provides a vantage point from which to reflect on the theme of the last ITMS Conference in Chicago, entitled "With Roots in Eternity: Merton, the Desert and City," and the works presented in this volume of *The Merton Annual* that continue the inquiry initiated there. Yi-Fu Tuan, retired Professor of Geography at the University of Wisconsin-Madison, studied the ways in which people feel and think about their place in the universe. As reflected in the title of another of his books, *Cosmos and Hearth*,[2] Yi-Fu Tuan understood place as a constructed habitat within the vast space of the universe. Understanding city and desert in this manner locates the city *within* the expansive desert. Furthermore, it situates Merton on the boundary of desert and city with a clear outsider/insider view of human affairs. It is from here that he engaged his contemporaries in conversation. This was no easy task. Merton had to work long and hard to find his place in the world. His writings, photography and calligraphy were the tools with which he created a *palace of nowhere*[3] – an opening into the city for the infinite Source of Life to freely flow with grace and truth.[4]

With this in mind, the reader may choose to approach the publications in this volume with attention to the relationship of desert and city, the ways in which contemplation and action collaborate, and the emergence of new forms of monasticism that seek to engage the world today. In order to dig deeper into our theme, I would also like to mention in passing something noted by Czeslaw Milosz. After reading *The Sign of Jonas*, Milosz sent Merton a letter stating what he believed readers were hoping to find in his books.

---

1. Yi-Fu Tuan, *Space and Place: The Perspective of Experience* (Minneapolis: University of Minnesota Press, 1977).

2. Yi-Fu Tuan, *Cosmos and Hearth: A Cosmopolite's Viewpoint* (Minneapolis: University of Minnesota Press, 1996).

3. James Finley, *Merton's Palace of Nowhere: A Search for God through Awareness of the True Self* (Notre Dame: Ave Maria Press, 1978).

4. Merton's calligraphy on the cover for this volume of *The Merton Annual*, as Roger Lipsey explains, is a fine example of what is here being said. For other examples, see Lipsey's *Angelic Mistakes: The Art of Thomas Merton* (Boston: New Seeds, 2006).

I suppose I was waiting until the last page of your book for something which by definition had been excluded in advance, so I am very unjust but I have to tell you frankly that I did not read your book as one reads a story and in this I am in agreement with your real purpose. To put it in a naïve way: I waited for some answers to many theological questions but answers not abstract as in a theological treatise, just on that border between the intellect and our imagination, a border so rarely explored today in religious thinking: we lack an image of the world, ordered by religion, while Middle Ages had such an image. This was not the aim of your diary and I have no reason to demand from one book of yours what can be demanded from all your work. But a reader (I can judge by introspection only) is eager to learn (gradually) what is the image of the world in Thomas Merton. In a period when the image accepted by majority is clear: empty Sky, no pity, stone wasteland, life ended by death. I imagine a reader who says: he possessed a secret, he succeeded in solving the puzzle, his world is harmonious, yet in his diary he tells already about sequences while we would be ready to follow him in 5 volumes through a very vision of the world redeemed by Christ.[5]

The reader of this volume of *The Merton Annual* will be exploring the border between the intellect and imagination in Merton's work and therein discover not only Merton's vision of the world redeemed in Christ but also the location of his hermitage situated in the desert just beyond city limits.

Desert and City

The following four articles provide insights into Merton's inquiry into the relationship between desert and city. **Patrick O'Connell** and **Malgorzata Poks** present us with studies of the third canto in *The Geography of Lograire*. While O'Connell begins with "East with Ibn Battuta," Poks' article continues with "East with Malinowski." Readers will find both articles helpful in understanding and appreciating one of Merton's most complicated and demanding works. It is a work that draws our attention to the essential unity of humanity and the ways in which that unity has been and continues to be violated by assertions of cultural, moral and religious superiority by one group over another. This conflict is at the heart of Merton's understanding of the relationship between the monastic life of the desert and the commercial life of the city. O'Connell

---

5.Thomas Merton and Czeslaw Milosz, *Striving towards Being: The Letters of Thomas Merton and Czeslaw Milosz*, ed. Robert Faggen (New York: Farrar, Straus & Giroux, 1997) 61-62.

compares the memoirs of Ibn Battūta, a fourteenth-century North African Muslim traveler, with Merton's account of those travels in *The Geography of Lograrie*. He does so in such a way as to reveal humanity's propensity for self-glorification and exploitation that is not only contrary to monastic life but periodically undermines the very existence of monasteries and the contemplative life. Poks, after identifying Merton as a poet-ethnographer, situates him within modern anthropological studies. The private diary of Malinowski revealed and initiated the undoing of Western privileged perceptions of the rest of the world. As Poks skillfully explicates, Merton's use of that diary in his poem provided him the opportunity to deconstruct the mentality of the West and, as she points out, to deconstruct his own worldview that was likewise shaped in and by the West. As a monk living in the desert, he could see all worldviews, including his own, as constructed, limited and flawed, and therefore in need of continuous attention and revision in light of the limitless horizon that the desert provides.

Hans Gustafson focuses our attention on Merton's sacramental spirituality. More specifically, his article clarifies how the monastic life influenced Merton's sense of place. As reflected in much of Merton's work, the place that he sought was more interior than exterior. One might say that he sought a spacious place wherein his awareness of the sacredness of the world could become increasingly apparent. Tracing the trajectories of Merton's quest for self and place, Gustafson underscores Merton's longing for a "home" that lies beyond the city. This longing led the young monk on a lifelong and arduous pilgrimage to the desert. It is from here, however, in the desert, that Merton's prophetic vision of the world enabled him to see possibilities of new life in the city. That new life for Merton was always present. The fecundity of creation and history allowed for humanity's habitat to be daily restored in Christ. **Christopher Pramuk**'s interesting article continues this line of thought by harmonizing the voices of Stevie Wonder and Thomas Merton in such a way that "our imaginations [are opened] to the life-worlds of people and places well beyond our habitual comfort zones." While this article could have fit just as nicely in the next section, I placed it here because it hints at something important regarding the way in which Merton understood the relation between desert and city. Quoting Merton, Pramuk writes: "Most of us are congenitally unable to think black, and yet that is precisely what we must do before we can hope to understand the crisis in which we find ourselves." The monk who lives in the desert, beyond all the constructs of us and them, is the one who is most able to hear, understand and appreciate the voices of others – voices that must be included for the world to be redeemed in Christ.

Voices to and from the Desert

The following articles seek to clarify not only Merton's voice but also the voices of those close to Merton who also spoke from the desert to life in the city. We begin with the transcript of one of Merton's conferences titled "Some Points from the Birmingham Non-Violence Movement," presented in the summer of 1964. Merton begins his talk in the following way:

> Well, I've got some interesting stuff today, a little unusual, but I think you have to get something unusual once in a while to get a good sense of perspective as to what we're doing in the religious life and to see other people who have a dedicated approach and who get into things that require a great deal of virtue and perfection.

His reference to getting a good perspective on the purpose of the religious life fits well with what is being said here. The monastery provides an invaluable perspective on life. As we know, for Merton, the monastic life was not a rejection of the city but rather the discovery of the city as "billions of points of light coming together in the face and blaze of a sun that would make all the darkness and cruelty of life vanish completely."[6] Note that he includes here the necessity of becoming aware of those persons outside the monastery who are engaged in activities that he later says are most relevant to the work of monks.

> These things are relevant for us. The things that these people did, we should be doing. Not quite in the same way. We're not engaged in this kind of particular social action, but we should be in this with people who are going through this kind of thing.

He is, of course, talking about persons involved in the civil rights movement. Here we find Merton sharing voices from the city with those in the desert, as if to say, "This is a conversation in which we must participate." Merton's "Letters to a White Liberal"[7] does just that. The interview with **Dr. Martin E. Marty** allows us an occasion to hear how that conversation went. Initially Marty had serious reservations about "Letters to a White Liberal." He questioned whether a cloistered monk is able to speak out as Merton did on this and other social issues. Marty eventually came to the conclusion that Merton was not "very wrong."

As we know, this is not the only conversation Merton had with the

---

6. Thomas Merton, *Conjectures of a Guilty Bystander* (Garden City, NY: Doubleday, 1966) 142.

7. Thomas Merton, *Seeds of Destruction* (New York: Farrar, Straus & Giroux, 1964) 3-71.

world. The articles by **David Belcastro** and **John Collins** show how Merton moved beyond conversation with the world to collaboration with those who like himself lived on the margins of society. While Belcastro focuses on Merton's work with Czeslaw Milosz and Albert Camus, Collins draws our attention to Merton's work with Camus and Walker Percy. In each case, Merton addresses the problem of nihilism and meaninglessness that had become the plague of the world described by Milosz as "empty Sky, no pity, stone wasteland, life ended by death." And, as Collins points out, it is the literary imagination that is at work in the efforts of these writers to rediscover the interior life where the search for meaning is satisfied.

Fiona Gardner's and **Robert Weldon Whalen**'s articles add two more marginal voices. While Gardner opens the correspondence between Merton and John P. Harris, who was a liaison between Merton and Pasternak, Whalen compares and contrasts Merton's *Conjectures of a Guilty Bystander* with Hannah Arendt's *The Human Condition*. The correspondence with Harris reveals that Merton's conversations with the world were guided by compassion and the desire for something more than just communication. He sought, as Gardner points out, "deep communion with the recipient." On the other hand, Whalen's comparison of Merton and Arendt makes clear the seriousness with which Merton approached conversations regarding the critical problems of the modern world that placed humanity under the apocalyptic threat of an atomic war.

Desert Spirituality and Urban Life

The following articles explore ways in which the contemplative life of the desert may find expression in the city today. **Hyeokil Kwon** begins this section by asking if desert spirituality is possible in the city. The question emerged from his awareness that much of urban life today is organized in such a way to make prayer and contemplation difficult if not impossible. Drawing on Merton's interest in the Desert Fathers, Kwon identifies ways in which those of us who live in the city may nonetheless maintain a contemplative practice and thereby rediscover the interior life of compassion and wisdom. **Nass Cannon** continues with an article that explores desert spirituality that is possible beyond the external walls and internal structures of a monastery. Recalling the words of Trungpa Rimpoche quoted by Merton in his last talk, Cannon explores how everyone "from now on . . . stands on his own feet." By everyone, Cannon means both monks and laity, both those within and beyond monastic enclosures with attention to those participating in the New Monasticism, the New Friars and the invisible monks that go unnoticed. **Joshua Hollmann** then takes up the discussion with a consideration of one of the significant values of desert spirituality for today's world. Desert spirituality, now as in the past, moves beyond the boundaries of ecclesiastical structures and theological articulations and thereby provides the space needed for conversations between the religious traditions. It is also here that contemplatives discover that they have much more in common than what is commonly thought. **Mary McDonald**'s article shares with us her thoughts on an unpublished piece by Merton on *lectio divina* that opens up possibilities for interreligious reading of sacred texts and the enrichment of those who live within and outside the monastery. **Daniel Horan**'s article points out how desert spirituality is able to enrich life in the city in a way that would surprise many. The celibate monk may very well be the one to assist society in rediscovering the mystery, beauty and sacredness of married life. Caught as we are between puritans and pornographers who both believe that sex is dirty, the former prohibiting it and the latter in response to the prohibition creating an industry, Merton's vision is capable of restoring the sacramental nature of marriage:

> The act of sexual love should by its very nature be joyous, unconstrained, alive, leisurely, inventive, and full of a special delight which the lovers have learned by experience to create for one another. There is no more beautiful gift of God than the little secret world of creative love and expression in which two persons who have totally surrendered to each other manifest and celebrate their mutual gift. *It is precisely in this spirit of celebration, gratitude, and joy that true purity is found.* The pure heart is not one that is terrified of eros but one that, with the confidence and abandon of a child of God, accepts this gift as a sacred trust, for sex, too, is one of the talents which Christ has left us to trade with until He returns.[8]

Joseph Raab, co-editor of *The Merton Annual*, presents us with an excellent bibliographic review essay and a fine collection of book reviews, all of which indicate that the conversation between desert and city continues and, as Raab points out, is rich with "wisdom at play in the rain of words." Merton's lifelong effort to engage us in this conversation has greatly changed our lives and our thinking. Perhaps more importantly he has brought to our awareness that we too can dwell on the outskirts of the city, in the silence and solitude of our hearts that we too can call home.

---

8. Thomas Merton, *Love and Living*, ed. Naomi Burton Stone and Brother Patrick Hart (New York: Farrar, Straus, Giroux, 1979) 117-18.

Some Points from the Birmingham Non-Violence Movement

Thomas Merton

Abbey of Our Lady of Gethsemani, Trappist, Kentucky
June 10, 1964

The transcript of the conference reproduced here has been done with the minimum of editing so as to keep as closely as possible to Merton's spoken word while, however, omitting certain repeated words and phrases which were characteristic of Merton's lecturing style but which would have distracted from his overall message. These conferences involved a certain amount of dialogue with the novices Merton was teaching. As a rule Merton's questions to the novices are audible, but their replies are not. As with many of Merton's lectures at Gethsemani he ends abruptly when the monastery bell rings. Delivered in the sixties, in an all-male environment, Merton observed the linguistic conventions of his day in regard to gender. If Merton were writing today he would, no doubt, be using inclusive language. The inclusivity of his message in this lecture rises above the exclusivity of his language.

* * * * * * *

Well, I've got some interesting stuff today, a little unusual, but I think you have to get something unusual once in a while to get a good sense of perspective as to what we're doing in the religious life and to see other people who have a dedicated approach and who get into things that require a great deal of virtue and perfection. Last year this time in Birmingham, they had this terrific series of demonstrations. The Negroes were going out and they were getting attacked by police dogs and getting attacked by hoses. Of course, something like this had to be planned. This wasn't one of these things where everybody just decided they were going to go out and do it. It was planned very carefully beforehand. The people who were in this thing had to be trained. And they had to have a very definite idea of what they were going to do and they had to have very definite motives as to why they were doing it. And very clear ideas, basing their actions on definite principles and oriented in a certain way so that this would really be possible to do, and to do well.

So, anybody who wanted to get into this thing had to sign a pledge promising to carry out the following program. Of course, the idea of the program is to get them so that they've got this full grasp on what they're doing and so they're really going to be dedicated in this thing. So they promise to do these various things, to live in this way while carrying out these demonstrations. Now, just from the monastic point of view this is very interesting indeed.

What do you suppose they're going to have on this list of things? What kind of things do you expect to find? Take a few guesses. I think you probably aren't going to hit high enough. [*answer*: general humanism.] Well, what do you mean by general humanism? I promise to look at this from the general love of man, or something like this. In other words, there's going to be some love that's going to get in there. That's important. They're going to have to make this a question of love and not politics. That's extremely important. That's the basis, that's the cornerstone of the whole thing. It was not simply political action. It was religious action. It was spiritual and it was based on love.

Well now, supposing you are organizing this, how are you going to form people so that they're going to be able to go into a thing like this without too much fear and they're going to have to have some kind of a religious basis? What would we do? Supposing you're going to go out of here and you're going to walk down to New Haven or go down to the distillery here and protest against the way the distillery is making a mess out of the moral atmosphere of Nelson County or something like that. You know they're going to get you with a hose or something. So how do you steel yourself for this ordeal? In other words, you're bringing God into it and you want to get God into it as close as possible to you, so that you are in this with God and it isn't just a question of you going down there with a political gripe and you're going to start some action. You want to get God into this. That's another thing that they want to get.

Well, let me just read through this. These things are relevant for us. The things that these people did, we should be doing. Not quite in the same way. We're not engaged in this kind of particular social action, but we should be in this with people who are going through this kind of thing. If you stop and think, this time last year we were sitting here giving conferences and talking about spiritual effects, and while we were sitting here talking about this jazz, down South, probably about this time of day these things would be hottest; down South, people were being bitten by police dogs and thrown into jail and bowled over by fire hoses and everybody was saying that they were all criminals and this was very bad and it was undermining the American nation. And they're getting treated badly and they're accepting this treatment for the love of God, which is a big thing. So in other words, a real profound Christian activity was going on at this time. We're supposed to be united with people who do this sort of thing, so we should have in our hearts very much the same kind of ideals and outlook.

Let me read the thing and then we'll talk about it. So if you were going to go into this now, you would have to sign this: "I hereby pledge myself, my person and body, to the nonviolent movement. Therefore, I will keep the following ten commandments." And here are the things that they have to do:

"1. Meditate daily on the teachings and life of Jesus." See, so that right away they sign up for a daily meditation.

"2. Remember always that the nonviolent movement in Birmingham seeks justice and reconciliation not victory." This is putting it on a completely disinterested basis.

"3. To walk and talk in the manner of love, for God is love.

"4. Pray daily to be used by God in order that all men might be free." Now, look at that. That's a terrific statement. It isn't just a question of "pray that we may win," or something like that, but pray and that's a very personal thing.

"5. To sacrifice personal wishes in order that all men might be free.

"6. To observe with both friend and foe the ordinary rules of courtesy.

"7. To seek to perform regular service for others and for the world.

"8. To refrain from the violence of fists, tongue or heart.

"9. To strive to be in good spiritual and bodily health." This is a very important thing, too. Think of all these things in connection with this movement.

"10. To follow the directions of the movement and of the captain on a demonstration." That's where the obedience part comes in; it comes in at another place there above, too.

"I sign this pledge having seriously considered what I do and with the determination and will to persevere." And then you sign and you put the address of your nearest relative and their phone number so that if you get conked, why, they can come pick you up. And then it says: "Besides demonstrations I could also help the movement by: run errands, drive car, fix food for volunteers, clerical work, make phone calls, answer phones, mimeograph, type, print signs, and distribute leaflets." So, right away, you are in contact with real life. We get so much into the way of sitting around thinking about the spiritual life and occasionally we get up and do something but most of the time it's all up here. We're thinking about it all the time. We're reading about it and here are these people. This stuff had to be practical. They didn't just promise they were going to think about these points. They said they had to do them.

Well now, it seems to me that this is right up the alley for monks. I mean, this is a monastic program. These people were committed to a kind of monastic program in the civil rights movement. So, comment on that a little bit. What does this have in common with the monastic life here? Think of the different points. While you're thinking about it, think of some of the things we haven't thought of. What's one of the things here that we perhaps neglect? You've got to face the fact that a lot of the monks who have been around for a long time have become, so to speak, ossified as regards to the ordinary rules of courtesy. There is such a thing as some of the senior professed and so forth who just don't see novices. Well, this is a pity but it's not their fault. They've lost interest in novices and I don't see particularly why they should be terribly excited when they see you coming along but still they should. It would be nice, but you've got to face the fact that a lot of them [have] kind of just lost the habit of paying too much attention when you go by. It's true. What's the purpose of this? Think of the context, please – "Observe with friend and foe the ordinary rules of courtesy." What's the situation where this is going to arise for these people? When they're getting clubbed and they've got to observe ordinary rules of courtesy when they're being hit over the head. This is not too easy. It should be relatively easy. It should be relatively easy around here to observe ordinary rules of courtesy when nobody's hitting you over the head. This is a program of heroism. The people who signed up and followed this out had to act heroically. A person who would sign up on something like this and carry it out for fully Catholic motives and hang on with the thing would be canonized. You're canonizable if you do this. Here you've got people who did it in ordinary everyday life and people also got killed for doing it – not too many but some – and children, six-year-old kids.

So anyway, the first thing is it's based on meditation. We meditate. There's no problem about that, except it has its own problems. They meditate on the teachings and the life of Jesus. That's their first point. Everything starts with that. So that means to say that the thing is a basically Christian program. It's a fundamentally Christian program meditating on Our Lord. We've got only one source of strength and this whole thing is based on the theological principle: you've got no strength except from God and from Our Lord, and you can't do these things without Him. These people are putting themselves into this position because they feel that Our Lord wants this of them and that He's going to give them the strength to do it, and down here it says: "To pray daily to be used by God." Now look at the ideal of that. That's the ideal of the religious life. A religious is a person who prays to be used by God, who wants to be used by God. Now, what does that imply? What's that got to do with our vow of obedience, for example? Is there any connection between this and religious obedience? Does there seem to be any? If I ask God to use me, how's He going to use me? How's He going to make known the ways in which He uses me? through superiors, through obedience? Of course, in this particular case, they don't have a vow of obedience, but still, if I'm asking God to use me, I'm saying, "Alright, I've put myself in Your hands, now use me." And then, I say this understanding that it's not going to be done through the means of an angel. It isn't going to be an angel [who] is going to appear in the Father Master's room and say, "Now, you've got to give this conference today," or something like that. It comes through superiors. The superior appoints you to this job or the superior gives you this thing to do or you're sent to this work, or circumstances arise and this is demanded. So if we pray God to use us, it means that we're going to remain open when He starts using us and sometimes we forget. We ask God to use us, and then all of the sudden, it's nice in the morning meditation, we've asked God to use us and so forth and all of the sudden someone comes up and says, "Hey, wash the dishes." "But it's not my turn to wash the dishes. I'm off this week," or something like that.

There is such a thing as what they call an examen of prevision which I don't recommend. I don't recommend all these stereotype methods and so forth, but there is such a thing. Look, we're here to be used by God. We've given ourselves to God, therefore He's going to use us for something or other, so it doesn't hurt to look ahead a little bit and say, "Well now, I've asked Him to use me. What's likely to happen today so that I won't miss?" What is coming up today and so forth? What are going to be the possible indications of His will? And then, of course, I'm going to be ready always for indications that I haven't expected because there are always going to be unexpected things. They're going out looking for it. That should be the monastic idea. Of course, actually, in a community, when you've got a well-run community, there isn't exactly an awful lot. If you run a foundation, there would be more. That's one of the things about a foundation. If you're in a community like this it's understood that most of it goes like clockwork. It's kind of automatic because it's a big community and everything is set up but, nevertheless, you're liable to be called upon to be used and if you're living the kind of life [of] a dedicated person around here, you're going to be used. And you want to look out sometimes that you don't stick your neck into too many things because that can happen, too. But if you're dedicated at all, you're going to be used, in some way or other. If you ask God to use you, He'll use you. There's no question about that. The only thing is, don't start asking if you don't mean it. If you want to be used, ask. If you don't want to be used, well stay out of it until you can get at it really from your own heart.

What about this second point of "remembering always that the nonviolent movement in Birmingham seeks justice and reconciliation, not victory"? What's that got to do with the monastic life? Has this got anything to do with our kind of monastic spirituality? [*inaudible*] Not looking for a personal gain, definitely, and of course, especially, the thing I'm emphasizing is this idea of remembering. Remember what you're here for. Remember what you're doing. Now this is a very important psychological and spiritual point that they bring up here, 'cause when you're in a thing like this, you get into something; remember what you're doing. So, remember your aim and you've got to have an aim and keep   ·
it in mind and of course the aim [is] not a selfish aim. You have to re-member that your aim is not for yourself. "We're not in this," they say, "for ourselves." This isn't just to win. This isn't just to defeat these other people. It's to seek justice and reconciliation because this is good for everybody.

Of course, this is the basic principle that you get in Pope John's *Pacem in Terris*. He's saying that the world problems have to be settled by people who are willing to seek justice and seek reconciliation and unity on a higher plane and not just be seeking that our side's going to win. We've got to defend ourselves against evil and all that sort of thing but on the higher plane we have to seek unity and reconciliation and universal justice.

So, well now, we should be in this. We should be in this. Here's an aim that isn't just something for these individuals. It's for everybody. These people are in this for everybody. They want everybody to have what's coming to them – justice. Okay, we should be thinking of that. Are there any other points that have struck anybody here particularly? Well, you've got this idea, for example, "sacrifice personal wishes in order that all men might be free." See, this is kind of a corollary for this business of being used. This is basically monastic. What are we in the monastery for? We're here to give up our wishes for the good of others, for the good of all men. It's sacrificing our way, our desires and so forth, in order that all men might be free. And you see they say all men. This is just Birmingham but they're thinking of everybody, thinking of the whole world. That, of course, gives you a powerful motive.

What happened in Birmingham? What actually was gained in Birmingham, really? What came of it? [*inaudible*] What did they actually get out of it? They got that agreement that a lot of things were supposed to be integrated. They haven't been. Materially speaking, they got very little out of it. But they got a great deal out of it, from two points of view. First of all, it was a great moral victory because it made the real meaning come out in the open. Hitherto, what had happened would be one Negro would get taken in jail and beat up and nobody [would] ever hear about it, and another one would get beat up and nobody would ever hear about that either. It's all in this, isolated, but nobody said anything about it. Now, these people in the thousands went out and stuck their necks out and for about a week the police tried to be nonviolent about it and finally they got out the police dogs and then it was all over the country. And it was absolutely clear and everybody saw it. Since that, the whole situation is different. And this had a big effect on a lot of white people in the South, too. It couldn't help but.

But the other main thing that it had was that it gave the Negroes this realization that they're important, the realization that they can come out and do something and it means something – that when they get out there and do something it has a meaning and it had a meaning for everybody and this is tremendously important, this having been done. Once this corner's been turned, it's never going to be the same again because now you've got the Negroes in this country [who] are aware of the fact that they mean something and that what they do cuts ice all over the world.

So, that's another thing. So, if a person has the conviction that when he's sacrificing his own wishes, this can have meaning for everybody in the world, this could have meaning for somebody in Africa and for somebody in China, and so forth, well then, he's doing this in a totally different way than if he just believes, "Well I do it because I got to do it." So, therefore, [the] conclusion for us is to renew in ourselves this kind of motive because this can sort of get lost in a monastic life – you know, the kind of a feeling that "well, it's all a very nice thing. Somebody preaches a sermon about it and it sounds great but, really, does it mean anything? Are the sacrifices that I make of my own wishes, are they really meaningful?" Seeking "to perform regular service for others and for the world" – again, you've got this worldwide aspect. These people have the courage to say, "What I am doing, the little act of service that I do, isn't just for these people, it's for the world." Again, this is most important for the monastic life. See, this is monastic spirituality. That's one thing that keeps a monk going, the realization that the service that he performs isn't just something to make himself look like a good monk in the community. This is a real service. This is my contribution to the human race. And again, we have to feel this.

See, all this is so important just from the ordinary psychological point of view. If you stop and think, when things get bogged down with us, we feel that, what's the meaning of it all? And what am I here for? And I'm wasting my time and that kind of thing. What it usually amounts to is that you've lost the sense that it can mean anything to anybody else. And then, of course, it gets to be individualistic. Finally it gets watered further and further down. You get down to the point of, "What am I getting out of it from the point of view of perfection? And what's the merit that I'm getting out of it?" Then finally, after that, you cease to be interested in the merit and you're looking for what's the immediate, how do I cash in on this here and now?

If I work in the refectory, well maybe I'll be able to get a glass of milk on the side, or something like that. When it gets down that far, it's really gone too far. When it's way down to that level, you're in trouble. You ought to start getting back up because there it's necessary to get this realization that what I do has a real meaning for the world.

Now, get this one too. What does this got to do with us? "To refrain from the violence of fist, tongue or heart." Well, there's not much violence of fist in the monastery but there can be. There has been in the past. It's possible. What strikes you as particularly useful for us? [*inaudible*]. "Violence of the heart." You see, this we don't bother with too much. I think there's a fair amount of it in the monastery. Tongue, well, usually we don't. That can happen. Violence of the tongue can burst out every once in a while, and so forth. Even in choir that has happened. No reference to any recent history, but I know in the past somebody in choir was telling his neighbor a few things about what he was going to do to him if he didn't shut up and so forth. So this can happen. Violence of the tongue can crop up in the monastic life; but especially violence of the heart, and this is very important; it's a real obligation for us. If we're looking for perfection and we're thinking about these things and we're thinking about these people who have to face this sort of thing, we can contribute something to this whole business of peace in the world by working very hard to be nonviolent in our hearts, and that is to say, not having aggressive thoughts about people. Now, that calls for really a whole conference actually. Because what does it mean? It means to say you've got to give this a little thought. How are we aggressive towards people? What is the violence that we have in our hearts? It isn't just necessarily cussing him up and down or anything like that. What are some of the standard forms of violence that we don't recognize as violence and that are violence of the heart, really? [*inaudible*] Well, it's rejecting. See, rejection is a form of violence. I mean to simply out-of-hand reject the person or even reject it before he says it, before he proposes it – "no." The answer's going to be "no" because it comes from this fellow. Or, especially, taking him apart – really, just systematically, everything he does: "That's wrong. That's wrong. Look, he did it that way, and so forth." See, this is a form of violence. This is a form of aggression on the person – in a certain sense, destroying his works. You can destroy what he does mentally. He gets up to sing. You say, "Ah, he's flat." He goes to do something. "He always does it the wrong way. Why does he do it that way? That's not the way it's supposed to be done," and so forth. You take him apart. So, in your mind, what has happened is that if your mind were the whole world and if you were God, by the time that poor guy got through there wouldn't be anything left. You would have completely destroyed the man. You have mentally destroyed the person. So, I would say this is a tremendously important thing: to learn not to be destroying people in our hearts; not to be taking them apart so that when we're though with them there's just nothing left. And this is something as monks, we should know. You don't expect people outside to think about this too much, although they probably think about this more than we do. But as monks this should be part of the program.

And then, finally, "strive to be in good spiritual and bodily health." Now, what's that got to do with anything? Is that important for the monastery? Why would you say that's important in the monastic life? What's the good of that? Has this got any reference; is it just a counsel for yourself, or what? [*inaudible*] You owe it to other people. You owe it to other people to be functioning properly if you can. If you're not functioning properly, somebody else is going to have to carry you. It's a question of both spiritual and bodily. They go together. It doesn't mean to say, you've got to be constantly worrying about your health or anything like that, but you've got to keep yourself in trim because you've got your job to do and if you don't do it somebody else is going to have to do it. Now, we're getting to the point where you begin to realize that. During the old days if somebody didn't show up for the dishwashing it didn't make too much difference. But now, if somebody's missing, nobody eats. So, it's getting to the point where we have to be able to handle the thing. You've got to be there and we've got to be in good spiritual health. That means, especially, I think we've got an obligation to the community to keep ourselves in trim from the point of view of morale – from the point of view of keeping up our spirits a little bit. We don't have to be corny about it, but there is such a thing as keeping ourselves a little bit on a more-or-less happy level. We have to keep ourselves a bit happy. You can't keep yourself totally happy; it's impossible. But if a person's morale is down and he's dragging around in the community, what happens? Again, he's got to be carried. Other people are going to have to put up with this. If a person is constantly down and constantly griping and constantly with a long face and so forth, if a person is constantly down like that, it's going to be a drag on everybody and everybody has to bear up with it and it's a weight on everybody. So, you see that something can be learned from these wicked people out in the world after all.

An Interview about Thomas Merton
with Dr. Martin E. Marty

Conducted by Vaughn Fayle, OFM
Edited by Joseph Quinn Raab

In 1964 Dr. Martin Marty published his *Varieties of Unbelief* (New York: Holt, Rinehart & Winston) and Thomas Merton published *Seeds of Destruction* (New York: Farrar, Straus and Giroux). Marty was meditating on the ways in which Christianity in America was itself becoming secularized and mutating into a kind of mythology at the service of patriotic nationalism and a justification for material privilege. Merton's book was prophetic in a slightly different vein; the monk was warning America that it was heading toward more violence and destruction. Merton argued that in spite of all the sincerity of white liberals in America, they would not be able to solve the "black problem" because they were part of the system, which itself was problematic. True liberation for blacks would require some destruction of institutionalized racism, a systemic evil, and this process would not be pleasant or pretty.

Merton reviewed Marty's book in *Commonweal* the very same week that Marty had reviewed Merton's book for the *New York Herald Tribune*, and as Marty later wrote to Merton "it turned out that you liked mine and I did not like yours."[1] In short, Marty had found Merton's "Letters to a White Liberal" too apocalyptic, too alarmist, too pessimistic. Events that followed, especially the riots in Newark and Detroit, caused Marty to revisit Merton's *Seeds of Destruction* and to see it in light of those events as being hauntingly accurate. In the August 30, 1968 issue of *The National Catholic Reporter*, Marty published an open letter to Merton, a public acknowledgment that Merton had indeed been "telling it as it is." The two expressed their mutual respect through a brief correspondence that followed.

In June 2010, Fr. Vaughn Fayle, OFM had the opportunity to interview Dr. Marty about his relationship with Thomas Merton. The interview was video-recorded by Michael Brennan, Director of the Chicago Chapter of the International Thomas Merton Society. The transcription of the interview that follows is an abridged version of the whole. It captures the

---

1. The reviews appeared in January, 1965, but Marty's comment that "I did not like yours" comes from his letter to Merton published in the *National Catholic Reporter*, August 30, 1968.

heart of the interview but some sections have been omitted. The entire interview is available in the archives at the Thomas Merton Center at Bellarmine University, Louisville, KY.

* * * * * * *

Vaughn Fayle: We are trying to do an ethnography of sorts and capture testimonies from people who were influenced by Thomas Merton in some way.

Martin Marty: I did a book of five hundred years of American History in 500 pages and it ends with Merton.[2]

VF: What was your impression of Catholicism as someone raised and schooled in the Lutheran faith, in the forties, fifties and sixties?

MM: I grew up in a little town in Nebraska which was exactly half-Catholic and half-Lutheran and we had good relations. It was a mysteriously different world; there were Czech Catholics and German Lutherans. Fr. Boesak would come by every now and then and meet with Pastor Oelschlaeger. We were good friends – my best friends were Catholic – but it never occurred to me until years later, when *U.S. Catholic* asked me to reminisce about it, that I had never been in any of their homes or vice versa. The great fear was inter-marriage. Everything else was fine. We played good basketball against each other.

Carrying that on, I went to what Catholics would call a minor seminary, a *Gymnasium* in the German style in Milwaukee – it combined boarding high school and junior college – and there my roommate, who was actually the first husband of my second wife – he died young, but he was a genius – and he and I started exploring and got to know Tom Stransky, CSP, who was much later to become head of the Paulists. Still later, at Vatican II, in the press conferences I would look at Tom and he would look at me with an "I know you, I know you" but we couldn't think of how. Then one day he resolved it: we remembered that he and his partner Tom Ziebarth had defeated us in the Midwest Debating championships, and you never forget who defeated you. That was a breakthrough because in those early years we became friends and worked with Junior Achievement and started a little newspaper together, and in cases like that the line was eroding a bit.

For me the beginning of the breakthrough was when I attended a very conservative Missouri Lutheran seminary in St. Louis and through

---

2. Martin E. Marty, *Pilgrims in Their Own Land: 500 Years of Religion in America* (Boston, Little, Brown, 1984).

artist Siegfried Reinhardt I met Water Ong, SJ and that was a total break-through.

VF: Had he started his work on *Orality*[3] at that point?

MM: I'm not sure, but you get the beginnings of it; he was interested in everything, whether it was drumbeats in Africa or whatever – his imagination was so rich. He was Catholic to the core, but never was that a barrier. He taught us that "catholic" is usually defined as "universal" geographically, but *kata holos* was the important thing – meaning it penetrates the "the whole" of the culture. He had a couple of books, one of them being *Frontiers in American Catholicism*.[4] By that time – it was 1952 when I graduated and was ordained – there were occasional Jesuit lecturers on campus, in events which had been unheard of even ten years earlier. But still the line wasn't completely broken until John XXIII and the Second Vatican Council.

VF: You were at the third session of the council, one of the very few representing the whole of the Protestant world.

MM: It was great being a Protestant at the council – I put on seventeen pounds! Every religious order wanted us to try out their chef.

VF: Do you happen to remember Archbishop Denis Hurley from South Africa? I think he was the youngest bishop at the Council.

MM: Yes. Decades later, the year before apartheid ended, I taught for six weeks at the University of Cape Town in South Africa and Archbishop Hurley was *huge* at that time. I did not meet Tutu at that time, but the leadership at the university was quite ecumenical.

VF: Back to the fifties then – this was a time when ecumenical and racial issues were at the fore . . .

MM: Well by 1954 with the U.S. Supreme Court decision *Brown vs. Board of Education* everything began to change significantly. There were not that many black Catholics in my circle, but whenever we would do a ride, like the March at Selma, we would always play a game on the bus – black, white, Catholic, Jew, agnostic – why are we all there? We would all go around and tell our stories and we would learn from each other and that was a deep bonding. I'll tell you one last thing – it may

---

3. Walter J. Ong, *Orality and Literacy: The Technologizing of the Word* (New York: Methuen, 1982).

4. Walter J. Ong, *Frontiers in American Catholicism* (New York: Macmillan, 1957).

not be good for ethnography but I can say it – we were scared, we were crossing Edmund Pettus bridge and you could see a line of cops there who wouldn't let us through, so we had a prayer there. There is a picture taken of me on that scene – trembling – next to Fr. Joseph Fichter, SJ from the department of sociology at Loyola University New Orleans, a hearty and husky guy, and years later I said to him, "I was so glad you were there because I was so scared, physically scared." He said "*You* were scared? I *shat green* I was so scared!"

Now these are the years when Merton is getting noticed on the social action front as his influence was already affecting monastic vocations.

VF: Let me ask you, what was the common Protestant attitude in America about monasticism, and monastic orders such as the Trappists, at that time?

MM: I don't think the average non-Catholic knew the difference between a diocesan priest and a person in a religious order. We knew about the sisters. They saved my father's life when he was in the hospital. He had peritonitis before penicillin and they tended him for ten days and managed to pull him through. Still when I go back to that little town I look up the sisters. There was also a Benedictine monastery, Elkhorn. There was no hostility, just unawareness about these people. But after the council every religious order was supposed to have a non-Catholic on their study group. In December of 1968 I was in Dubuque at the Trappist monastery for one of the groups; it was a snowy night, as quiet as can be, and I was busy reviewing a fat book on pacifism for *The New York Times*. I turned on a Dubuque station and heard that Thomas Merton had died. I think it was the same day that the greatest Protestant theologian of the era, Karl Barth, had died.

VF: Had you read much by Merton just casually other than the book you reviewed?

MM: Well everybody read *The Seven Storey Mountain* – everybody read that. Thanks to Robert Lax and Giroux, I was reading other things coming out, not so much the poetry, but mostly his prose writings.

VF: And, of course, *Seeds of Destruction*, which you reviewed and in which Merton raised concerns about the position of the white liberal, and you had responded that we didn't really need a white James Baldwin in a sense. You seemed to perceive it as an attack on the white Protestant liberal social engagement . . .

MM: It wasn't an attack on just Protestant liberals – it was on liberals,

Catholic liberal, Protestant liberal, it didn't matter. I was a liberal but very much for the peaceful side of things. And not all liberals were for the peaceful side; the line was very thin. In 1967 when Israel was attacked, immediately there was pressure, for example, to sign a petition saying the U.S. should defend Israel *no matter what*, and some did – Abraham Joshua Heschel, for example, did, and noted Presbyterian theologian and activist Robert McAfee Brown puzzled over it, I can remember. Here was the issue: we had just begun to make the point for peace in Vietnam and some of the first people to call for military response on the Israel front were liberals. And Merton, though *Seeds of Destruction* didn't call for violence, was right up to the edge with what he was saying on the race front. My question and those of us at *The Christian Century* was about the paradox of his being a cloistered monk speaking out in such polemical terms on the issue –we wondered if he really had the vision for it. We were on the ground so to speak. Marching was the beginning of it, but peace people like Jim Forest, Dorothy Day, the Berrigans, pushed things right to the edge. We at *The Christian Century* began thinking, "Where do we go now?" and Merton [in *Seeds of Destruction*] envisions a virtual holocaust, smoke from the camps, and for these reasons and their implications I criticized him. But the reason I wrote that somewhat famous letter a few years later was just to say "the way things turned out, he wasn't very wrong."

VF: Yes, you wrote, "I have been meaning to write for the past three years" and presumably those were very important years; all the chickens had come home to roost, and now you were almost saying that Merton was prescient.

MM: Yes, and we saw this more later, with respect to peace rallies than with race marches. It became clear later, due to the Freedom of Information Act, etc. . . . that the FBI and other government people were sometimes acting as *provocateurs.* We would be attending a peaceful rally and suddenly it would become boisterous, and we couldn't figure it out. Nobody coming to it was being boisterous and suddenly it erupted that way, and I think that's what we had not foreseen but Merton had foreseen.

VF: I'd like to explore this tension Merton talks about between "a police state" on the one hand which is easy to oppose, and this "un-Christian American Christianity" which sort of develops a theology of patriotism that denatures the gospel. He was very concerned about the latter because it's not so easy to see.

MM: Well, I think he was looking ahead. This all came to fruit in the

Vietnam protests, because then one after another – I think I have fifty books downstairs, I probably wrote several of them myself, on the end of American imperialism and criticizing this conflation of Christianity with American nationalism. What hadn't happened then yet was the rise of the Christian Right which seized all of these symbols. At first it was in the South, but it wasn't just the South; soon it went national.

VF: Where do you think we are now with race issues, now after the election of President Obama? Have we turned the corner?

MM: I think theologically we have turned the corner and among the elites it doesn't even arise as an issue. But you do have the rise of the Tea Party and that is racist to the core, no way around it, so it's not all behind us, and it still erupts and comes out in disguised forms.

VF: Merton and many others were concerned about the institutional level of embedded racism. Do you think on the institutional or cultural level we have turned the corner?

MM: We are in the thick of it. I gave a talk recently at DePaul University entitled ". . . Because I Am a Citizen." I got the title from an interview I had heard with a doctor who provides free medical services in his retirement and when he was asked why he does that he said, "because I am a citizen." So in the talk I looked at local, national and world citizenship. I contrasted this against Marx, not Karl but Groucho, who said "take care of me – I'm all I've got." This is where your question comes in. This is what we are up against. We have got a lot of this idea running around here. If the Tea Party were even a party I could handle it, but it is really anarchist (they don't know that), they are just *anti*-government, anti-everything. They have this notion that nothing good can come of it. Now being a citizen doesn't mean surrendering the right to criticize. Rather that is part of it. But we need good government and good citizenship.

VF: It is ironic because you have the Tea Party and the many movements that will surely come after it and these often appeal to people who have an anti-institutional bent. Merton, ironically, attracts many spiritual seekers who are disaffected with institutional religion, those who feel distant from organized religion, those who feel more "spiritual" than "religious," but he was a Catholic monk.

MM: Well yes, that is the attitude – anti-government, anti-institution, anti-organized religion; get rid of it all and get something new. But the one that's relevant here is religion, and I've always argued that Merton, the mediaeval mystics and others, they will be contemplative, they will be in hermitages, but they are *not* making up a new religion. They are living off of the prayers of the community, they are doing what the ancient prophets did, and they stand inside the tradition. They are doing what Paul Tillich said was the Protestant principle; they take the tradition and *turn it over*. I don't think you could ever understand Merton without seeing the way in which "the body of Christ," if not "the institution," is necessary for achieving wisdom.

VF: I recently heard Huston Smith criticizing those who prefer a generic spirituality over traditional religion because he said, whenever there is a crisis, "I see the Methodists, the Catholics, the Lutherans there doing something good; you do not see an abstract spirituality in action." Do you think Huston was on to something?

MM: Yes, I am very much with him. I always say that I like spirituality with adjectives, medieval, monastic, feminist, black. I don't care but if it has an adjective then you have a resource, a repository, a norm for judging. Many graduate students today doing work in spirituality are going back to Julian of Norwich, Mechtild of Magdeburg, each serving as *ressourcement*, because they see the problems with an ungrounded "spirituality."

VF: Many who appreciate Merton worry that his voice is now limited to being heard in a few courses offered at Catholic colleges, that his influence is waning. Where does Merton fit in the imagination of young people today?

MM: The first thing with any great person, and I can say we are talking about a great person, is the generation after him has to kick over the traces, like with Albert Schweitzer, Karl Rahner and Hans Urs Von Balthasar. Then you start selective retrieval. You take those things that were half-finished and you have that younger generation work out the implications.

VF: Some within the Church, even in high levels, think Merton is passé; that he is problematic, and we should ignore him. What is your impression?

MM: Come back in twenty years and see who is remembered! Of course this is the yin/yang, there will always be conflicting interpretations, but *a dismissal* of him would be absurd.

Pilgrimage, the Prophet, Persecutions and Perfume: East with Ibn Battūta and Thomas Merton

Patrick F. O'Connell

Just before leaving for Asia in September 1968, Thomas Merton sent his friend and publisher James Laughlin of New Directions the manuscript of his eighth volume of verse, the book-length sequence entitled *The Geography of Lograire*,[1] which appeared posthumously in 1969, the year after his death.[2] Merton himself describes the work in his introduc-

---

1. Thomas Merton, *The Geography of Lograire* (New York: New Directions, 1969) (subsequent references will be cited as "*GL*" parenthetically in the text); also included in Thomas Merton, *The Collected Poems of Thomas Merton* (New York: New Directions, 1977) 455-609 (subsequent references will be cited as "*CP*" parenthetically in the text). For a general overview, see Patrick F. O'Connell, "*The Geography of Lograire*," in William H. Shannon, Christine M. Bochen and Patrick F. O'Connell, *The Thomas Merton Encyclopedia* (Maryknoll, NY: Orbis, 2002) 169-74. Significant general studies include: James York Glimm, "Thomas Merton's Last Poem: *The Geography of Lograire*," *Renascence* 26.2 (Winter 1974) 95-104; George Kilcourse, *Ace of Freedoms: Thomas Merton's Christ* (Notre Dame, IN: University of Notre Dame Press, 1993) 184-95; Victor A. Kramer, "Thomas Merton's *The Geography of Lograire*: An Introspective Journey," *Exploration* 5.1 (1977) 15-27; Ross Labrie, *The Art of Thomas Merton* (Fort Worth: Texas Christian University Press, 1979) 147-67; Thérèse Lentfoehr, *Words and Silence: On the Poetry of Thomas Merton* (New York: New Directions, 1979) 115-34; Anthony T. Padovano, *The Human Journey: Thomas Merton, Symbol of a Century* (Garden City, NY: Doubleday, 1982) 136-65; Paul M. Pearson, "*The Geography of Lograire*: Merton's Final Prophetic Vision," *Thomas Merton: Poet, Monk, Prophet*, ed. Paul M. Pearson, Danny Sullivan and Ian Thomson (Abergavenny, Monmouthshire: Three Peaks Press, 1998) 80-94; Virginia F. Randall, "Contrapuntal Irony and Theme in Thomas Merton's *The Geography of Lograire*," *Renascence* 28.4 (Summer 1976) 191-202; Virginia F. Randall, "The Mandala as Structure in Thomas Merton's *The Geography of Lograire*," *Notre Dame English Journal* 11.1 (October 1978) 1-14; Bradford T. Stull, "Poetic Rhetoric and Baffling Illogic: Thomas Merton's *The Geography of Lograire*," *Religious Dialectics of Pain and Imagination* (Albany: State University of New York Press, 1994) 61-89; Walter Sutton, "Thomas Merton and the American Epic Tradition: The Last Poems," *Contemporary Literature* 14.1 (Winter 1973) 49-57. Malgorzata Poks' brilliant, theoretically sophisticated studies of the poem have brought a new depth of analysis to *Lograire*: see "*The Geography of Lograire* as Merton's *Gestus* – Prolegomena," *The Merton Annual* 22 (2009) 150-69, and "With Malinowski in the Postmodern Desert: Merton, Anthropology and the Ethnopoetics of *The Geography of Lograire*" immediately following in the present volume.

2. See the letter of September 9, 1968, the day before Merton left Kentucky for Arizona, Alaska, the west coast and Asia, in Thomas Merton and James Laughlin, *Selected Letters*, ed. David D. Cooper (New York: Norton, 1997) 357-58; while *The Geography*

tory "Author's Note" as "this wide-angle mosaic of poems and dreams [in which] I have without scruple mixed what is my own experience with what is almost everybody else's" (*GL* 1; *CP* 457). Its theme is both the global unity of humanity and the ways in which that unity has been violated, particularly by Western assertions of cultural and moral superiority. While Merton claims that the individual poems that make up the work "are never explicitly theological or even metaphysical" and that his methodology is "on the whole that of an urbane structuralism" (*GL* 2; *CP* 458), the spiritual implications of the work are never far beneath the surface, and the objective detachment implied by the phrase "urbane structuralism" in actuality masks a focused if largely unarticulated outrage at the dehumanization described repeatedly throughout the volume. The work is divided into four cantos based on the four compass points, preceded by a Prologue. Each of the cantos is subdivided into individual poems or sections, many of which depend closely on the historical and anthropological sources that Merton consulted. Because of the relative unfamiliarity of the incidents and movements described, the frequent lack of explicit comment on the material that is quoted and rearranged, and the obscurity of some of the more personal sections, this book probably makes greater demands on the reader than any other of Merton's works, whether poetry or prose. But its basic insight is clear: a failure to recognize, respect and foster the human dignity of every person leads not only to an estrangement from others but to an alienation from one's own most fundamental identity as an image of God.

The third, "East" canto of *Lograire* opens with a section entitled "East with Ibn Battuta," a series of seven excerpts, all but one reworked into verse, from the *Rihla*, the extensive memoirs of the fourteenth-century North African Muslim traveler Abu 'Abdallah Muhammad Ibn Battūta.[3]

---

of Lograire is often referred to as unfinished, since in his "Author's Note" Merton had called it "a purely tentative first draft of a longer work in progress, in which there are, necessarily, many gaps" (*GL* 1; *CP* 457), in this letter Merton writes: "This is the 'first draft' of *Lograire* but actually, glancing over it, I think it is about complete. I will certainly want to read it over carefully and perhaps make a few changes and slight additions, but I think as it stands it is as it should be." Two days later, in a note to Laughlin written on the plane, Merton reiterates: "About *Geography*: let me know if you think it is good just as it stands. Monkeying with it (except for a few minor changes and additions) might spoil it now – don't you think?" (359).

3. Ibn Battúta, *Travels in Asia and Africa: 1325-1354*, trans. H. A. R. Gibb (New York: Robert M. McBride & Co., 1929); subsequent references will be cited as "Ibn Battúta, *Travels*" parenthetically in the text. This is an abridged version of the work. Gibb later published three fully annotated volumes of a projected complete translation for the Hakluyt Society (up through Ibn Battūta's service to the Sultan of Delhi and appointment

Merton's evident attraction to Ibn Baṭṭūṭa's narrative lies at least in part in his largely straightforward, uncomplicated perspective on what he observes and experiences. Through selection, arrangement and subtle modification of the details of various incidents from Ibn Baṭṭūṭa's travels, Merton is able to construct a "slide show" of some high points of Ibn Baṭṭūṭa's experiences that is more complex and more revelatory than the narrator himself realizes, yet without violating the integrity of that narrator's voice and perspective. Merton makes use of only a tiny fraction, of course, of his source, but his choice of incidents provides both a sense of Ibn Baṭṭūṭa's geographical and temporal progress and an overview of the world of "the East" through the eyes of an observer who is conventionally pious but not particularly profound, observant but not remarkably reflective.[4] Ibn Baṭṭūṭa as "channeled" by Merton allows room for arriving at insights that he has not himself discovered, and so contributes to the pattern and theme of the work as a whole in ways that a writer of greater wisdom or more acute intellect might not have done.

Ibn Baṭṭūṭa[5] was born in Tangier in 1304 of a Berber family that had

---

as envoy to China); the edition was completed with a fourth volume plus a book-length index after Gibb's death by Charles Beckingham: *The Travels of Ibn Baṭṭūṭa – A.D. 1325-1354*, 5 vols., trans. and ed. H. A. R. Gibb and C. F. Beckingham (Cambridge: Cambridge University Press, 1958-2000); subsequent references will be cited as "Ibn Baṭṭūṭa, *Travels* [2]" parenthetically in the text.

4. It is instructive to compare Ibn Baṭṭūṭa with his younger contemporary, the Sufi master Ibn 'Abbād of Ronda (1332-1390), who also attracted Merton's attention in the 1960s and won his deep respect, and whose work Merton also reworked in a series of poetic adaptations. See "Readings from Ibn Abbad," in Thomas Merton, *Raids on the Unspeakable* (New York: New Directions, 1966) 141-51; *CP* 745-52; for an analysis, see Patrick F. O'Connell, "'A Son of This Instant': Thomas Merton and Ibn 'Abbād of Ronda," *The Merton Annual* 23 (2010) 149-83.

5. For an overview of Ibn Baṭṭūṭa's life, see "Ibn Baṭṭūṭa and his Work," the first section of Gibb's Introduction to his abridged translation (Ibn Baṭṭūṭa, *Travels* 1-15). A detailed recounting is provided by Ross E. Dunn in *The Adventures of Ibn Battuta, A Muslim Traveler of the 14th Century* (Berkeley: University of California Press, 1986); subsequent references will be cited as "Dunn" parenthetically in the text. A recent 45-minute IMAX documentary film entitled *Journey to Mecca: In the Footsteps of Ibn Battuta* (SK Films, in association with National Geographic, 2009), directed by Bruce Neibaur and narrated by Ben Kingsley, recreates the first part of Ibn Baṭṭūṭa's travels, the *hajj* to Mecca. Ibn Baṭṭūṭa's journey was also featured in the international edition of *Time* magazine's annual Summer Journey issue in 2011 (the entire issue is based on Ibn Baṭṭūṭa's itinerary; in particular see Reza Aslan, "World Wanderer"; Pico Iyer, "A Voyager for the Ages"; Michael Elliott, "Editor's Desk: An Islamic Odyssey" [http://www.time.com/time/specials/packages/completelist/0,29569,2084273,00.html]), with an accompanying five-part photo essay focusing on contemporary views of various locations included in his travels (http://lightbox.time.com/tag/ibn-battuta) [accessed January 22, 2013].

produced many generations of Islamic judges, or *qādīs*. In 1325 he embarked on the traditional pilgrimage to Mecca, the beginning of a journey that would keep him away from his homeland for the next quarter-century. In his travels he not only visited the entire Muslim world but journeyed as far as China. He discovered a passion for travel, but also opportunities for a successful career. As well as touring Egypt, Syria, Iraq, Persia, East Africa, Central Asia, even Constantinople, he spent three years of religious study in Mecca,[6] giving him credentials to become an authority on *sharia*, Islamic law, in any Muslim principality, and he soon obtained a lucrative if at times contentious position in the court of the Sultan of Delhi in India, where he remained for some seven years, until he was appointed an envoy of the Sultan to China in 1341. After a series of misadventures that found him in the Maldive Islands, Ceylon and Bengal, he finally made it to China, though his embassy was apparently of little consequence. In fact, rather than returning to Delhi he made his way to Syria in time to encounter the first ravages of the Black Death there in 1348, and eventually, after a seventh pilgrimage to Mecca,[7] found his way back to Morocco. His ambition to see every Muslim country led to brief subsequent trips north to Andalusia and south to the Niger region of Africa, after which he returned to Morocco where he settled down at last and functioned as a *qādī* until his death in 1368 or 1369. It has been estimated that in his travels Ibn Battūta covered some 75,000 miles,[8] a distance perhaps unmatched until the age of railroads, if not of jet planes. Interest in his exploits was so great upon his return to Morocco that the sultan instructed one of his own secretaries, Muhammad Ibn Juzayy, to commit his narrative to writing; thus Ibn Battūta did not actually record his story himself – it was an early example of the "as told to" genre, and the amanuensis evidently felt free to insert material from earlier accounts on occasion to provide supplementary details.[9] Ibn Battūta's veracity has sometimes been questioned, especially in his forays into non-Islamic territories such as Constantinople and China, but he is generally regarded as a largely trustworthy if somewhat credulous reporter.[10]

---

6. Dunn suggests, on the basis of various chronological anomalies, that Ibn Battūta may have spent only a single year (1327-28) studying at Mecca (106).

7. The accuracy of this number depends on the length of his residence in Mecca: Dunne says he made the *hajj* "at least four times" (11).

8. See Gibb's Introduction (Ibn Battūta, *Travels* 9).

9.See Gibb's Introduction (Ibn Battūta, *Travels* 11-13), and Dunn 3-4, 310-18.

10. See Gibb's Introduction (Ibn Battūta, *Travels* 13-14) and Dunn 314-16.

* * * * * * *

The first of the seven sections that make up "East with Ibn Battuta" is headed *"Cairo 1326"* (*GL* 82-83; *CP* 538-39) and provides observations on the religious life of dervishes living in the city, the first major stop on Ibn Battūta's itinerary. The material is arranged in three segments, the first of which focuses on the living conditions of these Muslim devotees:

> Cloisters (khanqahs) of Darvishes
> Built by aristocrats
> Have silver rings on their doors
> The mystics sit down to eat
> Each from his private bowl
> Each drinks
> From his own cup
> They are given
> Changes of clothing
> And a monthly allowance
> On Thursday nights
> They are given sugar
> Soap and oil
> For their lamps
> And the price of a bath. (1.1-15)

The focus seems to be particularly on the patronage of the dervishes by the rich, and the relative opulence of their living conditions. Merton substitutes "Cloisters" for the "convents" in his source (Ibn Battūta, *Travels* 51), thereby suggesting the implicit parallel with Christian monastic life both contemporary with Ibn Battūta and as experienced by Merton himself. "Built by aristocrats" compresses the original phrase "nobles vie with one another in building them" (Ibn Battūta, *Travels* 51), shifting the emphasis from the nobles' rivalry in performing pious deeds to the reliance of the religious on wealthy sponsors. Mention of the "silver rings on their doors" is actually imported from a description of one specific "monastery" mentioned later (Ibn Battūta, *Travels* 52), generalized to characterize these institutions in general. The subsequent details seem to undermine any sense of community, and perhaps of poverty as well. Whereas the identification of the "mystics" ("adepts in the mystical doctrines" in the original) is not directly linked by Ibn Battūta to their eating practices, the juxtaposition here seems to suggest inconsistencies between profession and practice: "each person is given his bread and soup in a separate dish" (Ibn Battūta, *Travels* 51) becomes "private bowl" and "his own cup" – with an implied possessiveness of personal property vs. communal ownership. The rest of the section suggests all their needs are taken care of, presumably by the same aristocrats already mentioned. Though the provisions are rather basic — clothing, a monthly allowance, sugar (specified for "cakes" in the original), soap ("to wash their clothes"), oil and "the price of a bath," there is a sense that the religious are sheltered and well provided for. While there is no indication that Ibn Battūta himself is at all critical of the mystics' comfortable living conditions, the ostentation of their silver door-knockers, the individualism of their "private" bowls and cups,[11] their dependence on aristocrats for sustenance, there is a clear if subtle satiric undertone here, without any overt commentary, that suggests a distance between the voice of the narrator and the perspective of the poet, quite aware from personal experience of how easy it is for "professional" religious to adopt a complacent, self-satisfied attitude of spiritual superiority.

The second segment describes what Ibn Battūta calls "the great cemetery of al-Qarāfa, which is a place of peculiar sanctity, and contains the graves of innumerable scholars and pious believers" (Ibn Battūta, *Travels* 51):

> In the great cemetery
> They build chambers
> Pavilions
> Hire singers
> To chant the *Koran*
> Day and night among the tombs
> With pleasant voices. (1.16-22)

Whereas in the original it is "the people" who build the pavilions, "They build" here, with its parallel to line 2, suggests that it is once more the aristocrats who are responsible for the construction, again highlighting the power of money to provide a kind of second-hand piety; they hire singers ("Koran-readers" in the original"), whose exact purpose is not specified (here or in the *Travels*), but who are apparently intended to create a sacred atmosphere by continuous chanting of the Qur'an. The impression is given that the rich are covering all their bases with this complementary enterprise – cloisters are built for living mystics, chambers and pavilions for religious service among the dead, an implied parallel to Christian nobility in medieval Europe as patrons of monasteries and as having Masses celebrated for their dead relatives. There is a kind of spark of recognition here, not, obviously, on Ibn Battūta's part, but for the poet and his primary audience. Remarkably similar behavior patterns imply comparable assumptions that paying for these devotional services

---

11. Though he does note: "none sharing with another" (Ibn Battūta, *Travels* 51).

fulfills their pious responsibilities. The juxtaposition of the two episodes thus functions quite differently in *The Geography of Lograire* than in the *Travels* (where they are also successive).

This impression is reinforced by the final segment of this first section, in which a particular convent (actually located not in Cairo but in upper Egypt) possesses relics of the Prophet Muhammad obtained at a presumably exorbitant price by the monastery's patron:

> Convent at Dayr at-Tin:
> A piece of the Prophet's
> Wooden basin with the pencil
> With which he applied kohl
> The awl
> With which he sewed his sandals
> Bought by the founder
> For a hundred thousand dirhams. (1.22-30)

The "relics" again suggest a parallel with Christian practices of the same era, and once more the focus is on conspicuous consumption for pious purposes. On the one hand, the expenditure is testimony to the honor in which Muhammad is held (Ibn Battūta's presumed focus), but in tandem with what has preceded, it appears as yet another instance of a wealthy "founder" ("builder" in the original [Ibn Battūta, *Travels* 53], probably altered both to avoid repetition and to highlight the element of financial support) attempting to "buy" spiritual stature, emphasized by making the (presumably) huge sum the final detail of the description. The simplicity of the Prophet himself, whose wooden basin has little in common with the silver door-rings mentioned earlier, and who stitched his own sandals, is in marked contrast to the extravagance of later followers who apparently think possessing the objects is equivalent to possessing the virtues they represent. This reflects the perpetual temptation, certainly not unknown in comparable Christian religious houses, to substitute sacralized objects for inner transformation, a temptation of which Ibn Battūta himself seems blithely unaware in his circumstantial recounting of the details, but which is apparently the motivation for the poet to select this particular episode to incorporate into his own narrative.

* * * * * * *

The second section is entitled "*Syria*" (*GL* 83; *CP* 539), where Ibn Battūta unexpectedly went after leaving Egypt, rather than journeying straight to Mecca as originally planned. The focus is on the religious divisions between Sunni and Shiʻite Muslims.[12] Here Ibn Battūta, as a pious Sunni, is unabashedly partisan, denouncing the "abominable Shiʻites / Who hate the Ten Companions / And every person called Omar" (2.2-4) (the one among these early companions[13] most responsible for bypassing the Shiʻite champion ʻAlī, Muhammad's son-in-law, as the Prophet's successor[14]). One might question the validity of this report from a hostile source, but if it is true the reason for the hatred is not the name *per se* but the evidence of allegiance to the hated oppressor. The following section mixes comments about commerce, a glimpse of the more "normal" aspect of the town's life, with more evidence of Shiʻites' prejudices:

> In Sarmín (where scented soap
> Is made and exported
> To Damascus and Cairo)
> These heretics so hate the Ten
> They will not even say "Ten"
> Their brokers at auctions
> When they come to "ten"
> Say "Nine-plus-one" (2.5-12)

This refusal even to pronounce the word "ten" initially does appear to reflect the absurd lengths to which such hostility is taken (though again one might wonder about the accuracy of the information). Certainly the reader's inclination is to reject, and even find ridiculous, such fanaticism and irrationality.[15] However the balance of sympathy shifts, for the reader if not for Ibn Battūta, in the subsequent scene:

> One day a faithful Turk
> At one of their markets
> Heard the broker call "Nine-plus-one"

---

12. In the unabridged version of the *Travels* these Shiʻites are explicitly described as "a sect of Rāfidīs, abominable persons" (Ibn Battūta, *Travels* [2] 1.93), whom Gibb identifies as "schismatic extremists of the Nusairī sect" (n. 98), the same group to be featured in the following section of "East with Ibn Battuta." Dunn notes that "Rāfidī" means "Turncoat" and was "a term of deprecation Sunnis commonly used" (90).

13. Gibb identifies the Ten Companions as "those to whom Muhammad gave the promise of Paradise, includ[ing] the first four caliphs, Abū Bakr, ʻOmar I, ʻOthmān, and ʻAlī" (Ibn Battūta, *Travels* [2] 1.93, n. 98).

14. ʻOmar I was the second caliph, succeeding Muhammad's close companion Abū Bakr; however in a detail included only in the unabridged version Ibn Battūta specifically mentions hatred for the Umayyad caliph ʻOmar II (717-20), who was buried in the vicinity (Ibn Battūta, *Travels* [2] 1.93).

15. Perhaps this may not simply be an absurd circumlocution but a way of distinguishing the revered ʻAlī from the rest of the companions.

He went for him with a club, shouting
"You bastard, say TEN!" (2.13-17)

The description of the Turk as "faithful" and the epithet "You bastard" are added to the original (see Ibn Battúta, *Travels* 61), but the fact that the en-forcer is a Turk is a detail that has more resonance than Ibn Battūta realizes or intends, given the later Turkish (Ottoman) hegemony over Syria and the Arab world generally – the "faithful Turk" becomes representative of the historical tendency of the conqueror to impose his will on those less powerful. The slight alterations in the concluding lines of the section have the effect (albeit not intended by Ibn Battūta) of reinforcing this identification with the underdog. The original reads: "he laid his club about his head saying 'Say "ten,"' whereupon quoth he 'Ten with the club'" (Ibn Battúta, *Travels* 61), which might evoke laughter from the audience, while in Merton's version – "'Ten with a club,' / Wept the broker" (2.18-19) – the Shi'ite forced to utter the forbidden word and anguished to the point of tears as a consequence, has become the victim of a hostility as intense as that shown by his own sect. The final focus on the weeping broker (there is no weeping in the original) tends to undercut the initial identification with the speaker's point of view and to win the victim a share of the poet's and the reader's sympathy, despite the narrator's evident unqualified approval of the proceedings. Again the poet's subtle and complex handling of his source reveals more than the narrator real-izes and evokes a more complex response to the material, without violating the "decorum" of the narrator's voice.

* * * * * * *

The third and longest section, still set in Syria, is headed *"The Nusayris"* (*GL* 83-85; *CP* 539-41) and focuses on a sect of extremist Shi'ites[16] who according to Ibn Battūta (in a detail not included by Merton) believe 'Alī to be divine (Ibn Battūta, *Travels* 62[17]). They exemplify a strain of mil-lenarian anticipation that recurs repeatedly throughout *The Geography of Lograire*[18] – the illusory dreams of oppressed peoples for vindication, and often, as here, for revenge, and the inevitable aftermath of shattered

---

16. These are the Alawites (see Gibb's Introduction: Ibn Battúta, *Travels* 39; see also Ibn Battūta, *Travels* [2] 1.111, n. 162), best known today as the sect to which the Assads belong, and so have a current resonance which of course neither Ibn Battūta nor Merton could have foreseen.

17. Gibb points out that such a claim "is a popular simplification of their Gnostic doctrine of emanation" (Ibn Battūta, *Travels* [2] 1.111, n. 162).

18. See "The Ranters and Their Pleads" ("North" III [*GL* 63-68; *CP* 519-24]), the Cargo materials of "East" (*GL* 91-116; *CP* 547-72) and the "Ghost Dance" sections of "West" (*GL* 131-37; *CP* 587-93).

hopes and increased suffering. The opening segment highlights their alienation from mainstream Islam:

> These heretics hate all true believers and when ordered
>   by the Sultan
> To build mosques build them far from their homes
> Keep asses and cattle in them let them fall into disrepair.
> If a true believer coming from another country
> Stops in a ruined mosque and sings the call to prayer
> The infidels say: "Stop braying,
> We will bring you a little hay." (3.1-7)

The introductory references to "heretics" and "hat[ing] all true believers" are more precise additions to the original; the other details are taken from the *Travels*, though Merton moves the reference to neglect after that about using the mosques as animal shelters, presumably to create a more progressive sequence. The terms "true believer" and "infidel" are also added, the latter the usual term for non-Muslim, here implying the more literal sense of those "unfaithful" to revelation. The insult to the "stranger" (as he is called in the original) is also made more pointed: "your fodder is coming to you" becomes "we will bring you a little hay," suggesting not only that he is no better than beast with his Sunni orthodoxy but that in his stubbornness and foolishness he is an ass.

In the lines that follow, the credulousness and fanaticism of the Nusayrīs are in evidence from their ready acceptance of the claims of a stranger to be the Mahdi, the long-expected hidden Imam of Shi'ism, whose coming marks the end times:

> Once a stranger came to the Nusayris and told them
>   he was the Mahdi
> He promised to divide Syria among them
> Giving each one a city or a town.
> He gave them olive leaves and said:
> "These will bring you success. These leaves
> Are warrants of your appointment."
>
> They went forth into city and town
> And when arrested, each said to the Governor:
> "The Imam al-Mahdi has come. He has given me this town!"
>
> The Governor would then reply: "Show me your warrant"
>
> Each one then produced his olive leaves
> And was flogged. (3.8-19)

In the *Travels* (62-63) this incident is set in a vague time period[19] and begins: "They tell a story that. . ." It seems to suggest an explanation for current social arrangements and behavior patterns. The sectaries' absolute, unquestioning trust in this stranger is evidently prompted by their fantasy of taking power, totally disregarding the flimsiness of the olive leaves as talismans. There is a kind of evangelical enthusiasm in their proclamation that the long-awaited Mahdi "has come" (added to the original), with of course the expected skepticism and rejection as a response. For the poet and his audience (though perhaps not for Ibn Battūta), olive branches are conventional symbols of peace, but here lead only to arrest, beatings and dismissal. But the Nusayrīs' naïve belief is not shaken by this ignominious result, and simply moves into a more violent phase, marked by even greater delusions:

> So the stranger told the heretics to fight:
> "Go with myrtle rods," he said
> "Instead of swords. The rods
> Will turn to swords at the moment of battle."
>
> They entered a town on Friday when the men were
>   at the mosque.
> They raped the women and the Muslims
> Came running out with swords
> And cut them to pieces.
>
> News was sent to the capital by carrier pigeon. The Governor
> Moved out with an army. Twenty thousand heretics
> Were slaughtered. The rest hid in the mountains.
> They offered one dinar per head if they were spared.
> This news went by pigeon to the Sultan
> Who said: "Kill them." (3.20-33)

The claim that the rods will become swords is even more fantastic than the instructions about the olive leaves, but "the heretics" still proceed with apparently no hesitation or doubt. They are presented by Ibn Battūta as incredibly deluded, out of touch with reality. They are also shown to be doubly dishonorable, shamefully attacking the town during the Friday prayers and more shamefully raping the women while the men are at the mosque. Ibn Battūta's comment that "the Muslims" (as opposed to the Nusayrīs, who are not counted as authentic followers of the Prophet) "seized weapons, and killed them as they pleased" (Ibn Battúta, *Travels* 63) becomes "Came running out with swords / And cut them to pieces,"

---

19. According to Gibb (Ibn Battūta, *Travels* [2] 1.112, n. 164), the uprising took place in 1317.

a pointed reminder that the myrtle rods did not in fact become swords. The subsequent wholesale slaughter of the "heretics" – not just the band of attackers, who have already been killed, but the members of the sect in general – as well as the stark command of the Sultan – "Kill them" (cold-blooded direct discourse altered from the more impersonal "ordering them to be put to the sword" in the original) – once again suggests a distinction between the narrator's perspective and that of the audience. Victimized first by the charlatan messiah, then by their much more powerful opponents, despite being perpetrators of violence themselves the sectaries are so ineffectual as to be pathetic, certainly no lasting threat. The disproportionate destruction visited upon them impresses the reader (though presumably not Ibn Battūta) as an example of "overkill." The purported Mahdi simply fades out of the picture; there is no indication that he did more than send them out, no suggestion of his own direct involvement in the military action. No explanation of his motivation is provided, leading to the question of whether it may even have been deliberate deception to send them to their deaths.

The final lines reveal the outcome of the conflict:

> But the General
> Said these people could be useful
> Working on the land
> And their lives were spared. (3.34-37)

In the *Travels* it is evident that the heretics were already peasants, whose disappearance would have negative economic consequences for the orthodox: "The chief commandant . . . represented to [the Sultan] that these people were tillers of the soil for the Muslims and that if they were killed the Muslims would suffer in consequence, so their lives were spared" (Ibn Battúta, *Travels* 63). Here, the implication is that as a consequence of their rebellion, the Nusayrīs are to be reduced to the state of peonage, so that the tale becomes an etiology for their oppressed status. Despite their own outrages their disproportionate destruction and subsequent subordination reflects at least as heavily on their opponents' savagery and domination as on their own crimes. Once again, Ibn Battūta has provided the material for a nuanced perspective that he himself does not share.

* * * * * * *

The central section of the sequence, appropriately located at "*Mecca*" (*GL* 85; *CP* 541), is the only one presented in prose, and is in fact taken word-for-word and without omission from the *Travels* (76), the only alteration being the division of the material into three separate paragraphs:

"The Meccans are very elegant and clean in their dress, and most of them wear white garments, which you always see fresh and snowy. They use a great deal of perfume and kohl and make free use of toothpicks of green arák-wood.

"The Meccan women are extraordinarily beautiful and very pious and modest. They too make great use of perfumes to such a degree that they will spend the night hungry in order to buy perfumes with the price of their food.

"They visit the mosque every Thursday night, wearing their finest apparel; and the whole sanctuary is saturated with the smell of their perfume. When one of these women goes away the odour of the perfume clings to the place after she has gone."

Juxtaposed with the conflict and violence of the two previous sections, this description of the "elegant and clean" appearance of the Meccans, in their flowing white garments, and particularly of the beauty, piety and modesty of the Meccan woman, who like their menfolk use perfume profusely, even if they have to go hungry to buy it, is particularly attractive. There are no signs here of doctrinal disagreement or of social or political strife. Mecca has an idyllic, almost paradisal atmosphere as seen through Ibn Battūta's eyes – and even more as sensed through his nose. In fact, despite being taken verbatim from the *Travels*, the selection seems to treat Ibn Battūta with gentle humor, in that (as the new paragraphing makes more obvious) he devotes twice as much attention to the women of Mecca as to the men, lingering particularly on the fact that the women's perfume continues to "saturate" the sanctuary of the mosque, and his own memory, after they themselves have left. At the very center of Islam, the most sacred place in the world for Muslims, Ibn Battūta is preoccupied with women, not in a perverse or sinister way, but as suggesting nonetheless a certain spiritual shallowness or superficiality, which paradoxically makes him a more appealing figure precisely because of his unselfconscious disclosure of what a more guarded, self-protective personality would have kept concealed.[20] There may not be much depth, but there is even less guile in Ibn Battūta.

* * * * * * *

The fifth of the seven segments moves on to "*Isfahan*" in Persia (*GL* 86; *CP* 542), where the prodigality of the natural world seems to be matched

---

20. Ibn Battūta's not untypically casual attitude toward, and practice of, marriage and divorce are evident throughout the *Travels*: see Dunn 39, 44, 62, 207, 233-35, 237, 247, 269.

only by the prodigality of its inhabitants:

> In Isfahan the fair
> Surrounded by orchards
> (Apricots and quinces
> Pears and melons)
> The people out-do one another
> In banquets
> "In the preparation for which
> They display all their resources"
> One corporation entertained another with viands
> Cooked over candles
> "The guests returned the invitation
> And cooked their viands with silk."

Whereas in the *Travels* Ibn Battūta calls Isfahán "one of the largest and fairest of cities" but then notes that "the greater part of it is now in ruins, as a result of the feud between Sunnis and Shiʻites,[21] which is still raging there" (Ibn Battúta, *Travels* 91), Merton evidently has no desire to reprise that theme and so concentrates only on the rivalry of different groups (identified by Ibn Battūta as trade corporations) in hosting dinners. For Ibn Battūta, this extravagant and conspicuous prodigality is clearly intended to be seen as commendable. He describes the residents as "exceedingly brave, generous, and always trying to outdo one another in procuring luxurious viands" (Ibn Battúta, *Travels* 91). But cooking a meal over candles obviously requires a huge number to generate sufficient heat, and thereby squanders resources better devoted to their intended purpose of providing light, while using silk for fuel shows an even greater disregard for economy, a profligate wastefulness. The narrator's evident admiration for this "generosity" takes no account of the artificiality and exhibitionism of this perverse concern for display, which ultimately contrasts with rather than emulating the natural abundance of the fruitful orchards described earlier. Once again the audience presumably evaluates the details differently from the way Ibn Battūta intends them to be regarded.

* * * * * * *

The penultimate segment, entitled *"Delhi"* (*GL* 86-87; *CP* 542-43), actually is inserted much later in the narrative (Ibn Battúta, *Travels* 226) after Ibn Battūta has left Delhi and the Sultan's service, when he's relating various stories of yogis' feats as part of his broader presentation of vari-

---

21. In the unabridged version Ibn Battūta specifically identifies the Shiʻite antagonists as Rāfidīs (Ibn Battūta, *Travels* [2] 2.295).

ous encounters with Hindus:

> In the Sultan's apartments
> I saw a *Júgí*
> Sitting in midair
> I fell in a faint
> They had to give me a drink
> To revive me (6.1-6)

For the first time in the sequence, Ibn Battūta refers to himself and uses the first person (as he will do in the final section as well). In the original he actually sees the yogi levitate, whereas here he seems to enter the room when he is already suspended, leaving the matter of how he got there even more open to question, but in both versions Ibn Battūta's reaction is the same, and in both versions he is revived by a drink (a "potion" [!] in the original). Any temptation on the part of the audience to take all this seriously is fatally undermined by the details that follow:

> And there he was
> Still sitting in midair
> His companion
> Took a sandal from a bag
> Beat it on the ground
> Til it rose in the air
> All by itself and poised
> Over the floating one
> And it began hitting him
> On the back of the neck
> Until he floated down
> And landed. (6.7-18)

For the reader – but not for Ibn Battūta – the performance has elements of slapstick farce worthy of the Three Stooges. The complete incongruity and fundamentally frivolous nature of the events certainly suggest the operations of a pair of master illusionists with their bag of tricks. There is not the least sense of any spiritual significance. It is the conspicuous display of the previous section transposed to an ostensibly religious context. Only a concern for Ibn Battūta's sanity prevents a succession of further marvels, suggesting the show may actually have been staged for his benefit:

> "I would tell them to do something else,"
> Said the Sultan, "If I did not fear
> For your reason." (6.19-21)

What is a sign of the preternatural for Ibn Battūta suggests to a more skeptical reader an exhibition of absurd buffoonery masquerading as spiritual "elevation" that reveals more about the narrator than about the true nature of the event, whatever it may have been. Here as elsewhere he appears to have missed the import of his own testimony. Ibn Battūta is an "unreliable" narrator not with regard to honesty or sincerity, but with respect to insight and perspicacity. Again Merton has done a masterful job of keeping the voice of the narrator consistent while allowing for, even implicitly calling for, a perspective divergent from that of the speaker.

* * * * * * *

The final section, entitled *"Calicut"* (*GL* 87-88; *CP* 543-44), relates the misadventures of Ibn Battūta as he attempts to embark on his voyage to China. He begins with a brief description of the harbor and of the Chinese junks which seem to be the medieval equivalent of luxury liners:

> Chinese vessels at anchor in the harbor
> One of the largest in the world. Malabar
> Coast of ginger pepper spice
> Four decks with cabins saloons
> Merchants of Canton Sumatra
> Ceylon stay locked in cabins
> With wives and slave girls
> Sailors bring their boys to sea
> Cultivate salads and ginger
> In wooden vats (7.1-10)

Here various details about the Malabar coast and the port of Calicut that are spread out over many pages of the *Travels* (231-36)[22] are compressed into a staccato succession of impressions, only moving to complete clauses when he focuses in on the human inhabitants of the ships and their contrasting domestic arrangements – the wealthy merchants consorting with wives and slave girls in privacy, juxtaposed with the sailors, the "working class" who are bringing their sons with them and growing their own food, probably to combat scurvy.

This panoramic scene is succeeded by the sudden eruption of personal details:

> In Calicut I missed my boat
> To China and my slave

---

22. See Dunn 213-40 (c. 10: "Malabar and the Maldives") for a clear presentation of the rather convoluted details of this entire segment of Ibn Battūta's travels.

> Girls were all stolen by the King
> Of Sumatra and my companions
> Were scattered over China
> Sumatra and Bengal (7.11-16)

This is a stripped-down version of a rather complex series of events (Ibn Battúta, *Travels* 236-40), involving shipwrecks of some of the junks, on one of which Ibn Battūta himself had initially booked passage – with a private cabin because of his own slave girls! – transferring his possessions to a smaller "*kakam*" only upon learning the cabin was "small and unsuitable"; the *kakam*, already at sea at the time of the wrecks, sailed away without Ibn Battūta but with his goods and his slaves, and he learned of their fate only much later (after suddenly joining a military expedition against Goa for three months, prompted, ostensibly at least, by the reading of a random verse of the Qur'an!). It's clear why Merton would choose to compress all this into the brief compass of these lines of verse, in which this string of misfortunes lead to a kind of purifying disillusion with the world of the great and powerful, the infidel world of Hindu sultans who steal one's slave girls, and prompt a retreat to a simpler and purer realm:

> When I saw what had happened
> I sailed for the Maldives
> Where all the inhabitants
> Are Muslims
> Live on red fish lightly cooked
> Or smoked in palmleaf baskets
> It tastes like mutton
>
> These natives wear no pants
> Only aprons
> Bathe twice a day
> Use sandalwood and do not fight
> Their armor is prayer. (7.17-28)

The Maldives are presented as a kind of edenic refuge of peaceful, simple, clean (and well-perfumed) inhabitants, whose prayer is their protection. In this idyllic setting Ibn Battūta's journey, for the time being at least, reaches a satisfactory climax. If the reality of the Maldives eventually proves to fall short of the vision described here, as it does in subsequent episodes from the *Travels* (Ibn Battūta comes into conflict with the ruler who has made him a *qádí*, has to flee, hatches unrealized plots to return with an invasion force [!], and subsequently moves on to Ceylon and finally to China), nevertheless the vision itself is a recognition of authentic values and a more authentic perception of what truly matters than Ibn Baṭṭūṭa has previously shown. The reshaping of Ibn Baṭṭūṭa's experience here moves into the realm of the mythic, finding an appropriate destination for a journey that is most fundamentally intended as a pilgrimage. It suggests that even in a fallen world (a Christian concept though not an Islamic one), one can still discover and strive for a way of life that embodies human dignity and promotes human flourishing. Such glimpses are caught only occasionally in the world of *Lograire*, but are to be cherished all the more for their relative rarity. Despite his limitations, his habitual naïvete and frequent narrowness of sympathy or of perception, Ibn Baṭṭūṭa is certainly a more appealing and sympathetic figure than the arrogant twentieth-century Westerners that patronize the Melanesians in the rest of the "East" canto, including the scatological anthropologist Bronislaw Malinowski whose *Diary* serves as the source for the following section, "East with Malinowski" (*GL* 89-90; *CP* 545-46), a parallel title that makes a comparison with Ibn Baṭṭūṭa almost inevitable.

In the end, the medieval Muslim pilgrim does make a significant contribution to envisioning and articulating an alternative to the way of self-glorification, exploitation and conflict that were prevalent in his day and age and, as Merton shows in great detail throughout his poem, have been no less prevalent in the centuries that have followed. Ibn Baṭṭūṭa plays a unique role in the overall mosaic composition of *The Geography of Lograire*. As the only source that predates the European arrival in the Americas, and the only source that does not either focus on Western experience itself or record, from one side or the other, the encounter between the West and various indigenous populations, he serves as a kind of control mechanism, a test case that at least suggests to what extent much of the exploitation and oppression recounted in the rest of the work is culture-specific to Christian (and post-Christian) Europeans and Americans and to what extent it is reflective of traits endemic to the human condition itself.

Postscript

There is actually one more excerpt from Ibn Baṭṭūṭa's *Travels* that is included, though without attribution, in *The Geography of Lograire*. The "East" canto uniquely has an extra introductory page, consisting simply of the epigraph:

LOVE OF THE SULTAN

A SLAVE
CUTS OFF HIS OWN HEAD
AFTER A LONG SPEECH

DECLARING HOW MUCH
HE LOVES THE SULTAN

A QUAINT OLD ASIAN CUSTOM

**LOVE
OF
THE
SULTAN!**
(*GL* 81; *CP* 537)

This is based on an incident from late in the *Travels* when Ibn Battūta visits the "infidel" Sultan of Mul-Jáwa, evidently located on the Malay peninsula:

> While this sultan was sitting in audience, I saw a man with a knife in his hand resembling a bookbinder's tool. He put this knife to his own neck, and delivered a long speech which I did not understand, then gripped it with both hands and cut his own throat. So sharp was the knife and so strong his grip that his head fell to the ground. I was amazed at his action. The sultan said to me "Does anyone do this in your country?" I replied "I have never seen such a thing." Then he laughed and said "These are our slaves, who kill themselves for love of us." . . . One of those present at this audience told me that the speech made by the man was a declaration of his affection for the sultan, and that he was slaying himself for love of him. (Ibn Battúta, *Travels* 277-78)

Without attribution, and coming (immediately) before "East with Ibn Battuta," the purpose of the epigraph is evidently not to provide insight on the narrator in particular but on "the East" in general. The implication seems to be that this sort of extreme self-abasement, offering one's life out of "love" for an absolute ruler (who reciprocates, in the original source, with a laugh), is behavior that typifies Oriental absolutism and servility. But such an interpretation is problematized by the editorial comment (so rare in *Lograire*) "A QUAINT OLD ASIAN CUSTOM," which seems to drip with irony, particularly as followed by the repetition of "**LOVE** / **OF** / **THE** / **SULTAN!**" – in bold upper-case, one word to a line. In fact the implication seems to be that this standard Western attitude toward the mysterious East will be challenged rather than reinforced by the material in the canto to follow – including the material from the very same source that provides this bizarre tale itself.

With Malinowski in the Postmodern Desert: Merton, Anthropology and the Ethnopoetics of *The Geography of Lograire*

Małgorzata Poks

Introduction: *The Geography of Lograire*

Published posthumously in 1969, and organized into four cantos named after the four cardinal points of the compass (South, North, East and West), Thomas Merton's long poem *The Geography of Lograire* was an attempt "to build or to dream the world in which he live[d]."[1] Intended as a "wide-angle mosaic of poems and dreams" in which Merton "without scruple mixed what is [his] own experience with what is almost everybody else's" (*GL* 1), *Lograire* juxtaposes the poet's personal memories with the dreams, myths and nightmares of the world's diverse traditional and modern cultures, including the consumer culture of America. Composed largely as a collage of quotations, "found" poems, and heavily edited versions of such narratives as the Amerindian Ghost Dance Movement, the Melanesian "Cargo" cults, the persecution of the English Ranters (a religious sect of the seventeenth century), Ibn Battuta's travels in the East, etc., the text allows divergent points of view to clash, even contradict one another. Dominant cultures and marginalized voices are placed side by side to construct their radically different cultural narratives. Within the poem the other is given a hearing; minority perspectives supplement official histories, exposing the ideological provenance of the latter. In a letter to a friend Merton called his new poem a "summa of offbeat anthropology."[2]

Introduction: Anthropology

Modern anthropology was born in the wake of geographical discoveries and its initial aim was to satisfy the Western world's insatiable curiosity about its "primitive" others – their ways of life, cultures and societal organizations. Assuming a common human essence but more often than not assigning non-white peoples an inferior rung on the evolutionary ladder

---

1. Thomas Merton, "Author's Note," *The Geography of Lograire* (New York: New Directions, 1969) 1; subsequent references will be cited as "*GL*" parenthetically in the text.

2. Thomas Merton, *The Hidden Ground of Love: Letters on Religious Experience and Social Concerns*, ed. William H. Shannon (New York: Farrar, Straus, Giroux, 1985) 235 [9/24/1967 letter to W. H. Ferry].

– even if not openly weighing their "animal" characteristics against their purely "human" traits – anthropology became a natural ally of colonial domination and was expected to provide justification of the imperialist project – the "white man's burden" and the corollary colonial exploitation of the "savage." Any discussion of the anthropological dimension of Merton's *The Geography of Lograire* is bound to revisit questions of colonialism, ideology and representation.

Merton and Anthropology

Anthropology started to engage Merton's imagination most intensely in the last decade of his life. It seems that his interest in modern anthropology in general and archeology in particular can be traced back to his intense engagement with Latin America. As early as 1958, impressed by Ernesto Cardenal's poetic recreation of the Mayan world and by the literary achievements of the Nicaraguan indigenist movement, Merton steeped himself in pre-conquest history and studied the art of ancient Mesoamerica. Archeologist Sylvanus Griswold Morley with his highly influential *The Ancient Maya* (1946)[3] was soon to emerge as Merton's most trusted guide through the maze of ancient Mesoamerican cultures.[4]

In the late 1960s, however, it was the structural anthropology of Claude Lévi-Strauss that held sway over Merton's imagination. In October 1967 the Frenchman emerged as "someone who has extraordinary views and is ahead of everyone (even though he may be 'wrong')."[5] At that time Merton was trying to plough through Lévi-Strauss's *Le Cru et le Cuit* (1964; translated as *The Raw and the Cooked* in 1969[6]), but got "snowed under the sheer mass of material." He was soon to revel, however, in the earlier monograph, *La Pensée Savage* (1962; *The Savage Mind*, 1966[7]), which he appreciated especially for its revaluation of neolithic thought – "more sophisticated and complex than some modern 'scientific' common-sense categorizing" (*LL* 299), as he put it.

---

3. Sylvanus Griswold Morley, *The Ancient Maya*, 3rd ed. (Stanford, CA: Stanford University Press, 1956).

4. See Malgorzata Poks, *Thomas Merton and Latin America: A Consonance of Voices* (2007; Saarbrücken, Germany: Lambert Academic Publishing, 2011) c. 6: "The Early Legend that Returns."

5. Thomas Merton, *Learning to Love: Exploring Solitude and Freedom. Journals, vol. 6: 1966-1967*, ed. Christine M. Bochen (San Francisco: HarperCollins, 1997) 299; subsequent references will be cited as "*LL*" parenthetically in the text.

6. Claude Lévi-Strauss, *Le Cru et le Cuit* (Paris: Plon, 1964); *The Raw and the Cooked*, trans. John and Doreen Weightman (New York: Harper & Row, 1969).

7. Claude Lévi-Strauss, *La Pensée Sauvage* (Paris: Plon, 1962); *The Savage Mind* (Chicago: University of Chicago Press, 1966).

Within his more immediate cultural context, Merton was discovering a spate of revisionist histories of the First Nations of North America, such as anthropologist Theodora Kroeber's story of the last of the Yana tribe, *Ishi in Two Worlds* (1961);[8] Peter Nabokov's *Two Leggings*, the story of a Crow Indian (1967);[9] *Black Elk Speaks*, a story, recorded by John Neihardt in 1932, of an Oglala Sioux medicine man;[10] and Cora Du Bois' account of the Ghost Dance movement (*The 1870 Ghost Dance*, 1939[11]). Moreover, his deep sympathy with African Americans struggling for basic human rights, his readings in Afro-American literature and culture, or his opposition to the American intervention in Vietnam allowed Merton to formulate the currently well-established connection between colonial and imperialist subjugation of the "exotic" other and the internal colonization of Afro-Americans and native Americans in the USA.

In October 1967 Merton was getting excited about the suddenly glimpsed convergences between such diverse events as the Caste War in the Yucatan (1847-1901),[12] the American Black Power Movement, and the Melanesian cargo cults[13] he was intensely studying at that time. "I want to write about this!"[14] he enthused. Four months later he wrote in his

---

8. Theodora Kroeber, *Ishi in Two Worlds: A Biography of the Last Wild Indian in North America* (Berkeley: University of California Press, 1961); see "Ishi: A Meditation," in Thomas Merton, *Ishi Means Man: Essays on Native Americans* (Greensboro, NC: Unicorn Press, 1976) 25-32; subsequent references will be cited as "*IMM*" parenthetically in the text.

9. Peter Nabokov, *Two Leggings: The Making of a Crow Warrior* (New York: Crowell, 1967); see "War and Vision" (*IMM* 17-29).

10. *Black Elk Speaks: Being the Life Story of a Holy Man of the Ogalala Sioux*, as told to John G. Neihardt (New York: Crowell, 1932).

11. Cora Du Bois, *The 1870 Ghost Dance* (Berkeley: University of California Press, 1939).

12. See "The Cross-Fighters" (*IMM* 35-52).

13. The "cargo" label is often contested as an essentially Western creation. Lamont Lindstrom of the University of Tulsa lists such alternative, nonstigmatizing names as: "nativistic movements, revitalization movements, messianic movements, millenarian movements, crisis cults, Holy Spirit movements, protonationalist movements, culture-contact movements, and the like" ("Cargo Cults" available at: http://www.berkshirepublishing. com/rvw/022/022smpl1.htm: accessed 4/27/2011); see also Lamont Lindstrom, *Cargo Cult: Strange Stories of Desire from Melanesia and Beyond* (Honolulu: University of Hawaii Press, 1993). For the purpose of this essay I will, however, preserve Merton's usage of the term "cargo," since it has gained widespread currency among Merton scholars.

14. Thomas Merton, *The Other Side of the Mountain: The End of the Journey. Journals, vol. 7: 1967-1968*, ed. Patrick Hart (San Francisco: HarperCollins, 1998) 6; subsequent references will be cited as "*OSM*" parenthetically in the text. See "Cargo Cults of the South Pacific," Thomas Merton, *Love and Living*, ed. Naomi Burton Stone and Brother Patrick Hart (New York: Farrar, Straus, Giroux, 1979) 80-94.

journal, "I am really turned on by social anthropology and cargo cults" (*OSM* 55). His reading in I. C. Jarvie's *The Revolution in Anthropology* (1964)[15] gave Merton insight into the crisis brought about by cargo in the professional world of anthropology and alerted him to the irony of the anthropologists' own cargo-like response to that phenomenon. Their "ritual methodological celebration," Merton concluded, helped disguise the professional world's helplessness in the face of a phenomenon far beyond the anthropologists' coping capabilities (*OSM* 55-56).

Following in the footsteps of Robert Daggy's famous description of the "French Cable" (#35)[16] as embedded at the very heart of Merton's antipoem *Cables to the Ace*,[17] I am tempted to forward an equally bold, though decidedly more problematic proposition concerning *The Geography of Lograire*. I want to argue that the "East with Malinowski" section (*GL* 89-90) – placed in the volume's "East" Canto between the narrative of the fourteenth-century Muslim traveler Ibn Battuta and the "Cargo" section, the latter itself richly interspersed with references to early colonial presence in Papua New Guinea – provides an important key to unlock some of *Lograire*'s many secrets.[18] Credited with starting the postmodern revolution in anthropology,[19] Bronislaw Malinowski's *Diary*[20] suffuses Merton's poem with an unmistakably poststructural and postcolonial sensibility and provides the necessary background for the discussion of cargo.

15. Ian C. Jarvie, *The Revolution in Anthropology* (New York: Humanities Press, 1964).

16. Thomas Merton, *Cables to the Ace* (New York: New Directions, 1968) 24-27.

17. Robert Daggy, "Hurly-Burly Secrets: A Reflection on Thomas Merton's French Poems," *The Merton Seasonal* 21.2 (Summer 1996) 23.

18. "East with Malinowski" is the title of Section II of *Lograire*'s "East" Canto and depicts Bronislaw Malinowski's boat trip to the Melanesian village of Tupuseleia on Wednesday February 10, 1915 and back to Port Moresby on the following day. Another segment excerpted from Malinowski's diary is to be found in the "East" Canto's section III, entitled "Cargo Songs," where it parasitically disrupts passages culled from Peter Worsley, *The Trumpet Shall Sound: A Study of "Cargo"Cults in Melanesia* (London: MacGibbon & Kee, 1957); subsequent references will be cited as "Worsley" parenthetically in the text.

19. See Grazyna Kubica, Wstep [Introduction] to Bronislaw Malinowski, *Dziennik w ścislym tego slowa znaczeniu* [*Diary in the Strict Sense of the Term*] (Kraków: Wydawnictwo Literackie, 2001) 26.

20. Bronislaw Malinowski, *Diary in the Strict Sense of the Term*, trans. Norbert Guterman (New York: Harcourt, Brace & World, 1967); Bronislaw Malinowski, *Diary in the Strict Sense of the Term* with a New Introduction by Raymond Firth (Stanford, CA: Stanford University Press, 1989); subsequent references to the latter edition will be cited as "Malinowski, *Diary*" parenthetically in the text.

Merton the Ethnographer

Before the late nineteenth century, the anthropologist was mostly an ethnologist – a scientist constructing general theories about humanity – and so was distinct from the ethnographer – a fieldworker, collector of data and report writer. Cultural historian James Clifford believes Malinowski to have been one of the first "new" anthropologists, in whom those two functions merged. "Squatting by the campfire; looking, listening, and questioning; recording and interpreting Trobriand life,"[21] Malinowski sanctions a new mode of anthropological authority – one based on participant observation – while his groundbreaking ethnographic narrative, *Argonauts of the Western Pacific*,[22] establishes a powerful new genre, at once "scientific and literary" (Clifford, *Predicament* 30). Ethnology was a powerful scientific project, but its successor, modern ethnography is, as Clifford explains, "from beginning to end, enmeshed in writing. This writing includes," as he clarifies, "minimally, a translation of experience into textual form. The process is complicated by the action of multiple subjectivities and political constraints beyond the control of the writer. In response to these forces, ethnographic writing enacts a specific strategy of authority. This strategy has classically involved an unquestioned claim to appear as purveyor of truth in the text" (Clifford, *Predicament* 25). As a result, ethnography is for Clifford a "compromised" science: allied with textuality, open to charges of inventing rather than describing its objects, sensitive to questions of representation and power.

Inspired by Clifford's definition of ethnographic practice as "diverse ways of thinking and writing about culture from a standpoint of participant observation" (Clifford, *Predicament* 9), I believe that a poet like Merton is an ethnographer.[23] In some parts of *The Geography of Lograire* he is more of an actual participant (e.g., "Queens Tunnel"), in others more of an observer, but whether writing from first-hand experience or participating only imaginatively in the lives and cultures he studies, the author invari-

---

21. James Clifford, *The Predicament of Culture: Twentieth-Century Ethnography, Literature, and Art* (Cambridge, MA: Harvard University Press, 1988) 28; subsequent references will be cited as "Clifford, *Predicament*" parenthetically in the text.

22. Bronislaw Malinowski, *Argonauts of the Western Pacific: An Account of Native Enterprise and Adventure in the Archipelagoes of Melanesian New Guinea* (New York: E. P. Dutton, 1922).

23. Clifford makes this claim about the William Carlos Williams of "To Elsie," a poem focusing on a racially mixed girl from New Jersey and the new America where everything is "out of place. A doctor-poet-fieldworker, Williams watches and listens to New Jersey's immigrants, workers, women giving birth, pimply-faced teenagers, mental cases. In their lives and words, encountered through a privileged participant observation both poetic and scientific, he finds material for his writing" (Clifford, *Predicament* 6).

ably "finds himself off center among scattered traditions," attempting to make sense of "the condition of rootlessness and mobility" (Clifford, *Predicament* 3) characteristic of the postmodern era. Written from positions of cultural undecidability, *Lograire* dramatizes the historical and cultural hybridity of the (post)colonial world, in which all identities are "inauthentic." It can, therefore, be read in terms of an ethnography of conjunctures, which Clifford opposes to the totalizing project of classical (Western) anthropology. "Constantly moving between cultures," the Cliffordian ethnography of conjunctures is "perpetually displaced, both regionally focused and broadly comparative, a form both of dwelling and of travel in a world where the two experiences are less and less distinct" (Clifford, *Predicament* 9).

The Scandal of Malinowski's *Diary* and
a Revolution in Anthropology

Bronislaw Malinowski (1884-1942) is widely acclaimed as one of the founding fathers of modern anthropology. Between 1914-1918, during his pioneering fieldwork in Melanesia, he transformed the ethnographic practice by pitching a tent in the middle of a native village, rather than staying in a mission house and meeting his native informants on its verandah, as was the custom of the day. No longer in a position of privilege (a white man's house in a native settlement; an elevated verandah suggesting Western culture's superiority), Malinowski became part of the society he studied, trying to understand it from "the native's point of view" – with scientific objectivity and without prejudice.

This myth of an unbiased fieldworker crumbled with the posthumous publication of that anthropologist's field diary. Written in Polish mixed with a considerable heteroglot input, the diary was not intended for publication.[24] In 1967, however, at the height of the Malinowski cult, his literary executor decided to have the diary published in English and in a much abbreviated form: the English version consisted of only two notebooks covering the period crucial to the evolution of the discipline: the Mailu and the Trobriand Islands notebooks.

Reviews of *Diary in the Strict Sense of the Term* varied from, at best, judging it a mere "footnote to anthropological history"[25] to, at worst,

---

24. The original diary consisted of seven separate notebooks spanning a ten-year period between 1908, when Malinowski took his doctoral degree at the University of Krakow, through to his brief recuperative stay in the Canary Islands, his studies in Leipzig, Germany and at the London School of Economics, and his extended fieldwork in Melanesia between 1914-18.

25. Raymond Firth, Introduction to Malinowski, *Diary* xviii; subsequent references

proclaiming Malinowski "a crabbed self-preoccupied, hypochondriacal narcissist."[26] Accusations of racism abounded. More perceptive reviews were rare. An isolated voice would point to the cathartic function of diary-writing for an individual stranded in an alien culture and left "alone with his instincts." Having worked through conflicting emotions by writing about them, continued the reviewer, Malinowski was thus much more capable of empathizing with the cultural "other" (quoted in Firth xxiv). Another sympathetic chord was struck by Anthony Forge, a practicing fieldworker himself, who recognized his own conflicting emotional states in Malinowski's notes (quoted in Firth xxvi). But the majority of the anthropological world was up in arms, mostly because the *Diary* repeatedly dismantles Malinowski's mythical status by portraying him as a fully embodied and largely imperfect human being: sickly, grumpy, demotivated, imperialistically-minded, obsessed by sexual fantasies, drugged by escapist fiction. To better understand the ambiguities of Malinowski's field experience, however, it should be noted that that Polish-born citizen of the Austro-Hungarian Empire, surprised by the outbreak of World War I while on an ethnographic expedition in the Britain-controlled region of Papua New Guinea, was considered an "enemy alien" and could neither return to Europe nor remain in Australia outside an internment camp. His only remaining option was a protracted ethnographical expedition. In consequence of unfavorable historical circumstances, this cosmopolitan European, affiliated professionally with the London School of Economics, spent three consecutive years on the colonial frontier, in a situation of cultural liminality, grappling with incompatible cultures and languages, and struggling against personal and cultural disintegration.

Two decades after the publication of Malinowski's *Diary*, Clifford, writing from a transformed historical and theoretical awareness, was to introduce the term "ethnographic self-fashioning" as a way of approaching the apparent aporias of ethnographic fieldwork.[27] Championing ethnography as the practice of writing (*gráphō*) about a particular people (*ethnos*) at a particular place and time, Clifford claims that anthropologists, like other writers, invent rather than represent the objects of their study.[28] He finds it natural that within this textual framework Malinowski should have

---

will be cited as "Firth" parenthetically in the text.

26. Clifford Geertz, quoted in Firth xxvi.

27. The chapter from Clifford's *Predicament of Culture* is entitled "On Ethnographic Self-Fashioning: Conrad and Malinowski," and draws intriguing parallels between those two famous Poles stranded between languages and cultures.

28. James Clifford and George E. Marcus, eds., *Writing Culture: The Poetics and Politics of Ethnography* (Berkeley: University of California Press, 1986) 2; subsequent references will be cited as "Clifford & Marcus" parenthetically in the text.

assumed – ironically, as he perceptibly notices – diverse colonial masks, including that of "Kurtz-like excess" (Clifford, *Predicament* 105).

But by the end of the 1980s, Malinowski's *Diary* had already become a focal point for a fascinating theoretical debate. Far from being a mere footnote to anthropological history, it emerged as a canonical text articulating a new ethnographic subjectivity – one situated within and circumscribed by the ethnographer's own culture, no matter how hard s/he should try to see things "from the native's point of view." In *The Predicament of Culture*, a work that momentarily assumed a canonical status in cultural anthropology, Clifford helpfully attributes the importance of Malinowski's *Diary* for the postmodern and poststructural discourse to its being written at "the moment [the 1910s] when the ethnographic (relativist and plural) idea [of culture] began to attain its modern currency" (Clifford, *Predicament* 10). Revealing the constructedness of cultural identity and thus corroborating post-structuralist theories of the de-centeredness of cultures and subjectivities, it was bound to deal a blow to traditional anthropological assumptions. In short, in 1967, the year of its publication, the professional milieu's opposition to Malinowski's *Diary in the Strict Sense of the Term* was almost unanimous because the text ruthlessly dismantled two myths most cherished by the discipline: that of cross-cultural understanding and that of a self-possessed, coherent subjectivity. Both proved to be rhetorical constructs enmeshed in situations of ambivalence and power (Clifford, *Predicament* 112).

Anthropology's "Experimental Moment"

By the mid-sixties the crisis of representation was beginning to register in many related disciplines as the traditional means of describing social realities were being challenged by the eclipse of "grand narratives" and as sensitivity to difference and close attention to detail, contextuality, irregularities and indeterminants demonstrated the inadequacy of accepted theories. As argued by Marcus and Fischer in their informative *Anthropology as Cultural Critique*, anthropology's "experimental moment," i.e. the discipline's involvement with experimental ethnographic writing, is reflective of the overall crisis of representation and therefore revealing of "the current conditions of knowledge."[29] Predictably, the publication of Malinowski's *Diary* yielded a crop of essays reflecting on the anthropologist as author. In a work thus subtitled cultural anthropologist Clifford Geertz analyzes in retrospect the "strategy of anthropological text-building" that Malinowski's *Diary* made manifest in the 1960s. Contrary

---

29. George E. Marcus and Michael M. J. Fischer, *Anthropology as Cultural Critique* (Chicago: University of Chicago Press, 1986) 5.

to the myth of scientific objectivity, as Geertz argues, the ethnographer had to construct his or her story of native life within and out of complex situational and cultural contexts. Factors naturally registering on ethnographic representations of native lives include, according to Geertz, the combined effects of: landscape, the sense of isolation, the presence of a local European population, one's memories of home and what one has left behind, the sense of vocation and future life, the unpredictability of human emotions, the fragility of one's physical and spiritual condition, the vagaries of one's thoughts.[30] This realization helped the author formulate a new paradigm of interpretive anthropology. Since "man is an animal suspended in webs of significance he himself has spun," he declares: "I take culture to be those webs, and the analysis of it to be therefore not an experimental science in search of law but an interpretative in search of meaning."[31] As a result, Geertz considers ethnographies to be "interpretations, or misinterpretations . . . as inherently inconclusive as any others" (Geertz, *Interpretation* 23).

Anthropology and the Historical Moment

By the mid-1960s, the Western world was not completely unprepared for the shock delivered to the anthropologist profession by Malinowski's *Diary*. World War II had contributed to the dismantling of the colonial system, while political independence had empowered the newly emergent nations to question Western constructions of native cultures and identities. As a result, important insights into the complex relations between culture, class and race were being offered by "Third World" intellectuals. It is worth remembering, though, that African Americans had been involved in shaping cultural and racial politics at least since the Harlem Renaissance in the 1920s, and that 1961 saw the publication of the founding text for the emerging postcolonial studies: Franz Fanon's *The Wretched of the Earth*.[32] By the mid-1960s the universality of the term "culture" –

---

30. Clifford Geertz, *Works and Lives: Anthropologist as Author* (Stanford, CA: Stanford University Press, 1988); subsequent references will be cited as "Geertz, *Works*" paenthetically in the text.

31. Clifford Geertz, *The Interpretation of Cultures* (New York: Basic Books, 1973) 5; subsequent references will be cited as "Geertz, *Interpretation*" parenthetically in the text.

32. Franz Fanon, *The Wretched of the Earth* (New York: Grove Press, 1963). Merton read Fanon and even used a chapter from *The Wretched of the Earth*, entitled "Colonial War and Mental Disorders," in his interpretation of Albert Camus' *The Stranger* (see Thomas Merton, *The Literary Essays of Thomas Merton*, ed. Patrick Hart, OCSO [New York: New Directions, 1981] 299-301; subsequent references will be cited as "*LE*" parenthetically in the text).

in the singular and limited to the Western world only – was being hotly debated. In 1966 another important opening was made. A year before the publication of Malinowski's *Diary*, French philosopher Jacques Derrida proclaimed the "event" of rupture in Western philosophy.[33]   His three important books followed in 1967: *Speech and Phenomena, Of Grammatology* and *Writing and Difference*.[34] With Derrida's announcement of "The end of the Book and the beginning of Writing,"[35] the theory of textuality was rapidly spreading beyond its Parisian nursery.[36]

Malinowski and the Historical Moment

It is against those developments that one should situate the "rupture" and "scandal" of Malinowski's *Diary*. There is little doubt nowadays that the author's morbidly honest presentation of his ever renewed and never fully successful attempts to articulate a coherent subjectivity and a coherent vision of a society thorough the multiple, often conflicting sites of "language, desire, and cultural affiliations" (Clifford, *Predicament* 102) began to transform anthropology from the older model of an exact, verifiable science to the humanistic discipline it is today – a discipline engaged in a continual effort of "ethnographical self-fashioning." In a chapter from *The Predicament of Culture* entitled "On Ethnographic Self-Fashioning," Clifford observes that Malinowski's *Argonauts of the Western Pacific*, the anthropological fruit of his fieldwork in Melanesia, "giv[es] wholeness to a culture (Trobriand) and to the self (the scientific ethnographer)" (Clifford, *Predicament* 112) at the cost of a lie. That lie was the exclusion of the diary material from his ethnographic work on the Trobriand society. With this exclusion all the disrupting contradictions and incoherencies of the complex cultural-anthropological picture presented in *Argonauts* became conveniently suppressed. Thus, concludes Clifford,

---

33. Jacques Derrida, "Structure, Sign and Play in the Discourse of the Human Sciences," a talk delivered at the Johns Hopkins Symposium of 1966, in Jacques Derrida, *Writing and Difference*, trans. Alan Bass (Chicago: University of Chicago Press, 1978) 278-95; rept. in *Modern Criticism and Theory: A Reader*, ed. David Lodge (London and New York: Longman,1991) 108-23; subsequent references to the latter source will be cited as "Derrida, 'Structure'" parenthetically in the text.

34. Jacques Derrida, *La Voix et le Phénomène: Introduction au Probléme du Signe dans la Phénoménologie du Husserl* (Paris: Presses Universitaires de France, 1967); Jacques Derrida, *De la Grammatologie* (Paris: Éditions de Minuit, 1967); Jacques Derrida, *L'Écriture et la Différence* (Paris, Éditions du Seuil, 1967).

35. Title of the opening section of Derrida's *Of Grammatology*.

36. Merton was not ignorant of the new developments: in 1967 he was reviewing Roland Barthes' *Zero Degree of Writing* (see "Roland Barthes – Writing as Temperature" [*LE* 140-46]) and, as I shall argue elsewhere, drifting close to the premises of textuality.

the discipline of fieldwork anthropology, in constituting its authority, constructs and reconstructs coherent cultural others and interpreting selves. If this ethnographic self-fashioning presupposes lies of omission and rhetoric, it also makes possible the telling of powerful truths. . . . The best ethnographic fictions are, like Malinowski's, inherently truthful; but their facts, like all facts in the human sciences, are classified, contextualized, narrated, intensified. (Clifford, *Predicament* 112-13)

Ethnographic fictions, those inescapable half-truths, are recorded by embodied, positioned subjects both affected by and affecting the lives they study.

In 1986, almost twenty years after the shock caused by *Diary in the Strict Sense of the Term*, Clifford looks at a photograph depicting Malinowski poised at his writing table inside his celebrated tent to observe, in a passage strikingly resembling Derrida, that "[w]e begin, not with participant-observation or with cultural texts (suitable for interpretation), but with writing, the making of texts" (Clifford & Marcus 2). Clifford's conclusion is irresistible: with the crumbling of the ideology of transparency of representation and cultural codes, "writing has emerged as central to what anthropologists do both in the field and thereafter." Like any other writers, anthropologists invent rather than represent (Clifford & Marcus 2).

Ethnocentrism, Metaphysics and the Post-Structuralist Moment

When Merton was composing *Lograire*, the social sciences lay in the overwhelming shadow of structuralism and the anthropology of Claude Lévi-Strauss, the author of *Tristes Tropiques* (1955),[37] *Anthropologie Structurale* (1958)[38] and *La Pensée Sauvage* (1962), with his impressive four-volume *Mythologiques* starting to come out in 1964 (*Le Cru et le Cuit*). Merton's attempt to deploy an "urbane structuralist" tactic in his new poetry was hugely influenced by the Frenchman's structuralist anthropology, as attested by Merton's fascinating struggle with Lévi-Strauss recorded in the pages of his working notebook. Known as the "Cargo" Notebook #30, it attests to Merton's attempt to reconcile Lévi-Strauss' "totemic thinking" with his interest in a-historical structures and relations (which Merton calls syntax), and the hermeneutic of Paul Ricoeur with his "historic event thinking" rich in content (semantics). On October 12 Merton wonders: "If the analogy of language gives key to understanding

---

37. Claude Lévi-Strauss, *Tristes Tropiques* (Paris: Plon, 1955).
38. Claude Lévi-Strauss, *Anthropologie Structurale* (Paris: Plon, 1958).

of parental systems, will it also give key to art, religion and all cultural phenomena?"[39] A few days earlier in the pages of his journal he had just eulogized the founder of structural anthropology for having "extraordinary views" and being "ahead of everyone" (*LL* 299).

Decidedly, by the late 1960s Lévi-Strauss was very much *the* anthropologist within the Western world, and Merton's uneasy *agon* with his model of anthropology was in itself a sign of the contemplative monk's keen attunement to the spirit of the time. It is not without significance for the exegesis of *Lograire* that Jacques Derrida used the anthropology of Lévi-Strauss to support his thesis of the decentering of Western culture. In his talk "Structure, Sign and Play in the Discourses of the Human Sciences," he located a significant post-structuralist moment in Lévi-Strauss' writings. According to the philosopher, the "scandal" that destabilizes the project of structural anthropology is, as Lévi-Strauss himself admitted, the incest prohibition, a concept that escapes the nature/culture opposition fundamental to Western philosophy. Lévi-Strauss believed that the incest prohibition belongs to the realm of culture in so far as it is a system of rules and norms (a prohibition), but he also realized that by virtue of its universality – the fact that incest is prohibited in all known societies – it seems to have been instituted by nature itself. To Derrida's regret, however, rather than follow suit and plunge "outside philosophy" to, consequently, begin to dismantle the system of binaries on which Western philosophy is founded, Lévi-Strauss preserved the opposition as a useful methodological tool while denying it any truth value. This double bind launches Derrida's inquiry into other inconsistencies in the anthropologist's discourse, which results in the deconstructionist philosopher's conviction that Lévi-Strauss ultimately abandoned "all reference to a center, to a subject, to a privileged reference, to an origin, or to an absolute archia" (Derrida, "Structure" 115-16). It is in this context that Derrida links the twentieth-century revolution in anthropology with the end of metaphysics, proclaiming: "there is nothing fortuitous about the fact that critique of enthocentrism – the very condition of ethnology – should be systematically and historically contemporaneous with the destruction of the history of metaphysics (Derrida, "Structure" 112). For Derrida, the question that needs to be addressed is the future of anthropology when "the name of man . . . [is] the name of that being who, throughout the history of metaphysics or of ontotheology – in other words, throughout his entire history – has dreamed of full presence, the reassuring foundation, the origin and end of play" (Derrida, "Structure" 122).

---

39. Thomas Merton, "Cargo" Notebook 30 (September-November 1967) (Thomas Merton Center [TMC] archives, Bellarmine University, Louisville, KY).

What can *Lograire* – written at that critical moment of history, that swelling juncture of multiple concerns that made themselves manifest at the emergence of "the as yet unnameable which is proclaiming itself" (Derrida, "Structure" 122) – offer its readers? What wisdom, what vision, what "saving fiction" can it offer to the world in crisis?

Merton and Malinowski

"There are good observations in Malinowski's diary," notes Merton on February 26, 1968. "I laugh at him, but he was really working things through in his own life and this [fragments from the *Diary* copied in Merton's journal] shows it" (*OSM* 59). The ethnographer's heroic efforts to control his ailing body and flagging spirits in an alien environment by imposing an almost monastic self-discipline must have won Merton's grudging admiration. The following observation that Merton culled from Malinowski sounds eerily close to Zen or some wisdom of the desert: "To get up, to walk around, to look for what is hidden around the corner – all this is merely to run away from oneself, to exchange one person for another." "Good!" notes the monk with appreciation (*OSM* 59-60). But his overall attitude to the anthropologist is marked by ambivalence. What the monk and contemplative appreciates – the honesty, the struggle, the hard-won disappointing truth[40] – the artist must "use" in a way that suits his poetic vision. Even though Merton has "[n]othing against" Malinowski, he admits: "I use him nevertheless, perhaps a little ruthlessly, in *Lograire*." He further explains that his objective is to use the anthropologist as an epitome of "a certain kind of mentality, pre-war European, etc. in confrontation with Cargo" (*OSM* 59).[41] That this mentality was essentially that of a quintessential English gentleman adds a personal note to Merton's experiment. In the pages of the "East" Canto of *Lograire* Merton is, in effect, reconstructing a mentality he himself shared as a one-time aspiring member of the English intellectual elite who was being groomed for diplomatic service. Although he would later laugh at the Oakham chaplain's exegesis of 1 Corinthians 13, which substituted "gentlemanliness" for charity,[42] and would see in the "gentlemanly" Eng-

---

40. *Diary in the Strict Sense of the Term* ends with Malinowski's recognition of defeat: "Truly I lack real character" (Malinowski, *Diary* 657).

41. Merton repeatedly applies this procedure in his "antipoetry." Already in the early *Original Child Bomb* (New York: New Directions, 1962), he "used" the US Fleet Admiral William D. Leahy in a similar fashion. Within that poem, the admiral's professed lack of belief in the atomic bomb serves as an incentive to the Manhattan Project team to work even harder towards success. Merton never even alludes to Admiral Leahy's strong opposition to the use of the bomb on Japan.

42. Thomas Merton, *The Seven Storey Mountain* (New York: Harcourt Brace, 1948)

land of his adolescence a "moral fungus" that bore the fruit of war (*SSM* 126-27), he used to be fascinated, e. g., by the worldliness and cultural refinement of his English guardian, Tom Izod Bennett, who was very much *the* gentleman and Merton's role model in those days. Bennett, and to some extent the young Merton himself, would thus emerge as other correlates of that pre-war European mentality that *Lograire* attempts to deconstruct by drawing on the intimate diary of Bronislaw Malinowski, another cosmopolitan European and a member of the elitist academic establishment.[43]

Pre-War European Mentality Reconstructed

"East with Malinowski" echoes the title of the poem's previous section, "East with Ibn Battuta" (*GL* 82-88). But while the fourteenth-century travel narrative richly fulfills its promise and introduces the reader to vivid images and – yes – a participant-observer's experience of cultures and places, of politics, religious beliefs, customs, legends, cuisine and daily life of almost half the hemisphere (there are vignettes of Cairo, Syria, Mecca, Isfahan, Delhi and Calicut), the other narrative, six centuries into the future, fails to deliver. "We tack into the lagoon" (*GL* 89) – the story begins in a classic ethnographic fashion. The rest, however, thwarts the expectations created by the opening. Instead of following with details of the unfamiliar new world he has just entered, the narrator turns within, to his inner landscape: "Shipping water I am ready / To throw up" (*GL* 89).

Unlike Ibn Battuta's, Malinowski's narrative is dominated by the physiological functions of a body transplanted into an alien and incomprehensible environment. In between vomiting, urinating and emptying his bowels, he claims to be "Having / The time of [his] life" (*GL* 89). This claim seems rather absurd unless one attends to images suggesting the European narrator's dominance over the exotic environment, such as urinating "from a height of 13 feet" or emptying the bowels "From a privy above the water" (*GL* 90). The elevated position of his body suggests authority, including the ethnographic authority to represent the cultural other. There is no doubt who is in control, who has taken metaphorical possession of the place – "no man shall sit higher in Trobriand than I,"

73-74; subsequent references will be cited as "*SSM*" parenthetically in the text.

43. In an unpublished November 4, 1962 letter to the Dutch psychoanalyst Joost Meerloo, Merton writes: "You speak very much for the world in which I grew up and to which I still belong: pre-war Europe with its particular heritage and traditional outlook" (TMC archives).

sarcastically comments Merton in Malinowski's voice (*GL* 95).[44]

It soon becomes clear that by analyzing acts of language and drawing radical conclusions from the diarist's rhetoric, Merton uses Malinowski to reveal the abiding colonialist mentality of the supposedly unbiased Europeans (whether anthropologists, colonial agents or missionaries), their irredeemable cultural situatedness, and hidden assumptions concerning the "primitive" societies they study / invent. In the canto's section III Malinowski becomes simply "the anthropologist" (*GL* 91, 92, 93, 95). Divested of his proper name, his function is limited to merely spelling out the characteristics of the colonialist-patriarchal mentality characteristic of pre-war Europe. Despite his obsessive self-preoccupation, the narrator of the Tupuseleia section has an artist's eye for details, is not unappreciative of natural beauty, and sporadically articulates this appreciation in poetic language – like the observation that at high tide the Kurukuru-covered houses "Dip their long thatch beards / In the water" (*GL* 90). But this beauty deserves no more appreciation (and no more space in the travel notes) than the novelty of urinating from the raised platform when the tide is low. Nor does the visionary landscape with "gentle hills" and "Sprawling spidery trees" at high tide the next morning prevent him from emptying his bowels "straight into the sea" (*GL* 90) – which he evidently does with a touch of excitement. The familiar reality has remained behind, in the metropolis; what confronts the anthropologist on the cultural frontier is the exotic and the bizarre, which dictates a different code of behavior than that of the high Georgian society of his adopted England.

The historical Malinowski, like Mr. Kurtz – that iconic colonial character from Joseph Conrad's *Heart of Darkness* – was keenly aware of the seductive pull of desire on the colonial frontier. His rigorous, though not always successfully maintained, self-discipline was meant to be an antidote to the Conradian realm of "the horror," whose presentiment haunts the pages of *Diary in the Strict Sense of the Term*. Merton's anthropologist figure, however, lacks Malinowski's nuance and real-life drama. Thus, for instance, when Merton's Malinowski, outraged at the Melanesian natives' lack of cooperation, confesses: "My feeling towards them: exterminate the brutes" (*GL* 95), Merton both misquotes Malinowski's actual words,[45] and leaves out the despair and dark irony of his original confession to make the desired generic profile more convincing.

---

44. Merton parodies here governor William MacGregor's famous claim "Nobody shall sit higher in New Guinea than I," quoted in Worsley 51.

45. "My feelings towards the natives are [on the whole] decidedly tending to 'exterminate the brutes'" (Malinowski, *Diary* 69).

Yes, Merton uses Malinowski rather ruthlessly,[46] but he does so with an eye to exposing the dark lining of the "civilized" Western mind. By selecting, condensing and rephrasing snatches from Malinowski's diary and arranging them in meaningful configurations, the author of *Lograire* allows some "intricately truthful" fiction to emerge, as James Clifford would put it (Clifford, *Predicament* 112).

This truthful fiction is the result of Merton's skillful editorial work. Not without significance is the fact that Merton's selection and arrangement of the *Diary* material encodes Malinowski's desire for absolute control over "his" territory – an ambition he shares in the poem with other European travelers (see especially "Place Names" [*GL* 96-97]) – in his body language. It is body language that qualifies him as a dominant male who urinates to mark his territory and parades his alpha status by towering over the submissive herd (in one vignette from Tupuseleia he shares a canoe with a native policeman "And another savage" [*GL* 89]). But the instinctive adoption of an animal male's boundary-staking strategy undermines the anthropologist's claim to refinement and high culture. The latter are expected to belong in the realm of "civilization" as opposed to the primitive realm of desires, bodily drives and naked instincts, and yet, has Malinowski not just demonstrated that he belongs with the same naked natives that his "civilized" mind dismisses as cultureless "savages"? Even if he has, this recognition does not haunt his conscious mind. The self-styled arbiter of culture feels an abysmal distance between himself and the naked "Bronze bodies" (*GL* 90) glimpsed inside the kurukuru-covered huts. Anonymous and dehumanized in his vision, the natives almost blend into a homogenous mass, safe for the occasional and rather unsavory sight of "firm breasts stick[ing] out" (*GL* 90).[47] But postcolonial theory would see his instinctive shrinking from this state of "savagery" as a recoil from the shadow, a disgust caused by the vague recognition of a "distant kinship"[48] with the civilized world's uncanny double. In his anticolonial

---

46. Academic honesty requires that a corrective be added to this one-sided picture of the "early" Malinowski. Archeologists Nancy Scheper-Hughes and Philippe Bourgois reclaim the broader picture by stressing that in his later years "Malinowski sided with the anticolonialist revolutions of the mid-twentieth century. He argued passionately against the archeologist as a neutral and objective observer and 'bystander' to the history of colonial violence and the suffering that is visited upon the people and cultures with whom anthropology had cast its lots" (Introduction to *Violence in War and Peace: An Anthology* [Malden, MA: Blackwell, 2004] 7).

47. Malinowski suffered from a "Fear of pointed objects" (*GL* 90).

48. This is how Chinua Achebe diagnoses Conrad's Marlow's troubled description of natives lining the shores of the Congo: see Chinua Achebe, "An Image of Africa: Racism in Conrad's *Heart of Darkness*," *Massachusetts Review* 18 (1977) (rpt. in *The Norton*

reading of Conrad's masterpiece, Nigerian critic Chinua Achebe makes an observation bearing directly on this point. "The meaning of *Heart of Darkness* and the fascination it holds over the Western mind," specifies the critic, "lies in the following comment made by the novel's narrator: 'What thrilled you was just the thought of their [the Africans'] humanity – like yours . . . Ugly'" (Achebe 1786). The West's negative projection of itself is what cosmopolitan Europeans of Conrad's and Malinowski's generation find on the colonial frontier and what they recoil from.

Ambiguity, ambivalence and postmodern, ontological irony saturate the whole section of Merton's poem. Upon entering the village of Tupuseleia, Merton's anthropologist reports: "Dark inside / Bronze bodies appear / At the doors" (*GL* 90). This sight apparently activates his worst racialist self: "Do not shoot," we hear him comment in a parenthetical aside, "Til you see the whites of their eyes" (*GL* 90). This Kurtz-like excess, an evocation of the central character of Conrad's *Heart of Darkness*, is Merton's skillful contribution to the presentation of a composite Western mentality, whose strengths and weaknesses Kurtz, to a large degree, epitomizes. "All Europe contributed to the making of Kurtz,"[49] confides Marlow, the Conradian narrator, when referring to the mixed background of the novel's protagonist. In a very real sense, the diabolically intelligent Kurtz is an epitome of the colonialist, pre-war mentality. His drive to absolute control over the natives, culminating in his demand that they worship him as a god, fits in with the anthropologist's sense of royal superiority expressed in the slogan: "No man shall sit in Trobriand higher than I." Additionally, Conrad's character seems to embody the colonialist myth of "white man's burden" gone sour better than anyone else.

On a different note, one would be hard pressed to find those exact words, "Do not shoot, / Til you see the whites of their eyes," in Malinowski's diary – not the sentiment, though. This statement is historically attributed to General William Prescott at the time of the Battle of Bunker Hill. Re-contextualizing this phrase, so closely associated with the American Revolutionary War and the poorly armed colonists' determination to prevail against the superior military potential of the British forces, Merton invests Malinowski's colonial encounter with some fearful symmetry: oppressor and oppressed collapse in this double-edged act of semantic violence. The suggestion is, once again, that any identity is constructed in opposition to the demonized Other. Moreover, Merton's use of this famous phrase interest-

---

Anthology of Theory and Criticism, ed. Vincent Leitch [New York: W. W. Norton, 2001) 1789]); subsequent references will be cited as "Achebe" parenthetically in the text.

49. Joseph Conrad, *Heart of Darkness*, *The Norton Anthology of English Literature*, 8th ed., vol 2, ed. Stephen Greenblatt (New York: W. W. Norton, 2006) 1926.

ingly illustrates the textual provenance of the poem: *Lograire* is a narrative of "language that speaks man" (Heidegger) and a narrative of man as an "être parlant" (Lacan, Bachelard)[50] – a speaking subject, always already constituted by the codes of culture. In a larger sense, Merton's entire poem is a labyrinth of "signifyin" practices (Henry Louis Gates, Jr.): of (mis) quotations, parodies and imitations of other voices and other narratives in the differential repetition of which the strategies of the original discourses are reversed and the repressed traces of alterity reclaimed.

Back in Port Moresby, the town removed from the dangerous "savagery" of the frontier, the anthropologist is self-composed and self-possessed again. With other refined European males he converses about "sun and moon / And the causes of things" (*GL* 90) while enjoying cold drinks and other desirable "cargo" in the luxury setting of McCann's Hotel – a hotel, no doubt, for whites only. Even in this decently regulated, "civilized" environment, however, some other prejudices, equally foundational for the fiction of the West's cultural integrity, come to light. "That woman / Vulgar beyond endurance" (*GL* 90) – this is how the anthropologist summarily dismisses an unidentified female. Tellingly, this is the only flesh-and-blood European woman in the entire East Canto. There are evocations of other white women in the canto's section III, but they function as either nostalgic correlatives of boyhood safety (Malinowski's mother) or male fantasies of ideal womanhood (as epitomized by Miss Nussbaum in her "glacier blue outfit" [*GL* 93]). There is more than a hint of misogyny in the patriarchal mentality of the empire.

In between the view of Tupuseleia at high tide and the image of its bronze-bodied inhabitants comes this cryptic passage: "*Stimmung* – desertion / (Death in Venice)" (*GL* 89) to contribute a touch of decadence to the composite portrait of the Western traveler. Fin-de-siècle moods characterize cultures in crisis – decadent, dying cultures, morbidly drawn to death. Decadence was fashionable in the artistic circles of the high modernist society in which the historical Malinowski moved, whether in his native Poland or in his adopted England. Merton's explicit allusion (not to be found verbatim in Malinowski's *Diary*) to Thomas Mann's novella *Death in Venice* – no doubt inspired by the lagoon-like landscape of the coast – grounds the anthropologist's high modernist status while undermining his society's claim to superiority, especially in its confrontation with the vibrant, vital cultures, uninfected by the Stimmung. The combined effect

---

50. In September 1967 Merton comments on Bachelard's *La Poetique de l'Espace*: "Trivializing of contemplative life when it either gets lost in words or loses the sense of man as *être parlant* and of the truly human as logos" ("Cargo" Notebook #30 [Sept.-Oct. 1967] [TMC archives]).

of such words as "desertion" and "death" would be enough to highlight the morbid condition of the West and its representative – the hypochondriac anthropologist. But adding this allusion to the Mann novella, the erudite Merton is reinforcing this impression by enmeshing Malinowski in a significant cultural intertext. The leitmotif of *Death in Venice* is an aging intellectual's obsession with a beautiful adolescent boy[51] and the ongoing association between Aschenbach's corrupted love for the boy and an outbreak of cholera in the Italian city of art and romance. Impressed by Nietzsche's views on decadence and decay, Mann was notable for his insights into the soul of the European artist and intellectual and was a closeted homosexual himself. Thus, with the evocation of *Death in Venice*, Merton broadens the range of objective correlatives for the turn-of-the-century European mentality, while simultaneously hinting at Malinowski's troubled sexuality and homosexual inclinations vis-à-vis native informants, especially his favorite informant/masseur Igua.[52]

Intricately Truthful Fiction

The above is a shorthand portrait of the Western anthropologist's world of privilege. On the one hand, this is an exclusive white man's club, a highly selective fraternity – whose lingering influence could still be felt in the several boarding schools attended by Thomas Merton, at the Cambridge of 1933/34, and perhaps most pervasively in the household of Tom Izod Bennett, Merton's godfather, guardian and role model after Owen Merton's death. On the other, it is a world of surfaces, hypocrisy and corruption of values officially cherished as "civilized." Reconstructing this mentality, the Malinowski section of Merton's *Lograire* lays bare some of the underlying causes of professional anthropology's failure in its confrontation with Cargo. It is no coincidence that at the very moment when, according to Peter Lawrence, the Cargo movement was entering the phase of the "third belief" in the nearby Madang province,[53] the profes-

---

51. The stunningly beautiful boy, whose name is Tadzio, is a young Pole staying in Venice with his parents. This is an interesting coincidence, although totally unrelated to Merton's interest in that other Pole, Bronislaw Malinowski. Being a Pole myself, I feel excited to be finding the (rather implicit) Polish allusions in so limited a fragment as "East with Malinowski."

52. Polish cultural anthropologist Joanna Tokarska-Bakir traces Malinowski's coded autoeroticism and hints of homosexual practices in her article "Malinowski, czyli paradox kłamcy" ["Malinowski, or the Liar's Paradox"], *ResPublica Nowa* 11 (October 2002) (Warszawa: "Polityka" Spoldzielnia Pracy) 60-67.

53. Peter Lawrence, *Road Belong Cargo: A Study of the Cargo Movement in the Southern Madang District, New Guinea* (Manchester: Manchester University Press, 1964) 63-86.

sional ethnographer of Merton's meditation, authorized to understand and describe the cultural other, "lay low, / Shivered under the hot compress / Read Bronte and pissed black / . . . thinking of French chophouses in Soho / Of anything in fact / But Trobriand Islanders and coral gardens" (*GL* 91).

Yet, even when criticizing and distancing himself from it, Merton is conscious of having been shaped by that very mentality as a culturally situated subject. If he devotes so much effort to (re)inventing it in the pages of the Malinowski section, it is because the imperialist figure of the anthropologist is the "other" within himself, whose trace is only partially erased within the agonistic and open-ended process of his subjectivity construction.[54] The jingoist, hypochondriac and disintegrating anthropologist, at least in Merton's "intricately truthful" fiction of Malinowski, is therefore the monk-poet's and his culture's disavowed "other." In the psychoanalytic process of identification "the subject of desire is never simply a Myself," postcolonial critic Homi Bhabha reminds us; and vice versa, "the Other is never simply an It-self, a front of identity, truth or misrecognition."[55] Identification is a process of "negotiation at the borders," famously claims Bhabha; it takes place "in-between disavowal and designation" (Bhabha 72). Bhabha's post-Lacanian theory helps us to navigate the complex process of Merton's psychological identification as reflected in *Lograire* and to identify "Malinowski" as that part of his cultural makeup that the poem's implied author rejects.

Merton, Malinowski and Battuta: Negotiation at the Borders

The similarities between both cosmopolitan Westerners stranded between various cultures and languages are notable. Born in the French Pyrenees to an American mother and a New Zealand father with Welsh ancestry, Tom straddled cultures and languages from his earliest childhood. He was brought up in America, educated at prestigious schools in France, England and the USA, and groomed for the diplomatic service. He travelled widely in Europe before withdrawing from the world of activism to the monastic margin. The sickly Malinowski, born in the part of Poland that belonged to the Austro-Hungarian empire, shuttled constantly between the metropolitan city of Kraków, the nearby Tatra mountains with their distinct culture and pronounced dialect, and the health resorts of Italy, Africa and the Canary Islands; he studied at Leipzig and London before

---

54. French intellectual Julia Kristeva first introduced the concept of *sujet-en-procès* (in the double meaning of subject "in process" and "on trial") in *Polylogues* in 1977.

55. Homi Bhabha, The *Location of Culture* (1994; London and New York: Rutledge, 2010); subsequent references will be cited as "Bhabha" parenthetically in the text.

leaving on an anthropological expedition to Australasia where he was to receive the status of enemy alien. Malinowski's and Merton's early exile from the bourgeois values of the West conferred on both a degree of cultural difference, which facilitated their assumption of the ethnographic position – the position of distance vis-à-vis the cultures and societies they visited and lived in.

Although shaped by many cultures, both identified most profoundly with the Anglophone world. In addition, both received thorough, elitist education, belonged to avant-garde intellectual and artistic circles, kept in touch with the newest intellectual trends and developments, at various points of their lives maintained rigorous monastic (Merton) or quasi-monastic (Malinowski) discipline, and helped redefine their respective professional fields: monasticism and anthropology. On top of that, both kept private diaries, which have since been published to become acclaimed classics. The diaries of both articulate, albeit in different idioms, insights into the spiritual turmoil of the postmodern age, as their authors are seen struggling with the decentering, disintegrating forces within modern subjectivity caught in an ongoing movement of ambivalence and contradiction. How, under those circumstances, could Malinowski's *Diary* not be the repressed trace, the displaced, disavowed other of Merton's literary and literal self?

On the other hand, it is imperative to note that "East with Malinowski" is placed in a dialectical relationship with the section symmetrically entitled "East with Ibn Battuta." Both sections constitute complementary narratives of traveling east.[56] Importantly, though, if both are subject to close scrutiny, the fourteenth-century Muslim from Morocco might emerge as no less ethnocentric and no less biased than the modern anthropologist, and his style will probably be deemed just as infected by cultural projection as Malinowski's. Like the anthropologist, although decidedly in a subtler fashion, Ibn Battuta cannot help seeing the other through the prism of cultural expectations and prejudices. Thus, for instance, his narrative elevates Islam over other religions when the hazardous lifestyle of cosmopolitan Calicut forces him to escape to the Maldives "Where all the inhabitants / Are Muslims" (*GL* 87) and where life is predictable

---

56. James Clifford sees Ibn Battuta's "traveling East" as a "trajectory of a different cosmopolitanism": non-western, non-white male, non-middle-class. Additionally, Battuta's travel notes appear to elude the fraught polarizations into West and East, empire and colony, oppressor and oppressed that so heavily inform Malinowski's notes (*Travel and Translation in the Late Twentieth Century* [Cambridge, MA: Harvard University Press, 1997] 5; subsequent references will be cited as "Clifford, *Travel*" parenthetically in the text).

and livable again. Moreover, he distinguishes between "true believers" and "heretics," and misrepresents the Shi'ite minority, repulsive to his mainstream Sunni sensitivity, as "abominable"[57] (*GL* 83).

Yet, Ibn Battuta's big advantage over Malinowski is that he traveled through a predominantly Islamic world, which spoke the same sacred language and whose "exoticism" was thus seriously delimited. Consequently, Battuta's cultural identity was not seriously undermined in the course of his journey. This both saved him from Malinowski's extreme self-consciousness and conferred on his narrative a greater degree of objectivity. In contrast, the author of *Diary in the Strict Sense of the Term* was, during his prolonged stay among the Trobriand, immersed in cultures and languages vastly different from his own and almost totally unknown to most Westerners of his generation. This is why the effect of cultural difference is incomparably stronger in his section of Merton's ethnopoetic meditation. Yet, if Merton implies that "the anthropologist" never manages to leave the West behind and that he keeps "traveling West," in the sense of projecting his distinctly "Western" worldview on the "exotic" other, the travel narrative of the fourteenth-century African Muslim is, *mutatis mutandis*, not quite free from similar defects of perspective. It is interesting that Merton never seems to notice it. What is more, the juxtaposition of the two travelers and their narratives clearly favors the medieval Muslim to the discredit of the modern ethnographer from Europe. Merton, who in 1968, when the poem was being composed, was a seasoned traveler East, albeit more in spirit than in flesh, quite obviously sympathizes with what he considers to be the more open-minded and affirmative attitude of Battuta. But it is precisely at this point that Homi Bhabha's assertion about identification taking place "in-between disavowal and designation" (Bhabha 72) can become helpful in understanding Merton's *sui generis* interstitial identity. "Malinowski," as a correlate of the turn-of-the-twentieth century racialist mentality of the West that has shaped Merton, continues to persist within the author's identity in the form of a displaced, disavowed trace; "Ibn Battuta," whose travel narrative complements and critiques Malinowski's, articulates a sort of "discrepant cosmopolitanism" (Clifford, *Travel* 36) which is much closer to Merton's sensitivity. One feels that the poet's sympathy gravitates toward the Moroccan and the

---

57. This word carries a warped echo of what English Puritans saw as "ABOMINABLE PRACTISES" (*GL* 65) of the Ranters, a millenarian sect persecuted in 1650s. Merton seems to be relativizing historical experience by his play on perspective: the sympathetic cosmopolitan Ibn Battuta and the cruel persecutors of Ranters stigmatize the incomprehensible other with the same harmful word. In both instances semantic violence opens the way to actual violence.

East while his cultural affiliation with the West is fraught with ambivalence. This agonistic process of "negotiation at the borders" is a form of Merton's personal self-fashioning, as well as a reminder that "identity is conjunctural, not essential"[58] (Clifford, *Predicament* 11).

Ethno-poesis of *Lograire*

In his introduction to *The Predicament of Culture*, Clifford revisits one of the key notions of ethnography, namely, the notion of orientation. Derivable from "Orient," it is "a term left over from a time when Europe traveled and invented itself with respect to a fantastically unified 'East'" (Clifford, *Predicament* 13). In the twentieth century an orientation so defined was to be seriously challenged by the new practices of dwelling and traveling that had brought the Oriental (along with other "exotic" peoples) into the very heart of the West. In effect, as Clifford notices, nowadays "difference is encountered in the adjoining neighborhood, the familiar turns up at the ends of the earth" (Clifford, *Predicament* 14). Ethnographic modernity is thus de-centered and dis-oriented; it can no longer claim any privileged Archimedean point for its cultural analysis. When Malinowski was researching Kiriwinian culture, the "West" as represented by missionaries, colonial agents and anthropologists had already struck deep roots within the "East," transforming, translating and hybridizing its culture(s). In *Lograire*'s "East" Canto this idea is effectively dramatized by the cargo movement, which was well under way in Melanesia in the 1910s, just when "The anthropologist lay low" (*GL* 91), too self-preoccupied to notice. Given the spatial dis-orientation of modernity as theorized by Clifford, it is symptomatic that the East invented in the pages of Merton's poem makes no claim to totality. Far from yielding a complete picture of that geopolitical entity, Merton's canto evokes an outrageously fragmentary and radically imbalanced view of that region, privileging Papua-New Guinea to the exclusion of cultures generally considered more "typically" Oriental, for instance India, China or even Japan. To illustrate the point, let it suffice to say that out of the canto's ten sections, only one offers a panorama of snapshots – in themselves highly selective and discontinuous – of a broader Islamic world of the East, while its remaining sections focus exclusively on Melanesia. The list of absentees would be too long to compose also with respect to religious traditions. Indeed, the "East" fashioned in Merton's meditation seems to exclude more than it includes, as important traditions as Hinduism, Buddhism or Shinto have been disregarded altogether. If Merton chose not to

---

58. The process of self-fashioning is also central for the elected Welshness of the speaker in the "Prologue" to *Lograire* (*GL* 3-6).

use the large geopolitical canvas for his *Lograire* and to attend to highly localized, not to say idiosyncratic, hi/stories instead, this strategy may rightly strike one as avant-garde, even prophetic in the late 1960s, when the postmodern paradigm shift in anthropology was still in progress. More than three decades after Merton's death, in an essay aptly entitled "The World in Pieces," Clifford Geertz insists that such ethnocentric formulas as the East or the West are in fact vastly complex and often contradictory realities and "conglomerate[s] of differences . . . resistant to summary."[59] Within a world in which neat systems broke down to yield an endless play of difference, Geertz pleads for ways of thinking and doing anthropology that would be "responsive to particularities, to individualities, oddities, discontinuities, contrasts, and singularities" (Geertz, "World" 224). The intimacies of local knowledge, Geertz believes, will contribute to our better understanding of cultures and societies.

It is well worth remembering that Geertz was one of the first anthropologists to mine the textual potential of ethnography, and, equally importantly, that his research sealed the death of structural anthropology by helping shift the discipline's attention from the structures to the interpretation of cultures, from ethnography as science to ethnography as a form of writing. In 1973, only four years after the publication of *Lograire*, he famously launched the interpretive paradigm in anthropology by declaring the discipline to be "not an experimental science in search of law but an interpretative in search of meaning" (Geertz, *Interpretation* 5). Given the general concurrence on the significance of Malinowski's *Diary* to the emergence of the new interpretive anthropology, Merton's appropriation of Malinowski as much as his poetic ventures in ethnographic modernity deserve an in-depth research which would open up an exciting – postmodern, poststructural and postcolonial – reading of his late poetry.

More than exciting, such a reading might well prove to be both urgently needed and somehow belated – which conviction was insightfully articulated in 1995 by Georg de Nicolò in the following words: "The fact that Merton utilizes unusual anthropological insights for *The Geography of Lograire* is a hint as to which direction the project was taking. Merton was not merely looking to the past for solutions as so many poets have done before him. . . . He focused rather on recent anthropological studies for a way out of the crisis of modern society and culture."[60] This is also

---

59. Clifford Geertz, "The World in Pieces: Culture and Politics at the End of the Century," *Available Light: Anthropological Reflections on Philosophical Topics* (Princeton: Princeton University Press, 2000) 224; subsequent references will be cited as "Geertz, 'World'" parenthetically in the text.

60. Georg de Nicolò, "Thomas Merton's Anti-Poetry: Genetic and Functional As-

my conviction and with its irresistible logic it returns me to that haunt-
ing question, which like a refrain should recur now, at the conclusion of
my preliminary venture into Merton's ethnopoetics: what wisdom, what
vision, what "saving fiction" can *Lograire* offer to the (Western) world
in crisis? The bold claim with which I started this essay – about the
centrality of the "Malinowski" section for Merton's *Lograire*, a section
seemingly insignificant and frequently overlooked by scholars – rests
on this conviction, especially in view of the fact that, unlike the other
three cantos, the "East" Canto relies almost exclusively on a collage of
anthropological materials.

Concluding, I merely wish to emphasize that what has been written
with reference to the "East" Canto is true of Merton's entire "work in
progress" (*GL* 1), in which drastically incomplete and selective portrayals of the four geopolitical regions are made up of sections radically
fragmented in themselves, each section being divided into discrete units
of information disconnected from others, which juxtapose disparate narratives and incompatible points of view. As a consequence, *Lograire* is
a discontinuous collage of fragments, which fact mimics "the world in
pieces" and the mosaic character of postmodern/postcolonial perception
with its localized knowledges of reality.[61]

---

pects of *Cables to the Ace* and *The Geography of Lograire*," unpublished master's thesis
(Regensburg-Harting, Germany: Universitat Regensburg, 1995) 198.

61. The splintered world of late modernity and the fragmentation of history and
syntax enacted in *Lograire* have fascinating theological-spiritual potential. David Tracy
believes that fragments depict "the spiritual situation of our times" and as such contain
"a sign of hope, perhaps . . . the only signs of hope for redemption" (David Tracy, "Fragments: The Spiritual Situation of Our Times," *God, the Gift, and Postmodernism*, ed.
John D. Caputo and Michael J. Scanlon [Bloomington: Indiana University Press, 1999]
173). I plan to develop the theological-spiritual dimension of *Lograire* in another essay.

Place, Spiritual Anthropology and Sacramentality in Thomas Merton's Later Years

Hans Gustafson

Thomas Merton, perhaps most known for his contemplative and monastic writings, had the remarkable ability of finding beauty, order and religious significance in even the most ordinary and seemingly insignificant events in life. For instance, he reflects on

> watching pro football on TV – at midnight!! The Packers beat the Dallas Cowboys – and it was, I must say, damn good football. . . . Football is one of the really valid and deep American rituals. It has a religious seriousness which American religion can never achieve. A comic, contemplative dynamism, a gratuity, a movement from play to play, a definitiveness that responds to some deep need, a religious need, a sense of meaning that is at once final and provisional; a substratum of dependable regularity, continuity, and an ever renewed variety, openness to new possibilities, new chances. It happens. It is done. It is possible again. It happens. . . . Final score 31-27 is now football history. This will last forever. It is *secure* in its having happened. And we saw it happen. We existed.[1]

Though a reflection on a seemingly ordinary ("non-spiritual") event, this journal entry illustrates a side of Merton, a true and authentic side, that surfaces often in his journals. The burden of this essay will be to offer a case study examining how Merton's sacramental spirituality concretely influenced his sense of "place" and orientation in the world. To assist in conceptualizing "place" (geographical place), I draw on Mircea Eliade's *The Sacred and the Profane*,[2] and in particular his elucidation of one's *axis mundi*, for it provides a constructive framework within which to approach the concept of "home" as such in the context of Merton's later years.

Merton espoused an anthropological vision in which persons are called to seek knowledge of the self via knowledge of God – that is, in knowing the true self more intimately, one knows God more intimately.

---

1. Thomas Merton, *The Other Side of the Mountain: The End of the Journey. Journals, vol. 7: 1967-1968*, ed. Patrick Hart (San Francisco: HarperCollins, 1998) 160-61; subsequent references will be cited as "*OSM*" parenthetically in the text.

2. Mircea Eliade, *The Sacred and the Profane: The Nature of Religion*, trans. Willard Trask (San Diego, CA: Harcourt Brace Jovanovich, 1987); subsequent references will be cited as "Eliade" parenthetically in the text.

In so doing, they might see the world sacramentally. This connatural[3] knowing of God and self hinges on contemplation. Merton's spiritual anthropology as laid out in *The New Man* and his explanation of contemplation in *New Seeds of Contemplation* are examined and applied to the personal narratives from his journals. *The New Man* presents the theological anthropology, *New Seeds* provides the contemplative theory, and his journals provide the practice or the data from his own life. Thus, the project here is to relate his theology and theory with his practice. Merton's consideration of "place" and where he should "be" consumes much of the content of the later journals as he frequently considers the possibility of moving to another "place" on earth, most notably northern California, Alaska, Latin America or even Asia. The journals offer insight into times and "places" as this occurred for Merton. They report when and where Merton understood the world sacramentally. In order to properly situate his journals, I shall first offer a brief review of his spiritual anthropology in *The New Man*[4] and contemplation in *New Seeds of Contemplation*.[5]

Merton's quest for self and place offers a window into the human condition of restlessness; thus many will resonate with the anthropological traits he exhibits such as dissatisfaction, restlessness, the sense of and longing for home, and the search for rootedness. Merton's quest for a new home, set within the context of his spirituality and sacramental vision, provides a striking glimpse into his quest for the "self," which remains a central concern for much of his contemplative theory.

Spiritual Anthropology

In the *New Man*,[6] Merton lays out his most complete theo-philosophical treatment of spiritual anthropology. He begins with the basic question: what does it mean to be human within a theological context? In so doing, he casts an anthropological vision that draws heavily on the tradition

---

3. By the concept connatural knowledge, I intend coming to knowledge of something by way of imitation, experience and practice. Connatural knowledge of God refers to coming to God by imitating and practicing godly attributes. For instance, by loving *agapeically*, one comes to know the *agapic* love of God and thus knows God more intimately.

4. Thomas Merton, *The New Man* (New York: Farrar, Straus and Cudahy, 1961); subsequent references will be cited as "*NM*" parenthetically in the text.

5. Thomas Merton, *New Seeds of Contemplation* (New York: New Directions, 1961); subsequent references will be cited as "*NSC*" parenthetically in the text.

6. Lawrence Cunningham points out that "the 'new man' of the title is an implicit rebuke to the Marxist claim to building a 'new man' – the theoretical capstone of a classless society. Merton's 'new man' is, in short, an alternative vision to the oft discussed 'new Soviet man' of the Cold War era" (Lawrence S. Cunningham, *Thomas Merton and the Monastic Vision* [Grand Rapids, MI: Eerdmans, 1999] 82).

of "Catholic Substance"[7] in positing the potential sacramentality of all persons via the Pauline notion of "putting on Christ" (see Gal. 3:27, Rom. 13:14). It is perhaps too hasty to say at this point that the "putting on of Christ" is similar (certainly not the same) to the Eastern Christian understanding of *theōsis*, or divinization, which broadly refers to a person living in and through Christ, or rather having Christ living in and through that person. However, the concept of "putting on Christ" is often interpreted metaphorically to refer to the immersion into, and the becoming similar to, Christ, not by nature, but by adoption and participation. Christ functions as mediator in the hypostatic union and incarnation – thus persons can understand themselves as potential sacramental mediators in the world; however, this by itself is not identical to the Eastern understanding of *theōsis*. Merton understands the human person as existing in a state of conflict, caught up in a tension between life and death, or rather existence and non-existence. In this sense, Merton does not deviate from the classical Augustinian and Thomist emphasis on *esse* (being) and the understanding of evil as non-being (privation). In other words, to live is to be, and to not-be is to not exist.

Anthropologically, this idea might be rephrased in the following way: we do not know ourselves because we do not know God, and we do not know God because we do not know ourselves; thus knowing God and knowing oneself are inherently wrapped up with one another. In other words, discovering God entails discovering one's self as well. Merton writes: "In order to find God, Whom we can only find in and through the depths of our own soul, we must therefore first find ourselves" (*NM* 63). This is the classic notion of connatural knowledge, the idea that one knows God through knowing one's self and vice-versa, or in common street parlance, "it takes one to know one."[8] Merton embraces connatural knowing in his advocating that the solution to knowing the self entails an attainment of connatural knowledge via "putting on Christ." This participatory path remains sacramental in its retention of the possibility that persons might become divinized via Christ through sacramental participation in Christ. In putting on Christ, one participates in a godly reality in which all things, steeped in God's sacramental self via grace, are seen fully and completely. A Christian believer, such as Merton, might proclaim this way of seeing as the way God intended the world to be seen; that is, this way of seeing entails seeing the world in the manner that Jesus spoke of when he espoused the imminent "Kingdom of God" in the New Testa-

---

7. Used by Paul Tillich in contrast to "the Protestant Principle"; sometimes it is also referred to as "the sacramental principle."

8. Peter Kreeft, "Aquinas and the Angels" (speech, ChristiFideles, April 1999).

ment. This vision includes one's own vision of the true self.

Mystically, in one's union with Christ (via the putting on of Christ) s/he becomes a living sacrament and (re)presents Christ in concrete space and time. The result is a new way of seeing[9] – a sacramental illumination in which all things are understood as potential avenues through which the divine is present and communicates. Did Merton ever truly find his true self? Though not the central question of this article, it should not pass without notice; that is, did Merton arrive at connatural knowledge of himself and God? If so, then how might it relate to his spirituality and search for place? Perhaps his later journals can offer some insight to these questions.

Contemplation

In *New Seeds of Contemplation*, Merton examines the practice and goal of contemplation in an accessible manner for monastics and non-monastics alike. It progresses from negative (*via negativa*) statements about contemplation (what contemplation is not) towards affirmative statements about what contemplation is. For Merton, contemplation "cannot be taught," but "only be hinted at" (*NSC* 6). It does not simply lie in pure passivity nor is it a mere psychological passivity. "The contemplative is not merely a man who likes to sit and think, still less one who sits around with a vacant stare" (*NSC* 9). Contemplation is not a pure prayerfulness nor the contentedness found in liturgical rites. It is not arrived at through "practical reason" alone, nor is it found in trance, ecstasy, emotion or enthusiasm. It is not the gift of prophecy. It is not a mere acceptance of the way things are in order put one at ease, and it is certainly no pain-killer. Contemplation is not Cartesian epistemology,[10] but rather is more

---

9. Robert Barron claims that "Christianity is, above all, a way of seeing. . . . What unites figures as diverse as James Joyce, Caravaggio, John Milton, the architect of Chartres, Dorothy Day, Dietrich Bonhoeffer and the later Bob Dylan is a peculiar and distinctive take on things, a style, a way, which flows finally from Jesus of Nazareth. Origen remarked that holiness is seeing with the eyes of Christ, Teilhard de Chardin said, with great passion, that his mission as a Christian thinker was to help people see, and Thomas Aquinas said that the ultimate goal of the Christian life is a 'beatific vision,' an act of seeing" (Robert E. Barron, *And Now I See: A Theology of Transformation* [New York: Crossroad, 1998] 1).

10. Merton places the Cartesian formula for the proof of one's own existence (*dubito ergo cogito ergo sum)* the furthest outside the reality of one experiencing her own existence because it clearly and distinctly reduces oneself to an objective concept only to be grasped via cognitive insight. Furthermore, it reduces God to a mere concept, to a *what*. However, for Merton, "'God is not a *what*,' not a 'thing.' . . . There is 'no such thing' as God because God is neither a 'what' nor a 'thing' but a pure '*Who*'" (*NSC* 13). Thus contemplation, as a means towards knowing the true self and God's true self, must

similar to the existential experience of subjective being. In making clear what contemplation is not (partially), Merton offers an understanding of contemplation that involves transcendence and knowledge of the true self in a subjective manner. Contemplation assists in knowing that one's false self is not the true self, but proceeds in an experiential way. "Contemplation," he writes, "is precisely the awareness that this 'I' is really 'not I' and the awakening of the unknown 'I' that is beyond observation and reflection and is incapable of commenting upon itself" (*NSC* 7).

In addition to this *via negativa*, he highlights three additional important themes for grasping what contemplation is. They are: (1) the relationship between faith and theology; (2) union with Christ; and (3) the vision of a pansacramental cosmology.[11] Each remains important in so far as it relates to Merton's journal narratives on "place" and spirituality.

First, the relationship between faith and theology is crucial for understanding contemplation. Faith is the first step towards contemplation since it marks the transition between theology and faith. In a certain sense, faith steps beyond the limits of theology. Faith, on its own, begins in "intellectual assent" and picks up where theology leaves off. In other words, faith commences in theology but eventually moves beyond it. Although faith begins in an "intellectual assent," it is not wholly intellectual. Theology can only proceed to a limit in the religious quest. Ultimately, it is to be left behind at a certain point at which it is radically purified or altered. "Radically purified" here is what Merton intends when he writes, "Here theology ceases to be a body of abstractions and becomes a Living Reality Who is God Himself" (*NSC* 148). The higher stages of faith, bordering on contemplation, put to rest analogies and technical theological language about God and seek to rest in the living presence

---

retain an emphasis on "the experiential grasp of reality as *subjective*" (*NSC* 8). To do this adequately, God's self must be understood as a subject (as a "Who"). Merton maintains that pure rationalism, such as one might find in Cartesian epistemology, undermines the project to know the self, since "For the contemplative there is no *cogito* ('I think') and no *ergo* ('therefore') but only *SUM*, I Am" (*NSC* 9).

11. Merton does not refer to this term, but offers a cosmic vision compatible with a pansacramental cosmology. In his essay "Symbolic and Sacramental Existence," Martin Buber coins the term "pansacramentalism" to clarify the distinct features of Hasidic sacramentality. (Martin Buber, "Symbolic and Sacramental Existence," in *The Origin and Meaning of Hasidism*, trans. Maurice Friedman [New York: Harper & Row, 1966] 178). More recently, I have made the case for the compatibility of a pansacramental panentheistic theological cosmology within a classical Thomist Christian theology in "Collapsing the Sacred and the Profane: Pan-Sacramental & Panentheistic Possibilities in Aquinas and their Implications for Spirituality," *The Heythrop Journal* (Sept. 16, 2011) (accessed at: doi:10.1111/j.1468-2265.2011.00684.x).

and reality of God's self. Theology is purified when all of the crutches of theological language and analogy are stripped away to reveal a deeper, truer reality of God. "Faith goes beyond words and formulas and brings us the light of God Himself" (*NSC* 129). Faith becomes a step towards contemplation, which is ultimately a lived theology – an existential participation in God's own self.

Second, union with Christ remains the heart and goal of the contemplative experience, which is attained by shedding the false self and "putting on Christ" and sharing in his divinity. To put on Christ is to model oneself after the inner life of the Trinity in having one nature, yet multiple persons (modes of relationality). In so doing, the contemplative (re)presents Christ. The contemplative becomes his/her true self, while the false self fades into its own illusion. Thus, contemplation provides a means through which one comes to be and to know the true self. In this way, kenosis entails *theōsis*. Merton writes, "In order to become myself I must cease to be what I always thought I wanted to be, and in order to find myself I must go out of myself, and in order to live I have to die" (*NSC* 47). However, contemplation goes beyond this, for it is an awareness (a *way of seeing*) of the world that renders to each thing its proper relation to God's self.

Third, this new *way of seeing* is a vision of the cosmos[12] as pansacramental. "[A]s we go about the world," writes Merton, "everything we meet and everything we see and hear and touch, far from defiling, purifies us and plants in us something more of contemplation and of heaven" (*NSC* 25). All cosmic things contain the potential to express God in temporal time and space. "God is everywhere," according to Merton; "His truth and His love pervade all things as the light and the heat of the sun pervade our atmosphere" (*NSC* 151). Contemplation is an awareness – a new *way of seeing* – of what is "really there" in the world. It allows one to grasp reality in an authentic manner. Through the eyes of the contemplative, the world is seen as in God. Further, for the contemplative, the world simply *is*; that is, God just IS, simply being (*esse*), and the recognition of this, albeit at some level profoundly simplistic and incomplete, holds the essence of contemplation.

---

12. I am using the term "cosmos" here in the manner that Raimon Panikkar uses the term "kosmos." I employ cosmology (and Panikkar employs Kosmology) "in the sense of the subjective genitive: the *logos*, the word of the kosmos that Man should try to hear and to understand by attuning himself to the music of this world, to the mysteries of the kosmos" (Raimon Panikkar, *The Rhythm of Being* [Maryknoll, NY: Orbis, 2010] 369). I do not intend the currently popular definition of the term which refers to knowledge resulting from scientific reasoning applied to the physical data of cosmos.

Merton's Later Journals

In Merton's final journals a constant inner debate (struggle) surfaces over where and how to be in the world. This may surprise those who expect an experienced monk, such as Merton, to be among those who are the most rooted and the least restless.[13] For instance, Merton reflects, "I struggle in myself with my own future – and with the fear I will be discovered before I can get away (irrational) – or even that I may die or be shot" (*OSM* 163). Eerily, he wrote these words four months prior to his death in Bangkok. Further, this passage reflects his restlessness and, to a certain degree, his non-rootedness. By looking at (a) home, (b) contemplative awareness, and (c) Merton's quest for a place in the world (in particular his journal narratives on the places and times he experienced the world in its pansacramentality), we can rediscover Mircea Eliade's religious categories of the *axis mundi* and the sacred and profane.

(a) "Home"

Eliade remains a giant in the field of religious studies for his phenomeno-logical study of religion. His classic text on the study of sacred place, *The Sacred and Profane*, has been foundational in the development of categories and terms used for analyzing religion. One major concept is the *axis mundi*, "the image of a universal pillar . . . which at once connects and supports heaven and earth and whose base is fixed in the world below" (Eliade 36). For many traditions, this axis is recognized as located in specific geographical places such as a certain mountain top,[14] town or river. However, Eliade makes clear that although this remains a fundamental feature of religiously oriented persons, it also manifests itself in those who adopt a nonreligious view of the world. In this way, "profane spaces" (secular, non-religious) can take on religious meaning to the extent that they become an *axis mundi* for certain individuals or groups. This might be, for instance, "a man's birthplace, or the scenes of his first love, or certain places in the first foreign city he visited in youth" (Eliade 24). These places may be understood as *axes mundi* of a person's individual universe or cosmic orientation.

Though he endlessly pondered the possibility of making a permanent move beyond Kentucky, the Abbey of Gethsemani remained his *axis mundi*. It had become the place around which he oriented his life and

---

13. Like Augustine, Merton typifies one of Augustine's most fundamental claims regarding the human condition of restlessness.

14. E.g. Bighorn Medicine Wheel of the Lakota & Sioux in Wyoming (USA); the sacred mountain Machhaphuchhare outside Pokhara (Nepal), a local sacred place to the God Shiva, etc.

world; it was at the center of his universe. He writes, "I remain a monk of Gethsemani. Whether or not I will end my days here, I don't know – and perhaps it is not so important" (*OSM* 166). Later, when in India reflecting on his future, he writes,

> so far the best indications seem to point to Alaska or to the area around the Redwoods. . . . I do not think I ought to separate myself completely from Gethsemani, even while maintaining an official residence there, legally only. I suppose I ought eventually to end my days there. I do in many ways miss it. There is no problem of my wanting simply to "leave Gethsemani." It is my monastery and being away has helped me see it in perspective and love it more. (*OSM* 282)

These passages portray a Merton oriented around a place that carries some sense of "home" despite his lack of desire to permanently reside there in his final years. Perhaps he understood Gethsemani as his "home" in the way many nostalgically orient themselves to their place of childhood. For instance, I orient myself to the geographical place of Minnesota, since it was the place of my childhood, most of my family and friends reside there, and I have spent most of my adult life there. Even when I lived on both coasts of the US, I still understand Minnesota as my "home." I orient myself psychologically, both consciously and unconsciously, around its geographical location; that is, I understand all other places on earth in relation to its orientation to Minnesota. Thus, Minnesota is at the center of my psychological map; to a certain degree it is my geographical *axis mundi*. Merton does this as well. He writes, "For solitude, Alaska really seems the very best place. . . . The idea of being in Alaska and then going out to Japan or the U.S. strikes me as a rather good solution" (*OSM* 252). Here Merton points out the utilitarian advantage of settling in Alaska in that it provides easy access[15] both to his "home" in Kentucky and to Asia, a place Merton was becoming increasingly interested in.[16] Thus, the pull of Kentucky, as a fixed point of orientation (*axis mundi*), remained an influence on his future considerations of place.

b) Contemplative Awareness

Prior to his travels in Asia, Merton traveled extensively within the western United States, spending significant time in New Mexico, Alaska and on

---

15. At the time of writing, Anchorage often served as a mid-way point between the US and much of the Eastern world as passenger airplanes often had to refuel there.

16. Though Merton probably ruled out Alaska for a number of reasons, perhaps one was that it would have been a disadvantageous compromise to settle in a particular place due to its proximity to two more desirable places.

the coast of northern California. He titled his journal during this period, *Woods, Shore, Desert*,[17] which included poems, impressions, memoirs, travelogues and photographs he had taken. It provides a unique glimpse into Merton's experience of exciting new places in the context of a pivotal point in his life as one searching for a new "place" in the world. Further, it demonstrates his attentiveness to seemingly mundane ordinary passages of time. For instance, while on the coast in northern California, he writes, "A huge shark lolls in the swells making his way southward, close in shore, showing his dorsal fin. Faint cry of a lamb on the mountain side muffled by sea wind" (*OSM* 98). What might be understood as descriptions of insignificant events were intentionally recognized by Merton and logged in the journal. In these episodes, Merton pauses and sees the world in a new way via contemplation.

There are many instances prior to *Woods, Shore, Desert* which demonstrate this contemplative awareness. Perhaps the best-known account, a key turning point in the life of Merton, is the experience that has come to be known as the "Vision in Louisville," or the realization "at the corner of Fourth and Walnut." It is a reflection which came to Merton in March of 1958 while in downtown Louisville. He writes,

> In Louisville, at the corner of Fourth and Walnut, in the center of the shopping district, I was suddenly overwhelmed with the realization that I loved all those people, that they were mine and I theirs, that we could not be alien to one another even though we were total strangers. It was like waking from a dream of separateness, of spurious self-isolation in a special world, the world of renunciation and supposed holiness. . . . Not that I question the reality of my vocation, or of my monastic life: but the conception of "separation from the world" that we have in the monastery too easily presents itself as a complete illusion: the illusion that by making vows we become a different species of being, pseudoangels, "spiritual men," men of interior life, what have you.[18]

Here, perhaps for the first time, Merton recognizes not only a collapse of the sacred and non-sacred, but the collapsing of the monastic/non-monastic dualism of the world. He realizes that his monastic vocation does not negate his connection to, and responsibility for, persons living

---

17. Thomas Merton, *Woods, Shore, Desert: A Notebook, May 1968*, ed. Joel Weishaus (Santa Fe, NM: Museum of New Mexico Press, 1982); this material was later included in *The Other Side of the Mountain*.

18. Thomas Merton, *Conjectures of a Guilty Bystander* (Garden City, NY: Doubleday, 1966) 140-41; subsequent references will be cited as "*CGB*" parenthetically in the text.

outside the monastery. Ten years later, in April of 1968, after visiting a Louisville burger joint, Merton reflects,

> When I was in Lum's I was dutifully thinking, "Here is the world." Red gloves, beer, freight trains. The man and child. The girls at the next table, defensive, vague, aloof. One felt the place was full of more or less miserable people. Yet think of it: all the best beers in the world were at their disposal and the place was a *good idea.* And the freight train was going by, going by, silhouetted against an ambiguous sunset. (*OSM* 78)

Merton takes note of the world around him and sees things in themselves. "Here is the world," he writes of its brute hard reality. He sees the world in its *is-ness*, its being. In the passage above, it is almost as if the world is staring back at Merton echoing the monotonic refrain: "Here I am. This is the World. What are you going to do about it?" He recognizes the persons around him as living in the world. Similar to his Fourth and Walnut experience, he affirms the reality of the world beyond Gethsemani, no matter how "ordinary."

On December 4, 1968, six days prior to his death in Bangkok, while in Ceylon (Sri Lanka) observing the rock formations, sculptures and carvings near the temple of Gal Vihara, Merton describes an onslaught of contemplative awareness,

> Looking at these figures I was suddenly, almost forcibly, jerked clean out of the habitual, half-tied vision of things, and an inner clearness, clarity, as if exploding from the rocks themselves, became evident and obvious. . . . The thing about all this is that there is no puzzle, no problem, and really no "mystery." All problems are resolved and everything is clear, simply because what matters is clear. The rock, all matter, all life, is charged with *dharmakaya*[19] – everything is emptiness and everything is compassion. I don't know when in my life I have ever had such a sense of beauty and spiritual validity running together in one aesthetic illumination. (*OSM* 323)

Here Merton experiences this "new way of seeing" as described in *New Seeds*; that is, he welcomes the vision of seeing all things in what he perceives to be their true reality as coming together in God. He describes this experience as one of the most beautiful and spiritually valid he has ever seen, and it comes six days prior to his departure from mortal life. These experiences demonstrate clear instances in which Merton recognized the world through a contemplative lens.

---

19.   Ultimate Truth (literally "body of truth" or "truth-body").

c) Merton's Quest for a "Place" in the World

"Tell me where you are to be found and I will tell you who you are,"[20] writes Emmanuel Mounier, the twentieth-century French Personalist philosopher. This line is a favorite among philosophers, anthropologists and sociologists of place when seeking to understand a person in the context of their physical and geographical location. However, the context of Merton is more difficult to discern than that of most. He was born in France and spent his youth moving around New York, France, Bermuda and England. He spent his last twenty-seven years at Gethsemani prior to his death in Bangkok at the young age of 53. Thus, the task of articulating who Merton was based on his context is rather complex due to the lack of any fixed place of youth and childhood. If a "home" is to be affixed to Merton, in any sense of the term, then it would arguably be Gethsemani, the place where he spent the majority of his life. Merton recognizes some sense of this in 1962 when he writes:

> Returning to the monastery from the hospital: cool evening, gray sky, the dark hills. Once again I get the strange sense that one has when he comes back to a place that has been chosen for him by Providence. I belong to this parcel of land with rocky rills around it, with pine trees on it. These are the woods and fields that I have worked in, and walked in, and in which I have encountered the deepest mystery of my own life. And in a sense I never chose this place for myself, it was chosen for me (though of course one must ratify the choice by personal decision). (*CGB* 234)

Since Merton lacked a place to be "from," the nuanced adage, "tell me where you are *from* and I will tell you who you are," might be reasonably negated. However, this would not rule out Mounier's claim. In other words, Merton's "home," to the best of one's knowledge, was Gethsemani.

If Merton was rooted in Gethsemani, then why might he have been inclined to find a new place? He cites several reasons in his journals, the most frequent of which pertain to a lack of privacy and dissatisfaction with the leadership and administration of the monastery. Thus, he sets out for the western United States with several destinations for the purposes of giving talks, correspondence and leading retreats.[21] Apart

---

20. Emmanuel Mounier, *The Character of Man* (New York: Harper and Brothers, 1956) 70-71.

21. For a well-written and synthesized exposition on this West Coast tour and Merton's thematic teachings, see Bonnie Thurston, "'I Spoke Most of Prayer': Thomas Merton on the West Coast (September 11–October 15, 1968)," *The Merton Seasonal*

from these talks and retreats, another theme emerges in his journals. It becomes evident that Merton also uses the trip as an opportunity to explore the possibility of finding another "place." What was he searching for? What type of place? Among the various places he visited, New Mexico, Alaska, northern California and even Asia received the most attention in his journals, and perhaps exerted the strongest pull on him. For instance, the vast empty spaces of the New Mexican desert impelled Merton to write, "New Mexico is one of the places where I might eventually settle" (*OSM* 163). However, despite a couple of visits to New Mexico, the impression made becomes largely overshadowed by both Alaska and northern California.

The desire for solitude persisted throughout his travels as he reflected on future locations to settle. He notes, "More than anything I want to find a really quiet, isolated place" (*OSM* 142). Alaska, he concluded, due to its isolation and lack of population, provided the greatest opportunity for seemingly unlimited solitude. He writes, "[I]t is clear that I like Alaska much better than Kentucky and it seems to me that if I am to be a hermit in the U.S., Alaska is probably the place for it. The SE is good – rain and all" (*OSM* 193).[22] Yet, he remained guarded against the possibility of being too isolated, for earlier he had written, "I have no special urge to be a hermit in Alaska, but it is an obvious place for solitude" (*OSM* 153), and "I tend to find myself thinking a lot about how to live in Alaska. . . . The thing is that I can't make sense out of a purely private endeavor to be completely alone, un-bothered, etc. This is nonsense" (*OSM* 154). Merton visited several places throughout Alaska including the Southeast, the tundra and near Anchorage. He found several places that would provide his sought-after solitude and escape from Kentucky; however I suspect none of them struck him as quite right. There is an analytical pickiness that seeps from his journal in his notation over their advantages, though always finding something inadequate about them. For example, when in Yakutat he wrote, "Frank Ryman has a quarter acre of land he offered me – and it is enough to put a trailer on. But it is right at the edge of the village. If I lived there I would become very involved in the life of the village and would probably become a sort of pastor" (*OSM* 192). This option was, I suspect, too public for him. He wanted more solitude, but not too much.

Merton spent the last weeks of his life in Southeast Asia, mostly in India. Prior to departure, in Kentucky, he writes, "In eight weeks I am

---

22. "SE" here is in reference to "Southeast Alaska" (i.e. the panhandle), known for its lush evergreen rain forests and abundant wildlife.

to leave here. And who knows – I may not come back. Not that I expect anything to go wrong – though it might – but I might conceivably settle in California to start the hermit thing . . . . Really I don't care one way or another if I never come back" (*OSM* 147-48). He had been preparing and looking forward to this trip for a long time. His journals give the impression that he had a true sense of destiny or fate about his trip to Asia; it was as if he expected to find something there that he had been searching for his whole life. Reflecting on his flight from the San Francisco airport, he writes, "We left the ground – I with Christian mantras and a great sense of destiny, of being at last on my true way after years of waiting and wondering and fooling around. . . . I am going home, to the home where I have never been in this body" (*OSM* 205). Perhaps this is best explained by the understandable excitement and romanticization of one's first trip to the East, or perhaps we should take seriously his reported sense of destiny. Regardless, we might easily imagine Merton in the airplane sitting at the edge of his seat for hours over the Pacific staring out the window while making the occasional recording in his journal, such as "When the stewardess began the routine announcement in Chinese I thought I was hearing the language of Heaven" (*OSM* 208).

Could he have subconsciously known that he was not to return? Could he have subconsciously known that he was indeed headed "home" in a very definite and ultimate sense?[23] While in Asia, Merton provided few insights about becoming a hermit there. If anything, I suspect Merton overcame his "honeymoon phase" and romanticized view of Asia and decided that there was no long-term place for him there. He did spend a few days in a secluded guesthouse in the Himalayan foothills of northern India outside Darjeeling; however, while there he came to the following conclusion: "With my reaction to this climate at its best and with the noise of the Indian radio in a cottage across the road from the hermitage, I guess it's still Alaska or California or Kentucky for me" (*OSM* 293).

Despite an overly-idealistic vision of Asia, the perfection of solitude in Alaska, and the vast empty nothingness of the New Mexican desert, northern California seemed to resonate with the deepest chord in Merton. In particular, the coastal area due south of Mendocino point caught the

---

23. Merton's last public words demonstrate this eerie destiny towards his ultimate home, which are now famous: "So I will disappear *from view and we can all have a coke or something.*" The first four words are found in Thomas Merton, *The Asian Journal*, ed. Naomi Burton Stone, Brother Patrick Hart and James Laughlin (New York: New Directions, 1973) 343; however, the complete sentence, which includes the italicized words, is found in the recorded presentation as found in *Merton: A Film Biography*, dir. Paul Wilkes and Audrey Glenn (New York: First Run Features, 1984) [2004 DVD: minute 51:28].

eye of Merton. It is the rugged coastal wilderness area known as "the lost coast," which Merton points out is the closest point of the lower 48 states to Asia. While visiting a Cistercian women's monastery (Our Lady of the Redwoods), Merton was introduced to Bear Harbor, which looked out over Needle Rock.[24] The following journal entry captures both the place within the imagination of Merton and his contemplative awareness of that place:

> About a mile from Bear Harbor, there is a hollow in which I am now sitting, where one could comfortably put a small trailer. A small loud stream, many quail. The calm ocean . . . very blue through the trees. Calla lilies growing wild. A very active flycatcher. The sun shines through his wings as through a Japanese fan. It is the feast of St. Pachomius. Many ferns. A large unfamiliar hawktype bird flew over a little while ago, perhaps a young eagle. (*OSM* 99)

The comfortable setting is illuminated well by Merton and, if he had moved there, one might easily imagine his seamless transition into the rhythms of coastal life. Later, back in Kentucky, he continues to describe the location in more detail:

> Northern California was unforgettable. I want very much to go back. Especially to Bear Harbor, the isolated cove on the Pacific shore where the Jones house is and which, I think, can be rented: the barrier, the reef, the eucalyptus trees, the steep slopes crowned by fir, the cove full of drift-redwood logs – black sand, black stones, and restless sea – the whole show, those deserted pyramids, the hollow full of wild iris, the steep road overhanging the sea, Needle Rock. (*OSM* 117)

The trip to Bear Harbor left such a great impression on him that, when back at Gethsemani, he devotes the majority of his journal entries to dreaming, analyzing and recapturing those memories. He reflects, after developing his Needle Rock photographs from the first trip, "The Agfa film brought out the great *Yang-Yin* of sea rock mist, diffused light and half hidden mountain – an interior landscape, yet there. In other words, what is written within me is there, 'Thou art that.' I dream every night of the west" (*OSM* 110).

His old home in Kentucky seemed to pale in comparison to what he imagined may be possible on the coast of northern California. He plots and justifies a move to the Pacific under several different arguments, some serious and others not. For example, he appeals to practicality when he

---

24. Today this location is both federally and locally protected within the King Range National Conservation Area and Sinkyone Wilderness State Park.

asks, "Would I do better creative work alone out by the Pacific? I have a feeling I probably would" (*OSM* 129). Similarly, he points out a symbolic and spatial justification in its geographical orientation; he writes, "Needle Rock is, I guess, within sight of Cape Mendocino and hence is one of the points south of Canada that are nearest to Asia" (*OSM* 130). Less seriously, he notes the seeming inferiority of his Kentucky surroundings when he writes, "Then I arrived back here in Kentucky in all this rain. The small hardwoods are full of green leaves, but are they real trees? The worshipful cold spring light on the sandbanks of Eel River, the immense silent redwoods. Who can see such trees and bear to be away from them? I must go back. It is not right that I should die under lesser trees" (*OSM* 112). Throughout, he peppers his journal with direct affirmations of his preference for Bear Harbor with statements such as, "I can think of nothing I'd like better than to fly back to California" (*OSM* 127), and "But what I want most of all is to spend a couple of months entirely alone somewhere on the shore of the Pacific" (*OSM* 132).

Merton's longing to return to the coast for an extended period of time takes on a language of one longing for a home and place of belonging. In addition to the reasons given at the outset of this section (e.g., solitude), perhaps this is explained by Merton's spiritual yearning. Perhaps he perceived himself as having spiritually plateau-ed in his ongoing quest for the self. Philip Sheldrake, in his article "Human Identity and the Particularity of Place," recognizes that one element that "home" represents is "our need for a location where we can pass through the stages of life and develop our fullest 'self.'"[25] Sheldrake's explanation supports, and perhaps clarifies, Merton's restlessness of place and longing to find a new "home." Merton's spirituality of self calls for putting to death the old self and finding the newer, supposedly more real, self in Christ. Thus, the real self is acquired through a negation of self. Fittingly and correspondingly, concerning the concept of place and home, Merton writes, "The country which is nowhere is the real home; only it seems that the Pacific Shore at Needle Rock is more nowhere than this, and Bear Harbor is more nowhere still" (*OSM* 110).[26] Bear Harbor must have provided something that none of the other locales could – a sense of nowhere, yet at the same time, a very definite sense of somewhere. Whatever it was,

---

25. Philip Sheldrake, "Human Identity and the Particularity of Place," *Spiritus: A Journal of Christian Spirituality* 1.1 (Spring 2001) 49.

26. Some have suggested the possibility that Merton is playing around with words here in his use of "nowhere." "Nowhere" can be broken up to "now here" and when used in this journal passage it functions well in describing a place where Merton felt content in the moment. Present contentment is a popular lesson drawn from Buddhism.

there is some indication that Merton thought he had found a place where he could feel at home. He recognized this back in Kentucky, "Lonely for the Pacific and the Redwoods. A sense that somehow when I was there I was unutterably happy – and maybe I was. Certainly, every minute I was there, especially by the sea, I felt I was at home – as if I had come a very long way to where I really belonged" (*OSM* 122).

I suspect that if Merton did return from Asia, he would not have ended up in Alaska, New Mexico or even somewhere in Central or South America as he sometimes toyed with, but would have worked out a temporary to semi-permanent arrangement in northern California. He certainly gave it the most attention in his journals and sought to justify it in a variety of ways, for it seemed to retain a stronger call than the other candidates on Merton's short list. In no other place did Merton record such vivid contemplative accounts as he did in northern coastal California. One such account that demonstrates his contemplative awareness combined with his longing for a new home and place is as follows: "It was a bright day and the sea was calm, and I looked out over the glittering blue water, realizing more and more that this was where I really belonged. I shall never forget it. I need the sound of those waves, that desolation, that emptiness" (*OSM* 120). Regardless of his musings over Alaska and California, Gethsemani remained his home, around which he oriented his life.

Conclusion

For one who wrote and spoke extensively on "the self" and being at home in the world, Merton was, to a certain extent, rather restless and not perfectly comfortable with being "at home" in the world. Perhaps Merton did not know himself as well as he let on, or at the very least, as well as others would have liked him to have known himself. Perhaps this restlessness is demonstrated by his quest for a new place in the later years of his life. His journals contain the constant questioning of who he was and where he was going. On August 5, 1968 he writes, "Maybe I am no true solitary, and God knows I have certainly missed opportunities, made mistakes – and big ones too!" (*OSM* 150-51). This restlessness, though perhaps disturbing to some (especially those who romantically envision the monk as the human striving for perfection), provides a very human side to Merton the monastic, in a similar way to Augustine who, in his *Confessions*, demonstrates his proneness to sexual gallivanting and the human delight found in stealing pears as a boy. Thus, it may not be surprising that it was Augustine who made one of the most profound statements about the human condition when he prays to God, "For Thou hast made us for Thyself and our hearts are restless till they rest in Thee."[27] Like Augustine, Merton will remain an enduring figure in the history of anthropological study and it may not be for his spiritual theology, but rather for his open candor about self, world and place. Like Augustine, Merton offers a window into the psyche and inner struggle of the human condition placed in the context of existential being in the world while striving to transcend it.

Recall Merton's opening reflection on the religious validity and significance of the football game. He was fascinated with its finality, fixity, and quality of lasting security in the logs of football history – and for this reason, he recognized its religious significance. In a similar fashion, perhaps Merton was searching for security and finality in a new place and new home to lay down new, though impermanent, roots. Places, due to their rootedness in the cosmos, contain the tremendous power to provide one with an *axis mundi* around which orientation of life and self is possible. Merton's quest, with his open candor and transparent journals, provides not only inspiration, but the opportunity for all to catch a little glimpse of their own self and place in the world.

---

27. Augustine, *Confessions*, trans. F. J. Sheed, ed. Michael P. Foley (Indianapolis: Hackett, 2006) 3.

"The Street Is for Celebration":
Racial Consciousness and the Eclipse of Childhood in America's Cities

Christopher Pramuk

Much of the real germinating action in the world, the real leavening is among the immobilized, the outsiders. Where the good may come from is perhaps where evil is feared. The streets. The ghettoes.

Thomas Merton, *Learning to Love*[1]

In 1976, Motown recording artist Stevie Wonder released a double-album masterpiece called *Songs in the Key of Life*, giving brilliant and beautiful voice to the joys and struggles of life in inner-city America. With an original working title of "Let's see life the way it is," the album's seventeen songs reveal a world largely hidden from suburban, middle-class, white America. I was twelve years old when *Songs in the Key of Life* debuted at number one on the pop music charts, and remember well listening to the record with my older brother in our suburban home in Lexington, Kentucky. I was mesmerized by the music, even where I did not or could not understand the social and racial complexity of the songs. Almost forty years later, I am still mesmerized. The album's third track, for example, "Village Ghetto Land," juxtaposes disturbing images of "life the way it is" in the city over the serene instrumentation of a chamber quartet:

> Would you like to go with me / Down my dead end street
> Would you like to come with me / To Village Ghetto Land? . . .
> Children play with rusted cars / Sores cover their hands
> Politicians laugh and drink / Drunk to all demands.[2]

Two tracks later, as if to say, don't even think you understand me now, or where I come from, Wonder delivers "Sir Duke," an incomparably funky and joyful tribute to the genius of Duke Ellington and other black artists, followed by "I Wish," his playful remembrance of growing up on the streets of Detroit. "Isn't She Lovely" celebrates the birth of Wonder's daughter, Aisha, followed by "Joy Inside My Tears," "Pastime Paradise,"

---

1. Thomas Merton, *Learning to Love: Exploring Solitude and Freedom. Journals, vol. 6: 1966-1967*, ed. Christine M. Bochen (San Francisco: HarperCollins, 1997) 231, 221; subsequent references will be cited as *"LL"* parenthetically in the text.

2. Stevie Wonder, *Songs in the Key of Life* (Detroit: Motown Records, 1976).

and "Black Man" – all hymns to what it *feels like* to be black in America. Like turning a many-faceted diamond, now this way, now that, Stevie refracts the mosaic colors of life as it is for many in inner-city America, life held down to street level.

Life in the Key of Black

Listening to the album today, one might be tempted to celebrate just how much things have changed in a so-called post-racial America, where a black man resides with his beautiful family in the White House and projects American military power across the world stage. Or one might lament how far too little has changed at street level for people of color in the United States in areas such as education, incarceration or political disenfranchisement. In any case, what interests me here is not the insight into "ghetto life" that Stevie Wonder's music gives us, gives me, as a middle-class white person in America. What interests me is the critique of the *racially unconscious white listener* embedded everywhere in his music. For listeners like myself, Wonder's artistry facilitates a powerful and potentially painful realization: namely, my own nearly complete isolation from black experience, my "confinement in the prison built by racism,"[3] and the degree to which my own white *"habitus"* or groupthink – what Thomas Merton called the "conspiracy of the many"[4] – conditions my very manner of seeing and judging reality.

In other words, the opening of "Village Ghetto Land" – *Would you like to go with me, down my dead end street?* – still resonates today as both an accusation and an invitation: an accusation of social blindness but also an invitation to wake up, to come and see life as it is more clearly than I have seen it before from my perspective of social privilege. To say yes to the invitation is to discover that what is at stake is not strictly my grasp of ghetto life so much as the music of life itself, life in the key of humanity, black, white, brown, red or yellow. It is about the music of human relationships, sorrowful and joyful, broken and redeemed.

In this essay I consider life as it is in the cities and streets of America by juxtaposing Stevie Wonder's music with select writings of Thomas Merton (1915–68), the Catholic monk and spiritual writer whose prophetic commentaries on race remain remarkably and sadly relevant today. Wonder and Merton are both artists, albeit of a very different kind. What

---

3. The phrase is borrowed from Eduardo Bonilla-Silva's superb study, *Racism without Racists: Color-Blind Racism and Racial Inequality in Contemporary America* (Lanham, MD: Rowman and Littlefield, 2010).

4. See Thomas Merton, *The Behavior of Titans* (New York: New Directions, 1961) 83-84.

joins them is their remarkable capacity to open our imaginations to the life-worlds of people and places well beyond our habitual comfort zones. An elder African American woman in my parish recently reminded me of Merton's significance as a voice for justice during the civil rights movement. She told me that for her, as a young black woman growing up in a racially explosive Cincinnati in the 1960s, Merton's *Conjectures of a Guilty Bystander* was her "bible." "I carried it with me everywhere," she added, with a pained look on her face. "Merton *got it*, when few others did."[5]

There is some irony to that fact. As a cloistered monk living in a remote monastery in rural Kentucky, Merton was about as distant geographically from urban America as one could be. It is true that before he entered the monastery in 1941, Merton had lived the better part of his life in cities throughout Europe and then for five years as a student and teacher at Columbia University in the heart of New York City. Indeed he even considered taking up residency in Harlem, living and working among the poor.[6] But Merton's deep sensitivity to the black situation

---

5. Several factors contribute, in my view, to Merton's enduring trustworthiness on matters of race. First, he never described black experience (or "Negro experience," in the parlance of the day) in a monolithic, naively romantic or sociologically detached way. That Merton saw and rejected the dangers of race essentialism (black or white) is clear (see for example a remarkable passage from the hermitage on January 31, 1965, his fiftieth birthday, in Thomas Merton, *Dancing in the Water of Life: Seeking Peace in the Hermitage. Journals, vol. 5: 1963-1965*, ed. Robert E. Daggy [San Francisco: HarperCollins, 1997] 200-201; subsequent references will be cited as *"DWL"* parenthetically in the text). Second, removed from the public fray as he was, Merton's commentary was comparatively clear-eyed and free of bias. He could be just as critical of the nihilist rhetoric of the black power movement as he was of the ignorance and complicity of white Christian liberals. In fact, he was suspicious of any rhetoric that elevated ideals, principles or social constructs (including race) over *persons*. Third, Merton recognized with epistemic humility that he was in many respects an alien and stranger to the struggles of the city, an outsider looking in, a guilty bystander. Reflecting on Malcolm X in 1967, for example, he noted, "I realize I don't fully know what I am talking about" (*LL* 233). Nevertheless he risked the attempt to understand life as it is for many blacks in this country, even where his social location prevented full comprehension. "I ought to learn to just shut up and go about my business of thinking and breathing under trees," he wrote in 1967. "But protest is a biological necessity" (*LL* 240).

6. For the considerable impact of Harlem on Merton's consciousness and emerging sense of vocation during these years – especially the influence of Catherine de Hueck Doherty – see Thomas Merton, *The Seven Storey Mountain* (New York: Harcourt, Brace, 1948) 337-52, 357-60; Thomas Merton, *Run to the Mountain: The Story of a Vocation. Journals, vol. 1: 1939-1941*, ed. Patrick Hart (San Francisco: HarperCollins, 1995) 384-85, 448-51, 455-56, 464-65; also "Holy Communion: The City" and "Aubade –Harlem," in *The Collected Poems of Thomas Merton* (New York: New Directions, 1977), 39-40,

during the 1960s was rooted not in geographical proximity so much as in basic human empathy, that is, in his radical openness to the life-worlds of others. "Most of us," as he wrote in 1964, "are congenitally unable to think black, and yet that is precisely what we must do before we can even hope to understand the crisis in which we find ourselves."[7]

Merton and Harlem: 1964

As detailed in his autobiography, *The Seven Storey Mountain*, it is clear that when Thomas Merton entered the Trappist monastery of Our Lady of Gethsemani in 1941, he saw his vocation in the traditional way as *fuga mundi*: flight from the world. By the late 1950s, however, Merton's awareness was turning dramatically back toward the secular world, to the realities of "life the way it is" for ordinary people in America who struggle simply to make ends meet and live with some kind of dignity. Like the Catholic Church on the eve of Vatican II, he was learning to re-discover God in unexpected places, which is to say, *everywhere*. The Christian contemplative way is not an escape from the world after all, Merton discovered, but a deepening grasp of all things in God, inclusive of the world's social and political problems.

Most casual readers of Merton will be familiar with that pivotal moment in March of 1958 at the corner of Fourth and Walnut in Louisville, Kentucky, when he suddenly heard the music of the city in a new key, a key resonant with Christianity's gospel of incarnation.[8] But there is another urban epiphany of sorts that I would like to consider here. Detailed in Merton's private journals, it is much more hidden and, to be sure, rather less idealized than the famous Fourth and Walnut passage. It happened in the summer of 1964, when Merton boarded an airplane for New York City for a meeting at Columbia University with Zen scholar D. T. Suzuki, with whom he had engaged in serious interreligious dialogue for many years. Flying over the city at 35,000 feet, Merton noted in his journal, hearkening back to his life before Gethsemani, "I suddenly realized after all that I was a New Yorker." Arriving at Columbia in late morning, he found his way to his room in Butler Hall, overlooking the streets of Harlem. He writes:

82-83; subsequent references will be cited as "*CP*" parenthetically in the text.

7. Thomas Merton, *Seeds of Destruction* (New York: Farrar, Straus & Giroux, 1964) 60; subsequent references will be cited as "*SD*" parenthetically in the text.

8. See Thomas Merton, *Conjectures of a Guilty Bystander* (Garden City, NY: Doubleday, 1966) 140-42 (subsequent references will be cited as "*CGB*" parenthetically in the text); also Thomas Merton, *A Search for Solitude: Pursuing the Monk's True Life. Journals, vol. 3: 1952-1960*, ed. Lawrence S. Cunningham (San Francisco: HarperCollins, 1996) 181-82.

[T]he noise of traffic and the uninterrupted cries of playing children, cries of life and joy coming out of purgatory, loud and strong the voice of a great living organism. Shots too – and there is no rifle range! Frequent shots – at what? More frequent than in the Kentucky woods behind the hermitage in hunting season. And drums, bongos, and the chanting of songs, and dogs barking and traffic, buses like jet planes. Above all the morning light, then the afternoon light, and the flashing windows of the big new housing developments. (*DWL* 114-15)

The passage is vintage Merton. Notice how Merton observes everything and seems to find something beautiful even in the "flashing windows of the big new housing developments." But there were gunshots too – at what, he wonders. But then, "drums, bongos, and the chanting of songs." In sum, *the incomparable music of Harlem*: "Cries of life and joy coming out of purgatory, loud and strong the voice of a great living organism."

Just a month later, back at the monastery, the key darkly changes:

Jim Forest sent me clippings from Monday's *New York Times* about the big riots in Harlem last weekend. It all took place in the section immediately below Butler Hall. . . . The police shot thousands of rounds into the air but also quite a few people were hit, and one man on a roof was killed. In the middle of all the racket and chaos and violence a police captain was shouting "Go home! Go home!" A Negro yelled back "We *are* home, baby!" (*DWL* 130)

Suddenly the description of Harlem as "purgatory" – a place of "purification" – bears much more ominous meaning.

"The Street Is for Celebration"

These memories of Harlem must have been fresh in Merton's mind when in the fall of 1967 he wrote "The Street Is for Celebration," an essay originally intended to serve as the preface for a picture book entitled *Summer in the City*, celebrating Monsignor Robert Fox's work with children in Spanish Harlem. Though the book was never published, Merton certainly had this setting in mind, and surely the children of Harlem as well, when he wrote the piece, which finally came to print in the posthumous collection *Love and Living*.[9]

---

9. Thomas Merton, *Love and Living*, ed. Naomi Burton Stone and Brother Patrick Hart (New York: Farrar, Straus, Giroux, 1979) 46-53; subsequent references will be cited as *"L&L"* parenthetically in the text. Monsignor Fox's associate Mary Cole did publish a book entitled *Summer in the City* (New York: P. J. Kenedy, 1968), that ended up being a kind of substitute for the originally planned picture book – without Merton's contribution – which she sent to Merton with a letter of June 13, 1968 (archives, Thomas Merton

On the surface "The Street Is for Celebration" is a much gentler read than Merton's fiercely prophetic commentaries on race such as "Letters to a White Liberal" (*SD* 3-71). Indeed, race is never mentioned at all. Rather Merton focuses our attention on cities and streets themselves as reflections of *what human beings do with space*. How we arrange and navigate the physical spaces of our cities, he suggests, reveals a great deal about who we are, what we value, and what we do not value in the everyday practices of our lives. The essay hinges on a distinction Merton draws between "alienated spaces," where people simply submit, and "inhabited spaces," where people actually live and can participate in the creation of their lives. The question at hand is this: "Can the street be an inhabited space?" Can the street be a place for living, for creativity, even for celebration? He writes:

Suppose the street is an impersonal no-man's-land: a mere tube through which a huge quantity of traffic is sucked down toward the glass walls where business happens. Suppose the street is a tunnel, a kind of nowhere, something to go through. Something to get out of. Or a nightmare space where you run without getting away.

Then the street cannot be an inhabited space. . . . [Then] the street is not where they live but where they have been dumped.

When a street is not inhabited it is a dump.

A street may be a dump for thousands of people who aren't there.

They have been dumped there, but their presence is so provisional they might as well be absent. They occupy space by being displaced in it. . . .

An alienated space, an uninhabited space, is a space where you submit.

You stay where you are put, even though this cannot really be called "living." You stop asking questions about it and you know there is not much point in making any complaint. (Business is not interested in your complaint, only in your rent.) "I live on X Street." Translated: "X Street is the place where I submit, where I give in, where I quit." (*L&L* 46-48)

Note the crucial point about persons living an alienated life: "their presence is so provisional they might as well be absent." To whom in American society today would such a description apply? To how many children

Center, Bellarmine University, Louisville, KY). I am indebted to an anonymous reviewer of this article for providing me valuable details on the genesis of Merton's 1967 essay, and other references to his early experiences in Harlem.

residing in our inner cities? How about the millions of young men of color locked behind bars inside our sprawling prison system?

Here I pause to mention two contemporary authors who have opened my eyes to the trajectory of this line of thought as it applies to systemic racial injustice in the United States today. The first is Jonathan Kozol, whose books have long cast an ominous spotlight onto the plight of minority children and the state of public education in our cities. The titles of Kozol's books – *Death at An Early Age*; *Savage Inequalities: Children in America's Schools*; *The Shame of the Nation: The Restoration of Apartheid Schooling in America*[10] – tell the story of whole populations of young people, disproportionately black and Latino, whose presence in America "is so provisional they might as well be absent." The second is legal scholar Michelle Alexander, whose critically acclaimed study, *The New Jim Crow: Mass Incarceration in the Age of Colorblindness*,[11] details the devastating effects of mass incarceration and systematic disenfranchisement on communities of color in the United States. Like Kozol, Alexander's painstaking scholarship unmasks patterns of injustice directed against whole populations that most of us would rather not see, and many simply choose to deny.

Fifty years ago the face of racial animosity was epitomized in openly racist organizations like the Ku Klux Klan, in men like Bull Connor, the bigoted public safety commissioner of Birmingham, Alabama, and in horrific tragedies like the bombing of the Sixteenth Street Baptist Church in Birmingham. Then it was quite clear what racial hatred and violence meant: it meant to will the nonexistence of black people, to seek their *erasure*. Merton's poem, "And the Children of Birmingham" is a powerful lament for this kind of race hatred; likewise his "Picture of a Black Child with a White Doll," an elegy for Denise McNair, one of the four children killed in the church bombing.[12]

---

10. Jonathan Kozol, *Death at an Early Age: The Destruction of the Hearts and Minds of Negro Children in the Boston Public Schools* (Boston: Houghton Mifflin, 1967); Jonathan Kozol, *Savage Inequalities: Children in America's Schools* (New York: Crown, 1991); Jonathan Kozol, *The Shame of the Nation: The Restoration of Apartheid Schooling in America* (New York: Crown, 2005); see also Jonathan Kozol, *Amazing Grace: The Lives of Children and the Conscience of a Nation* (New York: Crown, 1995).

11. Michelle Alexander, *The New Jim Crow: Mass Incarceration in the Age of Colorblindness* (New York: New Press, 2010).

12. For "And the Children of Birmingham," written before the bombing, see Thomas Merton, *Emblems of a Season of Fury* (New York: New Directions, 1963) 33–35 (subsequent references will be cited as *"ESF"* parenthetically in the text); *CP* 335-37. For "Picture of a Black Child with a White Doll," see *CP* 626–27. See also John Howard Griffin, *Black Like Me* (Boston: Houghton Mifflin, 1961), a riveting account of Griffin's experiment in

Today racial animosity manifests much more subtly than this, though its effects are no less quotidian, oppressive, or potentially violent, as Kozol and Alexander demonstrate in unflinching detail. In the decades since the civil rights movement, racism's implicit strategy has not been the erasure of the feared and marginal other (e.g., young black men) so much as their *eclipse* from meaningful participation in society. To eclipse is to ignore, to refuse to deal with a person as a person, as a somebody – a Child of God, as we say – who matters. To eclipse is to blot out the light. As the great Howard Thurman often noted, to destroy a people I don't have to kill them, I only have to convince them that they are not worth anything – to hold a bushel basket relentlessly over their light.[13] It is this form of violence, violence by systematic neglect and creeping despair, which concerns Merton here: *X street is the place where I submit, where I give in, where I quit.*

To his credit, Merton acknowledges the temptation to violence among the marginalized, violence as a means of reminding the world "that you are there, that you are tired of being a non-person" (*L&L* 49). Yet violence cannot succeed in making the city inhabitable, he continues, because "it accepts the general myth of the street as no-man's-land, as battleground, as no place." Violence is "another kind of submission . . . another way of giving up" (*L&L* 50).[14] How, then, can the street become an inhabited space, a place where people are present to themselves, with full identities, as real people, as happy people? Merton begins to gesture toward a positive answer, toward hope.

To acquire inhabitants, the street will have to be changed. . . . The people who are merely provisionally present, half-absent non-persons must now become really present on the street as *themselves*. They must be recognizable as people. . . .

Instead of submitting to the street, they must change it. . . . [T]hey must transform the street and make it over so that it is livable.

"becoming black" in the deep South during the 1950s. A close friend of Merton and his original authorized biographer, Griffin's story is one of the most compelling, yet strangely overlooked, narratives of cross-racial solidarity during the civil rights era. Both the book and a recent documentary, *Uncommon Vision: The Life and Times of John Howard Griffin*, dir. Morgan Atkinson (Louisville, KY: Duckworks, 2010), expose the question of social empathy (our capacity for it and our resistance to it) in US society.

13. See Howard Thurman, *Howard Thurman: Essential Writings*, selected with an Introduction by Luther E. Smith (Maryknoll, NY: Orbis, 2006).

14. The film *Crash*, dir. Paul Haggis (Lions Gate, 2005), brilliantly dramatizes intersecting racial tensions and the cumulative impulse to violence across the color line in contemporary Los Angeles – even while illuminating the humanity and latent impulse for good in the most racially bigoted of the characters.

The street can be inhabited if the people on it begin to make their
life credible by changing their environment.
Living is more than submission: it is creation.
To live is to create one's own world as a scene of personal hap-
piness. (*L&L* 48-49)

Here we come to the heart of things. Living, says Merton, is more than submission: it is creation. And here he contrasts the streets of modern America as places of alienation with the first Mayan cities of North America, which were places of festival and celebration. What is celebration? Celebration "is the creation of a common identity, a common consciousness. . . . Celebration is when we let joy make itself out of our love. . . . Celebration is the beginning of confidence, therefore of power" (*L&L* 53). He continues, redirecting our imaginations back to the streets of urban America:

When we laugh at them, when we celebrate, when we make our lives beautiful, when we give one another joy by loving, by sharing, then we manifest a power they cannot touch. We can be the artisans of a joy they never imagined.

We can build a fire of happiness in this city that will put them to shame. . . .

Can the street become an inhabited space?

Yes, when it becomes a space for celebration. (*L&L* 53)

Of course to remake the street and one's own life in the face of creeping despair will not be easy. "We can dance in the street, but that will not change the fact that our buildings are lousy, the rent is too high, the garbage is not taken away, and the back yards look like bomb craters." Nevertheless, Merton continues, "We [can] begin to discover our power to transform our own world. He who celebrates is not powerless. He becomes a creator because he is a lover" (*L&L* 52).

Invoking the theme of power as Merton did here was to engage the aims and rhetoric of the Black Power movement. Implicitly Merton is wrestling with the question of subjugated populations everywhere during the revolutionary 1960s: what are the conditions of the possibility for the empowerment of the poor, for justice and equal opportunity, for positive social revolution? Does Christianity, at its heart *a narrative of power through love and redemptive suffering,* have any wisdom to offer the black community? What are the implications, by contrast, when the demand for justice is framed by the logic of violence and revolution "by any means necessary," as it was by the Black Power movement? Implicitly Merton is making the case here, in the tradition of Jesus, Gandhi, Day and King, for nonviolent resistance through interracial solidarity and love: love not in the abstract, but love as it sings and marches and rises up fiercely in an embodied, joyful, hopeful people.[15]

Two further points are worth noting about this remarkable essay. First, by the middle of the piece Merton is no longer analyzing the situation objectively, as it were, from an abstract, third-person distance. Like Stevie Wonder, Merton draws his audience into the streetscape itself, inviting us, through a kind of imaginative empathy, to identify ourselves with the occupants of the alienated street: *We can build a fire of happiness in this city that will put them to shame.* Second, note how Merton gradually shifts the locus of power from the impersonal to the personal, from behind the shiny glass walls of skyscrapers "where business happens" to the inner landscape of lives and relationships down at street level, where hope can catch flame and burst forth again in human hearts. Yet such an outcome remains tenuous and unpredictable. Merton lays the burden of hope partly, if implicitly, upon the reader. Can I identify *myself*, my own kind – "'Kind' which means 'likeness' and which means 'love' and which means 'Child'" (*SS* 182)[16] – with my suffering brothers and sisters in the city?

The Divine-Human Child

In all of Merton's writings there may be no more poignant or powerful symbol of our shared personhood in God than the symbol of the Child. "We do not hear the soft voice, the gentle voice, the merciful and feminine. . . . We do not see the Child who is prisoner in all the people."[17] The

---

15. In "Gandhi and the One-Eyed Giant," Merton cites Laurens Van Der Post's thesis "that the white man's spiritual rejection and contempt for the African is the result of his rejection of what is deepest and most vital in himself" (Thomas Merton, ed., *Gandhi on Non-Violence: Selected Texts from Non-Violence in Peace and War* [New York: New Directions, 1964] 77). Author James Douglass takes his cues from Merton's prophetic unmasking of state violence in *Raids on the Unspeakable* (New York: New Directions, 1966) (subsequent references will be cited as "*RU*" parenthetically in the text) to examine both Gandhi's and John F. Kennedy's resistance to Western militarism: see James W. Douglass, *Gandhi and the Unspeakable: His Final Experiment with Truth* (Maryknoll, NY: Orbis, 2012); James Douglass, *JFK and the Unspeakable: Why He Died and Why It Matters* (Maryknoll, NY: Orbis, 2008).

16. This is from the original version of Merton's Fourth and Walnut epiphany of March 18, 1958.

17. Thomas Merton, *Hagia Sophia* (Lexington, KY: Stamperia del Santuccio, 1962) (*ESF* 63; *CP* 365); see also "The Time of the End Is the Time of No Room" (*RU* 65-75). For a close study of Merton's theological anthropology as it rises from the convergence of Christ-Wisdom-Sophia in his life and thought, see Christopher Pramuk, *Sophia: The Hidden Christ of Thomas Merton* (Collegeville, MN: Liturgical/Michael Glazier, 2009)

Christ of Merton's mature writings is the Christ Child of the Nativity, who hides especially in those for whom there is "no room" in society, no inhabitable space for dignity, creativity and happiness: the children of Harlem, for example, with their "cries of life and joy coming out of purgatory." What *kind* of purification, Merton might ask today, are we requiring of the nation's black and Latino children? Whose sins are being paid for as we build more and bigger prisons, fill them with young black and Latino men, and staff them with working-class whites who desperately need the jobs?

In one of my favorite passages in all his journals, Merton reflects on some children's drawings that were sent to the monastery from "somewhere in Milwaukee." After noting that the pictures are the "only real works of art I have seen in ten years," he continues, quite poignantly: "But it occurred to me that these wise children were drawing pictures of their own lives. They knew what was in their own depths. They were putting it all down on paper before they had a chance to grow up and forget."[18] What is Merton getting at here? What is it that lives and shines forth especially in children that we "grow up and forget," that we – academics, pundits, common-sense adults – fail to behold in ourselves, firstly, but especially in the strange and marginal other?

Perhaps it is that same translucence and secret innocence that Stevie Wonder beheld in his newborn daughter and celebrates in the song "Isn't She Lovely?": "*I can't believe what God has done / through us he's given life to one / but isn't she lovely made from love?*" Her name, Aisha, the song tells us, means simply "Life," life made from love. What we grow up to forget is that diamond-like image of God that hides in all people, without exception, the inner potentiality and latent freedom in which God invites each of us *to be* and to participate fully in the discovery, creation and celebration of our lives. As Merton confessed of the passersby at Fourth and Walnut, "If only they could all see themselves as they really *are*. If only we could see each other that way all the time" (*CGB* 142).[19]

(subsequent references will be cited as "Pramuk, *Sophia*" parenthetically in the text).

18. Thomas Merton, *The Sign of Jonas* (New York: Harcourt, Brace, 1953) 341.

19. The theme of innocence and the image of the child figure significantly in Merton's theological anthropology (see Pramuk, *Sophia* 200–202). Closely related and also prominent in the Fourth and Walnut passage is the phrase *le point vierge*, roughly the "virgin point" or secret heart of creation where God invites all things into being. With such terms Merton does not mean to suggest a regression to the freshness of childhood, in a naïve or narcissistic sense, still less a denial of sin. They speak rather to the divine image or spark in us, deeper and more primordial than sin, at once both gift (already given) and invitation (not fully realized). It is "a new birth, the divine birth in us" that grounds our freedom and creativity in history as co-creators before God.

Notice the integral link Merton uncovers between discovery of our true self and discovery of the other. Yet how often we live under the shadow of eclipse, where neither "you" nor "I" appear as our authentic self, as a person who matters infinitely in the eye of God. *To eclipse is to blot out the light.*

How then to live more fully in the light? How to identify myself more empathetically and compassionately with the occupants of the alienated street, and so discover myself in discovering them? Merton reminds us (citing theologian Karl Rahner) that it is not enough for the Christian to spiritualize the struggle, to "build a little chapel for himself inside the Church to make things more tolerable" (*LL* 147). One cannot listen to Stevie Wonder records in the suburbs, pray for peace "down there" in the city, and consider oneself sanctified. Nor is it enough to pontificate from the ivory tower, taking refuge in the "[i]llusory dignity of the well-fed spokesman who justifies himself by diagnosis, planning and exhortation" (*LL* 262). Much less can we be content with the arm-chair punditry of so many social commentators today, who "reduce everything to zero" (*LL* 259) and show little desire to engage those perceived from afar as strange, and dangerously different. In a word, the Gospel calls us to risk the kinds of *attachments* to people that will cost us something. Christ calls us to be transformed from beyond ourselves by love, by an embodied and active solidarity.[20]

Defending God's Image in the Other

A few years ago I heard black Catholic theologian Sr. Jamie Phelps frame the question quite simply and beautifully this way: "What work are we doing to help re-establish a sense of the image of God in people of color?"[21] Throughout the 1960s Merton confronted his readers, and confronted them theologically, with the same question: "How, then, do we treat this other Christ, this person, who happens to be black?" (*SD*

---

20. Innumerable gospel passages leap to mind: Jesus' encounter with the rich young man, the parable of the Good Samaritan, the judgment scene of Matthew 25 and so on. The word "love" as I use it here is analogous to the terms "solidarity" and the "preferential option for the poor," persistent themes of Catholic social teaching. Solidarity is not simply an ethical command so much as a *response* to the gift and wonder of life itself and God's love. We love because we have come to know God's love and mercy for us intimately through Jesus (1 John 4:19).

21. See *Uncommon Faithfulness: The Black Catholic Experience*, ed. M. Shawn Copeland, with LaReine-Marie Mosely and Albert J. Raboteau (Maryknoll, NY: Orbis, 2009), for Phelps' seminal essay on Catholic identity and mission with respect to social and racial transformation.

17).[22] In the process he angered and alienated a great many of his white Catholic readers. Yet he chose to speak, knowing full well he was treading into dangerous waters. Today Merton still challenges us, especially those of us who are white, to look carefully into the mirror of our own neighborhoods, churches, businesses and schools, and to recognize the signs of our self-segregation from peoples of color, our sad confinement in the prison built by racism. That prison is in no way a black or brown problem confined to the ghetto, as Merton recognized; it is a human problem, woven into the whole fabric of society.

What will it take for us to venture outside well-worn comfort zones and to linger for a while in places and with people that we habitually, from good "common sense," take pains to avoid? What work will I do to help re-establish the sense of the image of God in people of color? What work can we all do to cultivate racial and economic justice in our cities?[23]

Would you like to come with me to Village Ghetto Land?

Living is not submission to "the way things are." Living is creativity and celebration. It is when we let joy make itself out of our love. May God free us from every hesitation, and may God's own creativity and joy make itself out of our love.

---

22. Note the phrasing of the question: what matters first is the *person*, this "other Christ," who "happens to be black." We might also say that what matters ultimately for whites is not one's socially constructed whiteness but the discovery of one's true, Christ-like self, who also happens to be white. And yet for whites the need for heightened racial consciousness is especially acute since, as Merton long ago observed, whites are most inclined to be unconscious of the hidden privileges of their "normative" whiteness. Thus what Merton wrote in 1964 seems to me no less true today: "Most of us are congenitally unable to think black, and yet that is precisely what we must do before we can even hope to understand the crisis in which we find ourselves" (*SD* 60).

23. The opening to the rich histories and cultural horizons of peoples of color can take place for whites, of course, in many ways, and is certainly not limited to urban or U.S. contexts. My own religious imagination has been deeply shaped by participation in African American and Mexican American Catholic parishes, global immersion in places like Honduras and Haiti, as well as study of black literature, art and theology. I have tried to sum up what I have learned from these experiences, and give a little back, in Christopher Pramuk, *Hope Sings, So Beautiful: Graced Encounters Across the Color Line* (Collegeville, MN: Liturgical Press, 2013).

Voices from the Desert: Merton, Camus and Milosz

David Joseph Belcastro

Thomas Merton collaborated with two public intellectuals who, like himself, lived on the margin of society and from there resisted twentieth-century movements that prevent human life from flourishing. His correspondence with Czeslaw Milosz[1] and his reading of Albert Camus[2] presented Merton with an opportunity to study their critical reflections on the modern world. He found in Milosz and Camus perspectives that provided insight into the root causes of the violence that plagued the twentieth century, sacrificing countless innocent men, women and children to the ideologies of sociopolitical movements. Equally important, he found in Milosz and Camus friends outside the monastery that sought to articulate not only in words and actions but also within themselves a sense of *being* that affirms life and opposes the reduction of humanity to vague abstractions. This article will provide a brief history of the relationship between these three men that focuses on the common ground that they shared at the margin of society, their distinctive voices as writers addressing the world of the twentieth century, and their critique of modernity as the loss of our true self.

The titles given to Merton's private journals[3] present his life as a

---

1. Thomas Merton and Czeslaw Milosz, *Striving towards Being: The Letters of Thomas Merton and Czeslaw Milosz*, ed. Robert Faggen (New York: Farrar, Straus & Giroux, 1997); subsequent references will be cited as "*STB*" parenthetically in the text.

2. Merton's "Seven Essays on Albert Camus" are collected in Thomas Merton, *The Literary Essays of Thomas Merton*, ed. Patrick Hart, OCSO (New York: New Directions, 1981) 179-301; subsequent references will be cited as "*LE*" parenthetically in the text.

3. Thomas Merton, *Run to the Mountain: The Story of a Vocation. Journals, vol. 1: 1939-1941*, ed. Patrick Hart (San Francisco: HarperCollins, 1995); Thomas Merton, *Entering the Silence: Becoming a Monk and Writer. Journals, vol. 2: 1941-1952*, ed. Jonathan Montaldo (San Francisco: HarperCollins, 1996); Thomas Merton, *A Search for Solitude: Pursuing the Monk's True Life. Journals, vol. 3: 1952-1960*, ed. Lawrence S. Cunningham (San Francisco: HarperCollins, 1996) (subsequent references will be cited as "*SS*" parenthetically in the text); Thomas Merton, *Turning Toward the World: The Pivotal Years. Journals, vol. 4: 1960-1963*, ed. Victor A. Kramer (San Francisco: HarperCollins, 1996) (subsequent references will be cited as "*TTW*" parenthetically in the text); Thomas Merton, *Dancing in the Water of Life: Seeking Peace in the Hermitage. Journals, vol. 5: 1963-1965*, ed. Robert E. Daggy (San Francisco: HarperCollins, 1997); Thomas Merton, *Learning to Love: Exploring Solitude and Freedom. Journals, vol. 6: 1966-1967*, ed. Christine M. Bochen (San Francisco: HarperCollins, 1997); Thomas Merton, *The Other Side of the Mountain: The End of the Journey. Journals, vol. 7: 1967-1968*, ed. Patrick

journey through various periods of formation: *Run to the Mountain* [pre-monastic years of discernment], *Entering the Silence* [early monastic years of formation], *A Search for Solitude* [maturing and deepening of contemplative life], *Turning Toward the World* [expanding of contemplative life beyond monastic walls], *Dancing in the Water of Life* [becoming a hermit], *Learning to Love* [falling in love], and *The Other Side of the Mountain* [journey to the East]. The period described as "turning toward the world" was anticipated by his Fourth and Walnut experience of March 18, 1958, narrated in the preceding journal, *A Search for Solitude* (*SS* 181-83). The juxtaposition of this epiphany and the subsequent turning indicates that for Merton the maturing of his monastic vocation required the branching out into the modern world.

During this period, the books that Merton was reading reflected his shift of attention toward the world and his interest in the problem of nihilism. For example, on August 11, 1962, Merton noted in his journal: "Henry Miller's tremendous essay on Raimu deeply significant, touches the real nerve of our time, the American nihilist, the movie dreamer, who commits crime in his sleep, a bomb wrapped in ideals" (*TTW* 237). On December 11, 1962, he wrote:

I have been shocked at a notice of a new book, by Rachel Carson [*Silent Spring*], on what is happening to birds as a result of the in-discriminate use of poisons. . . . Someone will say: you worry about birds: why not worry about people? I worry about *both* birds and people. We are in the world and part of it and we are destroying everything because we are destroying ourselves, spiritually, morally and in every way. It is all part of the same sickness, and it all hangs together. (*TTW* 274)

Another book that caught Merton's attention was *The Captive Mind* by Czeslaw Milosz.[4] Written in Paris during 1951-1952, when French intel-lectuals were seriously looking at Stalin's communist Russia as a vision of the new world order, Milosz focused his attention on the vulnerability of the twentieth-century mind to seduction by sociopolitical doctrines and its readiness to accept a totalitarian world for the sake of a hypothetical future (see Milosz, *Captive Mind* v). The book explores the cause of this vulnerability and finds it in the modern world's longing for certainty, anything that will provide a sense of certainty, even the most illusory. This longing for certainty is understood in the context of a world torn by

---

Hart (San Francisco: HarperCollins, 1998).
    4. Czeslaw Milosz, *The Captive Mind* (New York: Vintage Books, 1981); subsequent references will be cited as "Milosz, *Captive Mind*" parenthetically in the text.

a great dispute, a world where people have come to believe that they must conform to one or the other of the systems advocated by the participants in the debate – systems equally, though differently, totalitarian. Milosz's book is a search for a third position, a position of integrity for the individual who longs for a place to stand in the modern world.

Merton responded to Milosz's book with enthusiasm. After reading *The Captive Mind*, he initiated a correspondence with Milosz that extended from 1959 to the end of his life, published in 1997 as *Striving towards Being*, a title that expresses a primary concern of the two writers to which they returned time and again. It is also a title that defines in part the third position that occupied their attention. It is this striving for the third position of being that drew Merton to Milosz. His first letter stated without reservation his intention to join with the Polish writer and others "who risk our heads and our necks and everything in the difficult, fantastic job of finding out the new position" (*STB* 4) as they confronted the social malaise of the twentieth century.

Merton and Milosz quickly became friends, as reflected in the closing lines of their letters that read: "I am glad that you exist / with love [Czezlaw]" (*STB* 63); and from Merton to Milosz: "Deep affection and solidarity in Christ – Tom Merton" (*STB* 20), as well as other expressions of endearment throughout the letters. The relation would soon include a third writer, a close friend of Milosz. In a letter dated February 28, 1960, Milosz writes:

> By the way, I would like to convince you to comment upon *La Chute* de Camus, a very ambiguous book, which is a cry of despair and treatise on Grace (absent). Perhaps it would be useful if you write a theological commentary. I am far from wishing to convert you to Manichaeism. Only it is so that the palate of your readers is used to very strong sauces and le Prince de ce monde is a constant subject of their reflections. That ruler of Nature and of History (if laws are different, necessity is similar) does not annoy you enough – in your writings. (*STB* 65)

Responding to what Milosz believed to be Merton's lack of attention to evil in history and nature, we see here Milosz encouraging Merton to read the works of Albert Camus. Merton took Milosz's advice and found Camus much to his liking. In a letter dated May 6, 1960, Merton writes:

> I enjoy and respect Camus, and think I understand him. What you said about *La Chute* struck me very forcibly when I read it: it is a fine piece of Manichaean theology and very applicable to this (Trappist)

kind of life. . . . I was deeply saddened by his death. In politics I think I am very much inclined to his way of looking at things, and there is in him an honesty and a compassion which belies the toughness of his writing. (*STB* 70-71)

By the summer of 1964, Merton had read Camus' novel *The Plague*. While he would not write his first essay on Camus until two years later,[5] his notebooks after this date record a considerable amount of attention to Camus' novels, short stories and essays. During this period, his opinion of Camus took shape. He came to consider Camus "the greatest writer of our times."[6] In Merton's opinion, Camus sufficiently embodied the contemplative life that he would refer to him as "that Algerian cenobite"[7] and include him in his select hermitage library. Eventually Merton would write seven literary essays on the works of Camus with the intention of publishing a book, a project left unfinished due to Merton's untimely death. Perhaps just as important to note is the friendship, odd as it might sound, that developed *within* Merton between these two men who had never met, since Camus had died in January 1960.[8] Commenting on the relationship, Merton wrote:

[A] monk today stands much closer to someone like Camus . . . than he does, for example, to someone like Billy Graham . . . . [I]t is easy for me to take his kind of position: that of a man who at once loves the world yet stands apart from it with a critical objectivity which refuses to become involved in its transient fashions and its more manifest absurdities.[9]

In addition to their concern for the modern world, Camus and Milosz shared what Merton describes here as "stand[ing] apart." All three writ-

---

5. The mimeographed text of "Terror and the Absurd: Violence and Nonviolence in Albert Camus" (*LE* 232-51) is dated August 1966; for an overview of the first phase of Merton's writing on Camus, including this essay, see David Joseph Belcastro, "Merton and Camus on Christian Dialogue with a Postmodern World," *The Merton Annual* 10 (1997) 223-33.

6. See David D. Cooper, *Thomas Merton's Art of Denial: The Evolution of a Radical Humanist* (Athens, GA: University of Georgia Press) 208.

7. Thomas Merton, *Day of a Stranger* (Salt Lake City: Gibbs M. Smith, 1981) 35.

8. Camus' talk to friars at the Dominican Monastery of Latour-Maubourg in 1948 reveals that while he was clear regarding his position as a non-Christian, he was nonetheless open to dialogue with Christians (see Merton's essay "Camus and the Church" [*LE* 261-74] for his reflections on this address). We find the same openness in Merton, so it is not difficult to imagine a conversation between them.

9. Thomas Merton, *Contemplation in a World of Action* (Garden City, NY: Doubleday, 1971) 227; subsequent references will be cited as "*CWA*" parenthetically in the text.

ers, while speaking to the world, lived on the margin of that world, in a solitude both imposed and willingly accepted. In a letter to Milosz dated March 28, 1961, Merton writes: "We have to get used to our total moral isolation. It is going to get worse. We have to regain our sense of *being*, our confidence in reality, not in words. . . . Bear your solitude. It is a great pain for you & there is great strength in it" (*STB* 115). The encouragement to "bear your solitude" was deeply personal and, as Merton knew, true for all three writers. As with Milosz and Camus, who had become marginalized because of the positions that they had taken on current affairs, he too had become marginalized for the same reason. Merton however understood his marginal position as a desert experience and therefore an invaluable perspective that provided common ground with Camus and Milosz. Merton shared their solitude and found with Milosz and Camus a solidarity of support in their mutual striving for being. Merton writes to Milosz:

> as far as solidarity with other people goes, I am committed to nothing except a very simple and elemental kind of solidarity, which is perhaps without significance politically, but which is I feel the only kind which works at all. That is to pick out the people whom I recognize in a crowd and hail them and rejoice with them for a moment that we speak the same language. Whether they be communists or whatever else they may be. Whatever they may believe on the surface, whatever may be the formulas to which they are committed. I am less and less worried by what people say or think they say: and more and more concerned with what they and I are able to be. (*STB* 40)

The recurring focus of the letters on the ability to be, the regaining a sense of being, and the "striving towards Being" (*STB* 133) indicates the problem with modernity that concerned the three writers. The modern world with its focus on the future creates totalitarian systems that reduce human beings to servile subjects of agendas for productivity whether it is for the future of a communist state or the success of a capitalist corporation.

In opposition to totalitarian movements of any sort, Merton, Milosz and Camus chose to live at the margin of these movements, in a monastic desert of their own making, and to speak from there to life in the city. It is here, in solitude and silence, that they each discovered the third position of being, a position of integrity, which refuses subjection to the pressures of totalitarian regimes. Perhaps more importantly, it was here that the three writers discovered in their own ways the place, which is no-place, from which true freedom flows and life flourishes.

In addition to the difficult task of finding the third position, the three writers were faced with the additional challenge of finding a voice in the desert that could be heard in the city. In a letter to Milosz, Merton writes:

> If there is one ambition we should allow ourselves, and one form of strength, it is perhaps . . . to *be* a complete piece of systematic irony in the middle of the totalitarian lie – or the capitalist one. And even the official religious one. . . . It gets back to the fact that we all have our game with Caesar, the Little Father who is no longer human and who therefore *ought* to be cheated, in the name of humanity. (*STB* 56-57)

In different yet complementary ways, each became a piece of systematic irony in the middle of the totalitarian lie. And, in the case of these three writers, the form of irony may best be understand as a kind of "Socratic" irony whereby the three writers raise questions, pretending not to fully understand, to lure the modern reader into an opening that reveals the deeper reality of Being.

Camus took on the problem of the absurd in the modern world. From nihilists to evangelists the opinion was that the world is absurd and not a fitting place for humankind. Consequently, programs were constructed to transcend this world with movements that would eventually transform the world or provide an escape route to another. While these movements would anoint themselves as saviors of the world, the institutions that they constructed embodied the very absurdity that they sought to transcend and so became instruments of death and destruction. Camus saw through this and would point to the folly of these movements. With novels, short stories and essays, he labored to awaken the reader to the absurd as not in the world but within us. We experience the world as absurd because we have "divorced" ourselves from it. The absurd is our problem and can only be resolved according to Camus by returning to the Mediterranean world of the past and living a life of moderation that accepts life on its own terms, challenged by the hardships and sustained by its graces – following Sisyphus up the hill with the boulder before us and walking with him down the hill with a sense of satisfaction and happy with our lot in life – striving to live a good life and die a happy death.

Milosz sees the modern world fragmented by its own contradictions that inevitably leave us separated from life itself. Faced with the contradictions of the modern world, contradictions that he was unable to reconcile, he chose simply to witness in his poetry to those disconnects but with the intention of awakening the reader to the loss of meaning that follows, a loss that contributed in his opinion to the loss of the sacred, the human soul, the deepest dimension of our lives.[10]

Milosz's work reveals a poet in quest of the sacred space in a world now defined by Copernicus and Darwin. While the astronomer's discovery deprived our world of its heavenly vault and subterranean worlds, as well as its central place in the universe, the biologist's theory drew into question the significance and meaning of human life and death. Accepting the insights offered by both scientists, Milosz laments the loss of that "other" space in his last collection of poems, entitled *Second Space*. This loss is understood by Milosz to be something of importance, believing as he does that what has been lost was/is essential to human nature and happiness. Summarizing decades of reflection, Milosz's poem entitled "Scientists" raises a question that inevitably leads the reader to the folly of the modern world and, if attentive, to an opening into the sacred that is present in this world:

> The beauty of nature is suspect.
> Oh yes, the splendor of flowers.
> Science is concerned to deprive us of illusions.
> Though why it is eager to do so is unclear.
> The battles among genes, traits that secure success, gains and losses.
> My God, what language these people speak
> In their white coats. Charles Darwin
> At least had pangs of conscience
> Making public a theory that was, as he said, devilish.
> And they? It was, after all, their idea:
> To segregate humans, write off as a genetic loss
> Some of their own species and poison them.
> "The pride of the peacock is the glory of God,"
> Wrote William Blake. There was time
> When disinterested beauty by its sheer superabundance
> Gratified our eyes. What have they left us?

10. In his introduction to Czeslaw Milosz, *Legends of Modernity: Essays and Letters from Occupied Poland, 1942-1943*, trans. Madeline Levine (New York: Farrar, Straus and Giroux, 2006), Jaroslaw Anders writes: "the old feeling of unity between the material world and the human spirit, between reason and imagination, between history and transcendence, has been taken away from man, possibly forever, and that striving to reconstruct that unity from the heap of broken fragments is both futile and dangerous. Though intellectually at odds with modernity, he seems to accept modernity's chief message: not everything adds up; some contradictions will never be reconciled; some gaps are not meant to be closed. In a letter written in the last years of the war, the young writer mapped out, in touchingly modest terms, what would become his epic intellectual journey of the next sixty years: 'I am satisfied with sketching contradictions; a stroll through the garden where "pro" and "contra" grow side by side suffices me'" (xvi).

Only the accountancy of a capitalist enterprise.[11]

Motivated by a love of the sensuous experience of earthly pleasures and a need for something enduring beyond such experiences, Milosz pursued this lifelong quest for the sacred in the world, not outside the world and certainly not one artificially constructed by an official agency of a government or the commercial enterprise of a corporation but one found by turning to this world. Recognizing that the geography of this place cannot be located with map and compass, he chose to explore the border between the intellect and the imagination within the interior life. This search eventually led him to Merton. In a letter to Merton, Milosz shares a concern of great importance after reading *The Sign of Jonas*:[12]

> I waited for some answers to many theological questions but answers not abstract as in a theological treatise, just on that border between the intellect and our imagination, a border so rarely explored today in religious thinking: we lack an image of the world, ordered by religion, while Middle Ages had such an image. This was not the aim of your diary and I have no reason to demand from one book of yours what can be demanded from all your work. But a reader (I can judge by introspection only) is eager to learn (gradually) what is the image of the world in Thomas Merton. In a period when the image accepted by majority is clear: empty Sky, no pity, stone wasteland, life ended by death. I imagine a reader who says: he possessed a secret, he succeeded in solving the puzzle, his world is harmonious, yet in his diary he tells already about sequences while we would be ready to follow him in 5 volumes through a very vision of the world redeemed by Christ. (*STB* 61-62)

Merton identified with Camus' and Milosz's search for the sacred in the world and their perspective on modernity as fragmented and thereby lacking the wholeness necessary for the flourishing of human life. As indicated in *Contemplation in a World of Action*, he was deeply concerned about the fact that "Modern man is not in agreement with himself [and that he] has no one voice to listen to, but a thousand voices, a thousand ideologies, all competing for his attention in a Babel of tongues" (*CWA* 27). Merton turns to the world, understanding that his responsibility to modern men and women begins with and within himself, and that he must recognize that the problems of the modern world are also his, and refuse imagining that

---

11. Czeslaw Milosz, *Second Space: New Poems*, trans. Czeslaw Milosz and Robert Hass (New York: Harper Collins, 2004) 25.

12. Thomas Merton, *The Sign of Jonas* (New York: Harcourt, Brace, 1953).

he lives in a totally different world. He knew that these problems would not to be solved merely in words, however carefully crafted into essays and poems, but must be lived through until the answer is found within himself, embodied in his life. It was the very nature of Merton's vocation to embody an interior life whereby the sacred that was lost would be rediscovered, an interior life that provides, as Milosz suggested, a vision of the world redeemed by Christ.[13] While we have the literary works of Camus and Milosz, it is his life as a vision of redemption by Christ that Merton leaves us and which continues to attract readers – as a systematic irony in the midst of the totalitarian lie.[14]

---

13. Merton had been considering this issue for some time, as is reflected in numerous essays such as *Day of a Stranger*, "Rain and the Rhinoceros" (Thomas Merton, *Raids on the Unspeakable* [New York: New Directions, 1966] 9-23) and "Vocation and Modern Thought" (*CWA* 26-55); see also "Christian Humanism," Thomas Merton, *Love and Living*, ed. Naomi Burton Stone and Brother Patrick Hart (New York: Farrar, Straus, Giroux, 1979) 149-50.

14. An earlier version of this essay was presented on June 11, 2011 at the Twelfth General Meeting of the International Thomas Merton Society at Loyola University, Chicago, IL.

Two Antiheroes:
Meursault and Binx Bolling Viewed
through Thomas Merton's Literary Imagination

John P. Collins

In the mid-1960s, Thomas Merton was encouraged by Jacques Maritain to pursue literary criticism and creative writing as a method of conveying his theological and philosophical ideas. He remarked to James Laughlin in a letter dated October 8, 1966, "I am pleased with the idea and it seems to make sense."[1] Czeslaw Milosz wrote to Merton urging him not "to write theological treatises" but rather to utilize the medium of literary criticism for his accomplishments.[2] Merton had "been on the edge" of literary criticism most of his adult life, with his strong university background in English literature received at Columbia University and his continued reading of literature as a monk at the Abbey of Gethsemani. However, as Michael Mott suggests, Merton had been mainly an occasional literary reviewer up to the time when he wrote his seven essays on Albert Camus. Spending close to a year reading the Camus canon, Merton became a serious literary critic, according to Mott.[3] In a 1982 interview, Matthew Kelty, OCSO extols Merton's talents as a literary critic. Speaking of the Sunday afternoon conferences at the abbey, Kelty had this to say about Merton after interviewer Victor Kramer mentioned William Faulkner: "Faulkner. I've read a comment by people, I think John Eudes [Bamberger] said it, that this was where he was superb, as a literary critic, apart from his spiritual area, which was probably the best. But as a literary critic, he was very gifted, and that's what he was doing on Sunday afternoons."[4]

---

1. Thomas Merton and James Laughlin, *Selected Letters*, ed. David D. Cooper (New York: Norton, 1997) 301.

2. Thomas Merton and Czeslaw Milosz, *Striving towards Being: The Letters of Thomas Merton and Czeslaw Milosz*, ed. Robert Faggen (New York: Farrar, Straus & Giroux, 1997) 142; subsequent references will be cited as "*STB*" parenthetically in the text. It should be noted that even though Milosz encouraged Merton to utilize literary criticism, he "had grave doubts about the value of literature and poetry in relation to salvation" (*STB* vii).

3. Michael Mott, *The Seven Mountains of Thomas Merton* (Boston: Houghton Mifflin, 1984) 477.

4. Matthew Kelty, OCSO, "Looking Back to Merton: Memories and Impressions: An Interview," interviewed by Victor A. Kramer, ed. Dewey Weiss Kramer, *The Merton Annual* 1 (1988) 69.

The purpose of this essay is to present two anti-heroes[5] as literary archetypes,[6] as described by Merton in his writings about the novelists Albert Camus and Walker Percy. The flawed protagonists presented by Camus and Percy resonate with the suggestions made by Maritain and Milosz regarding the value of literary imagination. The presentation of the two archetypes will be against the backdrop of Thomas Merton's literary essays describing the merits of literary imagination in creating symbols pointing to spiritual values. Among Merton's Camus essays is one entitled "The Stranger: Poverty of an Antihero,"[7] in which the "single-minded Algerian clerk" Meursault, the main character of Camus' novel *The Stranger*,[8] is portrayed by Merton as a man with no interiority and no God. Although Meursault is without an interior spiritual life, Merton offers an interpretation that is, at least, a partial redemption of this seriously flawed character. The second anti-hero, Binx Bolling in Percy's *The Moviegoer*,[9] is not presented by Merton through a formal essay in literary criticism, but rather is described by commentary in two letters, one to Percy[10] and the other to Merton's former mentor at Columbia University, Mark Van Doren.[11] Merton recognizes Binx Bolling as a person who is onto something through his labyrinthine search for meaning in his life.

Before examining Merton's presentation of Meursault and Binx Bolling, it would be instructive to briefly discuss Merton's writings relative to

---

5. "The [anti-hero is the] protagonist of a modern play or novel, who has the converse of most of the traditional attributes of the 'Hero'" (C. Hugh Holman, *A Handbook to Literature* [New York: Bobbs-Merrill, 1972] 32; subsequent references will be cited as "Holman" parenthetically in the text).

6. "The literary critic applies the term [archetype] to an image, a descriptive detail, a plot pattern, or a character type that occurs frequently in literature" (Holman 40-41).

7. Thomas Merton, *The Literary Essays of Thomas Merton*, ed. Patrick Hart, OCSO (New York: New Directions, 1981) 292-301; subsequent references will be cited as "*LE*" parenthetically in the text. See also "Camus and the Church" (*LE* 261-74) and "Terror and the Absurd: Violence and Nonviolence in Albert Camus" (*LE* 232-51).

8. Albert Camus, *The Stranger*, trans. Stuart Gilbert (New York: Vintage Books, 1954).

9. Walker Percy, *The Moviegoer* (New York: Vintage Books, 1998); subsequent references will be cited as "Percy" parenthetically in the text.

10. Thomas Merton, *The Courage for Truth: Letters to Writers*, ed. Christine M. Bochen (New York: Farrar, Straus, Giroux, 1993) 281-82; subsequent references will be cited as "*CT*" parenthetically in the text.

11. Thomas Merton, *The Road to Joy: Letters to New and Old Friends*, ed. Robert E. Daggy (New York: Farrar, Straus, Giroux, 1989) 47; subsequent references will be cited as "*RJ*" parenthetically in the text. There is also a brief commentary about *The Moviegoer* in one of Merton's journals: see Thomas Merton, *A Vow of Conversation: Journals 1964-1965*, ed. Naomi Burton Stone (New York: Farrar, Straus, Giroux, 1988) 15-16.

the significance of literary imagination as a way of conveying his "theological and philosophical ideas."[12] George Kilcourse states that "Spirituality and the literary imagination gradually became more intimately connected in Merton's vision for contemplative life" (Kilcourse 127-28). He lists eleven novelists that Merton was reading, including Percy and Camus.[13] Several years ago in one of my ITMS Chapter meetings,[14] the question was raised by one of the participants about the value of literary imagination as an antecedent for a fruitful prayer life. I must confess that my response was short on specifics, albeit I brought forth the "usual suspects" in my overly generalized commentaries. Although the topic would merit a full-length essay or even a book, I offer briefly the following ideas from Thomas Merton.

A neglect of imagination in our schools was recognized by Merton in his own mentoring of young novices at the monastery and, accordingly, he introduced them to the writings of outstanding novelists and poets. About the novice candidates at the monastery, Merton had this to say:

> We have to recognize that today many candidates come to our monasteries without adequate training in the humanities. And we must not make the mistake of thinking that "training in the humanities" means simply a "classical education" – or a knowledge of Latin. Something has to be done for those who are deficient in a rudimentary appreciation of literature, art, and other humane studies. These have a definite relevance for the spiritual life of the monk.[15]

Merton considers the importance of the imagination for the monk's spiritual life in his essay "Is the Contemplative Life Finished?" in *Contemplation in the World of Action* (*CWA* 331-84). Merton makes the case that the imagination has a place in the contemplative life, although he makes subtle distinctions between contemplative prayer and meditation or "*lectio divina*." On one hand, pure contemplative prayer, as explained by St. John of the Cross, is bereft of all images derived from the imagination. Merton suggests reading the Bible as a "work for the imagination."

---

12. For a more complete development of this topic, see the chapter entitled "Son of the Widowed God: Merton's Sapiential Reading of Fiction" in George Kilcourse, *Ace of Freedoms: Thomas Merton's Christ* (Notre Dame, IN: University of Notre Dame Press, 1993) 127-53; subsequent references will be cited as "Kilcourse" parenthetically in the text.

13. The other novelists include Boris Pasternak, James Joyce, James Baldwin, Flannery O'Connor, William Melvin Kelley, J. F. Powers, William Styron, Julien Greene and William Faulkner (Kilcourse 128).

14. ITMS Chapter at St. Mary's Parish in Shrewsbury, MA.

15. Thomas Merton, *Contemplation in a World of Action* (Garden City, NY: Doubleday, 1971) 201-202; subsequent references will be cited as "*CWA*" parenthetically in the text.

He states: "There is plenty in the Bible that appeals to the imagination, and the psalms are full of imagination. Anything poetic, anything literary, anything creative . . . is full of imagination" (*CWA* 345).[16] Merton defines imagination as the task of "making symbols, joining things together" in a creative way and providing illumination which enables one to see new relationships (*CWA* 345).

This of course is also the work of gifted novelists, as Merton makes clear in his seminal essay "'Baptism in the Forest': Wisdom and Initiation in William Faulkner" (*LE* 92-116), in which he discusses the power of symbols, that have "provided patterns for the myths in which man has striven to express his search for ultimate meaning and for union with God" (*LE* 98). In his essay "Symbolism: Communication or Communion," Merton states that "The realm of symbol is the realm of wisdom in which man finds truth not only in and through objects but in himself and in his life, lived in accordance with the deepest principles of divine wisdom."[17] *Sapientia*, "the Latin word for 'wisdom,'" Merton explains, "is the highest level of cognition. It goes beyond *scientia*, which is systematic knowledge, beyond *intellectus*, which is intuitive understanding. . . . It embraces the entire scope of man's life and all its meaning. It grasps the ultimate truths to which science and intuition only point" (*LE* 98-99). Merton goes on to say that "creative writing and imaginative criticism provide a privileged area for wisdom in the modern world,"[18] and echoes the insights of Maritain and Milosz about the merits of imaginative literature as an alternative way of expressing religious values: "Sapiential awareness deepens our communion with the concrete: It is not an initiation into a world of abstractions and ideals. . . . Wisdom . . . supposes a certain intuitive grasp of *unconscious motivations*, at least insofar as these are embodied in archetypes and symbolic configurations of the

---

16. Although Merton does not use the term "*lectio divina*" here when he mentions reading the Bible as a suitable role for the imagination, the term is commonly employed as a preliminary activity for contemplative prayer. See his extensive discussion of *lectio* in Thomas Merton, *Monastic Observances: Initiation into the Monastic Tradition* 5, ed. Patrick F. O'Connell (Collegeville, MN: Cistercian Publications, 2010) 149-58.

17. Thomas Merton, *Love and Living*, ed. Naomi Burton Stone and Brother Patrick Hart (New York: Farrar, Straus, Giroux, 1979) 68.

18. While Merton heralded the value of imaginative literature as a method of conveying religious values, he refused to compromise the autonomy of the artist for the purpose of "prostitut[ing] art as propaganda." Merton "avoided any suggestion of confusion between art and the sacred. In a 1956 essay [entitled 'Notes on Sacred and Profane Art'] he declared that the subject of art, even when it represents a 'sacred event,' does not make it sacred. 'It can be said that a secular piece that has life and character is itself more sacred than a religious piece that is without either one'" (Kilcourse 132).

psyche" (*LE* 100).

Merton's interest in Albert Camus was a result of a need to develop a humanism that went beyond a "theistic framework" to fulfill his attraction to a "post-Christian ethos." After a methodical reading of Camus' works covering many questions in the realm of ethics, philosophy, politics, religion and aesthetics, Merton concluded that he was "the greatest writer of our time."[19] In a summary statement from his essay on *The Stranger*, Merton contends that this existentialist novel is about an alienated man who decides not to justify his alienation and in his refusal to do so is subsequently condemned by society.[20] Meursault, the novel's protagonist or antihero, according to Merton has no interior or inner life – a man without God, he is a man without purpose, unable to make choices, and even his crime is so mechanical that it is really not his act. This is truly a man without identity, and the vacuum is filled by a society that gladly manufactures an identity for him. This false identity portrays Meursault as a born criminal, and he is officially designated as such by the prosecution. The "stranger," Meursault, is finally able to make a choice by refusing to accept the contrived identity given him by society, and according to Merton "freely elects to *affirm his own absurdity*" rather than submit to a convenient but false definition which claims to explain him (*LE* 293).

Merton affirms a Camusian definition of the "absurd" – it "is the gap between the actual shape of life and intelligent truth" (*LE* 268). To clarify his definition, Merton explains that Camus revolted against the incongruity of men professing to be Christians who believe in "love, mercy, forgiveness and peace" and who at the same time embrace the "secular ideologies of hate, cruelty, revenge, and war" (*LE* 268). The absurdity of justice in *The Stranger* is exemplified by the chaplain, who is complicit with the prosecution and jury in the final condemnation of Meursault. The fact that the prisoner did not weep at his mother's funeral took on more importance than the murder itself. The chaplain adds insult to injury when he attempts to make Meursault a complete penitent by trying to convince him that the justice of the jury was congruent with the justice of God. Being assailed by the chaplain as a man with a "blinded heart," Meursault reacts violently to the deprivation of his personhood by everyone involved. He perceives that the justice of a bourgeois society is, indeed, the justice of the chaplain's so-called God (*LE* 261-62).

---

19. See David D. Cooper, *Thomas Merton's Art of Denial: The Evolution of a Radical Humanist* (Athens, GA: University of Georgia Press) 208.

20. Merton identifies *The Stranger* "as a typical 'existentialist novel' (in spite of all Camus' protests that he was neither an existentialist nor a 'philosopher of the absurd')" (*LE* 293).

Merton describes Meursault as a man plagued with *acedia*, which he defines as "the demon of psychic exhaustion, listlessness, void, thirst, and the moral impotence which attacks the ascetic when he has been entirely burned out by the desert sun and seeks at all costs to find a little shade and clear water" (*LE* 294). According to Merton, Meursault, the acedic, was motivated to seek the shade and cold spring water protected by the Arab. It was not murder, but rather a sense of unity with nature, to be in the same place with the Arab, that Meursault sought. Merton's interpretation of Meursault's unconscious motivation towards unification resonates with the theme of unity evident throughout the Merton canon. In *The Inner Experience*, Merton states that because man was created as a contemplative, the "fall from Paradise was a fall from unity . . . into the multiplicity, complication, and distraction of an active, worldly existence."[21] In a conference given to religious in Alaska during the last year of his life, Merton asserts, the "final integration and unification of man in love is what we are really looking for."[22] He adds that we need to develop people "full of love who keep the fire of love burning in the world" (*TMA* 149). Implied in Camus' portrayal of Meursault as a "rebel" against false societal norms is the foreshadowing of a "unity in love" which Merton indicates was forthcoming in the future works of the French novelist (*LE* 297). Camus' theme of love is presented by Merton in a quotation from one of Camus' Notebooks: "If someone here told me to write a book on morality, it would have a hundred pages and ninety-nine would be blank. On the last page I should write 'I recognize only one duty, and that is to love.' And as far as everything else is concerned I say *no*" (*LE* 241).

If Meursault's search for authenticity is that of a person amidst the clamor of false societal and religious norms, then one can find a search for authenticity on the part of Binx Bolling as a major theme in Walker Percy's *The Moviegoer*.[23] In a January, 1964 letter to Percy, Merton praises

---

21. Thomas Merton, *The Inner Experience: Notes on Contemplation*, ed. William H. Shannon (San Francisco: HarperCollins, 2003) 35.

22. Thomas Merton, *Thomas Merton in Alaska: The Alaskan Conferences, Journals, and Letters*, ed. Robert E. Daggy (New York: New Directions, 1989) 147; subsequent references will be cited as *"TMA"* parenthetically in the text.

23. Percy acknowledged his indebtedness to European philosophical novelists and admits in a number of interviews that Camus had an influence on his style and technique; see "A Talk with Walker Percy: Zoltan Abadi-Nagy/1973," in *Conversations with Walker Percy*, ed. Lewis A. Lawson and Victor A. Kramer (Jackson, MS: University Press of Mississippi, 1985) 73. Tony Tanner states that Percy utilized the strategies of Camus's *The Stranger* when he describes characters in *The Moviegoer*: see *Walker Percy*, ed. Harold Bloom (New York: Chelsea House, 1986) 9. Kieran Quinlan states: "Percy . . . drew on Camus for precision and style" in his novels: see Kieran Quinlan, *Walker Percy, The Last*

the virtues of the book, published four years earlier:

With reticence and malaise . . . I think your book is right on the target. . . . You are right all the time, not just sometimes. . . . Never too much of anyone. Just enough of Sharon. The reason the book is true is that you always stop at the point where more talk would have been false, untrue, confusing, irrelevant. It is not that what you say is true. It is neither true nor false, it points in the right direction, where there is something that has not been said and you know enough not to try to say it. Hence you are one of the most hopeful existentialists I know of. I suppose it was inevitable that an American existentialist should have a merry kind of nausea after all, and no one reproaches you for this or anything else. (*CT* 281-82)

Merton conveys his enthusiasm for *The Moviegoer* to Mark Van Doren in a Februry 11, 1964 letter; he writes that Binx, the protagonist, is portrayed as "a supreme dope of some sort for going to so many movies, but in the end it turns out that he is the only smart one, in a wild existentialist kind of way" (*RJ* 47).

In 1965 Merton published an article in *The Critic* entitled "The Many Faces of Existentialism," later included in *Mystics and Zen Masters* under the revised title "The Other Side of Despair: Notes on Christian Existentialism."[24] Hence, existentialism was very much on Merton's mind about the time he read and critiqued Percy's novel. Christian existentialism, according to Merton, is "active not only in philosophy but also in the renewed Biblical theology which has been so eloquent and so salutary in the years of Vatican II" (*MZM* 256). He admits that the term existentialism is difficult to define; he asserts that it is not a system of thought but rather "an experience and an attitude," and it defies journalistic clichés about "existentialist nihilism, pessimism [and] anarchism" (*MZM* 258). Merton makes the point that the most significant religions have "been marked by 'existentialist' insights into man's current situation" (*MZM* 270). Although Merton's definition of Christian existentialism is a polar opposite of Jean-Paul Sartre's atheist version, both rejected collectivism

---

Catholic Novelist (Baton Rouge, LA: Louisiana State University Press, 1996) 89. Martin Luschei declares that "The voice in *The Moviegoer* owes a good deal to Albert Camus, as Percy has acknowledged"; in a footnote on the same page, Luschei compares the opening sentences of *The Moviegoer* and *The Stranger* to make his point: see Martin Luschei, *The Sovereign Wayfarer* (Baton Rouge, LA: Louisiana State University Press, 1972) 15, n. 40 (subsequent references will be cited as "Luschei" parenthetically in the text).

24. Thomas Merton, *Mystics and Zen Masters* (New York: Farrar, Straus and Giroux, 1967), 255-80; subsequent references will be cited as "*MZM*" parenthetically in the text.

and scientific positivism. However, Sartre's rejection of collectivism was characterized by a lack of dialogue, without any genuine communion with others. Apparently, it was "the cool assertion of one's privacy" (*MZM* 276). Merton was especially wary of the danger of the Church being reduced to an institution whereby the members merely acknowledge religious truths and dogmas as a substitute "for any kind of intimate and personal surrender to God. Religion thus becomes a matter of formalities and gestures" (*MZM* 271). After moving away from other forms of existentialism, Merton describes Christian existentialism or existential theology as manifesting a power of grace reconciling one's self with Christ, "with one's true self, one's neighbor, and with God" (*MZM* 278). There is an authentic "communal life" and the community members are ready to confront and "participate in all the most cogent concerns of the world" (*MZM* 280). Merton's understanding of the authentic Church, therefore, required intersubjective love among its members, leading to a true sense of community.[25]

Percy is described by Merton as a hopeful existentialist, through his characterization of Binx Bolling in *The Moviegoer*; conversely, Camus' protagonist Meursault is without hope and apparently without any interior life. At least Binx has some semblance of an interior life as he is onto the search.[26] Early in the novel, Binx describes the search in his alienated world:[27]

The search is what anyone would undertake if he were not sunk in the everydayness of his own life. . . . To become aware of the possibility of the search is to be onto something. Not to be onto something is to be in despair. The movies are onto the search, but they screw it up. The search always ends in despair. . . . What do you seek – God? You ask with a smile. (Percy 13)

The possibility of the search by Binx is, therefore, a hopeful sign, as he is aware that he must get out from under the "everydayness" of his life. There are two kinds of searches revealed by Percy in his novel. The vertical search is made through the study of science; after understanding the

---

25. In his Alaska talk "Building Community on God's Love," Merton contrasts "the old institutional community" (*TMA* 96) with "a community built on God – because that is really the center of Christianity" (*TMA* 97).

26. Both Meursault and Binx are alike in temperament: both "are laconic, basically indifferent to religious and moral values" (J. Donald Crowley and Sue Mitchell Crowley, *Critical Essays on Walker Percy* [Boston: G.K. Hall, 1989] 126).

27. For a discussion of Percy's malaise in connection with Merton's theme of alienation, see John P. Collins, "Thomas Merton and Walker Percy: A Connection through Intersections," *The Merton Annual* 15 (2002) 166-93; subsequent references will be cited as "Collins" parenthetically in the text.

universe, one discovers, "I myself was left over." Conversely, the hori-
zontal search is an existential quest "addressed to the concrete realities
of existence." In other words, who am I? (Luschei 88-90). The malaise
of "everydayness" is explained by Lewis Lawson as the masquerading of
happiness and as one not being aware that he/she is in a state of despair.
Such people are "desperately alienated from themselves."[28] Indeed, the
epigraph of the novel is a quotation from Soren Kierkegaard: "the specific
character of despair is precisely this: it is unaware of being despair." In
a September 12, 1959 letter to Czeslaw Milosz, Merton revealed that he
was very much aware of the "hopefulness" of despair – an oxymoron that
he shared with Percy. Merton writes:

> We should all feel near to despair in some sense because this semi-
> despair is the normal form taken by hope in a time like ours. Hope
> without any sensible or tangible evidence on which to rest. Hope in
> spite of the sickness that fills us. Hope married to a firm refusal to
> accept any palliatives or anything that cheats hope by pretending to
> relieve apparent despair. (*STB* 52)

The terse comment "What do you seek – God? You ask with a smile"
is but one example in the novel of Merton's assertion that Percy knows
where to stop, and that "more talk would have been false, untrue, confusing, irrelevant." Percy refused to allow his novels to morph into religious
handbooks, but rather, the spiritual longing of his characters was a means
of diagnosing the "malaise" of our society. Listen to what Binx Bolling
has to say about the malaise: "What is the malaise? You ask. The malaise
is the pain of loss. The world is lost to you, the world and the people in
it, and there remains only you and the world and you no more able to
be in the world than Banquo's ghost" (Percy 120). Merton mentions the
malaise in his letter to Percy and he may have recognized *The Moviegoer*
as "a fictional counterpart to [the] alienation theme evident in his works"
(Collins 178). Binx, as an existentialist, is having his own merry kind of
nausea[29] and exhibits, from time to time, his disdain for the collective,
as described in Merton's essay on existentialism. In one of the many
humorous parts of the novel pointing to a "merry kind of nausea," there

---

28. Lewis Lawson, *Following Percy* (Troy, NY: Whitston, 1988) 9.

29. In a later part of his January 1964 letter to Percy, Merton mentions Sharon, one
of Binx's many girlfriends in *The Moviegoer*; my interpretation of Merton's phrase a
"merry kind of nausea" is the narration of the frivolous events associated with Binx and
Sharon in the novel. There are other humorous events as well in the novel that contribute,
in my view, to a "merry kind of nausea." For a more esoteric interpretation of the phrase,
see George Kilcourse, "Merton's 'True Spirit' or a Calculated 'Official Pedestal'?" *The
Merton Annual* 16 (2003) 221-44.

is a description of Binx's acceptance into a college fraternity, but in the end his existential instincts take over and we find him sitting on the front porch of the fraternity "bemused and dreaming," having contributed nothing to the group (Percy 38).

Although the novel is virtually without plot, we find Binx, near the end of the book, coming close to finding his authentic self after stumbling through numerous episodes of exhibiting, in Merton's words, his false self. In Kierkegaardian terms,[30] Binx has made an existential leap from the aesthetic, consumer-driven level of existence to the religious sphere, as he muses about a middle-class Negro who has received ashes on Ash Wednesday. Ralph Wood states: "Binx wonders whether this black man is seeking to make his way into the white man's world of business contacts and economic advancement, or whether he has come to repent his sins, to confess that he is made of dust and shall return to it, and thus to embark on the repentant life that leads to resurrection."[31] After observing the incident, Binx admits, "It is impossible to say" (Percy 235) whether he has witnessed a moment of grace or if it was just another Catholic emerging from a church like so many other Catholics fulfilling their Lenten ritual. As Merton observed, Percy stops "at the point where more talk would have been false, untrue, confusing, irrelevant." If we accept it, as a "dazzling trick of grace," Binx and his wife Kate have embarked on a new journey, still part of the search towards "intersubjective love and true sense of community."

Although he never met or corresponded with Camus before the French author's tragic death in 1960, the tone of Merton's seven essays on Camus is dialogical in nature. David Belcastro observes that Merton was hopeful "of discovering in dialogue with Camus conditions under which communication between Christians and people of other traditions, both religious and secular, may conceivably be more authentic and creative."[32]

---

30. Percy borrowed the three stages of existence from Soren Kierkegaard. The following description of the stages relates them to Percy's presentation as found in *The Moviegoer*: "The aesthetic sphere can be best described as 'the happy consumer' [Binx] who does all the right things; has the right clothes . . . and car – all designed to make a statement. The ethical sphere is represented by Aunt Emily . . . who personifies the Stoic philosophy which 'includes charity, compassion and reason.' The religious sphere is where one realizes a faith in God but cannot or will not express this faith" (Collins 185-86). When Binx realized the possibility of God's "trick of grace" outside the church on Ash Wednesday, he simply said, "It is impossible to say" (Percy 235).

31. Ralph C. Wood, *Literature and Theology* (Nashville, TN: Abingdon Press, 2008) 22.

32. David Joseph Belcastro, "Merton and Camus on Christian Dialogue with a Postmodern World," *The Merton Annual* 10 (1997) 224.

Conversely, Merton and Percy corresponded, and met on one occasion. Indeed, Merton felt a kinship with Percy as they were the same age, both attended Columbia University, and both were converts to Catholicism. Although Merton asserted that Camus did not understand the Christian Gospel, he embraced the novelist's repugnance toward for violence and the declaration that his one duty was "to love." Certainly Merton's kinship with Percy was primarily through reading *The Moviegoer* and I surmise that the monk may have had an epiphanic moment as he read about Binx Bolling's discovery of the search – that is, "To become aware of the possibility of the search is to be onto something."

In sum, the 1960s had been a fruitful literary period for Thomas Merton. During this period he had encouragement from Jacques Maritain and Czeslaw Milosz to express his theological and philosophical ideas through literature and literary criticism. The seven Camus essays had been written during this period, which according to Michael Mott, were indications that Merton was a serious literary critic. Through commentary in letters to Percy and Mark Van Doren, as well as a journal entry, Merton critiqued Percy's novel *The Moviegoer*, albeit the critique did not have the rigor manifested in the Camus essays. In the mid-1960s, Merton wrote his influential essay proffering the term "sapiential" as a preferred word over "religious" in expressing ultimate truths.

In this discussion, I have singled out Meursault and Binx Bolling as antiheroes or flawed protagonists who symbolize the "sapiential" in their search for authenticity. Merton intuits a search for unity in nature on the part of Meursault as a partial redemptive quality of Camus' stranger. With Binx Bolling, Percy stops short of portraying his character, near the end of the novel, as one who now has decided to genuflect before the altar of God. Instead we are left with irresolution and with even the possibility of Binx and Kate embracing the bourgeoisie. Camus would have been disappointed, of course, because Meursault had been clear about his disdain for the norms of the bourgeois society, buttressed by the institutions of court and Church. Both antiheroes have a concern for their identity, a key to their authenticity. Meursault rebels against the false identity imposed upon him by society, whereas Binx had created his own false identity through a consumer-driven aestheticism. Both Meursault and Binx are interpreted by Merton as representing "communion with the concrete" and he cleverly presents their "unconscious motivations" – Meursault's search for unity in nature and Binx's sometimes on, and sometimes off, search for authenticity through "the thin gas of malaise" (Percy 18).[33]

---

33. This essay is based on a presentation on March 29, 2012 at the College English Association annual meeting in Richmond, VA.

You Are You: That Is the Most Important Thing – Everything Is in It Somewhere: An Analysis of the Correspondence from Thomas Merton to John Harris

Fiona Gardner

The collection of letters from Thomas Merton to John Harris published in *The Hidden Ground of Love*[1] encapsulates Merton's ability to establish an immediate empathy and intimacy with a previously unknown correspondent. What is particularly interesting about this correspondence is that Merton elicits very quickly the underlying reason for the initial contact made by Harris, and his replies lead to a life-changing transformation for Harris. It is Merton's extraordinary capacity to get so quickly to the very heart of the issue that is explored in this paper. When Merton writes "you are you" and the sentences that follow, he is at that moment in deep communion with the recipient, and that communion calls forth an equally deep spiritual connection for Harris and between the two men. It is in particular this exchange that opens Harris to the guidance of the Spirit, and leads to Harris' conversion to the Catholic Church.

There are three suggestions about what is happening in this correspondence: firstly, that Merton's use of language is in itself his way of conveying his own experience of a deeper truth, and thematic discourse analysis is used to explore this; secondly, that the spirit of Boris Pasternak permeates and influences the entire correspondence, and this is evidenced by drawing on Merton's literary essays on Pasternak; thirdly, that the psychodynamics between Merton and Harris affect the outcome, and psychoanalytic theory is used for this exploration.

John P. Harris (1923–2003) was born in London, and at the time of his correspondence with Merton was working as a language teacher at a progressive school in Devon, and following that in Cornwall. He later became known as the author of a number of books and a BBC broadcaster about life in the center and south of France. In the 1950s Harris wrote

---

1. Thomas Merton, *The Hidden Ground of Love: Letters on Religious Experience and Social Concerns*, ed. William H. Shannon (New York: Farrar, Straus, Giroux, 1985) 384-401; subsequent references will be cited as "*HGL*" parenthetically in the text. Both sides of the original correspondence are available at the Thomas Merton Center, at Bellarmine University, Louisville, KY; for a summary and list of items, see: http://merton.org/Research/Correspondence/y1.aspx?id=856.

to Boris Pasternak (1890–1960) after reading his book *Dr. Zhivago*. Pasternak, the Russian poet and writer born in Moscow, won the Nobel Prize for literature in 1958 for this novel but withdrew his acceptance of the award so that he could remain in Russia. He was seen as an artist at odds with the political establishment of the time. Pasternak in response to Harris' letter asked him to contact three people, one of them Thomas Merton, "whose precious thoughts and dear bottomless letters enrich me and make me happy" (see *HGL* 384). (The limited edition book *Six Letters: Boris Pasternak, Thomas Merton* contains their correspondence.[2]) Pasternak asked Harris to relay a message to Merton, and in turn Merton could make use of Harris to convey greetings and support to Pasternak, as Harris, acting as a go-between, would not attract the attention of Soviet authorities as Merton would. Alongside this pragmatic reasoning it is possible that there was some aspect or quality in that initial letter that alerted Pasternak to a deeper need in Harris that had been touched by his reading of the novel. So in December 1958 Harris initiated a correspondence with Thomas Merton which was to last ten years.

An overall reading of the letters gives the "storyline" of the sequence, and what might be called the generative vitality of the dialogue. The transformative vitality lies in the first half of the correspondence, as if the necessary energy to effect the conversion happens immediately. Again this highlights Merton's capacity not to "just" respond to surface information, or what might be called the manifest level, but rather to read and intuit the subtext or latent meaning in the letters he received.

After Merton's initial welcoming letter, the second letter picks up the issue of conversion and the "official" concern about the status of Harris' earlier marriage, which might preclude permission to receive the sacraments. In this second letter, Merton separates the "official" view from a deeper reality of what it means to be a Christian, and this theme continues in letters 3 and 4. By letter 5 Merton has a picture of the Harris children on his desk and is sharing ideas on prayer and what it really means to be "in" the Church. In the second half of the correspondence the pace slows, and there is exchange on "life in Christ," the interweaving of ideas, news of holidays taken by the Harrises, exchanges of photos, and Merton's interest in the Harris children, especially Arthur, "our trusty secret agent in Cornwall" (*HGL* 400 [4/10/1967]), to whom Merton sends stamps

---

2. *Six Letters: Boris Pasternak, Thomas Merton*, ed. Naomi Burton Stone and Lydia Pasternak Slater (Lexington, KY: King Library Press, 1973); Merton's letters to Pasternak are also found in Thomas Merton, *The Courage for Truth: Letters to Writers*, ed. Christine M. Bochen (New York: Farrar, Straus, Giroux, 1993) 87-93; subsequent references will be cited as "*CT*" parenthetically in the text.

that he suggests jokingly could possibly be impregnated with opiates and secret messages.

There are three aspects to this correspondence that merit deeper examination.

1. Merton's use of language: discourse analysis is an umbrella term used to describe different ways of studying texts. The term "discourse" is sometimes used to refer to patterns of meaning and it can be used to deconstruct linguistic patterns, and the way someone writes or speaks. In this instance it is not restricted to language but is also used as a way of understanding social interactions. Thematic analysis is one type of discourse analysis, and is a way of exploring the recurring and meaningful themes in a text. The first two letters sent by Merton can be analysed in this way where the significant words are categorized into six themes and the percentages given.

Letter 1 (*HGL* 384-85 [12/4/1958]) is an extraordinarily generous offering by Merton: 23% of the words are positively warm and welcoming. They include: "wonderful," "welcome," "joy," "relief," "treasure," "valued," "overjoyed," "confidence," "enjoyed," "gratitude," "lovely" and "loved." Another 23% are words that convey compassion and reaching out. This creates an immediate chain of connection and bonding between Merton and Harris. They include: "your," "our," "every one of us," "our lives," "great sorrow" and "pain."

32% of the words are inspirational – words used that would take the recipient of the letters out of the ordinary into the extraordinary. They include: "surprise," "everything," "extraordinary," "reaching everyone," "portent," "immense," "significance," "greatest," "sign of hope," "first star," "new dawn," "much truth," "inspired," "significance," "great meaning," "without measure." The use of various forms of repetition is generally seen as a basis for cohesion, for example "lovely" and "loved," "joy," "enjoyed" and "overjoyed." It is not just the words themselves that are significant, but the sound of the words and the emotional resonances for the reader. Other themes that begin to emerge in letter 1 are the author's voice, the voice of Merton as his own person, which is 15% of the material. However there is only 3.5% reference to what could be categorized as Christian values and truths, and the same amount for the opposition within the Church to Christian values and truths. So in summary, 78% of the words used in that first letter are either warm, convey a quality of reaching out, or are inspirational. The use of these categories of words is in no way to be seen as calculated, but rather stems from the genuine person of Merton. The implication is that it is then hardly surprising that Harris can immediately turn to Merton as someone who can be entrusted with his search for and acceptance by God.

In letter 2 (*HGL* 385-87 [1/31/1959]), Merton responds by immediately re-framing the connection between the two men by his use of "you" and "your," and then beginning to use words linked to the theme of Christian values and truths. These are words such as: "adequate," "straight," "thoughtful," "clear," "Christian," "Christ," "personal." In the second paragraph Merton also introduces in contrast words and phrases that are in opposition to his experience of Christian values and truths. These are negative controlling words and phrases such as: "officials," "official declarations," "official answers," "no one is officially saved," "cannot be," "not claiming," "solve all," "false position," "official solutions," "declarations," "not sound," "official." Throughout, to cohere and contrast these two opposing themes, there is a continuing use of connections and words and phrases that reach out to the recipient, such as: "you bring up," "your questions," "your problems," "you probably believe," "your problem," "you doubt," "account to yourself," "you believe in." In this letter is the now-conscious assumption that this is a Christian discourse with phrases such as: "finds himself in God," "same God" and repetition of "God." This repeated pattern of the two opposing Christian discourses continues in paragraphs three and four. The percentages linked to the six themes have completely changed in this letter. The two highest groupings are those of Christian values and truths at 28%, with the opposing Christian discourse at 24%; 13% is the author's voice, 6% inspirational and 2% warm and welcoming. The proportion of words that convey compassion and reaching out is 27% and thus slightly higher than in letter 1. Throughout this letter Merton connects to Harris and keeps high the level of intimacy. The destination and peak of the whole letter is contained in the last paragraph where five of the six themes are contained, and where the main theme is inspirational, but with Christian values and truths and a deep reaching out included within it. Merton's words here deserve close attention: "Do not hesitate to write if there is anything I can do for you, or send you." Here is the real connection and generosity. There is within this context a reaching out by Merton in a deeply spiritual manner. Following this opening he appeals to the very core of Harris, beyond the "official" rulings and restrictions, writing: "The important thing is who are you: you are not a 'man with a problem,' or a person trying to figure something out." Instead Merton tosses aside the clichéd descriptions to focus on the actual individuality of Harris. He locates him and places him as a unique person when he writes: "you are Harris, in Devonshire, and that means you are not and cannot be another in a series of objects, you are you and that is the important thing." Here Merton jumps to the crux of each person's particular and personal relationship with God. The individual is no longer anonymous or reduced to a category, but each person is seen rather as a child of God, individually loved for who they are and the person they are meant to be. In his next sentence Merton reaches to the heart of what it means to be in relationship with another person and with Christ, immersed in the world and immersed in God: "For, you see, when 'I' enter into a dialogue with 'you' and each of us knows who is speaking, it turns out that we are both Christ." This is the heart of Merton's gift. This is not just a gift to Harris, but also to each person who reads and reflects on Merton's words. Here is the evidence of the fruits of contemplation with the connection that goes beyond dialogue into deep communion, where the true self of each unites with and as part of Christ. As Merton concludes in this paragraph: "This, being seen in a very simple and 'natural' light, is the beginning and almost the fullness of everything. Everything is in it somewhere. But it makes most sense in the light of the Mass and the Eucharist." Here is the true meaning of life and life in Christ, the fullness of all experience.

Thematic analysis can be applied to the whole correspondence; certainly in letters 3 and 4 (*HGL* 387-88 [3/14/1959]; 388-90 [5/5/1959]) the high levels of reaching out are maintained, and letter 4 in particular is full of inspirational language. This letter 4 also rises to a discourse peak in the last paragraph which includes Merton's understanding of the emptiness that contains everything.

2. The influence of Pasternak: the link is firmly established with Pasternak as the trigger for the correspondence. His underlying influence permeates the first six letters where Pasternak is mentioned. It then resurfaces only once again, in letter 9 (*HGL* 396-97 [6/17/1960]), which includes discussion of Pasternak's funeral. However it is not the actual references to Pasternak that influence the correspondence, but rather his underlying spirit. Merton was in correspondence with Pasternak between 1958 and 1960 and wrote as a "kindred mind." "It is as if we met on a deeper level of life on which individuals are not separate beings. In the language familiar to me as a Catholic monk, it is as if we were known to one another in God" (*CT* 87-88). The feeling was reciprocated by Pasternak who replied that Merton's letter had seemed, "wonderfully filled with kindred thoughts" (see *CT* 87). The letter from Harris is mentioned by Merton in December 1958, the link between the three brothers in Christ.

In his essay entitled "The Pasternak Affair,"[3] Merton analyses not

---

3. Thomas Merton, *Disputed Questions* (New York: Farrar, Straus and Cudahy, 1960) 3-67; subsequent references will be cited as "*DQ*" parenthetically in the text.

only the Russian's writing, but also his spirituality. The suggestion is that the kindred-spirit aspect recognized by Merton is then in turn reflected in his letters to Harris. Merton found Pasternak a genuinely spiritual man whose "religious" character was "mysterious" and "existential," and who through his work stirred up in others a spiritual longing. This clearly was the effect on Harris.

How the spirituality that Merton experiences in Pasternak is reflected in the correspondence to Harris is now explored in four ways. The first is picking up on Pasternak's cosmic mysticism. So, for example, when commenting on *Dr. Zhivago* Merton writes, "it is in some way about everybody and everybody is involved in it" (*DQ* 8), there are echoes of "everything is in it somewhere." This is intense awareness of all cosmic and human reality as "life in Christ." Secondly, Merton picks up on Pasternak's ability to present a spirituality that is opposite to passive conformity. This is a central feature of the Merton letters to Harris – the forces of officialdom that oppose genuine Christian truths. In the essay on Pasternak Merton writes of "people with watch chains" (*DQ* 7) who thrive on conformity and who oppose life that is genuinely revolutionary in the sense that it constantly strives to surpass itself. When Merton writes the superlative paragraph at the end of letter 2, he seems to tap into this same energy as, in Pasternak's words, the "irresistible power of the unarmed truth" (*DQ* 16, 17). Thirdly, Merton writes of the ingeniousness and spontaneity of a spirituality that has never become quite conscious of itself. To illustrate he quotes from *Dr. Zhivago* about Lara: "She was here on earth to grasp the meaning of its wild enchantment, to call each thing by its right name, or, if this were not in her power, to give birth out of love for life to successors who would do it in her place" (*DQ* 18).[4] Through "life in Christ" love becomes the only dynamic and creative force, and indeed it is in the second half of the correspondence with Harris that we see the lack of self-consciousness where Merton is friend and quasi-family member, and the same unarmed truth is demonstrated in terms of "everyday reality." The fourth aspect to comment on is Merton's use of language, in particular the inspirational words and phrases looked at earlier. It could be said that when Merton turns to inspirational language he also becomes poet. The central character Yurii in *Dr. Zhivago* is also a poet. Pasternak sees the poet's vocation as dynamic and contemplative, and Merton comments on the poet who utters the voice of God and the incarnation, "it is the transfigured, spiritualized and divinized cosmos that speaks through [the poet] and . . . utters its praise of the Creator" (*DQ* 20-21). For Pasternak,

---

4. The original passage is quoted from *Dr. Zhivago* (London: Collins Fontana, 1958) 89.

language is the home and receptacle of beauty that turns "wholly into music" (*DQ* 21); likewise some of the peak discourse in this correspondence is wholly music.

3. The psychoanalytic discourse: psychoanalytic ideas can help to open up different levels in any relationship between and within people. In this context undoubtedly there were positive transferences (by transference is meant the unconscious projection onto another person based on earlier significant relationships). There are positive transferences from Harris to Merton, and Merton to Harris, and in the background the transference Merton held toward Pasternak and Pasternak to Merton. One might surmise that as kindred souls all three felt as brothers. The later correspondence suggests Merton as a benevolent uncle and family friend to the whole Harris family.

However the aspects to highlight in the correspondence are what Merton offers to Harris. There are three aspects to briefly explore. The first is that Merton offers Harris a transitional space in his conversion. This is space in between being in one state or another. The English psychoanalyst D. W. Winnicott wrote about the use of transitional objects in infancy[5] that allow us to negotiate into a new state of consciousness about who we are, and the same ideas can be applied to the conversion process. Merton opens up a space for dialogue about what it means to be a Christian, and he offers a space outside of the official doctrinal boundaries. In other words Merton in this transitional space offers an alternative. Harris waits a long time for the doctrinal issues to be resolved, and Merton commends him for his patience. Yet such patience is possible because Merton gives Harris another perspective and space to be. The space allows Harris to move with Merton's support from a place of passive dependency into a state of independence as a Christian, and the second part of the correspondence confirms this change of status.

The second aspect is that Merton demonstrates an ability to play. Using psychoanalytic thinking, we recognize that Merton finds, creates, matches up ideas, improvises his thinking, and then discards some of it. He refines what he is saying, and finds images that help him describe and convey to Harris the reality of this life in Christ. In his spontaneous and genuine style, Merton offers lots of ideas, reading materials and insights from thinkers outside of the Christian tradition. In his later letters he models that family life can be as much part of life in Christ as any official Church traditions. The third aspect is that Merton becomes for Harris the person through whom God's transformational action takes

---

5. See D. W. Winnicott, "Transitional Objects and Transitional Phenomena," in *Playing and Reality* (London: Penguin, 1971) 1-30.

place. Conversion is subjective and that's what gives it such power, but Merton became significant for this action in Harris' life. Using analytic discourse, one might say that Merton became the transformational object whom Harris could make use of at a crucial time in his life.

In conclusion, any analysis of Merton's letters reveals rich depths and much fruitful analysis, whatever approach is taken. Merton's responses to Harris contain a generosity and depth of spirit that takes the reader well beyond the limitations of the actual literal meaning. As one correspondent wrote to Merton, "your silence speaks well between the lines; and your words mean more than they seem to mean."[6]

---

6. Thomas Merton and Catherine de Hueck Doherty, *Compassionate Fire: The Letters of Thomas Merton and Catherine de Hueck Doherty*, ed. Robert A. Wild (Notre Dame, IN: Ave Maria Press, 2009) 54.

Thomas Merton and Hannah Arendt: Desert and City in Cold-War Culture

Robert Weldon Whalen

Thomas Merton was "the twentieth century's most eloquent and accessible spiritual figure," critic Michael Higgins claims, and he's probably right.[1] During the long Cold War, Fulton Sheen and Billy Graham were by far the greater celebrities, but for people interested in the life of contemplative prayer, Merton was an iconic figure. Merton was, however, as Robert Inchausti writes, "a man of many contradictions."[2] For example, Merton the monk-poet-mystic was also a political thinker. Merton, of course, shared the views of his multiple circles: his passion for nuclear disarmament, his advocacy of civil rights, his angry opposition to the Vietnam War, his feminism and environmentalism were, one might argue, typical of his Beat, literary, radical Catholic circle. Merton's thought, though, went beyond the predictable. His views were, surprisingly, also akin to the kind of in-depth social critique practiced by one of the most remarkable of Cold War America's many counter-cultures.

Beat poets and left-wing Catholics were not the only counter-cultures in Cold War America. Merton's own monastic life was certainly a kind of counter-culture (Higgins 86-88). One of the most peculiar and influential counter-cultures might be called "Weimar in exile." Its denizens were those German intellectuals who fled from Hitler to America, who then became fascinated with and outraged by America, and whose thoughts on American public life would have an immense impact both on scholarship and politics. A tight, though by no means homogeneous sub-culture, bound together by their Central European sensibilities, Weimar roots and experience of persecution, "Weimar in exile" first took root in Manhattan and in Los Angeles. Theodor Adorno, Max Horkheimer, Erich Fromm and others from the Frankfurt School, would have enormous influence on American thought.[3] Hans Morganthau became 1950s America's

---

1. Michael W. Higgins, *Heretic Blood: The Spiritual Geography of Thomas Merton* (Toronto: Stoddart, 1998) 2; subsequent references will be cited as "Higgins" parenthetically in the text.

2. Robert Inchausti, *Thomas Merton's American Prophecy* (Albany: State University of New York Press, 1998) 1.

3. For the definitive history of the Frankfurt school, see Martin Jay, *The Dialectical Imagination* (Berkeley: University of California Press, 1996). The "Frankfurt School" is the nickname for the Institute for Social Research (Institut für Sozialforschung) created

best known "political realist." Paul Tillich would have a major impact on American culture and politics, as a 1959 *Time* magazine cover story about him explained.[4] The American left would be inspired, for a time, by Herbert Marcuse; the right, for a longer time, would be inspired by Leo Strauss.

One of the most influential members of "Weimer in exile" was Hannah Arendt; Dana Villa describes Arendt as "one of the most original and influential thinkers of the twentieth century."[5] After the publication of her *Origins of Totalitarianism*,[6] in 1951, Arendt rocketed to academic fame. Her later work established her as an important political philosopher; *Eichmann in Jerusalem*,[7] serialized in *The New Yorker* in 1961, brought Arendt celebrity and plunged her into controversy.[8]

Merton and Arendt never met. Merton knew and admired some of Arendt's work; while Arendt may have heard of Merton – he was famous, after all – she never seriously engaged with his work. They were contemporaries with European pasts, and both would have an enormous impact on their adopted American homes, but Merton and Arendt were very different people with very different biographies and passions. Merton, educated in France, Britain and the United States, was a Christian, a poet and a mystic. Arendt, educated in Weimar Germany, a student of Martin Heidegger and Karl Jaspers, was a non-observant Jew, a philosopher and a religious skeptic. It is all the more striking, then, that their understandings of Cold War America would intersect so often.

This article will explore some of these Merton-Arendt intersections by focusing on two almost contemporary texts, Arendt's *The Human*

in 1923 by political scientist Carl Grünberg, and affiliated with the Frankfurt University. By the 1930s, the Institute's leaders were Theodor Adorno and Max Horkheimer. Adorno, Horkheimer and their colleagues were "engaged" social scientists, convinced that their task was both to describe and critique society. Influenced especially by Marx, the Institute's scholars also drew on Freud, Hegel, Kant and the long tradition of Central European social criticism, including both Christian eschatology and Jewish messianism. Exiled to the United States during World War II, the Frankfurt School scholars had an enormous impact on post-war American social criticism.

4. See "A Theology for Protestants," *Time* (March 16, 1959) 46-52.

5. Dana Villa, "Introduction: the Development of Arendt's Political Thought," in *The Cambridge Companion to Hannah Arendt*, ed. Dana Villa (New York: Cambridge University Press, 2002) 1; the entire volume is a useful introduction to her thought.

6. Hannah Arendt, *The Origins of Totalitarianism* (New York: Harcourt, Brace, 1951).

7. Hannah Arendt, *Eichmann in Jerusalem* (New York: Viking Press, 1964).

8. For a biography of Arendt, see Elisabeth Young-Bruehl, *Hannah Arendt: For Love of the World* (New Haven: Yale University Press, 2004).

Condition,[9] published in 1958, and Merton's *Conjectures of a Guilty Bystander*,[10] based on his journals of the late 1950s and early 1960s, and published in 1966. One could hardly juxtapose two more drastically different texts. *The Human Condition* is sober philosophy; *Conjectures* is a collage of reflections, intuitions and observations. Arendt's book is a single, complex, earnest, impersonal argument. Merton's is episodic, disjointed, impressionistic, occasionally comic and highly personal. Arendt refers to contemporary affairs, like "Sputnik," only in passing; reflections on contemporary affairs weave their way throughout *Conjectures*. Oddly enough, Arendt's text seems the more ethereal, the more unworldly, though it is her purpose to defend worldliness; of the two, Merton's ostensibly spiritual text actually seems the earthier.

Merton and Arendt – one could hardly imagine an odder couple. As different as they were, contemporary concerns drew them together. I'll argue that in at least three thematic areas – I'll call them "Apocalypse," "*Polis*" and "Revelation" – Merton and Arendt share, if not answers, then at least questions. More surprisingly, I'll suggest as well that not only Merton's politics, but Arendt's as well, lead them and their students off into the realm of the spirit.

I. Apocalypse

"Supposing, for a moment," Merton writes, "that our society is headed for cataclysm. One is supposed not to think that it is, yet at the moment everyone is talking about fallout shelters. (Build one in your backyard, come out after two weeks and resume the American Way of Life amid the ashes). What kind of attitude should one take . . . ?" (*CGB* 173).

Merton's *Conjectures* is not consistently apocalyptic. He writes about literature and prayer; the new altar in the novitiate chapel and the mauve snow in the farm fields. But a deep melancholy runs throughout *Conjectures*. Humanity, in Merton's lifetime, twice plunged into catastrophic world wars, and the evil spirits that inspired those two disasters, Merton worries, were preparing a third. Merton's concerns are not merely speculative. The looming atomic apocalypse Merton sees as yet one more chapter in the ghastly political history of the twentieth century. "Into this crisis I was born," he says, thinking of his birth in France in 1915, in the midst of World War I. "By this crisis my whole life has been shaped. In this crisis my life will be consumed" (*CGB* 57). He remembers his

---

9. Hannah Arendt, *The Human Condition* (Chicago: University of Chicago Press, 1958); subsequent references will be cited as "Arendt, *Condition*" parenthetically in the text.

10. Thomas Merton, *Conjectures of a Guilty Bystander* (Garden City, NY: Doubleday, 1966); subsequent references will be cited as "*CGB*" parenthetically in the text.

younger brother, John Paul, killed in World War II. A bomber crewman, John Paul's plane was shot out of the sky, and Merton recalls: "Eighteen years since the three survivors in John Paul's crew dropped his body off the lifeboat into the North Sea. His back was broken when the plane hit the surface" (*CGB* 175). Brooding about the recent past, Merton worries that past is prologue. He writes, "How long can the menace of war grow and grow, and still not end in war?" (*CGB* 235).

Merton, in *Conjectures*, is no fatalist; the disasters of the 1930s, and the impending disasters of the 1950s, are not products of impersonal forces or malevolent fate. We humans have made the fix in which we find ourselves; the evil spirits are us. What were we thinking? But there, Merton argues, is the problem – we weren't thinking. We may well have lost the capacity to think. We've lost the capacity to think clearly because of the specific contours of our history and culture. To be precise: "The central problem of the modern world is the complete emancipation and autonomy of the technological mind" (*CGB* 62).

Merton may be a Thoreauvian, but he is no Luddite. He does not simply demonize technology. He does worry, though, that a dangerous cultural shift has occurred in which thought has become thoroughly "instrumentalized." Within the iron cage of our technological society, we easily calculate means but are increasingly incapable of thinking about ends. "The basic inner moral contradiction of our age is that, though we talk and dream about freedom . . . our civilization is strictly *servile*. I do not use this term contemptuously, but in its original sense of 'pragmatic,' oriented exclusively to the useful, making use of means for material ends" (*CGB* 281).

Our ability to think in ways other than instrumentally is so atrophied, we cannot think critically or, as he says, maturely. For example, Merton writes: "The core of the race problem as I see it is this: the Negro (also other racial groups of course, but chiefly the Negro) is victimized by the psychological and social conflicts now inherent in a white civilization that fears imminent disruption and has no mature insight into the reality of its crisis" (*CGB* 21-22). Our culture positively punishes mature insight. The culture industry – and here Merton echoes the social criticism of Theodor Adorno and his colleagues from the Frankfurt School – generates an infernal racket that confounds reflection and mobilizes the most primitive of instincts. "[W]hat did I leave when I entered the monastery? . . . . a society that is happy because it drinks Coca-Cola or Seagrams or both and is protected by the bomb" (*CGB* 36). Merton is appalled by social communication in post-war America. He writes: "The greatest need of our time is to clean out the enormous mass of mental and emotional rubbish that clutters our minds and makes of all political and social life a mass illness. Without this housecleaning we cannot begin to *see*. Unless we *see* we cannot think. The purification must begin with the mass media. How?" (*CGB* 64).

We have, inadvertently, created a cultural universe in which we can gaze but cannot see; in which we can calculate but cannot think. Our imaginations colonized by the mass media, our language infested with jargon, our spirits shrivel. To speak with William Blake, we have been conquered by the mythical character Urizen, that figure of despotic calculation; we have been infected with, as Merton says, "spiritual cretinism" (*CGB* 37) and, "Like Blake," as Michael Higgins says, "Merton worked for the dethronement of Urizen" (Higgins 75) and the liberation of spontaneity, creativity and awe. Merton's jeremiad is rooted in eschatology, not cultural pessimism. *Conjectures* is actually filled with hope. It is precisely that hope, though, that yearning for a better day, that fuels Merton's prophetic indictment of his own day.

Parallels between Merton's indictment and Arendt's argument in *The Human Condition* are striking. Arendt, like Merton, believes that we have come from "dark times"[11] and may return to dark times. She was convinced, as her biographer Elisabeth Young-Bruehl points out, that the disasters of the twentieth century, specifically the rise of totalitarianism, marked "a fundamental break" in human history.[12] Julia Kristeva refers to the "apocalyptic" strain in Arendt's thought; Kristeva notes that in her path-breaking *Origins of Totalitarianism* Arendt argued that what totalitarianism threatened was nothing less than human life as such, and that in *The Human Condition*, Arendt's purpose is to understand this threatened life so that we, perhaps, can rescue it.[13]

The Human Condition has little of *Conjectures'* pessimistic irony, but Arendt is no less alarmed than Merton, and she is alarmed for the same reasons. She begins *The Human Condition* by referring to Sputnik. She is struck by repeated comments in the media about space exploration as a way to "escape from men's imprisonment to the earth" (Arendt, *Condition* 1). She finds such comments unnerving because, as she says, "the earth is the quintessence of the human condition" (Arendt, *Condition* 2), and to flee the earth is to abolish humanity. The threat now is not from the totalitarians, but from fools – cousins, perhaps, to Merton's "spiritual

---

11. Hannah Arendt, *Men in Dark Times* (New York: Harvest Books, 1970).

12. Elisabeth Young-Bruehl, *Why Arendt Matters* (New Haven: Yale University Press, 2006) 9.

13. Julia Kristeva, *Hannah Arendt: Life as Narrative* (Toronto: University of Toronto Press, 2001).

cretins" – who cannot think about what they're doing. They cannot think because, Arendt says, epistemological paradigms of work – the mental structures of technology – have all but extinguished the possibility of what she calls "action." Arendt's task, then, in *The Human Condition* is "to think what we are doing" (Arendt, *Condition* 5) and this will take her to the "*polis*."

II. *Polis*

The "*polis*" is for Arendt the uniquely human habitat, and politics, the activity characteristic of the *polis*, is the uniquely human activity. Arendt distinguishes among three fundamental human capacities – labor, work and action. Labor is what we do to stay alive biologically; work is what we do to make the things we need or want. Action – the activity that defines human beings as human – refers to the engagement of humans among themselves, when they meet, publicly, as equals, in a condition of plurality (Arendt, *Condition* 7) and weave together those strands of meaning that Clifford Geertz, citing Max Weber, calls culture.[14]

Arendt does not dismiss labor or work. Arendt insists, though, that "action alone is the exclusive prerogative of man; neither a beast nor a god is capable of it" (Arendt, *Condition* 23). Action is public, communicative, revelatory and performative. We appear in public to each other; we communicate to each other; we enact plans and projects; and through all this we reveal to each other who – not what – we are. Indeed, who we are is not independent of this act of revelation; to the contrary, we become who we are through this process of mutual revelation. Politics is the only way that humans can achieve, not eternity (that is an attribute of the gods alone), but immortality – that is, memory embedded in narrative which, as mortals, is what fulfills our purpose on earth.

Though necessary, neither labor nor work makes us human. Action alone is what makes us human. But, Arendt warns, there is a grave threat to our capacity for action. Only certain cultures permit action, that is, politics; and alas, modern American culture is, increasingly, not one of them. Of course there is tremendous political noise in American life, but Arendt understands this noise as a media phenomenon, no longer really politics.

The problem is that work has usurped the role of action. Work is the realm of "*homo faber*" and fabrication. In this "world of work," *homo faber* makes objects, sells them, devours them or hoards them. *Homo faber* secretes a peculiar epistemology, an epistemology that is instrumental,

---

14. Clifford Geertz, *The Interpretation of Cultures* (New York: Fontana Press, 1993) 5.

utilitarian and manipulative. *Homo faber*'s entire energy is devoted to transforming stuff into things. *Homo faber* is all but incapable of thinking beyond instrumental calculation. There is nothing public, or communicative, or performative, or revelatory about this sort of work, which means that *homo faber*'s consciousness excludes politics, and thereby, ominously, the possibility of fulfilling our humanity.

If Merton shared with Arendt a deep suspicion of *homo faber*, Merton had very contradictory feelings about the *polis*. The city of his day is something from which he fled, and, almost twenty years after his flight, he was glad he was in Kentucky's woods and not in Manhattan's canyons. Merton was utterly unimpressed with the level of public discourse, especially as it occurred in the public media. "I question nothing so much as the viability of public and popular answers" (*CGB* v), he writes, and adds: "There is such a thing as a labyrinth of information . . . . One enters the labyrinth . . . and there is no rational way out. . . . The real violence exerted by propaganda is this: by means of apparent truth and apparent reason, it induces us to surrender our freedom and self-possession. It predetermines us to certain conclusions . . . . Propaganda *makes up our minds* for us" (*CGB* 216).

For Arendt, "world" and "worldliness" are positive terms; in the world is where we act. But regarding "world," Merton writes:

> For me the "worldly" attitude which I think is nefarious is not simply the "turning to the world" or even the total and would-be uncompromising secularism of the "honest to God" set. . . . What I mean by worldliness is the involvement in the massive and absurd mythology of technological culture and in all the contrived and obsessive gyrations of its empty mind. (*CGB* 259)

To be "worldly," then, for Merton was something akin to having "false consciousness"; to be "worldly" meant to be stuck in Plato's cave, to be a prisoner, in particular, of post-war America's belligerent and hedonistic culture. Fretting about the nuclear arms race in the early 1960s, Merton could be absolutely scathing in his comments about American culture. On September 9, 1961, he wrote in his journal:

> I fear the ignorance and power of the U.S. . . . [I]t has quite suddenly become one of the most decadent societies on the face of the earth. . . . full of immense, uncontrolled power. Crazy. . . . The mixture of immaturity, size, apparent innocence and depravity, with occasional spasms of guilt, power, self-hate, pugnacity, lapsing into wildness and

then apathy, hopped up and wild-eyed and inarticulate and wanting to be popular. You need a doctor, Uncle![15]

He adds, in *Conjectures*, "to my way of thinking, 'the world' is precisely the dehumanized surface" (*CGB* 234) and "The realm of politics is the realm of waste" (*CGB* 74). As for "the city":

> Cities, even Louisville (which, being the city nearest to home is in some sense my city), leave me with a sense of placelessness and exile. . . . [T]he purpose of a city seems to be to guarantee that everyone has to travel about eighteen to fifty miles a day just in the performance of the routine duties of everyday life. . . . Even where war has not yet touched, cities are in devastation and nonentity. (*CGB* 234-35)

The term "city," or "*polis*," would have, for Arendt, positive connotations – not for Merton. He concludes his thoughts on the "city": "The city is the place where the mythology of power and war develop, the center from which the magic of power reaches out to destroy the enemy and to perpetuate one's own life and riches. . . . Urban culture is then committed to war. . . . We live, of course, in the most advanced of all urban cultures" (*CGB* 123-24). Merton, a disciple of William Blake, is sympathetic to the nature/city dichotomy, and within that dichotomy, he is on the side of nature. Throughout *Conjectures*, Merton's sensitivity to nature is quite remarkable,[16] while for Arendt, in *The Human Condition*, the natural is the realm of labor – biologically necessary but utterly inadequate, by itself, to provide meaning for humans.

And yet – Merton, in *Conjectures*, reports that he has encountered the work of Dietrich Bonhoeffer, and Merton is struck by Bonhoeffer's comments on "worldliness." What Bonhoeffer writes about is, Merton says, "a 'Christian worldliness' with which I thoroughly agree" (*CGB* 183). There are cities, too, it would seem, that are not like other cities. Merton drifts backward and inward as he remembers his origins: "There are times when I am mortally homesick for the South of France, where I was born" (*CGB* 168). These French memories conjure up Paris. "I came into this world because of Paris," he writes, "since my father and mother met there as art students. Certainly the sign of Paris is on me,

---

15. Thomas Merton, *Turning Toward the World: The Pivotal Years. Journals, vol. 4: 1960-1963*, ed. Victor A. Kramer (San Francisco: HarperCollins, 1996) 160; subsequent references will be cited as "*TTW*" parenthetically in the text.

16. *Conjectures* is filled with quite lyrical descriptions of birds, trees and snow: see, for instance, Merton's comments about a heavy snow in central Kentucky (132-33). For more on Merton and ecology, see Monica Weis, *The Environmental Vision of Thomas Merton* (Lexington: University Press of Kentucky, 2011).

indelibly!" He thinks of Paris as a city of philosophy, art and spirit, and this "archetypal and inescapable Paris" (*CGB* 164) he loves. Because of Bonhoeffer and Paris, Merton, grudgingly perhaps, acknowledges that the "worldliness" of the city has validity: the "tradition of *contemptus mundi* . . . needs to be re-examined" (*CGB* 34), he thinks, and adds with regard to the "world-denying world of the monastic enclosure" that "the good that is in it is perhaps more 'worldly' than we think" (*CGB* 161-62). Merton notes that "what Aristotle gave to Christian thought in the thirteenth century was its '*turning to the world.*'" Thomas Aquinas, Merton adds, shares with Aristotle a certain "worldliness," an affirmation of the "concrete and sensuous reality of the world," which Merton sees as a "Christian affirmation of creation" (*CGB* 185). Aquinas was, Merton adds, a "theologian in the city" (*CGB* 187). But Merton still has his doubts. He writes: "the Church had better acquire a healthy and articulate respect for the modern world. . . . But in what does this respect for the world consist?" (*CGB* 35).

In June, 1960, Thomas Merton was studying Hannah Arendt's *The Human Condition*. His brief and sometimes cryptic observations, recorded in his journal, are fascinating. He took "pages of notes" (*TTW* 11). He admired her incisive commentary on modern times, particularly her insight that the "active life" (which to her meant vigorous civic engagement) had degenerated "from *political action* to *fabrication* to *laboring* and finally to that completely empty activity of *job holding*" (*TTW* 11). He agreed with her that human beings had become, in some fundamental way, "*alienated from the world*" (*TTW* 11) (though in his journal he does not try to distinguish between his often critical use of the term "world" and Arendt's often positive use of the same term). He was struck by Arendt's comments on Christianity, especially the ways in which Christianity contributed to the decline of the classical *polis*, and the ways in which Christianity's stress on the "sacredness of life and its emphasis on forgiveness" had important political implications (*TTW* 11).

Above all, Merton was fascinated by Arendt's notion that the classical *polis* was a "space" in which people became "real" through their interactions with others (*TTW* 6). One of Arendt's key intuitions was that humans are free to shape their lives not in the realms of family or work, but in the realm of the political, where people openly, freely and vigorously debate about, and construct, their shared futures. Arendt's idea that we need some sort of "space" in which we can become "real" through our lives with others, and that in such a space we can move from mindless "process" to "Being," sounded to Merton like a defense not only of the "political" but also of what Merton thought of as the "contemplative" life.

He noted in his journal on June 12, 1961: "finished the *Human Condition* today. It is the deepest and most important defense of the contemplative life that has been written in modern times. That covers a great deal of ground!" (*TTW* 11).

Hannah Arendt, of course, never knew about Merton's reading of her advocacy of the *polis* as a defense of the contemplative life. Perhaps she would have complained that he had misunderstood her. But perhaps she would have been sympathetic. In the mid-1960s, after the publication of *The Human Condition*, in the last years of her life, Arendt was hard at work on a book she called *The Life of the Mind*.[17] She died before it was completed. *The Life of the Mind* is an exploration of the "inner life," the world of imagination, intellect and will, and among the writers she discusses are Augustine, Aquinas, Duns Scotus and St. Paul. At the very time that Arendt in *The Life of the Mind* was trying to relate the *vita activa* to the *vita contemplativa*, Merton was struggling to relate "contemplation" to the "world of action."[18] Coming from quite different directions, Arendt and Merton, had they ever met, would have found themselves, in the last years of their lives, passionately engaged with remarkably similar concerns.

III. Revelation

Perhaps the Church's respect for the modern world, not necessarily the world as it is but as it might be, could be rooted in the world's capacity for revelation. Merton was never really non-political, and as the 1950s flowed into the 1960s, Merton's involvement with the radical causes of the day became more intense. His political engagement was not without hope. "[O]ne can, after all," he writes, "recover hope for the other dimension of man's life: the political" (*CGB* 194). Merton's fragile hope for the *polis* was at least partly confirmed by one of the odder experiences of his very odd life – his famous 1958 "Louisville epiphany" which he recounts in *Conjectures*: "In Louisville, at the corner of Fourth and Walnut, in the center of the shopping district, I was suddenly overwhelmed with the realization that I loved all those people" (*CGB* 140).[19]

Hannah Arendt would not have been surprised by this urban epiphany,

---

17. Hannah Arendt, *The Life of the Mind* (New York: Harcourt Brace Jovanovich, 1977).

18. See Thomas Merton, *Contemplation in a World of Action* (Garden City, NY: Doubleday, 1971).

19. All Merton's biographers comment on this event: see, for instance, William H. Shannon, *Thomas Merton: An Introduction* (Cincinnati: St. Anthony Messenger Press, 2005) 37-38.

because for her, the *polis* is preeminently the place of revelation. The *polis* is the place for human action. "With word and deed," she writes, "we insert ourselves into the human world, and this insertion is like a second birth" (Arendt, *Condition* 176). A kind of "revelation" occurs, a human revelation to be sure, but not without a strange superhuman quality. The "who" that is revealed, Arendt writes, is not so much the mundane "who" that lives and works and shops hereabouts; no, "it is more than likely that the 'who' which appears so clearly . . . remains hidden from the person himself, like the *daimōn*, in Greek religion which accompanies each man through his life, always looking over his shoulder from behind and thus visible only to those he encounters" (Arendt, *Condition* 179-80).

Arendt closes her remarkable account of worldly action, that is, politics, with a surprise. The two parameters of human life, Arendt argues, are "mortality" and "natality." Humans die. But humans are also born. If humans fade to silence, they also emerge from silence. If mortality cautions us against *hubris*, natality proves that there is always something new. Mortality and natality are all we have. We have few fixed laws of behavior; we have fewer predictable outcomes. Without predictable outcomes, how do humans conduct their common lives, their political affairs? Arendt argues that humans call on two distinctive capacities which enable their political lives to continue. The first is the familiar notion of promise and contract; our social contracts provide a certain stability to our lives together. The second capacity is the surprise – it is, Arendt says, our capacity to forgive. The future is inherently unknowable and unpredictable; even the best intentions can lead to ruin. Therefore, an ability to forgive each other is essential to our lives together. Arendt does not add love to forgiveness; love, she argues, by its very nature is unworldly; it has a "non-human, superhuman quality" (Arendt, *Condition* 76). Love is exclusive and preferential, she thinks, and therefore is destructive of the equality and plurality characteristic of the *polis*. But if Arendt is cautious about love, she does argue that "respect," and more importantly "friendship," are essential to forgiveness and therefore to political life (Arendt, *Condition* 243); and, she writes, "the discoverer of the role of forgiveness in the realm of human affairs was Jesus of Nazareth" (Arendt, *Condition* 238).

Conclusion

Contemporaries, Thomas Merton and Hannah Arendt make a very odd couple. Merton, to be sure, admired Arendt's work, and refers to it several times in *Conjectures* (*CGB* 89, 93, 261, 264-65). Arendt did not know Merton's work. Their writing, their points of reference, their fundamental concerns, are all quite different. But as they discuss contemporary life, their thought intersects. Indeed, there might well be other, equally powerful, commonalities. Both are attracted to non-violence.[20] Both have a marked anarchic streak.[21] Both are struck by thoughtlessness as the special curse of their generation. One suspects that the kind of "thoughtfulness" Arendt aspired to, and the "mindfulness" Merton advocated, might well have something in common. But at the very least, one can conclude from this cursory comparison that Thomas Merton and Hannah Arendt, these very different representatives of two very different Cold War countercultures, share, surprisingly, if not conclusions, then at least fundamental concerns, concerns which lead them to second births, revelations, mystical moments of love and friendship, daimōns, and finally, forgiveness.

---

20. "Power has nothing to do with peace," Merton writes (*CGB* 30), arguing that power as violent coercion will not be the source of human happiness. Arendt uses "power" in a different way, and argues that "power" is that energy which arises to keep equals together, and is quite different from mere "force" (Arendt, *Condition* 200). Using different terminology, both Merton and Arendt agree that coercion cannot keep human beings together in peace.

21. Jeffrey C. Isaac, writing about Arendt and Albert Camus in *Arendt, Camus and Modern Rebellion* (New Haven: Yale University Press, 1992) 148, comments on the "anarchist" qualities Arendt and Camus share. Michael Higgins argues that Merton, like Blake, is fundamentally an anarchist at heart; "Merton the anarchist" (Higgins 247) is "the William Blake of our time" (Higgins 4).

Is Desert Spirituality Viable in the Twenty-First-Century City? The Legacy of the Desert Fathers in Thomas Merton

Hyeokil Kwon

Introduction

Nowadays, most people, especially those in advanced and developing countries, live in secular cities. Though an increasing number of city people have an earnest desire for spirituality, solitude, meditation and contemplation, the truth is that most cannot leave the cities for lengthy periods – to enter into the desert, woods, monastery or retreat center – like Henry David Thoreau, in order to lead a spiritual life. Is it then impossible for present-day urban dwellers to lead spiritual lives in these secular cities which have become darkened by collectivism and hyperactivism? To answer this question, I will investigate the life and work of Thomas Merton (1915-1968), a Trappist monk who withdrew into solitude to lead a contemplative life but shared his wisdom with other people through his writings. He was not only a disciple of the Desert Fathers but also himself a revived Desert Father. From the Desert Fathers, Merton learned the meaning of the desert, its relationship with society and its life-giving teaching. I believe that the desert spirituality of Thomas Merton can provide some of the wisdom we need to answer the question.

Merton was deeply influenced by the spirituality of the Desert Fathers, who entered into the deserts of Egypt, Palestine, Arabia and Persia in the fourth and fifth centuries. They lived as hermits or cenobites, seeking perfect surrender to God's will. Merton was introduced to the tradition of the Desert Fathers in the early days of his monastic life. He writes, in a 1965 letter to Nora Chadwick, a noted medievalist, "Certainly I agree with you about Cassian. Ever since I had him as a Lenten book in the novitiate, I have kept close to him, and of course use him constantly with the novices."[1] For Merton, John Cassian was a gateway to the desert tradition in that Cassian was the person who delivered the monastic tradition of the Egyptian desert to Western monks. He says, "Through Cassian I am getting back to everything, or rather, getting for the first time to monastic and Christian values I had dared to write about without

---

1. Thomas Merton, *The School of Charity: Letters on Religious Renewal and Spiritual Direction*, ed. Patrick Hart (New York: Farrar, Straus, Giroux, 1990) 283.

knowing them."[2] Also, he enthusiastically read the *Apophthegmata,* the sayings of the Desert Fathers, and translated parts of its Latin version, the *Verba Seniorum.*[3] He delved into the desert tradition, both to touch the root of the monastic tradition and to find wisdom for monastic renewal. As a result, Merton gave a series of conferences on John Cassian and the Fathers when he was master of novices.[4]

According to John Eudes Bamberger, who studied under Merton as a scholastic, "Merton did more than learn from them [the Desert Fathers]. He became a disciple and allowed himself to be formed by them, to enter into their experience so as to be himself transformed by their teaching. He became himself one with them."[5] Indeed, the Desert Fathers were his teachers and spiritual directors, well beyond the time and space of his spiritual and monastic formation. Their wisdom, thoughts and ways of life are both explicitly and implicitly reflected in many of his writings. Abbot Bamberger recalls a speech Merton made in earlier years, in the course of a conference in the novitiate: "these men from the Egyptian desert have more reality for me than the people living in Louisville" (Bamberger 443). Granting the possibility that Merton made that statement before his famous experience at the corner of Fourth and Walnut streets in Louisville on March 18, 1958, in which he mysteriously realized his oneness with all the people there,[6] this speech shows how Merton was deeply connected with the Desert Fathers. In this sense, James R. McNerney states that desert spirituality "provided the inner dynamism of [Merton's] monastic journey, and was the basis of his contemplative prayer. It forged his contemplative vision, and provided him a perspective on reality that enriched him."[7] What then are the legacies of the Desert Fathers in the

---

2. Thomas Merton, *A Search for Solitude: Pursuing the Monk's True Life. Journals, vol. 3: 1952-1960,* ed. Lawrence S. Cunningham (San Francisco: HarperCollins, 1996) 38; subsequent references will be cited as "*SS*" parenthetically in the text.

3. Thomas Merton, *The Wisdom of the Desert: Sayings from the Desert Fathers of the Fourth Century* (New York: New Directions, 1960); subsequent references will be cited as "*WD*" parenthetically in the text.

4. Thomas Merton, *Cassian and the Fathers: Initiation into the Monastic Tradition,* ed. Patrick F. O'Connell (Kalamazoo, MI: Cistercian Publications, 2005); subsequent references will be cited as "*CF*" parenthetically in the text.

5. John Eudes Bamberger, "Thomas Merton and the Christian East," in *One Yet Two: Monastic Tradition East and West,* ed. M Basil Pennington, Cistercian Studies [CS] Series 29 (Kalamazoo, MI: Cistercian Publications, 1976) 450; subsequent references will be cited as "Bamberger" parenthetically in the text.

6. See Thomas Merton, *Conjectures of a Guilty Bystander* (Garden City, NY: Doubleday, 1966) 140-42 (for the original journal version, see *SS* 181-82).

7. James R. McNerney, "Merton and the Desert Experience," *Review for Religious* 43 (July-August 1984) 605.

works by Thomas Merton? How can the legacies help contemporary city people lead a spiritual life?

The Desert of Emptiness

First, one of the greatest contributions of Thomas Merton for today's desert spirituality is his grasp of the existential meaning of the desert. The desert is certainly a geographical place into which one can withdraw for solitude, detachment, purification and union with God. The Desert Fathers left their societies and went into the actual deserts of Egypt, Palestine, Arabia and Persia. However, for the Desert Fathers, merely being physically in the desert did not guarantee tranquility, the object of the desert solitude. The desert is a more implicative symbol, and one not confined to a geographical locale. According to Patrick F. O'Connell, Merton believed that one's real desert is not merely an earthly location but an existential place in the human heart,[8] in which a person faces one's own weaknesses and limitations without any comfort or support from human cities.[9] Merton writes, "The 'desert' of contemplation is simply a metaphor to explain the state of emptiness which we experience when we have left all ways, forgotten ourselves and taken the invisible Christ as our way" (*CP* 115-16). In the emptiness of the desert one is able to encounter God. Thus, Merton asserts in his essay "Wilderness and Paradise" that the desert wilderness is "the place specially chosen by God to manifest Himself in His 'mighty acts' of mercy and salvation."[10]

Also, humans can reach their own real desert only with the guidance of God. It is a journey through which there is *no way, darkness and emptiness*. In his poem, "Macarius the Younger,"[11] Merton re-articulates

---

8. See Patrick F. O'Connell, "Desert," in William H. Shannon, Christine M. Bochen and Patrick F. O'Connell, *The Thomas Merton Encyclopedia* (Maryknoll, NY: Orbis, 2002)108-109.

9. See Thomas Merton, *Contemplative Prayer* (New York: Herder & Herder, 1969) 29; subsequent references will be cited as "*CP*" parenthetically in the text.

10. Thomas Merton, *The Monastic Journey*, ed. Brother Patrick Hart (Kansas City: Sheed, Andrews & McMeel, 1977) 145.

11. Merton wrote "Macarius the Younger" and its companion poem, "Macarius and the Pony," based on material from the *Historia Monachorum in Ægypto*, the Latin translation of an anonymous account of a journey taken by seven monks from Jerusalem to major monastic sites in Egypt in 394. The original Greek version of the *Historia Monachorum* has been translated into English by Norman Russell under the title, *The Lives of the Desert Fathers*, CS 34 (Kalamazoo, MI: Cistercian, 1980). For detailed comments on these poems and their background, see Patrick F. O'Connell, "More Wisdom of the Desert: Thomas Merton's Macarius Poems," *Cistercian Studies Quarterly* 40.3 (2005) 253-78; subsequent references will be cited as "O'Connell, 'More Wisdom'" parenthetically in the text.

a story from the Egyptian desert, where St. Macarius lived, and exhorts readers to set out on a journey to the most desolate desert, relying on signs from God:

> In wide open desert
> A day and night's journey . . . .
>
> No road, no path,
> No land marks
> Show the way there.
> You must go by the stars.[12]

Paradoxically, the journey to the "wide open desert" is "the walk in darkness, an apophatic journey, guided only by the celestial light of the stars" (O'Connell, "More Wisdom" 266). Merton signifies that the life in the desert, that is, the contemplative life, is opened to many people, even to those who are not in a monastery, but one should reach one's own actual desert through the apophatic journey.

In addition, he discloses the destructive power of today's deserts and cities. He intensely deplored that people destroyed wilderness, which God has blessed, with glittering towns that spring up overnight in the desert. The desert is then changed from a place where human beings cannot live without God's help, to a land promised by the devil where they can live on their own resources – money and technology – and without depending on God. Therefore, Merton contends that in today's context, "the desert itself moves everywhere. Everywhere is desert."[13] This means that whether people live in cities or the wilderness, they can find their own desert in each place where they face their limitations and vulnerabilities and must rely on God. Today's city dwellers can enter into their deserts even in their ordinary urban lives. In fact, the terrible pressures and problems of urban life often drive people into an existential wilderness. From his understanding of John Cassian, Merton said that living in the desert means "dwelling alone in the vast emptiness of total solitude" (*CF* 203). What is needed is the perspective to realize the desert in which one lives. Thomas F. McKenna properly points out that although our world and Merton's world are disparate, "What he offered was perspective. Individually and corporately, one can walk purposefully through the wilderness."[14]

12. Thomas Merton, *The Collected Poems of Thomas Merton* (New York: New Directions, 1977) 319; subsequent references will be cited as "*CPTM*" parenthetically in the text.

13. Thomas Merton, *Thoughts in Solitude* (New York: Farrar, Straus and Cudahy, 1958) 20.

14. Thomas F. McKenna, CM, "A Voice in the Postmodern Wilderness: Merton on

The Desert of Creativity

Second, such emptiness is "an abyss of creativity"[15] in which the true self emerges. The desert is a place where one confronts the power of the devil with no other defenses but those of faith. As shown well in the *Life of Antony*, the warfare with demons was an important aspect of the desert life; it is a way of a monk's spiritual formation. Also, as Benedicta Ward, translator of *The Sayings of the Desert Fathers*, points out: "The desert itself was the place of the final warfare against the devil, and the monks were 'sentries who keep watch on the walls of the city.'"[16]

It must be noted that for Antony and the Desert Fathers, to fight against demons was to contest with the enemy within themselves, rather than "out there." According to Peter Brown, for the desert monks the demons were "sensed as an extension of the self."[17] In this sense, Merton grasped that the ascetic life in the desert had spiritual and psychological dimensions. Confronting demons means confronting one's own false and empirical self. The life of sacrifice in the desert led the Fathers to transcend, to pass from an attachment to the unreal value of the self, to an emergence of the hidden reality of the self. Thus, Thomas Merton thought that a life of sacrifice in the desert "enabled the old superficial self to be purged away and permitted the gradual emergence of the true, secret self" (*WD* 8). Therefore, the desert is the place where the false self goes away and the true self eventually emerges.

In other words, the desert is a creative place in which one can become the person whom God originally intended when God created him/her. According to Merton, when St. Pachomius and the Desert monks went to the desert to be themselves, they went "out into the desert tormented by a need to know the inner meaning of their own existence."[18] Douglas Burton-Christie points out, "Solitude is for Merton a kind of paradise where we rediscover our true identity . . . a place of tremendous creativity."[19] Rediscovering or recovering one's true self gives one inner

Monastic Renewal," *The Merton Annual* 8 (1995) 136.

15. Thomas Merton, *Raids on the Unspeakable* (New York: New Directions, 1966) 71.

16. Benedicta Ward, foreword to *The Sayings of the Desert Fathers: The Alphabetical Collection*, trans. Benedicta Ward, CS 59 (Kalamazoo, MI: Cistercian Publication, 1984) xxv-xxvi.

17. Peter Brown, *The Making of Late Antiquity* (Cambridge, MA: Harvard University Press, 1978) 89.

18. Thomas Merton, "The Spiritual Father in the Desert Tradition," in *Contemplation in a World of Action* (Garden City, NY: Doubleday, 1971) 276; subsequent references will be cited as "*CWA*" parenthetically in the text.

19. Douglas Burton-Christie, "The Work of Loneliness: Solitude, Emptiness, and Compassion," *Anglican Theological Review* 88.1 (Winter 2006) 26.

freedom to faithfully lead a pure Christian life. In the desert of creativity, one is able to have "purity of heart," which is the ability to love God purely and to live for God alone.

A crucial way to awaken this true self is to reject "diversion," which the human society systematically provides its citizens. In his essay, "Notes for a Philosophy of Solitude," Merton offers the concept of "diversion" from Blaise Pascal's "divertissement," which refers to amusement or systematic distraction.[20] People plunge into a crowd, searching for diversions to avoid encounters with reality, because the way to the encounter is through the arid and dreadful desert. In the crowd or herd of false selves, they pursue to forget or disguise their limitation by assuming the mask provided by a collective mentality or by human technology. In other words, diversion is one of the greatest obstacles for people in leading a desert life. In this sense, Merton states, "The real desert is this: to face the real limitations of one's own existence and knowledge and not try to manipulate them or disguise them."[21] Therefore, one needs the courage to renounce the diversions offered by human society and to fight the demon, that is, to face one's false self in the arid desert.

In today's context, many people are seeking diversions by switching TV channels, clicking the computer mouse, or tapping the screen of their mobile device to find "fresh amusement" in an illusory space. Also, as Daniel P. Horan suggests, the false self often appears in the Millennial generations as "the digital self" which means "the identity (or identities) formed on Facebook, communicated in the 'tweets' of Twitter, and constructed as an avatar in virtual worlds like 'Second Life.'"[22] Thus, the legacies of the Desert Fathers in Thomas Merton challenge today's city dwellers, especially the digital generations, to search their true self not in the so-called *creative cyberspace*, but in *their own desert of creativity*, by disconnecting oneself from the network of diversion provided on TV or cyberspace and facing the digital self.

---

20. Thomas Merton, *Disputed Questions* (New York: Farrar, Straus and Cudahy, 1960) 178-79; subsequent references will be cited as "*DQ*" parenthetically in the text. In this essay, Merton deals primarily with monastic life but also broadens the readership to the general population. Merton wrote a note on this essay's title, "This could also properly be called a 'Philosophy of Monastic Life' . . . . I am speaking of the solitary spirit which is really essential to the monastic view of life, but which is not confined to monasteries. . . . [T]he 'solitary' of these pages . . . may well be a layman, and of the sort most remote from cloistered life" (177).

21. Thomas Merton, *Learning to Love: Exploring Solitude and Freedom. Journals, vol. 6: 1966-1967*, ed. Christine M. Bochen (San Francisco: HarperCollins, 1997) 309.

22. Daniel P. Horan, "Striving toward Authenticity: Merton's 'True Self' and the Millennial Generation's Search for Identity," *The Merton Annual* 23 (2011) 85-86.

The Desert of Compassion

For Merton and the Desert Fathers, both the hermits and cenobites, the desert was a meeting place of people in profound compassion. St. Antony was a counselor, teacher and healer for those who were in need and visited him, even though he gradually withdrew into "the Inner Mountain," a place far from towns and villages. Moreover, he visited Alexandria twice, to give strength to the Christian martyrs during the persecution of 311 and to preach against the Arians. In his famous article "The Rise and Function of the Holy Man in Late Antiquity," Peter Brown shows that holy men, especially the desert monks of Syria, played a social and political function in the late Roman empire.[23] Also, for John Cassian, monastic perfection was charity, which can be nurtured only in the pure heart and in *quies*, i.e., rest or tranquility. Thus, Merton writes that in the desert, "Charity and hospitality were matters of top priority, and took precedence over fasting and personal ascetic routines" (*WD* 16). Also, in his poem "Macarius and the Pony" (*CPTM* 317-18), Merton implies that one of the precious fruits of the desert life is the ability to see others as they really are (see O'Connell, "More Wisdom" 264). Such clear eyes are an important aspect of desert compassion, and he believed that there could be no compassion without solitude because people paradoxically escape from others by plunging into a crowd.

Further, Merton states, "The Desert Fathers did, in fact, meet the 'problems of their time' in the sense that *they* were among the few who were ahead of their time, and opened the way for the development of a new man and a new society" (*WD* 2-3). Though they left their cities in search of solitude, the Fathers faced the problems of fellow human beings living in faraway towns and villages. In his final lecture, "Marxism and Monastic Perspectives," presented in Thailand on December 10, 1968, Merton said, "I think we should say that there has to be a dialectic between world refusal and world acceptance. The world refusal of the monk is something that also looks toward an acceptance of a world that is open to change."[24] Such rejection and acceptance of the world were rooted in profound charity, out of which the Fathers and Merton participated in the world with their contemplative and prophetic perspectives. As such, the charity of the desert cannot be reduced to mere pity for others. Rather, charity surpasses sensual love and goes into the social and political dimen-

23. Peter Brown, "The Rise and Function of the Holy Man in Late Antiquity," *The Journal of Roman Studies* 61 (1971) 82-91.

24. Thomas Merton, *The Asian Journal*, ed. Naomi Burton Stone, Brother Patrick Hart and James Laughlin (New York: New Directions, 1973) 329-30.

sion of love, provoking social transformation. This wisdom can also be appropriated by the "city solitaries" who lead desert lives in contemporary cities. They can contribute to an inner transformation of their society by sharing the fruit, compassion, which is grown on their barren ground of the desert. Therefore, Merton urges his readers to "[g]o into the desert not to escape other men but in order to find them in God."[25] In this sense, Merton names his new desert *compassion.*[26]

The Desert as a River of Wisdom

Finally, the desert is a river of wisdom where ineffable spiritual experiences flow from spiritual masters to seekers. Merton understood that the Abba or spiritual Father in the desert was someone who had learned the secrets of desert life and so cared that the mysterious seeds of contemplation could truly grow and flourish in his disciples (see *CWA* 271). Merton highly appreciated the Fathers' life-giving teachings. He not only thought that for the discovery of inner solitude one may need such a spiritual director, but he also embodied the Fathers' life-giving teachings as a master of scholastics and novices. He was a wise teacher who helped his students bring out what was deepest in them.[27] Merton believed that the idea of spiritual fatherhood in the Desert Father tradition and the Russian tradition needed to be recovered, not only for his own teaching, but also for monastic renewal. He points out, "One who had made the discovery of his inner solitude, or is just about to make it, may need considerable spiritual help. A wise man, who knows the plight of the new solitary, may with the right word at the right time spare men the pain of seeking vainly some long and complex statement of his case" (*DQ* 147-48). Clearly, one who wants to dwell in one's own desert in a city needs the life-giving teaching of spiritual directors. Therefore, we need more "fathers" and "mothers" who can pass down the wisdom of the desert into contemporary cities. This desert as a river of wisdom will not only help the "city solitaries" but also enrich the life of other city dwellers by its overflowing compassion.

---

25. Thomas Merton, *New Seeds of Contemplation* (New York: New Directions, 1961) 53.

26. Thomas Merton, *The Sign of Jonas* (New York: Harcourt, Brace, 1953) 334.

27. Gloria Kitto Lewis, after an interview with seven of Merton's former students, concludes that "Merton can be described as a centered teacher who reverently explored interrelated spiritual and aesthetic subject matter, inviting his students to join him in humility and trust in a contemplative study which all knew would lead them into eternity" (Gloria Kitto Lewis, "Learning to Live: Merton's Students Remember His Teaching," *The Merton Annual* 8 [1995] 102).

Conclusion

The most difficult task in appropriating desert spirituality to today's city life is practicing the way of the desert life. The ways of life of the Desert Fathers and Thomas Merton are very different from that of most people in cities. However, the words and the ways of the Desert Fathers are not rigid but rather flexible and adaptable, according to each specific circumstance. As Benedicta Ward points out, the *Sayings of the Fathers* were originally delivered to individuals on specific occasions, so they should be understood within those contexts. Also, the practice of the desert life, which spread from the Mediterranean into northern Europe, was lived out through an adaptation to each specific circumstance, while the calling remained the same.[28] Merton also was well aware of the concreteness and particularity of the sayings, so he writes they are "precise keys to particular doors that had to be entered, at a given time, by given individuals" (*WD* 13). Hence, he did not apply the legacies of the Desert Fathers literally; rather he strove to adapt the spirit and essence of the desert wisdom into his own time and place. Therefore, in the prologue to his conferences on Cassian he said,

> Besides *renewal* of our own tradition we must of course obviously *adapt* ourselves to the needs of our time, and a return to tradition does not mean trying to revive, in all its details, the life lived by the early monks, or trying to do all the things that they did. But it means living in our time and solving the problems of our time in the way and with the spirit in which they lived in a different time and solved different problems. (*CF* 6)

I believe that such flexibility and adaptability make it possible to revive the legacies of the Desert Fathers in Thomas Merton within contemporary city life.

In addition, Robert E. Daggy notes that Merton is a stranger not only because his lifestyle is peculiar, but also because "he does almost nothing that society, as he sees it, considers respectable, acceptable and valuable."[29] Merton asserts, "The desert life was a life of non-conformity, it was a protest."[30] The essence of the way of desert life exists not in its external lifestyle but in its spirit, which rejects sensual materialism and the herd

---

28. Benedicta Ward, introduction to *The Desert Fathers: Sayings of the Early Christian Monks*, trans. Benedicta Ward (London: Penguin, 2003) xix.

29. Robert E. Daggy, introduction to *Day of a Stranger* (Salt Lake City: Gibbs M. Smith, 1981) 11.

30. Thomas Merton, *The Springs of Contemplation: A Retreat at the Abbey of Gethsemani*, ed. Jane Marie Richardson, SL (New York: Farrar, Straus, Giroux, 1992) 137.

mentality of cities and pursues the perfect Christian life of renunciation and the ideal of silence, solitude and direct dependence on God. Therefore, for contemporary city dwellers, to practice the way of desert life in a city means to embody the spirit of it in their own context. They will seem to be "strangers" to the eyes of other people as the Desert Fathers did.

Consequently, Merton was a person who revived desert spirituality in the twentieth century and was himself a revived Desert Father in a world of technology. Desert spirituality is not only possible in urban life, but is also helpful in saving city people from being deserted by the pressure of modern city life and the obsession over human technology. According to William Harmless, it was from the bustling city of Alexandria "that the literature of the desert was first disseminated, and it was through Alexandria that pilgrims . . . would pass."[31] The city was a gateway to the desert, and the seedlings of desert spirituality were planted and bore fruit in the city. The desert needs a city, and the city needs a desert. In sum, today's city people can embody desert spirituality by dwelling in the emptiness of solitude, facing the false self by rejecting diversion, rejecting and accepting the world out of compassion, and giving and receiving life-giving teaching. They can lead contemplative lives in their own city by *making the city a desert* like the early Egyptian monks who *made the desert a city.*[32]

---

31. William Harmless, SJ, *Desert Christians: An Introduction to the Literature of Early Monasticism* (Oxford: Oxford University Press, 1998) 4.

32. See Athanasius, *The Life of Antony and The Letter to Marcellinus*, trans. Robert C. Gregg, Classics of Western Spirituality (New York: Paulist Press, 1980) 14.

Stand on Your Own Feet!
Thomas Merton and the Monk
without Vows or Walls

Nass Cannon

"From now on, Brother, everybody stands on his own feet,"[1] proclaims Thomas Merton on the day of his death. He was quoting an abbot who gave this advice to the Tibetan monk, Chogyam Trungpa Rimpoche, confronted with fleeing or staying in the face of an advancing Chinese communist army. Merton interprets this saying to be "an extremely important monastic statement" and asserts that "The time for relying on structures has disappeared" (*AJ* 338). This paper explores the concept of a monk standing on his own feet without walls or vows. Traditionally, we view the monk as someone enclosed by physical boundaries, adhering to a particular spiritual tradition, bound by vows. However, stripped to its essentials, what constitutes the vocation of a monk? Can its essence be hidden within any vocation? With Merton as guide, this paper focuses on the basic elements of being a monk both for those in the monastery and for those in the world. It considers the visible monks in the world such as the lay monk, Brother Wayne Teasdale, those of the New Monasticism, and the New Friars, as well as those more hidden, invisible monks. Concentrating on Merton's thoughts in regard to purity of heart and reconciliation, the paper will review the transformational process which molds all monks and guides them to "final integration."[2]

An Atypical Traditional Monk

Thomas Merton is a model of a traditional although atypical monk who stands on his own feet. Secluded behind the walls of a monastery, he continues his vocation as a writer. His yearning for the freedom of solitude leads him into a hermitage. He advocates for peace by publicly decrying the Vietnam War and railing against the atomic bomb. He joins the civil rights movement. He studies Eastern religions. Through his writings and actions, he reflects someone who stands on his own feet, arrives at his

---

1. Thomas Merton, *The Asian Journal*, ed. Naomi Burton Stone, Brother Patrick Hart and James Laughlin (New York: New Directions, 1973) 338; subsequent references will be cited as "*AJ*" parenthetically in the text.

2.Thomas Merton, *Contemplation in a World of Action* (Garden City, NY: Doubleday, 1971) 205-17; subsequent references will be cited as "*CWA*" parenthetically in the text.

own conclusions, and speaks the truth with the light that he is given. On the surface, he appears to be an anomaly – an outspoken monk afloat in the cultural waters of the Cistercian tradition, who bridges monastic isolation through diverse activities, including a dialogue with people of good will from various faiths, traditions and cultures, rendezvous with the famous such as Joan Baez, and affection for a student nurse. Although he shatters the iconic image of a monk, Merton personifies an authentic selfhood congruent with his interior convictions, a man of integrity. From him, we learn that monks who live from the center of their authenticity reveal their true self which is the image and likeness of God, uniquely expressed through their personhood as it exists at a particular place and time in history. For Merton, this meant integrating within himself other cultures, traditions and religions as he sought to expand his interior boundaries to become more inclusive, as expressed in his comments on "final integration":

> The man who has attained final integration is no longer limited by the culture in which he has grown up. "He has embraced *all* of *life*. . . ."
> . . . He passes beyond all these limiting forms, while retaining all that is best and most universal in them, "finally giving birth to a fully comprehensive self." He accepts not only his own community, his own society, his own friends, his own culture, but all mankind. (*CWA* 212)

Merton realizes that the human race in all its diversity is the body of Christ, and that all of creation pulsates at its core with energy divine. "We must, first of all, see all material things in the light of the mystery of the incarnation. We must reverence all creation because the word was made flesh."[3] For Merton, the monk with this realization has begun his journey to attain final integration, which is not a discovery of the mind through words or images but an exploration of the heart.

He was a Trappist monk living in a monastery, within the enclosed walls of Our Lady of Gethsemani Abbey, at least most of the time. He was fed by the silence and solitude of a monastery which was "a tabernacle in the desert, upon which the *shekinah*, the luminous cloud of the divine Presence, almost visibly descends."[4] He felt both nourished and restrained by his environment. His writings suggest that at times he was dancing with angels, as when he proclaims, "Love sails me around the

---

3. Thomas Merton, *The Monastic Journey*, ed. Brother Patrick Hart (Kansas City: Sheed, Andrews & McMeel, 1977) 18; subsequent references will be cited as "*MJ*" parenthetically in the text.
4. Thomas Merton, *The Silent Life* (New York: Farrar, Straus & Cudahy, 1957) 34.

house. I walk two steps on the ground and four steps in the air. It is love."[5] On deep issues of conscience, he appears bridled by convention and the arbitrary whims of his superiors and censors, as illustrated by his lament to James Forest in the Cold War letters: "The orders are, no more writing about peace. This is transparently arbitrary and uncomprehending."[6] However, of greater importance, he was bound by ascetic vows:

> The whole ascetic life of the monk, in all its aspects both positive and negative, is summed up in his consecration of himself, his whole life, all that he has and all that he is, to God, by his five monastic vows. The life of the monk is the life of the vows. . . . Conversion of manners means striving to change one's whole life and all one's attitudes from those of the world to those of the cloister. . . . Obedience means the renunciation of our own will, in order to carry out in our whole life the will of another who represents God. Stability means renouncing our freedom to travel about from place to place, and binds us to one monastery until death. Poverty and Chastity are not explicitly mentioned in the Rule of St Benedict because they were considered by him to be included in conversion of manners, but they form an essential part of the monk's obligations. (*MJ* 30-31)

Particularly during his hermetic solitude, these vows challenged him to the very depths of his existence:

> The hermit, all day and all night, beats his head against a wall of doubt. That is his contemplation. . . . a kind of unknowing of his own self, a kind of doubt that questions the very roots of his existence, a doubt which undermines his very reasons for existing and for doing what he does. It is this doubt which reduces him finally to silence, and in the silence which ceases to ask questions, he receives the only certitude he knows: the presence of God in the midst of uncertainty and nothingness, as the only reality. (*MJ* 159)

In this desert, Tom Merton disappears (perhaps foreshadowing his last publicly spoken words before he is electrocuted [see *AJ* 343]) and is "swallowed up in" God (*MJ* 159). In union with the Holy Spirit, his liberated spirit radiates a creative openness to others, reaching fruition in his speech in Calcutta when he says "we are already one. . . . And what we have to recover is our original unity" (*AJ* 308). Transcending the limits of monastic formalism, a transformed Merton can ask: "Can there

---

5. Thomas Merton, *The Sign of Jonas* (New York: Harcourt, Brace, 1953) 120.

6. Thomas Merton, *The Hidden Ground of Love: Letters on Religious Experience and Social Concerns*, ed. William H. Shannon (New York: Farrar, Straus, Giroux, 1985) 266.

be a monastic life without vows? Is a monastic life with vows necessarily better and more authentic than one without vows?" (*CWA* 191). He continues with the observation, "In the earliest days of desert monasticism, there were no vows, no written rules, and institutional structure was kept at a minimum. The monastic commitment was taken with extreme and passionate seriousness, but this commitment was not protected by juridical sanctions or by institutional control" (*CWA* 191-92). Merton is "convinced that a monastic life without vows is quite possible and perhaps very desirable. It might have many advantages" (*CWA* 195). He wonders, "Why could not married people participate temporarily, in some way, in monastic life?" (*CWA* 192). Finally, he questions the very structure of monasticism: "A greater flexibility in the monastic structure would permit the development of ecumenical monastic communities. There is no reason why non-Catholics and even unbelievers should not be admitted to a serious participation – at least temporary – in monastic community life" (*CWA* 195).

In *A Monastic Vision for the 21st Century*, several prominent authors reflect on the future of monasticism with a focus on traditional monastic communities. As a group, they concentrate less on the form of future monastic communities and more on the guiding principles that will shape monastic life. For Michael Casey, those are to be seekers of God, to radically renounce the world, to live simply, and within a spiritual tradition.[7] Bonnie Thurston believes the monk's pursuit of purity of heart is an indispensable ingredient of all future monasticism (Hart, ed. 75). Joan Chittister thinks future monks must distinguish the concept of cloister, "as if place were the determining factor in the making of a contemplative," from that of contemplation, "as if Jesus was not a 'contemplative,' as if all of us are not called to be contemplative" (Hart, ed. 95). By contrast, Gail Fitzpatrick would retain monastic enclosure for its value "of guarding one's heart" (Hart, ed. 150). John Eudes Bamberger's "vision of Cistercian life for the 21st century is the monastery as a school of charity where all the essential, practical skills for attaining to union with God are acquired" (Hart, ed. 126-27). He views the task of the monk as "the recovery of the likeness to the Word of God" achieved "by developing the whole of our person, including the spiritual senses" (Hart, ed. 144). Similarly, Francis Kline views the lifetime work of the monk both now and in the future to be that of suffering and dying with Christ so that through the power of the Holy Spirit there is "the formation of the Risen Christ in the heart of

---

7. *A Monastic Vision for the 21st Century*, ed. Patrick Hart, OCSO (Kalamazoo, MI: Cistercian Publications, 2006) 24-25; subsequent references will be cited as "Hart, ed." parenthetically in the text.

a monk" (Hart, ed. 180). Although Merton would agree with all of these viewpoints, he appears to transcend the boundaries of traditional monasticism when he states that monastic life without vows may be desirable, married persons could participate, and non-believers would be welcomed. Merton points us to non-traditional monks.

Visible Non-Traditional Monks

Wayne Teasdale

As if in response to Merton's musings, self-declared monks in the world appear after Merton's death. One of these, Brother Wayne Teasdale, referred to himself as a hermit in the city. Influenced by both Merton and Abbot Thomas Keating in the 1960s, Brother Wayne was no ordinary hermit secluded from others; he taught at a number of institutions, including Catholic Theological Union in Chicago. After living in an ashram in India for two years, he became a Christian sanyasi under the influence of Bede Griffiths, who explained to him that "the real challenge for you, Wayne, is to be a monk in the world, a sanyasi who lives in the midst of society, at the very heart of things."[8] In 1989, the Archbishop of Chicago formally professed him to be a lay monk.

A contemplative, Brother Wayne was active in a variety of social issues such as the cause of the Dalai Lama, homelessness and the environment. He also espoused interfaith understanding through "interspirituality" which he viewed as the commonality of mystical experiences in diverse religions. He defines a monk as "a person who has dedicated his or her life to seeking God" (Teasdale, *Monk* xxvi). Teasdale asserts, "The daily tasks of earning a living, paying bills, saving money, getting along with others, being entertained, enjoying healthy recreation, and learning how to interact with difficult people are all part of an active life. So they must also be part of life for a monk in the world, at the crossroads of contemporary culture and experience" (Teasdale, *Monk* xxiv). For monks in the world, he suggests, "the question becomes how to integrate their glimpse of monastic peace into their everyday lives in the world, how to cultivate contemplation within an active life" (Teasdale, *Monk* xxvi). He thinks, "To achieve this integration requires the realization that the real monastery exists within them as a dimension of their own consciousness" (Teasdale, *Monk* xxvi). According to Brother Wayne, the structure of "Monasticism in all its forms – Eastern, Western, primitive, inventive, contemplative, active, and mixed – exists to nurture the development, fruition, and gifts

---

8. Wayne Teasdale, *A Monk in the World* (Novato, CA: New World Library, 2003) xxii; subsequent references will be cited as "Teasdale, *Monk*" parenthetically in the text.

of the inner mystic or inner monk" (Teasdale, *Monk* xxvii). He espouses Keating's pronouncement that "The essence of monastic life is not its structures but its interior practice, and the heart of interior practice is contemplative prayer" (Teasdale, *Monk* xxvii).

Similar to the desert fathers who went out to the desert and were tested by demons, Brother Wayne thinks that "in our age, the desert is the city – that is civilization" (Teasdale, *Monk* 13). He desires that there be more monks in the world because he believes, "A contemplative in the heart of the world has the opportunity to be aware of, to relate to, to touch and heal this suffering, to be a sign of love and hope to those who are so vulnerable in this difficult and indifferent world" (Teasdale, *Monk* 15). He advises those who wish to be monks in the world to focus their life of prayer on contemplative meditation, spiritual reading, the practice of nature, including walking and sky meditation and allowing for silence and solitude (see Teasdale, *Monk* 23-24). He counsels that an effect of contemplation is to root out the hidden motivations in our unconscious, the seeds of selfishness and negativity, and to further our integration (see Teasdale, *Monk* 41). A monk transformed by contemplation can envision a society of compassion, mercy and love, and be the leaven to radically transform the world by transforming others, eliminating cultural and economic selfishness (see Teasdale, *Monk* 135).

Teasdale views Merton as a forerunner of interspirituality through his study and appreciation of Eastern spiritual classics. Brother Wayne believed, "Thomas Merton was perhaps the greatest popularizer of interspirituality. Not only did he acquaint his readers with the rich and vast tradition of Christian contemplation . . . but he opened the door for Christians to explore other traditions, notably Taoism, Hinduism, and Buddhism."[9] He also believes that Merton's notion that "we are already one . . . and what we have to recover is our original unity" (*AJ* 308) goes beyond our cultural, psychological and religious differences, points to the future of monasticism and is key to transforming the world. To enable this transformation, Brother Wayne envisions a universal order of mystics or contemplatives which would "include people from all traditions and no tradition at all. They would include young and old, men and women, certain and skeptical, confused and enlightened" (Teasdale, *Monk* 218).

New Monasticism

Teasdale's vision is illustrated in the new monasticism movement. Although some of these communities date to the early 1970s, with a heritage

9. Wayne Teasdale, *The Mystic Heart: Discovering a Universal Spirituality in the World's Religions* (Novato, CA: New World Library 1999) 39.

going back to 1930, the term "New Monasticism" was popularized by Jonathan Wilson-Hartgrove in the 1990s. It is based on Dietrich Bonhoeffer's belief that "the restoration of the church will surely come only from a new type of monasticism which has nothing in common with the old but a complete lack of compromise in a life lived in accordance with the Sermon on the Mount in the discipleship of Christ."[10] In his brief book *Life Together*, Bonhoeffer discusses "directions and precepts that Scriptures provide us for our life together under the word."[11] He perceives Christianity as "community through Jesus Christ and in Jesus Christ" (Bonhoeffer, *Life* 21). Members of the fellowship spend the day with others in prayer and work and the day alone in meditation. He cautions, "Let him who cannot be alone beware of community; let him who is not in community beware of being alone" (Bonhoeffer, *Life* 77). As speech is essential for life in community, silence is essential for solitude. In the communal fellowship, Bonhoeffer proposes an atypical ministry which he refers to as "the ministry of holding one's tongue" (Bonhoeffer, *Life* 91), "the ministry of meekness" (Bonhoeffer, *Life* 94), "the ministry of listening" (Bonhoeffer, *Life* 97), "the ministry of helpfulness" (Bonhoeffer, *Life* 99), "the ministry of bearing" (Bonhoeffer, *Life* 100), "the ministry of proclaiming" (Bonhoeffer, *Life* 103), "the ministry of authority" (Bonhoeffer, *Life* 108). For the community to have spiritual depth, each member must acknowledge his or her sinfulness and partake in confession to be reconciled one to another and each to God. "Reconciled in their hearts with God and the brethren, the congregation receives the gift of the body and blood of Jesus Christ, and, receiving that, it receives forgiveness, new life, and salvation. . . . The life of Christians together under the Word has reached its perfection in the sacrament" (Bonhoeffer, *Life* 122).

Following Bonhoeffer's call, Wilson-Hartgrove proposes a new monasticism which would aim at healing fragmentation and eliminating the distinction of sacred and secular vocations. This would be accomplished by a small group of disciples who through intense theological reflection and commitment would lead contemplative and communal lives with a focus on hospitality and concern for the poor. In 2004, a number of existing communities formulated a rule of life, known as the twelve marks. They include living at the margins of society, sharing economic resources, hospitality, just reconciliation, submission to the church, a formative process like a novitiate, nurturing common life, support for

----

10. Dietrich Bonheoffer, *A Testament to Freedom*, ed. Geoffrey B. Kelly and F. Burton Nelson (San Francisco: Harper & Row, 1997) 424.

11. Deitrich Bonhoeffer, *Life Together* (San Francisco: Harper & Row, 1954) 17; subsequent references will be cited as "Bonhoeffer, *Life*" parenthetically in the text.

both celibate singles as well as married couples and children, communal geographical proximity of members, care of the local environment and support of local economies, peacemaking and conflict resolution, and commitment to a contemplative life.[12] Wilson-Hartgrove believes the work of a new monastic community "is to tend to a culture of grace and truth in the world" (Wilson-Hartgrove 135-36). Doing this requires a reliance on the church, where the "the church is called to be a people who love one another and make a life together, tending to a culture of grace in a world broken by sin" (Wilson-Hartgrove 145).

Among many others, the Iona Community and the Northumbria Community are examples of the new monasticism. The Iona Community, as described by Ronald Ferguson in *Chasing the Wild Goose: The Story of the Iona Community*, had Celtic monastic roots. The founder, Rev. George MacLeod, in 1938 led a group of craftsmen to rebuild a ruined medieval Iona Abbey on a small rocky island in the Scottish Hebrides, founding a community in the process. For its first twenty years of its existence, the community's activity centered on its restoration project. Later it became a community "bound together by a Rule of private prayer, economic sharing, and work for justice and peace."[13] This ecumenical community is concentrated in Scotland, England and Wales, with full members numbering in the hundreds, but there are also associates and friends of the community.

The Northumbria Community's beginnings are traced to the relation-ships of John and Linda Skinner and Andy Raine in Northumberland, England in the late 1970s and early 1980s, followed by the creation of the Nether Springs Trust with the involvement of Roy Searle and Trevor Miller. With a geographically dispersed community, "They attempt to find a practical modern expression of a new monasticism rooted in the vows of 'availability and vulnerability' and hold an uncompromising allegiance to the imperatives of the Sermon on the Mount."[14] Members progress in stages from being postulants to novices and finally to full companions. They follow a rule of "availability," being available to God in the cell of their hearts as well as to others, and "vulnerability," manifested as being teachable in prayer, and the "heretical imperative," by challenging as-

---

12. Jonathan Wilson-Hartgrove, *New Monasticism* (Grand Rapids, MI: Brazos Press, 2008) 39; subsequent references will be cited as "Wilson-Hartgrove" parenthetically in the text.

13. Ronald Ferguson, *Chasing the Wild Goose: The Story of the Iona Community* (Glasgow, Scotland: Wild Goose Publications, 2006) 35.

14. Richard Foster, *Sanctuary of the Soul: Journey into Meditation* (Downers Grove, IL: InterVarsity Press, 2011) 94.

sumed truth, living among others as "church without walls."

The New Friars

Another expression of this impetus may be the "New Friars." Scott Bessenecker believes:

> we are at the front edge of another missional, monastic-like order made up of men and women, many of whom are in their twenties and thirties, burning with a passion to serve the destitute in slum communities of the developing world – not from a position of power but from alongside them, living in the same makeshift housing, breathing the same sewage-tainted air, subject to the same government bulldozers that threaten to raze their communities. They are new friars, flying just below our radar because they have not come under any single denominational or suprachurch banner.[15]

Like their historic counterparts, he views this movement as having the same roots and reflecting the same qualities, which he describes as incarnational, devotional, communal, missional and marginal. Bessenecker thinks, "Slum communities are kinds of chapels in which one can meet face to face with Christ in the dispossessed" (Bessenecker 87). The new friars' spirituality revolves around Christ's pledge, "I tell you solemnly, in so far as you did this to one of the least of these brothers of mine, you did it to me" (Mt. 25:40). Their vocation is lived out over months or years alongside the destitute, those who are garbage scavengers, prostitutes, homeless, abused children, and those who are dying.

Brother Wayne Teasdale, the New Monastics and the New Friars appear to be heroic individuals who stand on their own feet, open to grace. They have responded to the invitation of Christ's Spirit to "Follow Me" as they serve Christ in their work with the poor and the marginalized. Although their numbers may be small, their hearts are large and their efforts like mustard seeds will have their fruition in the kingdom of God. These individuals are very visible monks in the world. But there are more invisible ones who, without vows or walls, live outwardly a very ordinary life.

Invisible Non-Traditional Monks

Merton's attestation on the day of his death – "From now on, Brother, everybody stands on his own feet. . . . The time for relying on structures has disappeared" – may herald the work of the Spirit generating invis-

---

15. Scott A. Bessenecker, *The New Friars* (Downers Grove, IL: InterVarsity Press, 2006) 16; subsequent references will be cited as "Bessenecker" parenthetically in the text.

ible non-traditional monks without walls or vows or monastic structure. Invisible monks, called to contemplation and solitude, live and work in all strata of society. Their external circumstances appear to be like those of their neighbors. They may work, marry, have children and socialize while nourishing a hidden vocation to live a life of prayer and to dwell in God's presence. The path of their work in the world and that of their interior life may appear in conflict early in their spiritual journey, with time set aside for solitude and contemplation stolen from time set aside for family or work. Ideally, at some point the inner and outer paths join so that in both being and doing their whole life becomes a living prayer.

The hidden vocation of this invisible monk is the same as that of the professed; it is to dwell in God's presence through a life of prayer. All monks quest to see the face of the Living God and this steadfast pursuit, either inside or outside the walls of a monastery, either with or without vows, characterizes this individual as a monk. The quest of the invisible monk is that of all monks who desire to be transformed into a new creation in which the old man becomes a new one dwelling in the presence of God.

The monastic monk, assisted by vows, monastic practices, the office, the liturgy and the support of his brothers, seeks God alone. However, even with monastic support, such a monk faces doubt, interior struggles and obstacles to his pursuit. Similarly a monk in the world faces these as well as worldly activities which often seek to separate him from God. For the invisible monk without walls or vows or a rule guaranteeing time set aside for prayer, much of his life may be consumed by an occupation or worldly concerns. However such a person discovers that the Spirit which calls one to contemplation also arranges time for silence and solitude. This individual with his whole life surrounded by the obstacles of a secular environment may find the core of his existence wound around the pursuit of the presence of God.

What sets both the visible and invisible monks apart is their focused response to the invitation of the Holy Spirit to pursue the beatitude, "Happy the pure in heart: they shall see God" (Mt. 5:8). The means to this end is contemplation, a flight of the will and mind and heart towards God. This lifetime journey begins with an assent to an invitation from the Holy Spirit to allow the divine fire of contemplation to burn them. Like fire burning a log, this spiritual fire as described by St. John of the Cross is oppressive to the soul as it burns away the grime and habits of sin.[16] This solitary work digs at the roots of sin and gives rise to self-

_____

16. See St. John of the Cross, *The Collected Works of St. John of the Cross*, ed. and trans. Kieran Kavanaugh & Otilio Rodriguez (Washington DC: ICS Publications,

knowledge of the interior division and strife and the self-hatred which results from sin. It uncovers the boundaries separating one from one's true self and from others and from God. As the Spirit breaks down these boundaries, monks open themselves more fully to the presence of God, particularly as expressed in the presence of others. This presence of God may be discerned not only in those like them but in those who differ, not only in Christians but in Buddhists and Muslims as well as agnostics and atheists – in all of creation and the family of man. The goal of a mature discernment would be to realize, as Merton did, that "we are already one" and we have to recover "what we are" (*AJ* 308).

Of course, the journey to this awareness may be turbulent, as monks falter and soar. They appear caught up in the liturgical cycle of the birth, death and resurrection of Christ as He comes to be born, to die and to rise in them as they live out their lives interpenetrated by sin and grace. Yet this spiritual work wrought in them by God's grace and His Spirit remains hidden from them. They see it dimly but do not know its fruits. In fact, their way of living in the world does not make sense even to themselves. They question their sitting, their meditation, their contemplation, their leisurely gazing and their dim awareness of the realization of the presence of God. They wonder about the futility of their existence as measured by the productivity of their more active brethren. Days, months, years, decades pass and it seems like they have not even made a beginning in the spiritual life. However they are at peace living this marginal life which appears to them to be not only marginal to the world but seemingly even marginal to God. They live in a no man's land at the interface between Eden where they witness to the light emanating there and a redeemed world darkened by sin. Somehow through the merits flowing from Christ's sacrifice, they hope to participate in His mediation.

Christian monks participate in that mediation by their interior exploration in which they encounter not only their own heart, but the heart of mankind in which both grace and sin abound. Although they may be aware of the presence of God and the light of grace, they are also in contact with the darkness of sin and its destructive power in themselves, the world and others. In some small measure, it is their mission to bring this darkness to the light of Christ. As a consequence of being a conscious meeting point of the light and darkness, monks seek reconciliation for themselves. In doing so, they become instruments of reconciliation for others. Theirs is a never-ending task. The solitary journey into the center of their own heart becomes a journey into the center of mankind's darkened heart as

1979) 350; subsequent references will be cited as "John of the Cross" parenthetically in the text.

they seek to discover the center of their true self where they find God. In their journey, every arrival becomes another departure.

Stand on Your Own Feet

With each arrival and departure, monks increasingly learn to stand on their own feet. They do this by withdrawing from a false self, concentrating through solitude on the exploration of an inner realm in which they seek God.[17] In the process they deepen their capacity for obedience, faith, freedom and love – all critical elements for monks to stand on their own feet before God.

Merton emphasizes that our false self originates in our disobedience to the call to be a true son or daughter of God. Our disobedience makes us afraid and we hide like Adam. We hide from God, we hide from our true self and we hide from others. We fear that we will be discovered, unmasked, unclothed, and be naked before the truth of God which is God's truth in us:

> The man and his wife heard the sound of Yahweh God walking in the garden in the cool of the day, and they hid from Yahweh God among the trees of the garden. But Yahweh God called to the man. "Where are you?" he asked. "I heard the sound of you in the garden," he replied. "I was afraid because I was naked, so I hid." "Who told you that you are naked?" He asked. "Have you been eating of the tree I forbade you to eat?" (Genesis 3:8-13)

This false self is the lie of our self-creation which results from our profound refusal to be the image and likeness of God. This wound of the false self has primitive roots extending back to the Garden of Eden.[18] As noted by John Eudes Bamberger (Hart, ed. 144), the restoration of this image and likeness is the primary defining task of the monk, whether living in the monastery or within the world. "God created man in the image of himself: in the image of God he created him, male and female he created them" (Genesis 1:27). Through obedience, the monk's task is to return to Eden, to return to the presence of God. The path to this restoration passes through a dark night of dread which arises from the realization that one's external identity is inauthentic and illusionary. Merton observes: "The purpose of the dark night, as St. John of the Cross shows, is not simply to punish and afflict the heart of man, but to liberate, to purify and to

---

17. See Thomas Merton, *Disputed Questions* (New York: Farrar, Straus and Cudahy, 1960) 177-207.

18. See Thomas Merton, *The New Man* (New York: Farrar, Straus and Cudahy, 1961) 50-68.

enlighten in perfect love. The way that leads through dread goes not to despair but to perfect joy, not to hell but to heaven."[19] At its secret roots, dread opens into faith. If one opts to live at the center of this dread, the dread itself becomes a school of faith. In this barren desert, faith blossoms within the obscure and opaque boundary between the ground of ourselves and the ground of our being, the interface between us and God.

Monks stand on their own feet through their growth in faith in God and dependence on Him and through their growth in faith in their community and dependence on them. Through the gift of faith monks encounter God whose Love is their freedom. Merton suggests that monks through their journey in faith realize that God is the supporting ground of their existence.[20] They may discover this support as expressed through others. Often, it appears, God stands such persons on their own feet by allowing them to lean on the backs of others, drawn from family, friends, workplace, community and church. However, paradoxically, the cement holding them in these relationships may dissolve as monks surrender their group identity for their unique individual identity, hidden in the mystery of their union with God. Later, these relationships may be recovered at a more profound level as they become more centered on God. They may even realize St. John of the Cross's pronouncement, "the soul knows creatures through God and not God through creatures" (John of the Cross 645).

As monks receive the gift of dependence on others, they share with them the gift of presence, not only their own but that of the risen Christ. By their fidelity to the quest of seeking the face of the living God, their union with God, however limited, allows them to become a transparent bearer of God to others. Merton notes:

> The presence of God in His world as its Creator depends on no one but Him. His presence in the world as Man depends, in some measure, upon men. Not that we can do anything to change the mystery of the Incarnation in itself: but we are able to decide whether we ourselves, and that portion of the world which is ours, shall become *aware* of His presence, consecrated by it, and transfigured in its light. We have the choice of two identities: the external mask which seems to be real and which lives by a shadowy autonomy for the brief moment of earthly existence, and the hidden, inner person who seems to us to be nothing, but who can give himself eternally to the truth in whom he subsists.

19. Thomas Merton, *Contemplative Prayer* (New York: Herder & Herder, 1969) 138; subsequent references will be cited as "*CP*" parenthetically in the text.

20. See James Finley, *Merton's Palace of Nowhere* (Notre Dame, IN: Ave Maria Press, 1978) 93.

It is this inner self that is taken up into the mystery of Christ, by His love, by the Holy Spirit, so that in secret we live "in Christ."[21]

Through interior exploration, monks recover their true self by the intervention of the Holy Spirit. For those in monasteries as well as those in world, the monk's journey entails a life of prayer, grace, silence and solitude. Prayer exposes their interior through self-knowledge, allows the mercy of God to heal their interior wounds,[22] leads them to union with God and communion with others. Grace liberates them from the false self through the actions of the Holy Spirit who prompts them to seek the truth of themselves as they seek the Truth that is God. Grace restores the lost innocence of Eden through the promptings of the Holy Spirit, their source of grace, their guide and their destination. Silence guides them to the solitude of their true self and the ground of their being where they encounter God and peace.[23] Through their interior exploration, they are hollowed out and experience their emptiness. Merton perceives the depths of this emptiness to be pure freedom and love. "The character of emptiness, at least for a Christian contemplative, is pure love, pure freedom. Love that is free of everything, not determined by anything, or held down by any special relationship. . . . This purity, freedom and indeterminateness of love is the very essence of Christianity" (*CP* 118-19).

To experience the reality that God became man that man may participate in the divine (so often expressed in the liturgy of Eastern rites) is the deepest aspiration of monks. Their whole solitary journey revolves around this notion. It forms the core of the "work of God" which has been traditionally expressed through the office, choir and liturgy, and assisted by monastic stability and the vows – all designed to facilitate an encounter with God through which monks are transformed. The monk without walls or vows may incorporate some of these practices as well as other paths seeking the same result. All of these means exist to provide the individual time, silence and focus, to seek God, be transformed by God through grace, and through union with God participate in his divinity, which is to participate in His Love. Merton suggests:

But in fact the Resurrection and Ascension of Christ, the New Adam, completely restored human nature to its spiritual condition and

---

21. Thomas Merton, *New Seeds of Contemplation* (New York: New Directions, 1961) 295.

22. See Thomas Merton, *Thomas Merton in Alaska: The Alaskan Conferences, Journals, and Letters*, ed. Robert E. Daggy (New York: New Directions, 1989) 160-61.

23. See Thomas Merton, *Love and Living*, ed. Naomi Burton Stone and Brother Patrick Hart (New York: Farrar, Straus, Giroux, 1979) 20-21.

made possible the divinization of every man coming into the world. This meant that in each one of us the inner self was now able to be awakened and transformed by the action of the Holy Spirit, and this awakening would not only enable us to discover our true identity "in Christ," but would also make the living and Risen Savior present in us. . . . Each one of us, in some sense, is able to be completely transformed into the likeness of Christ, to become, as He is, divinely human, and thus to share His spiritual authority and charismatic power in the world.[24]

With the recovery of their true self, monks stand on their own feet by discovering their real but hidden identity in Christ in which their spirit and God's Spirit become one (see *IE* 38). As they awaken to the mystery of the presence of God and increasingly live in this presence, they accelerate their maturity as sons or daughters of the Father. They have not attained to final integration but they are awake and aware of their shortcomings and strive to overcome them. They seek wholeness by pursuing integration of their bodies, minds and spirits subject to the Spirit of God, which enables openness to all persons of cultural and religious diversity, and love for the family of man. They hope for a final and complete integration through full union with the Divine – conscious within Consciousness – realized within Reality – Heaven – where they will experience the deepest aspiration of a monk, to stand on his or her own feet before God and see Him, face to Face.

---

24. Thomas Merton, *The Inner Experience: Notes on Contemplation*, ed. William H. Shannon (San Francisco: HarperCollins, 2003) 38; subsequent references will be cited as "*IE*" parenthetically in the text.

Searching for *Sophia*:
Nicholas of Cusa and Thomas Merton

Joshua Hollmann

In a letter to the Pakistani Sufi Abdul Aziz dated December 26, 1962, Thomas Merton notes with sadness the death of a shared friend, the famous Christian scholar of Islam, Louis Massignon.[1] Merton had become acquainted with Massignon in 1958 and corresponded with him until Massignon's death in 1962. Massignon had introduced Aziz to Merton, and Merton and Aziz corresponded from 1960 until Merton's death in 1968.[2] Merton and Aziz were mystics from different religious traditions, Merton of the Cistercian way and Aziz of the path of Sufism, while both Merton and Massignon were priests, Merton of the Latin Rite, Massignon of the Greek Catholic Melkite rite.[3] Merton, Massignon and Aziz were also bound by a deeper more innate desire: they were all three avid seekers of wisdom, *Sophia*, in all of its multivalent and mysterious manifestations. Massignon was famous for his work on the great Sufi al-Hallâj, *La Passion d'al Husayn ibn Mansour al-Hallâj: Martyr Mystique de l'Islam*, first published in 1922,[4] and for his landmark *Essai sur les Origines du*

---

1. Thomas Merton, *The Hidden Ground of Love: Letters on Religious Experience and Social Concerns*, ed. William H. Shannon (New York: Farrar, Straus, Giroux, 1985) 52-53; subsequent references will be cited as *"HGL"* parenthetically in the text. For an overview and study of Merton's correspondence with Abdul Aziz, see William Apel, *Signs of Peace: The Interfaith Letters of Thomas Merton* (Maryknoll, NY: Orbis, 2006) 9-27; subsequent references will be cited as "Apel" parenthetically in the text. See also Sidney H. Griffith, "'As One Spiritual Man to Another': The Merton-Abdul Aziz Correspondence," in Rob Baker and Gray Henry eds., *Merton and Sufism: The Untold Story* (Louisville, KY: Fons Vitae, 1999) 101-29; subsequent references will be cited as "Baker & Henry" parenthetically in the text.

2. On Merton and Massignon, see Herbert Mason, "Massignon and Merton," in *Louis Massignon au Cœur de Notre Temps*, ed. Jacques Keryell (Paris: Éditions Karhala, 1999) 247-58; Sidney H. Griffith, "Un Entretien sur Toutes Choses, Humaines et Divines: La Correspondance entre Louis Massignon et Thomas Merton" (Keryell 259-78); Sidney H. Griffith, "Merton, Massignon and the Challenge of Islam" (Baker and Henry 51-78) (subsequent references will be cited as "Griffith, 'Challenge'" parenthetically in the text); see also Apel 12.

3. Merton was ordained as Father M. Louis, OCSO on May 26, 1949, the Feast of the Ascension. Massignon was ordained in 1950.

4. Louis Massignon, *La Passion de Husayn ibn Mansûr Hallâj: Martyr Mystique de l'Islam*, 2nd ed. (Paris: Gallimard, 1975); ET: *The Passion of Al-Hallaj: Mystic and Martyr of Islam*, trans. Herbert Mason, 4 vols. (Princeton, NJ: Princeton University Press, 1982).

Lexique Technique de la Mystique Musulmane also first published in 1922 with a second, revised edition in 1954.[5] What Merton has to say about Massignon's death is also memorable, even prophetic. "It seems to me," Merton writes, "that mutual comprehension between Christians and Moslems is something of very vital importance today, and unfortunately it is rare and uncertain, or else subjected to the vagaries of politics" (*HGL* 53). Given the recent history of Christian-Muslim relations, "the vagaries of politics" have often obscured mutual comprehension. Massignon, Aziz and Merton remind seekers after peace that there exists, however hidden in the enigma of signs and things signified, the *"point vierge"*[6] of the human spirit where God and self are known in the merciful, compassionate One (*Bismillah al-rahman al-rahim*).

Upon hearing the news of the fall of Constantinople to the Ottomans in 1453, the philosopher and prelate Nicholas of Cusa (1401-64) (Latin: Cusanus) composed *De pace fidei,* in the form of an irenical dialogue between Christians and Muslims.[7] The fall of Constantinople,[8] the ancient capital of the Eastern Roman empire and home of the famous ancient church *Hagia Sophia*, sent shock waves throughout Western Europe and provoked calls for a crusade from Pope Nicholas V and the Roman Curia. Indeed these calls for crusade would continue throughout the fifteenth and well into the sixteenth century. Unlike many of his fellow churchmen,

---

5. Louis Massignon, *Essai sur les Origines du Lexique Technique de la Mystique Musulmane,* 2nd ed. (Paris: J. Vrin, 1954). An example of Massignon's comparison of Christianity and Islam is found in chapter four of this work, where he writes, "Si la Chrétienté est, fondamentalement (1), l'acceptation et l'imitation de Christ, *avant* l'acceptation de la Bible, – en revanche, l'Islam est l'acceptation du Qor'ân *avant* l'imitation de Mohammed" (139). For an English translation of the *Essai*, see Louis Massignon, *Essay on the Origins of the Technical Language of Islamic Mysticism,* trans. Benjamin Clark (Notre Dame, IN: University of Notre Dame Press, 1997).

6. See Thomas Merton, *Conjectures of a Guilty Bystander* (Garden City, NY: Doubleday, 1966) 117, 135-36, 142; subsequent references will be cited as *"CGB"* parenthetically in the text. The expression is taken from Massignon ("Foucauld au Desert: Devant le Dieu d'Abraham, Agar et Ismael," *Les Mardis de Dar-es-Salam* [1958-59] 57-71): see Griffith, "Challenge" 63-68.

7. *Nicholas of Cusa on Interreligious Harmony: Text, Concordance and Translation of De Pace Fidei,* trans. James E. Biechler and H. Lawrence Bond (Lewiston, NY: Edwin Mellen Press, 1990). *Nicolai de Cusa Opera Omnia,* vol. VII: *De Pace Fidei,* ed. Raymundus Klibansky et Hilderbandus Bascour, OSB (Hamburg: Felix Meiner Verlag, 1959) xiii-xxvi. *Nicolai de Cusa Opera Omnia iussu et auctoritate academiae litterarum heildelbergensis ad codicum fidem edita,* 22 vols. (Leipzig-Hamburg: Felix Meiner, 1932-2012).

8. This essay refers to the events of 1453 as the fall of Constantinople as this is how Cusanus and his contemporaries in Western Europe would have seen it. The event is also referred to as the Ottoman conquest of Constantinople.

however, Nicholas of Cusa responded to the fall of Constantinople not with a call to arms, but with an invitation to conversation. For a Church leader of his age and place, he was remarkably well versed in the thought and traditions of Islam. His personal library in Bernkastel-Kues, Germany contains various Western theological writings on Islam, as well as works by the great early-medieval Muslim philosopher Avicenna. In Cusanus's library, well-marked works by Arab philosophers such as Averroës and Al-Ghazali stand side by side with Aquinas' *Summa Theologiæ*, Plato's *Republic* and the sermons of Meister Eckhart.[9] Cusanus's library, and the *De pace fidei* in particular, guide seekers of peace to a shared font of Sophia as channelled through Abraham and Plato, revelation and reason, monotheism and mysticism.

On the common ground of Greek philosophy, the intellectual worlds of the three Abrahamic religious traditions interacted, creating similar patterns of thought in dealing with crucial religious concepts. Furthermore, the impact of Greek philosophy on Christian and Muslim theologians and philosophers provided them a shared synthetic and hermeneutical paradigm. For Cusanus, learned ignorance is the apophatic art of knowing that one does not know God. From Antiquity to the Middle Ages, during which time philosophy and religious thought were closely aligned and intertwined, the dynamic encounter between Greek philosophical tradition and the three Abrahamic religions shaped the contours of Western intellectual history, and this is especially true for Cusanus. As his library shows, on the common ground of Greek philosophy, he interacted with the intellectual traditions of Islam through such thinkers as Al-Ghazali and Averroës, and employed similar modes of thought in dealing with the doctrine of God and Wisdom, the Word and words, unity and plurality, Being and beyond Being.[10] For Cusanus, the three Abrahamic faiths – Judaism,

---

9. For the sometimes inaccurate catalogue to Cusa's library, which is still housed at the hospital which he bequeathed in Kues (Latin: Cusa, now Bernkastel-Kues on the Moselle River between Trier and Koblenz), see J. Marx, *Verzeichnis der Handschriften-Sammlung des Hospitals zu Cues bei Bernkastel a./Mosel* (Trier: Druck der Kunst- und Verlagsanstalt Schaar & Dathe, Komm.-Ges. a. Akt., 1905). Copies of the library are also found at The Hill Manuscript Museum and Manuscript Library, St. John's University, Collegeville, MN. See *Cod. Cus.* 177, ff. 108-11 (Plato's *Phaedrus* with numerous notes and markings by Cusanus); *Cod. Cus.* 178 (Latin translation of Plato's *Republic*, also with notes and markings by Cusanus – see especially f. 132r.: Book Six of Plato's *Republic*); on Thomas Aquinas, see *Cod. Cus.* 68, f. 124v (*Summa Theologiae, Pars Prima*, q. 93, with notes by Cusanus); see also *Cod. Cus.* 21, ff. 137r-172v (sermons by Meister Eckhart in Latin, with notes or markings by Cusanus on almost every page).

10. See *Cod. Cus.* 205 (writings by Arab philosophers); *Cod. Cus.* 298 (Avicenna, with note by Cusanus [f. 79v]); *Cod. Cus.* 299 (Avicenna's *Liber de Anima* with mark-

Christianity and Islam – are Western monotheistic religions shaped by the contours and categories of Greek thought. Thus, Greek philosophy, and, with regard to Cusanus, Neoplatonic dialectical and hierarchical thought in particular, provided medieval Christians, Muslims and Jews with collective insights into the mystery of the essence of God and the wonders of the cosmos;[11] and for Cusanus, the one in whom all things are unfolded and enfolded is the Word of God, Christ, Holy Wisdom, *Hagia Sophia*, enlightenment and enlightener, who is both God and man and the way to God, and God the unknowable, and according to *De pace fidei*, the very reconciliation and transcender of the many rites of the one religion.[12] The *point vierge* of Nicholas of Cusa's sapient dialogical approach to the interrelation between Christianity and Islam is centered in the enfolding and unfolding, the hidden-revealed Wisdom and Word of God as evocatively and dialectically explicated in Cusanus's *De pace fidei*.

Merton carefully studied Cusanus. He translated into English Cusanus's apophatic dialogue *De Deo abscondito* (*Dialogue about the Hidden God*) where God is ultimately unknown and yet, paradoxically, attainable.[13] The dialogue describes searching for God beyond mere names and words and leads the "pagan" in the dialogue to a deeper understanding of what God is by saying what God is not.[14] Ultimately, this is a *learned* ignorance, or the art of knowing which knows that one cannot know God.[15] Cusanus was deeply influenced by apophatic thought, especially

---

ings by Cusanus [f. 21v]); *Cod. Cus.* 107-108 (materials on Islam with numerous notes by Cusanus). Note also the dynamic interplay of Plato, Proclus and Denys in Cusanus' notes: *Cod. Cus.* 195 (*Liber de Causis* and Proclus's *Elements*, copied by the same scribe in the same script and meant to be read together, with notes and markings by Cusanus throughout; see especially f. 38r: notes on Prop. 20 of Proclus; ff. 4r, 7r, 8r: references to Plato in margins of *Liber de Causis*; ff. 5v, 8r: references to Pseudo-Dionysius); *Cod. Cus.* 185, ff. 89r, 91r, 93, 103r (notes and markings on Proclus's *Platonic Theology*).

11. For the centrality of Dionysian hierarchy in Cusanus, see *De concordantia catholica*, Bk. I, cc. 1-3.

12. *De pace fidei* II.7.

13. *Nicholas of Cusa: Dialogue about the Hidden God*, trans. Thomas Merton (New York: Dim Gray Bar Press, 1989); first published in *Lugano Review* (Summer 1966) 67-70.

14. *De Deo abscondito* 1.10-11, 15; cf. *De pace fidei* I.4.

15. *Learned Ignorance* is the title of Cusanus's most famous work, *De docta ignorantia* (1440). Cusanus describes learned ignorance as "a method of reasoning in theological matters" and states, "One will be the more learned, the more one knows that one is ignorant" (*De docta ignorantia*, prologus and Bk. I, c. 1, par. 4; see *Nicholas of Cusa: Selected Spiritual Writings*, trans. H. Lawrence Bond [New York: Paulist Press, 1997] 87, 89).

as found in the writings of Pseudo-Dionysius.[16] In a letter on New Year's day 1964 to R. J. Zwi Werblowsky, a prominent scholar of comparative religion, Merton also notes how the "pagan" character in the dialogue *De Deo abscondito* is a superficial Christian.[17] Merton writes how he found comfort in turning to Cusanus after reading Hannah Arendt on the Eichmann case and the moral disorientation of the West – indeed, as Merton writes, "a sordid examination of conscience of *the entire West*" (*CGB* 261). For Merton, though, reason and conscience must not give way to what he calls "the insane cruelties of our bureaucratic age" (*CGB* 261). The "West" may be burdened by bureaucracy, but for Merton and Cusanus, it also represented, at least at its best, a living repository and transformer of ancient Greek thought and Christian and Muslim revelation, an intellectual setting for mystical ascent, and modality of belief in one God. For Cusanus (and indirectly, for Merton) the superficial Christian is one who does not see that God is both hidden (unknowable, apophatic) and knowable in revelation (cataphatic). Thus, God may be found without by revelation both in Jewish and Christian Scripture, and, also, albeit conditionally or as it pertains to Christ, in the Qur'an, and within through contemplating the poetic muse of wisdom.[18] By way of Cusanus and other great thinkers and writers, Merton creatively borrowed the elastically recurring neologism of *coincidentia oppositorum*.

Christopher Pramuk's masterful study of Cusanus' Christology in *Sophia: The Hidden Christ of Thomas Merton*, succeeds in showing how *Sophia*, the unknown and unseen Christ, "centered and in many respects catalyzed Merton's theological imagination in a period of tremendous social, political, and religious fragmentation."[19] The same may be said of Cusanus concerning his Christocentric and sapiential understanding of Islam in *De pace fidei*: *Sophia*, the unknown and unseen Christ, the *Verbum Dei*, Jesus, centers, unifies, catalyzes the seeming *coincidentia oppositorum* of Christianity and Islam as one religion in a variety of rites in his own uncertain time rent by tremendous social changes such as in

---

16. See *Cod. Cus.* 43-45, 96 (works of "St. Denys"; for notes by Cusanus see v. 45, f. 89r; v. 96, f. 257r).

17. Merton writes, "I send you a mimeo of a translation of a very short piece of Nicholas of Cusa. Here again the intention is in no sense apologetic, where he pits a 'pagan' against a 'Christian.' In point of fact, one of the things that strikes the alert reason is that the 'pagan' is really a 'Christian' of the superficial type" (*HGL* 587).

18. In *Cribratio Alkorani* (1461), Cusanus sifts or searches the Qur'an for Christ and finds him therein.

19. Christopher Pramuk, *Sophia: The Hidden Christ of Thomas Merton* (Collegeville, MN: Liturgical Press, 2009) xxiii; subsequent references will be cited as "Pramuk" parenthetically in the text.

the discovery of the so-called "New World," the Renaissance, the advent of heliocentrism, and the nascent Scientific Revolution. Cusnaus's age was also rife with political challenges: the Hundred Years' War, the rise of Islam through the rapidly expanding Ottoman Empire. Most pressingly, Cusanus's troubled century witnessed religious fragmentation on a near apocalyptic scale: the papal schism, the subsequent conciliar movement of the fifteenth century, and the oncoming Reformation. According to orthodox and catholic Christian doctrine, as confessed by both Merton and Cusanus, the incarnation of the *Verbum* is indeed the ultimate *coincidentia oppositorum* of God and man; and yet, as God, Christ Jesus is also beyond every *coincidentia oppositorum* as the one infinitely and utterly unutterable and unknowable God. Chapter three of Pramuk's study, "In the Belly of a Paradox: The Archaeology of Merton's Sacramental Imagination" (Pramuk 77-129), aptly demonstrates how Merton's conviction that there exists an inherent relationship among all expressions of wisdom in and through the Wisdom of God extends to non-Christians, including pre-Christian Hellenic philosophers and Muslims. For Merton and Cusanus, the Logos, *Verbum, Sophia*, pulsates from the center which is both a center and not a center, and magnetically emanates inherent sublime power through existence.

Cusanus's *De pace fidei* begins and ends in Jerusalem, the place Pope Urban II in his sermon in 1095, announcing the First Crusade at the Council of Clermont, called the navel or center of the earth, the city holy to Jews, Christians and Muslims,[20] a city of violence and peace, discord and concordance. At the conclusion of *De pace fidei*, the representatives of the world's religions are sent back to instruct their peoples in the one religion in a variety of rites. They are then compelled to meet again in Jerusalem, the old and the new, literal and figurative city straddling heaven and earth. Beginning in Jerusalem, religious peace will then emanate to the ends of the earth. The dialogue of *De pace fidei* closes in Jerusalem with the opening of books. At the end of the dialogue, the representatives of the world's religions search the ancient Greek and Latin sources where they discover that from the very beginning of Western philosophy, all religious diversity consists in multiple rites rather than in the worship of the one God. One of the central conceptual religious frameworks used by Cusanus in *De pace fidei* is the city as nexus, as the political, temporal and eternal setting for the synthesis of religious

---

20. For the description of Jerusalem as "the navel of the earth," see Robert the Monk's chronicles of the events of the First Crusade and his rendition of the sermon by Pope Urban II at the Council of Clermont (*Robert the Monk's History of the First Crusade: Historia Iherosolimitana*, trans. Carol Sweetenham [Aldershot, UK: Ashgate, 2006] 81).

concord: the topography of realizing religious peace and the geography of dialectical discourse. Cusanus begins his mystical vision of *De pace fidei* in the flux of becoming, the dissimilarity of religious strife. The visionary, Cusanus himself, prays ardently for peace. He then, according to the dialogue, ascends intellectually by divine grace into the heaven of reason, the angelic, metaphysical realm of abstraction where peace is realized hierarchically and dialectically through the Word of God.[21] For Cusanus, religion presupposes the Word of God from whom, in whom, and by whom the peace of faith is achieved (both *fides qua creditur* and *fides quae creditur*[22]). Furthermore, Cusanus transmits the Greek archetypal idea of the *polis* as nexus of religious concordance. The two cities – Constantinople, which for Cusanus was the primary repository of Neoplatonic thought, and Jerusalem, which in the Western medieval mind was the center of the earth – spatially and symbolically mark the Greek-patterned geography for the social imaginary of Christian-Muslim dialogue in *De pace fidei*. For Cusanus the Logos of concordance extends by gradation to all being; so also religious peace as realized dialectically and hierarchically through the Logos extends from the city of Jerusalem to Constantinople and throughout the world – a hierarchical geography of the chain of being and the chain of cities. At one point in history, after the unsettling events of the fall of Constantinople and the troubles that religious persecution bring, Cusanus wrote how he saw a vision of what intellectually already is and pragmatically could be.[23]

There are broad conjectural and even urban similarities between Merton's and Cusanus's search for shared wisdom between Christians and Muslims. While different in tone and time, both mystics sought *Sophia* as a way of finding common ground and concordant peace. Merton wrote on the life of faith, "The tendency of our modern society and of all its thought and culture is to deny and to deride this simple, natural awareness, and to make man from the very beginning both afraid of faith and ashamed of it."[24] Indeed, by looking back to *Hagia Sophia* as found in the Abrahamic faiths and ancient Greek thought (revelation and reason), Merton retrieves the importance of faith found within. He presses on, "The first step to living faith is then, as it has always been one way or another, a denial and a rejection of the standards of thought complacently

---

21. *De pace fidei* I.1, 6; II.7.
22. "faith by which one believes" and "faith which is believed".
23. *De pace fidei* I.1, XIX.68.
24. Thomas Merton, *Life and Holiness* (New York: Herder & Herder, 1963) 96; subsequent references will be cited as "*LH*" parenthetically in the text. Merton dedicates this work *in memoriam* to Louis Massignon (d. 1962).

accepted by rationalistic doubt" (*LH* 96). For Merton, seekers of *Sophia* must press on beyond the vagaries of politics and the smog of modern doubt to discover the *"Point vierge."*[25] This brief essay has sought to introduce readers to the sapiential concordance between Cusanus and Merton in order to consider further theological and philosophical parallels between these two Catholic visionaries of religious peace. Cusanus waited in hope on the way to the perpetual peace, the way to Jerusalem. Merton too waited in hope for peace, and the providential God of peace was with him as he traveled to a great chain of cities *"from Prades to Bermuda to St. Antonin to Oakham to London to Cambridge to Rome to New York to Columbia to Corpus Christi to St. Bonaventure to the Cistercian Abbey of the poor men who labor in Gethsemani"*[26] even to as far as Bangkok. Indeed, Merton died while seeking religious concordance while attending a conference of Eastern and Western monks in Thailand. Cusanus's vision of *De pace fidei* and Merton's own interreligious search for *Sophia* ultimately coalesce with the *telos* of Scripture and the end of things, the sight of the new Jerusalem coming down from above, the eternal abode of peace, the time beyond time when the many will be One, and the journey to religious concord consummated.

---

25. Merton writes of "the *'point vierge'* of the spirit, the center of our nothingness where, in apparent despair, one meets God – and is found completely in His mercy" (*CGB* 136). Merton constructively proposes that the mystery of God's mercy may be a nexus of dialogue between Christians and Muslims.

26. Thomas Merton, *The Seven Storey Mountain* (New York: Harcourt, Brace, 1948) 422-23.

No Spouse Is an Island: Thomas Merton's Contribution toward a Contemporary Spirituality of Marriage

Daniel P. Horan, OFM

Introduction

It might at first seem counterintuitive to look at the work of a mid-twentieth-century American Trappist monk for insights in developing a theologically sound and pragmatically substantive spirituality of marriage. Yet the wisdom of Thomas Merton again demonstrates that despite such a natural inclination there exist at least some significant exceptions to that rule. Although Merton did not construct a sustained or systematic treatment on the theology or spirituality of marriage, as some scholars have since the Second Vatican Council's positive contributions to the subject in conciliar texts such as *Gaudium et Spes* and *Apostolicam Actuositatem*, his occasional reflections on marriage as sacrament and source of sanctity offer illuminating resources for those interested in developing a contemporary spirituality of marriage.[1] Merton's theological reflection on marriage is found in three primary forms: his book-length spiritual treatises, such as *No Man Is an Island*,[2] *The New Man*,[3] *The Ascent to Truth*[4] and others; his personal journal entries; and, perhaps in both the most diverse and pragmatic forms, his extensive correspondence with a variety of people. While the explicit references to marriage in Merton's writing, journals and correspondence offer a trove of valuable material, which has largely gone unexamined and without contemporary appropriation, his more broadly addressed work on the spiritual life also provides material valuable for the development of a spirituality of marriage today.[5]

---

1. All conciliar constitutions and decrees are taken from *The Documents of Vatican II with Notes and Index*, Vatican Translation (Strathfield, Australia: St. Paul's Publications, 2009); subsequent references to conciliar texts will include the document's Latin title (or its abbreviation) with paragraph numbers and page numbers of this edition.

2. Thomas Merton, *No Man Is an Island* (New York: Harcourt, Brace, 1955); subsequent references will be cited as "*NMI*" parenthetically in the text.

3. Thomas Merton, *The New Man* (New York: Farrar, Straus and Cudahy, 1961); subsequent references will be cited as "*NM*" parenthetically in the text.

4. Thomas Merton, *The Ascent to Truth* (New York: Harcourt, Brace, 1951).

5. More than twenty-five years ago, before Merton's journals were edited and published, Lawrence Martone published an article entitled "Merton's Insights Applied to Marriage," *Spiritual Life* 32 (1986) 105-10; subsequent references will be cited as

The aim of this paper is not to demarcate the definitive parameters of a spirituality of marriage according to Thomas Merton, but instead to highlight those areas of his writing fecund for appropriation in the contemporary theological enterprise of developing a spirituality of marriage, while also noting several trajectories worthy of further exploration. The dearth of scholarly engagement with Merton's thought in this area elicits a substantive treatment such as I propose below. It is my hope that this paper might provide the impetus for additional inquiry into what Merton's work might offer theologians and pastoral ministers today by way of resource and guidance.

The structure of this discussion is fivefold. First, we will begin with a look at the current state of the development of a spirituality of marriage from the dual lens of helpful contributions and challenges to the process. Second, we will examine Merton's contribution to the theological concept of vocation, particularly as it emerges in his writing with regard to marriage as a legitimate and holy vocation. Third, we will consider the way that Merton describes marriage as the place of divine encounter for spouses. Fourth, we will explore Merton's understanding of marriage as the locus for Christian sanctity. Finally, we will conclude with a recapitulative summary of Merton's contribution to a contemporary spirituality of marriage.

Spirituality of Marriage: Seeds and Challenges

Thomas Merton often uses the image of "seeds," a symbol frequently found in the Gospel parables and Christian tradition, to refer to myriad dimensions of the Christian life of contemplation. The image is helpful insofar as we recognize the inchoate and, at times, unclear features of the *vita evangelica* in its manifold form. Like the mustard-seed-sized faith of those about whom Jesus speaks in the Gospels (Matthew 13:31-32; Mark 4:30-32; Luke 13:18-19), there are aspects of our lives of prayer and Christian praxis that at once appear nascent, yet bear potential for extraordinary growth. The metaphoric use of seed in such instances provides a multivalent image that relies on concurrent factors for its sustenance and

---

"Martone" parenthetically in the text. It remains the only attempt to resource Merton's writing for use in relationship to marriage. Martone's article is helpful in that it is the first attempt, if preliminary, to look at Merton's work as a serious resource for a spirituality of marriage, but it lacks a broad and sustained engagement with both the Mertonian corpus and the post-conciliar theological texts that frame the discussion of marriage as sacrament and the parameters of a marital spirituality today. The only other treatment of Merton's view of marriage is the brief encyclopedia entry by Patrick O'Connell, "Marriage," in William H. Shannon, Christine M. Bochen and Patrick F. O'Connell, *The Thomas Merton Encyclopedia* (Maryknoll, NY: Orbis, 2002) 281-82.

growth, which could be taken to represent the liturgical life of the faithful, contemplative engagement with prayer, the support and participation of the community and so on. A seed does not grow on its own, but remains fragile and dependent on outside factors for its nurturing and development. The efforts to develop a contemporary spirituality of marriage, one that is not as restrictive or problematic as those found earlier in Christian history, culturally conditioned as they were, bear a resemblance to seeds: they are rich starting points that require assistance, support and reflection to grow into a comprehensive and adoptable spirituality.

At the same time, while certain beneficial seeds of marital spirituality have been planted in recent decades, there also exist numerous challenges to the efficacious nurturing and harvesting of these spiritual seeds. Among the diverse challenges of contemporary experience, one might count the confluence of cultural and social views of marital normativity brought into conflict as a result of increased globalization, the absence of sustained theological reflection on the role of married life in the post-conciliar Church, and the remaining specter, if not a reinvigorated reality in recent years, of a clericalism that subordinates so-called "secular" life, including marriage, in order to elevate clerical and religious life as objectively better or "more holy." In this section of the paper, I wish to briefly survey both the seeds and challenges that have emerged in recent years as theologians and others have consciously grappled with identifying sources for and the development of a spirituality of marriage.

Seeds of a Fruitful Spirituality of Marriage

Among the most important developments in the theology and spirituality of marriage in recent history is the way in which the Second Vatican Council addressed the subject of marriage in *Gaudium et Spes*, the Pastoral Constitution on the Church in the Modern World. Whereas previous conceptualizations of marriage focused on the inferiority of that state of life when compared to other states such as religious life, as well as a nearly exclusive emphasis on the procreative end of marriage as the institution's subject and purpose, *Gaudium et Spes* presents a more expansive and theologically rich understanding of the source, purpose and end of marriage. The Council Fathers explain: "For the good of the spouses and their offspring as well as of society, the existence of the sacred bond no longer depends on human decisions alone. For, God Himself is the author of matrimony, endowed as it is with various benefits and purposes" (*G&S* §48 [160]). The starting point for any reflection on marriage must begin with God as the source, the "author" as it is understood here, which bespeaks the inherent goodness and gift of this state of life.

Previous conceptions of marriage, many of which might unfortunately persist in our world today, understood marriage following the perspective offered by St. Augustine – namely, as a remedy for concupiscence.[6] This view considered the state of marriage as simply the least-bad option in response to the need for human sexual expressivity and for procreation. Furthermore, the operative understanding governing marriage for at least the four centuries prior to the Second Vatican Council was the notion of marriage as a contract.[7] This contract was the formal agreement between two parties – formerly between the groom and bride's father, if now between the bride and groom – that negotiated these two ends: procreation and the so-called "bodily-sexual rights" of the spouses.

In this regard, the Council moved beyond the previously held notion of marriage and the popular understanding of the contractual and subordinated nature of this state of life. It offered an image of marriage as primarily "a covenant of life and love" (see *G&S* §§47-52 [159-66] and Jeffery 35-75). However, as Peter Jeffery rightly notes, it seems that in the decades following the promulgation of *Gaudium et Spes* and the rest of the conciliar texts, the covenantal and richly theological understanding of marriage has "been concealed" (Jeffery 35). One of the seeds of a fruitful spirituality of marriage is found within the conciliar conceptualization of marriage.

Another seed of a fruitful spirituality of marriage might be found within the recent *ressourcement* efforts of theologians to identify trajectories within the Christian spiritual, theological and historical traditions that might help inform a contemporary understanding of marriage in relation to Christian discipleship and love.[8] There are rich resources available within the tradition to be re-appropriated in such a way as to aid in the il-

6. For an excellent historical study of the Church's developing understanding of marriage during this time, see Philip Lyndon Reynolds, *Marriage in the Western Church: The Christianization of Marriage during the Patristic and Early Medieval Periods* (Leiden: Brill, 1994) esp. 259-79.

7. See Peter Jeffery, *The Mystery of Christian Marriage* (New York: Paulist Press, 2006) 37; subsequent references will be cited as "Jeffery" parenthetically in the text.

8. For a helpful survey of recent literature, see the review essay: Monica Sandor, "Contemporary Marital Spirituality: A Survey of the Principal Themes," *INTAMS Review* 11 (2005) 238-55. Some of the more notable recent efforts to construct a contemporary spirituality of marriage in the English language include Richard Gaillardetz, *A Daring Promise: A Spirituality of Christian Marriage*, rev. ed. (Liguori, MO: Liguori Publications, 2007); Charles Gallagher, George Maloney, Mary Rousseau and Paul Wilczak, *Embodied in Love: Sacramental Spirituality and Sexual Intimacy* (New York: Crossroad, 1994); and *Christian Marriage and Family: Contemporary Theological and Pastoral Perspectives*, ed. Michael Lawler and William Roberts (Collegeville, MN: Liturgical Press, 1996) esp. 93-207.

lumination of the sacrament of matrimony's meaning and relevance today. There is, perhaps more than ever, a need in our own time to elucidate a spirituality of marriage from a Christian perspective, especially in light of the challenges popular culture, among others, present to spouses or would-be spouses in the Church.

Challenges to Constructing a Spirituality of Marriage

During the fall of 2011 much media attention was paid to the story of the short-lived marriage of socialite-turned-celebrity Kim Kardashian and professional basketball player Kris Humphries. Their 72-day-long marriage led to a media and internet frenzy of commentary and critique, much of which focused on the scandal or abuse of the institution of marriage caused by the brevity and ostensibly flippant treatment of this union.[9] The casual approach to marriage that this celebrity debacle represents – and it should be noted that this is simply one among many such instances – does not just affect the rich and famous, but informs and reinforces elements of a popular cultural influence that reaches to the ends of an entire society.

The Second Vatican Council Fathers realized the various challenges that face marriage in our modern world. Their most extensive treatment of the sacrament of marriage takes place under the heading of the second major section of the document, entitled "Some Problems of Special Urgency" (*G&S* §§46-52 [159-66]). This particular section on marriage, as it is understood within the hostile social climate of the world, begins with the assertion that human dignity and the value of the individual are directly tied to the institution of marriage: "The well-being of the individual person and of human and Christian society is intimately linked with the healthy condition of that community produced by marriage and family" (*G&S* §47 [159]). Among those matters that the Council decries as currently threatening marriage are counted polygamy, divorce, "so-called free love" and other "disfigurements," which the documents states all "have an obscuring effect" (*G&S* §47 [159]). It is difficult, we are told, for the wider culture to appreciate the sacredness of the bond and the sacramentality of the relationship of marriage due to these and other societal influences. Marriage is no longer presumed to be a lifelong and lasting institution, but, as demonstrated by the spectacle of the Kardashian and Humphries wedding and subsequent divorce, it is now popularly considered to be a no more than a contractual agreement that might be dissolved whenever the contracting partners see fit. So prevalent are the

---

9. See, for example, Monica Corcoran Harel, "I Do, Briefly," *The New York Times* (November 6, 2011) ST18.

misconceptions of the meaning and purpose of marriage that some like Ann Linthorst had begun to describe marriage as "an alternative lifestyle" as long as thirty years ago.[10] There are few social cues and cultural norms that overtly endorse a Christian view of marriage; this is indeed a great challenge today.

Another major challenge to marriage today that was identified by the Second Vatican Council is the notion of married love as having been "profaned by excessive self-love, the worship of pleasure and illicit practices against human generation" (*G&S* §47 [159-60]). Selfishness and the desire for immediate gratification play particularly insidious roles in the popular dissolution of the integrity of marriage. While these characteristics might not be limited to shaping a culture's understanding of marriage – for selfishness and the desire for immediate gratification also shape one's understanding of self, society and all relationships in turn – they have inexorably shaped the popular understanding of why one enters into marriage and what the purpose of that relationship should be.

These are simply preliminary observations of just two of the many challenges that face both the maintenance of a Christian understanding of marriage and the construction of a contemporary spirituality of marriage in our own day.

Having looked at both some positive seeds of a fruitful spirituality of marriage and samples of the challenges present to the efficacious nurturing and harvesting of those seeds, we now move to consider three ways in which the thought and writing of Thomas Merton offers us resources in moving toward a contemporary spirituality of marriage.

Marriage as a Legitimate Vocation

While the exclusive use of the term "vocation" to refer to clergy and consecrated religious has rightly been in decline since the Second Vatican Council's renewed emphasis on the place and dignity of the laity within the Church, which is the Body of Christ called People of God, there are some remnants of a disparity in dignity or value between the manifold expressions of Christian life in various states of living. One of the ways that Thomas Merton's work contributes to a contemporary spirituality of marriage rests in his broadening of the notion of vocation to extend beyond religious clerics such as himself to include marriage as a legitimate calling from God to live an authentically Christian life. His reflections on the subject of vocation, mostly written prior to the Council, presage the more popular appropriation of the term in the contemporary multivalent

---

10. Ann Linthorst, *A Gift of Love: Marriage as a Spiritual Quest* (New York: Paulist Press, 1979) 1-16.

way. For this reason, it might be helpful to return to Merton's insight to glean resources to aid women and men today in understanding the divine invitation to enter into the vocation of married life.

In his lesser-known book *Life and Holiness*, Merton writes, "Every baptized Christian is obliged by his baptismal promises to renounce sin and to give himself completely, without compromise, to Christ, in order that he may fulfill his vocation, save his soul, enter into the mystery of God, and there find himself perfectly 'in the light of Christ.'"[11] He makes the point early on in his writing that the term "vocation" should not be limited to the ministries and lifestyles of formal ecclesiastical roles. Instead, *all* Christians, every baptized person, has a vocation, albeit this vocation varies from person to person. Writing as he was in the late 1950s and early 1960s, Merton does exhibit a vestigial preference at times for what he refers to as a "special vocation," by which he means consecrated religious life (see *LH* 4-5). However, it should be noted that these comments are usually made in passing and take a subordinate place beside the expansive view of the Christian vocational horizon that Merton presents immediately afterward, as is the case in *Life and Holiness*. Shortly after naming the uniqueness of the religious vocation, Merton qualifies his statement, saying that all Christians are to take "the basic Christian vocation to holiness" seriously, something not reserved for just clerics and religious. Nowhere does Merton make this as explicit as he does later on in *Life and Holiness*:

The way of Christian perfection begins with a personal summons, addressed to the individual Christian by Christ the Lord, through the Holy Spirit. This summons is a call, a "vocation." Every Christian in one way or other receives this vocation from Christ – the call to follow him. Sometimes we imagine that vocation is the prerogative of priests and of religious. It is true that they receive a special call to perfection. They dedicate themselves to the quest for Christian perfection by the use of certain definite means. Yet every Christian is called to follow Christ, to imitate Christ as perfectly as the circumstances of his life permit, and thereby to become a saint. (*LH* 35-36)

---

11. Thomas Merton, *Life and Holiness* (New York: Herder & Herder, 1963) 3; subsequent references will be cited as "*LH*" parenthetically in the text. [Author's note: concerning gender-exclusive language, it should be noted that Merton wrote the texts cited in this paper almost half a century ago, prior to the widespread awareness of the need to use gender-inclusive language. Merton's words, in accordance with the policy of *The Merton Annual* and that of the Merton Legacy Trust, are quoted as originally written, though if Merton were writing today he would surely incorporate gender-inclusive language.]

Every Christian has a vocation given by God to live in a particular way in the world, striving as it were at all times to follow Christ as a disciple. Merton advocates for what the Second Vatican Council would later call the "universal call to holiness" shared by all believers, an articulation of this *a priori* relational vocation of the baptized.[12]

Elsewhere when Merton discusses this universal notion of vocation within the context of contemplation and the Christian life, it appears as something resembling Karl Rahner's conceptualization of an existential characteristic of human personhood.[13] In a similarly Rahnerian way, Merton presupposes the freedom that is integral to the idea of a universal Christian vocation. He suggests that it is our intentional response to a primordial and personal call that best constitutes what we mean when we talk about contemplation.

Hence contemplation is a sudden gift of awareness, an awakening to the Real within all that is real. A vivid awareness of infinite Being at the roots of our own limited being. An awareness of our contingent reality as received, as a present from God, as a free gift of love. This is the existential contact of which we speak when we use the metaphor of being "touched by God." Contemplation is also the response to a call: a call from Him Who has no voice, and yet Who speaks in everything that is, and Who, most of all, speaks in the depths of our own being: for we ourselves are words of His. But we are words that are meant to respond to Him, to answer to Him, to echo Him, and even in some way to contain Him and signify Him.[14]

It is important to observe the inclusivity of Merton's reflection here. This experience of the divine in contemplation and subsequent response to God's call is not limited to a select few, but is an offer extended to all humanity as a gift from God.

In other places, Merton identifies this divine call and our free response as an explicit invitation to share in Christ's ministry to inaugurate the Kingdom of God. In his popular book *No Man Is an Island*, Merton writes: "Each one of us has some kind of vocation. We are all called by

---

12. See *Lumen Gentium*, the Dogmatic Constitution on the Church, §§39-42 (52-57).

13. See Karl Rahner, *Hörer des Wortes: Zur Grundlegung einer Religionsphilosophie* in *Karl Rahner: Sämtliche Werke*, vol. 4, ed. Albert Raffelt (Freiburg: Herder and Herder, 1997).

14. Thomas Merton, *New Seeds of Contemplation* (New York: New Directions, 1961) 3; subsequent references will be cited as "*NSC*" parenthetically in the text. For a comprehensive study of the development of Merton's thought in *New Seeds* see Donald Grayston, *Thomas Merton's Rewritings: The Five Versions of Seeds/New Seeds of Contemplation as a Key to the Development of His Thought* (Lewiston, NY: Edwin Mellen Press, 1989).

God to share in His life and in His Kingdom. Each one of us is called to a special place in the Kingdom" (*NMI* 131). Writing nearly a decade before the Second Vatican Council, Merton anticipates some of the conciliar texts' best expression of the dignity and place of *all* members of the Body of Christ, described throughout *Lumen Gentium* as the People of God. It should be noted that Merton's inclusivity contrasts with the later post-synodal Apostolic Exhortation of Pope John Paul II *Christifideles Laici*, in which the particular expressions of the vocation of the laity are relegated to the last part of the text and treated very superficially, drawing only on a single passage from St. Francis de Sales' *Introduction to the Devout Life*.[15] This articulation of the "lay vocation," with only a passing reference to marriage in terms of Francis de Sales' text, is a very secularized and limited expression of what the meaning of a Christian calling by virtue of baptism means for all members of the Body of Christ. Merton, by contrast, even despite his focus at times on religious life, does not relegate married spouses to a place of clerical subordination within the *ecclesia*. Instead, his emphasis is on the genuinely grace-filled reality of married life that is intrinsically holy and a particular invitation to Christian discipleship inasmuch as ordained priesthood or consecrated religious life is.

Merton asserts that the problem with the popular conception of vocation does not stem from any inherent inequality or inferiority of state of life, but is instead engendered by something of a collective forgetfulness on the part of the Church to support and recognize marriage as a "truly spiritual vocation." For this reason, I would assert, the writing of the late Pope John Paul II in this regard – namely the continued subordination of married life to a "secular realm" and in a categorically inferior place to ordained priesthood and consecrated religious life – and those who follow a similarly antiquated and clerical trajectory of thought – do violence to the integrity of vocation as a constitutive element of human existence, something given by God prior to any human demarcation or ranking. Merton explains:

> Hence we must not imagine that married life is "life in the flesh" and religious life alone is "life in the spirit." The married life is a *truly spiritual vocation*, though in many ways it is accidentally rendered difficult by the fact that married people do not recognize their spiritual opportunities and often find no one to guide them in the right direction. (*LH* 147-48; emphasis added)

---

15. John Paul II, *Christifideles Laici* [December 30, 1988] §§55-56 (Washington, DC: USCCB Publishing, 1989) 166-71.

In an implicit way, he goes on to discuss the failure of the Church as a whole to support women and men in married life. The elevation of consecrated religious life has created what Merton calls a "tragedy," because it leads good women and men into thinking that they can never reach holiness, that they are in essence barred from a life of Christian perfection because they, naturally, "find it difficult or impossible to imitate the austerities, the devotions, and the spiritual practices of religious" (*LH* 148). It is entirely understandable that they would feel such a way of life "difficult or impossible," because that is not the way of life that God has called spouses to live. Their vocation looks different, is affectively expressed in other ways and is equally dignified and Christian. The problem lies with the Church's tradition of silence about (at best) and subjugation of (at worst) married couples in the community of faith.

Another concern that Merton identified in the history of marital spirituality is the extreme idealization that could also take place of the relationship and sacrament from the perspective of celibate clerics and religious. One thinks of Augustine and his suggestion that marriage suffices to morally respond to natural human concupiscence. Yet, as Merton notes in the correspondence with a woman named Mrs. Lytton, society also has its own idealization of marriage and what that type of relationship should look like and produce. Writing in the early 1960s, Merton describes his own take on his contemporary society's perpetuation of a certain view of marriage:

> I think that we live in a society which *makes* a problem out of love and marriage, whether one likes it or not. There is so much nonsense, explicit or otherwise, about sex: there is a myth of sex, it is glamorized, and impossible ideals are proposed, people get the idea that marriage is a failure unless one attains to utterly hopeless ideals of perfect adjustment, and so on. One has to face the fact that sex is both intoxicating and disconcerting, that it takes a person out of himself and leaves him in confusion. It is beautiful but it is also in some ways ugly. It is full of consolation and bliss, but it also arouses the power to hate. Love and hate go together, and sex is full of ambivalence. The real thing then is to learn to give oneself maturely, without futile idealization, accepting the unsatisfactory realities and the transient intoxications.[16]

---

16. Thomas Merton, November 21, 1963 letter to Mrs. Lytton, in Thomas Merton, *Witness to Freedom: Letters in Times of Crisis*, ed. William H. Shannon (New York: Farrar, Straus, Giroux, 1994) 309-10; subsequent references will be cited as "*WF*" parenthetically in the text.

Merton's frank approach to what he identifies as the problem of idealization of marriage and sex within his contemporary society sets the stage
for him to offer his salient advice to Mrs. Lytton. He writes, "The great
thing in marriage is not an impossible ideal of fulfillment and exaltation
but a mature rational Christian acceptance of the responsibilities and
risks of human love" (*WF* 310). Love plays a central role in Merton's
understanding of the sacrament of marriage. Marriage is both authentically human and an expression of Christian discipleship. At one point,
Merton even suggests that a vocation to married life presupposes "the
capacity for a deeply human love" (*NMI* 99). It is a legitimate vocation
that should not be subordinated nor elevated, but embraced and lived as
part of God's plan for humanity and salvation. In a 1965 letter to a woman
named Edith, Merton responds to her news that she is engaged with yet
another affirmation that marriage is indeed a vocation. He writes: "I am
happy to hear you have found someone you might marry. Certainly that
is a most beautiful vocation, but a difficult one in these days when love
is misunderstood so seriously."[17]

Ahead of his time, Merton articulated well what the Christian tradition
had long taught, but so many had forgotten: *all* Christians have a vocation.
Marriage, then, is not simply an external, contractual or convenient way
to live in the world, nor is it a subordinate form of life when compared to
consecrated religious life, but it is inherently dignified, sacramental and
legitimately vocational. Women and men have been called by God and
led by the Spirit into this way of expressing Christian love.

Marriage as the Place of Divine Encounter

The Second Vatican Council, in the Pastoral Constitution *Gaudium et
Spes*, identified married love as the location where the two spouses
primarily encounter God in Christ: "Authentic married love is caught
up into divine love and is governed and enriched by Christ's redeeming
power and the saving activity of the Church, so that this love may lead
the spouses to God with powerful effect and may aid and strengthen them
in the sublime office of being a father or a mother" (*G&S* §41 [161]).
Within the covenant of marriage, women and men both experience the
presence of God and are simultaneously brought into the life and love
of the Trinity. This is something that Thomas Merton, years before the
Second Vatican Council refocused the Church's theology and spirituality toward the inherent dignity and vocation of the marriage covenant,
identifies in his writings.

---

17. Thomas Merton, June 25, 1965 letter to Edith (unpublished correspondence,
Thomas Merton Center archives, Bellarmine University, Louisville, KY).

Perhaps one of the most succinct reflections that Merton offers on marriage as the place of divine encounter comes in what would eventually be posthumously published as *The Inner Experience.* This particular passage highlights Merton's understanding and presentation of the unique locus of Trinitarian love in marriage and the privileged place the sacrament provides to the spouses for experiencing Christ:

> It follows from this that for the married Christian, his married life is essentially bound up with his contemplation. This is inevitable. It is by his marriage that he is situated in the mystery of Christ. It is by his marriage that he bears witness to Christ's love for the world, *and in his marriage that he experiences that love.* His marriage is a sacramental center from which grace radiates out into every department of his life, and consequently it is his marriage that will enable his work, his leisure, his sacrifices, and even his distractions to become in some degree contemplative. For by his marriage all these things are ordered to Christ and centered in Christ.[18]

Prompted by reflection on the mode and place of contemplation in the lives of lay women and men, Merton posits that it is precisely the married life itself that serves as that location, as that privileged place within which Christ is most immediately encountered. Merton even goes so far as to suggest that married life provides the very condition for the possibility for all aspects of the spouse's work, relationships and leisure. So too will married life provide the foundation and location for the spirituality of the spouses, a notion that flows directly from the recognition of the legitimacy and integrity of marriage as vocation.

At certain points in his writing, Merton identifies by way of privation the meaning and purpose of marriage. As it concerns that privileged place of encounter with God, something oftentimes called contemplation, marriage should not be confused with popular or "worldly" conceptions of marriage. Merton keenly notes, "The union of two in one flesh is not chiefly for consolation and mutual support," a view that is widely held by some (*NM* 92). As attributes of the relationship, consolation and mutual support are not inherently bad, but they are not the primary reason why two spouses should enter into the covenant of marriage. There is also the temptation, if one fixates on those theses and other secondary aspects of marriage, to slip into a consumeristically or individualistically driven view of marriage. This is made more explicit in Merton's posthumously published book *Love and Living*: "The trouble with this commercialized

---

18. Thomas Merton, *The Inner Experience: Notes on Contemplation*, ed. William H. Shannon (San Francisco: HarperCollins, 2003) 140 (emphasis added).

idea of love is that it diverts your attention more and more from the essentials to the accessories of love. You are no longer able to really love the other person, for you become obsessed with the effectiveness of your own package, your own product, your own market value."[19] The flippancy and self-centeredness with which love is treated in popular culture distracts, as Merton observes, from the essential properties of marriage and relationship. At the core, Merton claims, is this encounter with God through married life. Meanwhile, what popular culture and many modern people focus on are the accidental or incidental qualities of married life and love. Merton speculates that one reason marriages break up so rapidly in his own day (and how much more so today) is this lack of recognition of the central reality of the encounter with the divine within married life. "For many people what matters is the delightful and fleeting moment in which the deal is closed. They give little thought to what the deal itself represents. That is perhaps why so many marriages do not last, and why so many people have to remarry" (*L&L* 31).

Merton situates marriage within the context of contemplative life to highlight the intrinsically spiritual nature of the covenant and sacrament. He describes marriage as inherently "creative and fecund," asserting that it is the intimate sharing and communication of marriage that "elevates marriage to that sublime spiritual level in which action and contemplation are capable of fusion in the brilliant darkness of mystery" (*NM* 92). Too often marriage is seen through the Augustinian or clerical lenses that claim such a relationship prevents or distracts from an "authentic spiritual life." Certainly this is an attitude reflected in Merton's own time in the pre-conciliar first-half of the twentieth century. Yet, Merton rejects this subordination and artificial demarcation in an effort to highlight that marriage itself is a locus of divine encounter.

> In the union of man and woman it is no longer words that are symbols of the mystery of God's holiness, but persons. God appears in them as sacred, not only in the sense that life itself seems sacred to us, because it is mysterious, but in the sense that the productive union of those who are humanly in love with each other is a sacred symbol of the infinite giving and diffusion of goodness which is the inner law of God's own life. (*NM* 92)

Not only do the spouses experience God in married life, but they themselves reflect the image of God to each other. It is in the strictly theologi-

---

19. Thomas Merton, *Love and Living*, ed. Naomi Burton Stone and Brother Patrick Hart (New York: Farrar, Straus, Giroux, 1979) 30-31; subsequent references will be cited as "*L&L*" parenthetically in the text.

cal sense that Merton uses the term "symbol" here. Instead of viewing the spouses as mere signs that point to something other than themselves (i.e., God in this case), they are understood to be symbols, realities that actualize that which they represent. The spouses help make God in Christ incarnate in their relationship and love. They do this for each other and they do this for the world as all Christians are called to do.

Another aspect of marriage as the place of divine encounter that Merton discusses in his writing is the physical, sexual relationship shared between the spouses. Certainly this is a topic that is usually avoided in most spiritual and theological literature over the centuries. Nevertheless, Merton takes this important component of married life very seriously and offers us a renewed and healthy Christian anthropological perspective that highlights the gift of sexuality and an opportunity for spouses to recognize God in their marital love. "The married love that is transfigured by the Church's sacrament reproduces something of this love by which Christ sanctified His Church, and the natural mystery of the communication of life by love becomes a supernatural mystery of the communication of holiness by charity" (*NM* 93).[20] Not only does marital sexual love reflect the love of God, but Merton claims it is an instantiation or "reproduction" of that divine love. He writes in *No Man Is an Island* that "In married life, divine love is more fully incarnate than in the other vocations" and that married love "becomes a sign of divine love and occasion of divine grace" (*NMI* 154).

Merton feels strongly about the immanent presence of God in marriage. When spouses enter into the covenant, they make a concrete, historical choice that is at one and the same time much more than a public commitment or contract. "When two [spouses] consciously make this choice, this spiritual choice, with regard to one another, then a great mystery and transformation takes place in the world and God is present in this mystery."[21] They enter into a new way of living in the world and ministering the love of God in Christ to one another. They enter into the Trinitarian life of God in a new way. They fulfill their baptismal call of Christian discipleship in a unique way.

---

20. Additionally, in *No Man Is an Island*, Merton writes: "But it is clear that married life, for its success, presupposes the capacity for a deeply human love which ought to be spiritual and physical at the same time" (*NMI* 99). A recurring theme, Merton often ties the spirituality of married life to the physical and sexual expression of marital love.

21. Thomas Merton, *A Search for Solitude: Pursuing the Monk's True Life. Journals, vol. 3: 1952-1960*, ed. Lawrence S. Cunningham (San Francisco: HarperCollins, 1996) 259 [2/13/1959].

Marriage as the Means by which Spouses Become Saints

The journey for all baptized Christians is ultimately a pilgrimage toward sainthood. Thomas Merton does not claim, of course, that everybody will necessarily enter the official canon of the saints, but that in the more Pauline sense of the term, we are all called or invited by God to be our truest selves, which, found in relationship with God, means striving to live who it is we were created to be. It is not at all unusual for many people to think that sanctity is something reserved for ordained priests and members of religious communities. However, Merton makes very clear in his writing that such a restriction on the concept of sainthood is not helpful nor is it supported by the Christian tradition. At one point, illustrating what he sees as the universal reality of human sanctification in Christ, Merton suggests that there will logically be many more married people that will become saints than those who are celibate priests and religious, because there are simply *more* married people in the world. He then asks the question, "How then can we imagine that the cloister is the only place in which men can become saints?" (*NMI* 99).

This notion that marriage provides the means by which spouses will become saints stems from the two previous points Merton makes about marriage, namely that it is a legitimate vocation and that it is the privileged location for the spouses' encounter with God. For Merton, what is at the heart of what it means to be a saint is for a person to *truly* be him or herself.[22] It is an intrinsic call that comes to be recognized more clearly through baptism and Christian discipleship and the true self comes to be known only in knowing God. Because Merton holds that the privileged place for spouses to encounter God is in their marriage, where the love of each spouse for the other becomes the symbol of divine love made manifest in relationship, then the discovery of one's true self in God is properly understood as recognizable in the sacramental nature of marriage. This response to God's invitation and encounter with God in marriage leads to a transformation in love, which offers an opportunity to discover one's true self and therefore move closer to sanctity. Merton explains the connection between God's love and becoming a saint: "I who am without love cannot become love unless Love identifies me with Himself. But if He sends His own Love, Himself, to act and love in me and in all that I do, then I shall be transformed, I shall discover who I am and shall possess my true identity by losing myself in Him. And that is

---

22. See *NSC* 31: "For me to be a saint means to be myself. Therefore the problem of sanctity and salvation is in fact the problem of finding out who I am and of discovering my true self."

what is called sanctity" (*NSC* 63). Spouses, by virtue of their calling to the married life and the encounter of God experienced in love, help each other to discover their true selves and become saints. Merton explains, "[W]e must come to recognize that the married state is also most sanctifying by its very nature, and it may, accidentally, imply sacrifices and a self-forgetfulness that, in particular cases, would be even more effective than the sacrifices of religious life" (*LH* 7). This notion of intrinsic means toward sanctity is true not only of typical forms of prayer and contemplation within the marital relationship, but in the physical and sexual exchange of love proper to the married life. Merton sees in the physicality of married life a gift from God that is a complementary characteristic or means to sanctity. He writes: "The existence of a sacrament of matrimony shows that the Church neither considers the body evil nor repugnant, but that the 'flesh' spiritualized by prayer and the Holy Ghost, yet remaining completely physical, can come to play an important part in our sanctification" (*NMI* 99-100). That's right, sexual expression of love within marriage is not only necessary (as a distorted Christian view might suggest because of the utility of procreation), but it is an actual contribution toward the spouses becoming saints. Elsewhere Merton reiterates this point, writing that "in authentic married love, two persons become not merely well-adjusted sexual partners, but they complete one another spiritually, they bring meaning and fulfillment to one another's lives by a unity which cannot be accounted for by the human and biological needs of the natural species."[23] In other words, marital sexuality is not simply the natural response of two adult human beings, but within the marriage precisely as *sacrament*, it becomes an expression of love and spirituality between the two mutually self-giving spouses. In effect, the physical expression of love shared by the couple is a symbol of God's unbounded love for humanity in creation.

Yet the physical, emotional and spiritual expression of sexual love shared by the married couple is not where the vocation of marriage and the encounter with God end. On the contrary, Merton believes that this love between spouses, emblematic of God's love for humanity in creation often illustrated theologically by Christ and the Church, should spill over into the world in concrete and charitable actions. Christian spouses live out their vocation and invite others to experience the loving, compassionate and self-giving face of God through their interactions in society and with others. This way of living in the world begins, however, within the marriage. Lawrence Martone picks up on this aspect of Merton's outlook in connecting marital commitment and relationship with that

---

23. Thomas Merton, *Redeeming the Time* (London: Burns and Oates, 1966) 57.

of the broader communal commitment that comes with baptism into the Body of Christ. The "marital and communal commitment each demand an other-directed spirituality wherein one shares the cross of the other. By concentrating on another's needs, one loses sight of his or her own individual problems. Merton suggests that the burden of the cross in relationships is negligible compared to carrying around the weight of one's own problems" (Martone 109). Martone's reading of Merton's insight suggests that it is in the day-to-day practice of Christian discipleship on the level of the spousal relationship that enables married individuals to develop what he calls "other-directed spirituality."

While the foundation of becoming a saint is located in the exhortation that "Every Christian is therefore called to sanctity and union with Christ, by keeping the commandments of God" (*LH* 4), Merton makes it clear in *Life and Holiness* as well as in other texts that Christian life is not limited to an individualistic union of one person and God. Similarly, Christian life cannot be authentically lived in a union of a married couple and God alone, but, as mentioned above, the love shared between the spouses should impel them to reach out in relationship to others.

The question naturally arises: *how* does one live out this life toward holiness? In what way or method can spouses reach out in relationship to others? Merton responds to this inquiry with some thoughts about the "methodology" of sanctity, noting from the outset that no concrete "method" exists (one, for example, can think of the myriad iterations of sanctity modeled by the canonized saints).

> The Christian "method" is then not a complex set of ritual observances and ascetic practices. It is above all an ethic of spontaneous charity, dictated by the objective relationship between the Christian and his brother. And every man is, to the Christian, in some sense a brother. Some are actually and visibly members of the Body of Christ. But all men are potentially members of that body, and who can say with certainty that the non-Catholic or the non-Christian is not in some hidden way justified by the indwelling Spirit of God and hence, though not visibly and obviously, a true brother "in Christ"? (*LH* 42-43)

In other words, there is no hard and fast method for Christian living other than charitably serving the needs of all whom a Christian encounters. At a time when the general Catholic disposition to non-Catholics and non-Christians more broadly was incredulous if not dismissive, Merton sought to expand the horizon of Christian action, positing the Gospel's universal law of love as the means to holiness in all places and when encountering all people.

> The will of God is therefore manifested to the Christian above all in the commandment to love. . . . This is the only ascetic "method" which Christ has given us in the Gospels: that all should show themselves his friends by being friends of one another, and by loving even their enemies (Mt. 5:43-48). If they should always behave in a spirit of sacrifice, patience, and meekness even toward the unjust and the violent, Christians are all the more strongly obligated to be charitable and kind to one another, never using vicious and insulting language toward one another (Mt. 5:20-26). (*LH* 43-44)

Merton makes clear that his reading of the Gospel according to Matthew, as well as the rest of Scripture, offers Christians a clear injunction toward living in the world, even if Christ does not make, and really could not make, explicit provisions for every instance a person might encounter on the pilgrimage of life.

At the heart of Christian life, then, is the realization that "we are all bound to seek not only our own good, but the good of others," and that "The whole Christian life is then an interrelationship between members of a body unified by supernatural charity, that is by the action of the Holy Spirit, making us all one in Christ" (*LH* 45). The notion that one cannot save one's self is not only an anti-Pelagian warning, but a recognition that every Christian's journey toward becoming a saint is centered on relationship with and within the *entire* Body of Christ, which Merton expands beyond the baptized to include all human persons.

In marriage the spouses recognize this command of love first and foremost with each other. As stated above, it is the love that is shared in the commitment to live out the vocation to which God has called the couple and the experience of the divine that takes place in the relationship that should lead toward the world and not simply end inwardly in marital isolation. Love and joy are naturally directed *ad extra*: their expression cannot be contained if it is a genuine experience of God's grace. What begins in marriage carries over to every aspect of the spouses' lives, which is how Merton explains the progression of Christian discipleship in the world. Merton writes that the Holy Spirit "leads us to the most perfect observance of [the law of love], to the loving fulfillment of all our duties, in the family, in our work, in our chosen way of life, in our social relationships, in civic life, in our prayer, and in the intimate conversation with God in the depths of our souls" (*LH* 38). Therefore, every aspect of life is transformed by the law of love, which, in the case of two spouses, originates and is nurtured in the sacrament of marriage.

Spouses are called to minister to each other, encouraging and supporting the other along the journey, while also being mindful to exhort and challenge the other when necessary. Just as the spouses are the ministers of the sacrament of matrimony, their ministry does not end after the exchange of vows, but commences in that rite and continues through life. Their goal is the same: to become saints. Their becoming saints begins and returns to their covenantal relationship, for it is the privileged place of encounter with God and the response to God's invitation to follow Christ in a unique way in the world.

Conclusion: No Spouse Is an Island

The title for this paper is of course an adaptation of the title of Merton's best-selling book, *No Man Is an Island*. His book's title, though, is explained only briefly in the text itself and it is in that explanation that Merton's contribution toward a contemporary spirituality of marriage can best be understood. Merton writes:

> And since no man is an island, since we all depend on one another, I cannot work out God's will in my own life unless I also consciously help other men to work out His will in theirs. His will, then, is our sanctification, our transformation in Christ, our deeper and fuller integration with other men. And this integration results not in the absorption and disappearance of our own personality, but in its affirmation and its perfection. (*NMI* 64)

The contribution that Merton makes toward a contemporary spirituality of marriage is the threefold identification of the particular instantiation of the Christian life of discipleship and love experienced in the sacrament shared by two spouses. This spirituality of marriage begins with the recognition and embrace of a divine call, an invitation from God to live a certain way in the world. It includes the realization that God in Christ is most immediately and primarily encountered in the marital relationship and expressed in the love shared by the spouses for each other. It culminates in what Martone calls "other-directed spirituality," or the living of Christian discipleship of charity, service, forgiveness and concern for all people. The whole flow of these three elements is not necessarily linear, but instead represents an interrelated matrix that moves in and out from each aspect of the marital relationship.

At the core of any contemporary spirituality of marriage is the acknowledgement that indeed no spouse is an island. Marriage is not something into which one person enters individually, but instead is a joint vocation to follow Christ in intimate partnership in the world. Marriage is not something devoid of or removed from God, but is in fact the location where a spouse can encounter the divine most immediately. Marriage is not an end in itself nor is it a self-enclosed partnership, but is the very means by which two spouses become saints through moving outward into the world to live a life of Christian love-in-praxis rooted in the shared spousal experience of Christian love.

There remains much work to be done in the area of developing a Christian spirituality of marriage that responds to the needs of women and men in our age. There are indeed seeds that we can discover planted deep within the Christian tradition and in the thought of contemporary spiritual writers and theologians. Thomas Merton offers us three themes, the depth of each of which could not completely be examined in this paper, but they have been introduced so as to offer a heuristic guide for further consideration of the twentieth-century Trappist monk's wisdom for a new time and audience. It is my hope that any future spirituality of marriage take seriously Merton's insights, which lead to the assertion that marriage is a legitimate vocation, the privileged place for spouses to encounter the divine and the primary means by which a married couple become the saints God has called them to be.

The Soul-Rich Monk/Priest:
Thomas Merton on *Lectio Divina*

Mary Murray McDonald

Has there ever been a time when we have been graced with such a great number of resources on *lectio divina*? Wonderful books by writers such as Michael Casey, Basil Pennington, Raymond Studzinski, Norvene Vest and so many more authors are most often directed toward lay persons and now even toward children.[1] They translate in great detail the four movements of Guigo the Carthusian and how best to begin this ancient form of prayer.[2] What a wonder, then, to see Thomas Merton in an unpublished manuscript on the subject go straight toward a very complicated and rich example.[3] He addresses a different audience, yet this difference allows us to see the rich world of the monk/priest and encourages us to enter into the mysteries of our faith with great respect, reverence and joy.

This manuscript, according to Merton Center Archivist Mark Meade, was found filed with a chapter on faith published in *Seeds of Contemplation*,[4] but there is no date on the manuscript itself. It is divided into two parts: the first where Merton outlines the subject of reading in general to a very wide audience, and the second where he considers exclusively *lectio divina*. Both are written in an outline format which would make the 1949 date credible as they are most likely lecture notes for his teaching monks studying to be priests.

Merton cared deeply about these future priests and gave them the

---

1. Michael Casey, *Sacred Reading* (Liguori, MO: Liguori, 1997); Basil Pennington, *Lectio Divina* (New York: Crossroad, 1998); Raymond Studzinski, *Reading to Live* (Collegeville, MN: Liturgical Press, 2009); Norvene Vest, *No Moment Too Small* (Boston: Cowley, 1994).

2. Reading (understanding the literal meaning), meditating (applying the reading to one's life), praying (for oneself and others), contemplating (resting in the words and in God). For Merton's own discussion of Guigo's work see "Appendix I: The *Scala Claustralium* " in Thomas Merton, *An Introduction to Christian Mysticism: Initiation into the Monastic Tradition* 3, ed. Patrick F. O'Connell (Kalamazoo, MI: Cistercian Publications, 2008) 332-40.

3. Thomas Merton, "*Lectio Divina* I & II" (archives, Thomas Merton Center, Bellarmine University Louisville, KY, n.d.) 1-33; subsequent references will be cited as "'*LD*'" parenthetically in the text (used with permission from the Thomas Merton Center and the Merton Legacy Trust).

4. Thomas Merton, *Seeds of Contemplation* (New York: New Directions, 1949) 77-82.

richest possible picture of what *lectio divina* can do – an analysis of the readings they would encounter on Septuagesima Sunday, which offers a whole, beautiful, enigmatic picture of salvation history. These students were taught by Merton to see the full spectrum of our salvation, as they had such a great task ahead of them through their lives of prayer and sacrifice. His view of *lectio divina* offers us a glimpse of how deeply he lived his faith.

His views offer some challenges to our understanding of *lectio divina* by virtue of their being offered to prospective priests and not to lay people: *lectio divina* was both public and private for Merton, and it meant the Mass and participation in the Mass. For Merton scholars, it is with great delight that we see him teaching the literary aspects of Scripture and even a deep acknowledgement and reverence for the words themselves. The manuscript as a whole ranges from general advice on reading to reverence for particular words themselves. How very much like Merton the poet and monk to isolate the most essential parts of *lectio divina* for the future priests alongside the literary fine points. His own appreciation and love for Scripture and prayer is apparent.

Septuagesima Sunday

In the traditional liturgical calendar, the third Sunday before Lent was referred to as Septuagesima Sunday, and, though scholars still cannot figure out why the term was used, as it is not literally seventy days before Easter, this particular Sunday offers a mindset for preparation for Lent. Its first mention is found in the Gelasian Sacramentary from the eighth century; in 1969 it was removed from the liturgical calendar. It sets our eyes on Easter, with the awareness that we will soon enter into a period of repentance through fasting, abstinence, prayer, almsgiving and acts of charity.

The history of this day Merton refers to as a function of the early Roman Church meeting the Oriental Church:

> 1) Under the influence of the Oriental Church, which had moved the beginning of the Lenten fast back to the opening of their liturgical year, the Church of Rome adopts the pre-Lenten liturgy. The reading of the creation narrative from Genesis springs from this fact.
>
> 2) When the Office and Mass were composed, the Church herself was in anguish. The political situation of the West, ravaged by wave after wave of barbarian invasions, was desperate. Everyone believed that the end had come. The sorrow and near-despair of a society pushed to the limit of endurance makes itself felt in this Office. This

extrinsic factor was used by the Holy Spirit to give a special fruitful-
ness to the Church's meditation of Scripture in this Office.

In doing so, the Church wrote an Office that admirably expresses
the sentiments of our own day.

Septuagesima is for us, par excellence, a starting point from which
we enter into the great Easter mystery. ("*LD*" 29)

Merton's emphasis is on the participation of the monk/priest in liturgy as
the purpose of *lectio divina*.

Merton's Teachings on *Lectio Divina*

What did Merton want these monk/priests to know about *lectio divina*?
Chiefly two things: first, that the reading of Scripture had primacy in this
ancient practice of prayer, and, second, that they were not conducting this
kind of prayer alone but rather within the Church, and they had to know
how and why the Church prays as she does.

The Primacy of Scripture

Merton begins by saying that his first section, on reading, is just a preparation for his discussion of *lectio divina*: "Only the reading of the Scriptures,
or at least reading which helps to penetrate God's revelation of Himself
in Scripture, can properly and strictly merit the name of *lectio divina*,
according to the monastic tradition" ("*LD*" 18); and further, "The Bible is
the only book in which God Himself has told us, in His own words, and
in detail, the way to sanctity, the way to contemplation, the way to union
with Him. Most of all, the Bible gives us God's own authentic way of
telling us Who He Himself is" ("*LD*" 20).

He insists that every Catholic should read Scripture: "The Catholic
must, then, be able in some way to read the Bible as his book, as a book
which, though often obscure, disconcerting, and difficult, will often
unexpectedly reveal its mysteries to the very depth of his being, so as to
change his whole life in its inmost depths and turn him anew to God"
("*LD*" 25). He says that, "When we read Scripture, with faith and in
union with the Church, the Holy Spirit gives the words of His revelation
a special dynamic force in our lives. He makes them 'living and efficacious,' penetrating with a spiritual action into the very deepest recesses
of our being, and opening our hearts to the sanctifying and illuminating
power of God, present in mystery" ("*LD*" 19).

Merton does a fair amount of refuting ideas surrounding the reading
of Scripture, and these take the form of objections and replies. In short,
despite all objections to seeing Scripture as the best reading for us, Merton

notes that "God willed, precisely, that His will for our sanctification should be revealed in this disconcerting way – by the history of His mysterious action in a world of sin" (*"LD"* 22); and "In a word, we cannot fully understand Scripture without the help of the Holy Spirit" (*"LD"* 24).

How the Church Prays

Merton makes the point that "the Church, before she teaches, first lives and meditates the great mysteries which she proclaims in her mysteries. The Catholic reads the Scriptures, not on his own (although they should indeed form the chief part of his private spiritual reading), but as a member of a community divinely enlightened and guided by the Holy Spirit" (*"LD"* 24). Here are the points that Merton makes for the monk/priests: "the Church selects special readings and appoints that they be read in connection with certain great mysteries" (*"LD"* 25); "Then the Church relates certain texts to one another, by placing them together in the same Office. . . . [V]ery special lessons are learned, which would otherwise never strike us" (*"LD"* 25); "the Church also intersperses the lessons of Scripture with antiphons, responsories, graduals, capitula, and other liturgical texts which use or adapt the scriptural themes of the Office in such a way as to reveal yet more of the liturgical mystery being celebrated" (*"LD"* 26); "The Church comments directly on Scripture texts" (referring to nocturns) (*"LD"* 26); "The moral implications and consequences of the mystery are usually brought out by an appropriate epistle in the Mass, or by lessons in the Nocturns" (*"LD"* 26); and finally, he mentions that "Offices are not always systematically put together, and sometimes the original arrangement of texts has been perverted or lost, so that in fact the texts not rarely have little real connection with one another, and the liturgists who find such connections are just exercising their pious imagination" (*"LD"* 26).

The Liturgy as the Highest Form of Lectio Divina

Merton understands the use of Scripture in liturgy as the Church's way "to adore God" (*"LD"* 26). The greatest use of *lectio divina*, according to Merton, is to "enter into the mystery in participation with Christ Himself, and . . . grasp the meaning of the sacred texts precisely in their relation to the act which He accomplishes, here and now, in the liturgical mystery!" (*"LD"* 27). He adds, "It is an awareness, an experience of the inmost reality of what is hidden in the words of Scripture in the liturgical text, and this awareness is arrived at by participation, through the Holy Spirit, in the mind of Christ, the mind of the Church" (*"LD"* 27). Finally, "Hence in a completely unique and incomparable manner, reading and chanting the inspired text in the liturgical celebration of the sacred mysteries, we enter into a union with Christ which reveals to us His presence in us, as a community and as individuals, our presence in Him, and last of all our union, through Him, with the Father" (*"LD"* 28).

Merton's Poetic Eye on the Readings for Septuagesima Sunday

To Merton, the beauty and literary aspects of Scripture are a symphony. He teaches monks to hear not just the message, but the cadences and tensions among the readings. He writes,

> The lessons begin with the beautiful, limpid sentences of Genesis. "In the beginning God made heaven and the earth . . . ." The responsories take the same tone. But in the II Nocturn, St. Augustine comes out with sad and thundering periods [a Latin rhetorical device] on sin. (Each of the first two lessons is made up of one long sentence.) These build up to a terrible climax of the whole "massa damnata" of the human race being carried away to hell with the rebellious angels. But it ends with a comforting thought that "God judged it better to make a good use of evil that [*sic*] to allow no evil to exist." (*"LD"* 31)

He lists more terrifying juxtapositions – the gospel of the workers in the vineyard (Mt. 20:1-16), St. Gregory's homily on "different ages of the world," the "frightening words" from the Gospel "Many are called, but few are chosen" (Mt. 22:14), and Paul's reminder in 1 Corinthians 9 that only Caleb and Joshua reached the Promised Land. Analyzing the group of readings, he says that "The combined effect of all these texts is not sadness or depression, but hope, confidence (together with compunction and sorrow). In the Church, even sorrow has a dynamic and constructive purpose" (*"LD"* 30).

After these readings, he tackles the responsories of the first nocturn, noting "all sorts of implied resonances from the Greek Fathers and St. Augustine" (*"LD"* 32). These four responsories, according to Merton, "give the clue to what the Church is thinking about the Genesis narrative" (*"LD"* 32). The emphasis Merton gives is that man was created good ("all things were very good"; "to His image and likeness"; "breathed with His own breath of life upon him"). In the third responsory, Merton notes that we should see the "Patristic doctrine on man being created for contemplation and rest in God" (*"LD"* 32) when we read that God rested on the seventh day.

In the last section, he turns to the readings of the second nocturn with their direct contrast: "'Mortis supplicium' – man is threatened with condemnation to death" (*"LD"* 32). Referring back to Genesis, the first responsory notes Adam's need to work and remain in paradise, and the second to the tree of life. The third "says quietly, 'It is not good for man to be alone – let us make him a helper like unto himself.' (And this is repeated.) How rich in surprising implications!!" (*"LD"* 33).

The second part on *lectio divina* ends here, although five further pages, single-spaced, refer to other texts on understanding Scripture and the power of Scripture. These pages were probably added later, as he draws from a book by Romano Guardini published in 1955, *Meditations before Mass*,[5] that emphasizes reverence for the words of Scripture themselves as selected by God. After passages from Guardini, Merton allows Scripture verses to pile up as if what he began in general advice ends in allowing Scripture to speak for itself.

Lectio Divina Notes as a Rhizome

While Merton's message may surprise readers in its emphasis on the intensity of the experience of *lectio divina*, particularly in Mass, his perspective that was shared with only monk/priests clarifies later works of Merton and can be seen as Merton's base for understanding how to pray as a Cistercian – like a plant's energy source, or rhizome, this piece stores the energy for his future growth.

The most poignant rendering of the message of the *"Lectio Divina"* notes is found in the posthumously published *Opening the Bible*, giving the exact same message of the need to understand the full message of Scripture, only using Faulkner to reach a wider set of readers. The *Sound and the Fury*, Merton writes, is "a modern work of art in which the experience of 'hearing the word' is described";[6] "The entire congregation responds to a sermon which, in its own crude and lovely poetry, condenses into a few moments the whole history of salvation – the whole Christian message about the meaning of life in love, redemption, reconciliation" (*OB* 47). With the monk/priests, he can revel in the beauty of Scripture, the daily monastic readings, and the saints; with the general public, he turned to a work of literature. Merton revealed his experience of *lectio divina* prayer in the notes, and then shared it with the world more quietly and less personally in *Opening the Bible*, *Bread in the Wilderness* and *Praying the Psalms*.

We watch his experience with *lectio* fan out in *Bread in the Wilder-*

---

5. Romano Guardini, *Meditations before Mass*, trans. Elinor Castendyk Briefs (Westminster, MD: Newman Press, 1955).

6. Thomas Merton, *Opening the Bible* (Collegeville, MN: Liturgical Press, 1970) 42; subsequent references will be cited as *"OB"* parenthetically in the text.

ness[7] and *Praying the Psalms.*[8] *Bread in the Wilderness* takes ideas from the notes and fully explains them, such as the acceptance of suffering and the presence of the Holy Spirit helping us to understand Scripture. The *"Lectio Divina"* notes most likely paved the way for *Bread in the Wilderness.* The pamphlet *Praying the Psalms* offers many of the same principles from the notes, such as the need for active participation in praying them, the need to pray and live them at a very deep level, and the reading of the psalms as leading us to contemplation. In both books, he offers readers tips on reading, which he does in great detail in the first part of the notes. What changes in these books are the references; whereas the notes reveal Merton's own priestly experience with *lectio*, the subsequent books offer more general examples of literary figures and theologians. The message itself does not change.

The second and third volumes of Merton's journals span the years these notes and these latter books were written, a range from 1949 through 1960. The tone of the notes and of the second volume is similar in that Merton conveys in 1949 that he was "in a big hurry to show all my treasures" to his students.[9] He also relates in June, 1951 that he himself has been changed the most due to his teachings: "The one who is going to be most fully formed . . . is [me]. . . . I am a grown-up monk and have no time for anything but the essentials. The only essential is not an idea or an ideal: it is God Himself, Who cannot be found by weighing the present against the future or the past, but only by sinking into the heart of the present as it is" (*ES* 460). In these comments, we hear Merton's gravity gained from the intense experience he has revealed in his notes.

In the third volume,[10] Merton often considers psychological aspects of his personality and the day-to-day life of the monastery much more than his own monastic formation; thus the notes were probably written sometime between 1949 and 1952. The reference to the Guardini volume that was published in 1955 looks like an addition to these notes – markedly different in appearance and subject matter.

---

7. Thomas Merton, *Bread in the Wilderness* (New York: New Directions, 1953).

8. Thomas Merton, *Praying the Psalms* (Collegeville, MN: Liturgical Press, 1956).

9. Thomas Merton, *Entering the Silence: Becoming a Monk and Writer. Journals, vol. 2: 1941-1952*, ed. Jonathan Montaldo (San Francisco: HarperCollins, 1996) 381; subsequent references will be cited as *"ES"* parenthetically in the text.

10. Thomas Merton, *A Search for Solitude: Pursuing the Monk's True Life. Journals, vol. 3: 1952-1960*, ed. Lawrence S. Cunningham (San Francisco: HarperCollins, 1996).

Conclusion

If this unpublished manuscript tells us anything about Merton, it is how respectfully and joyfully he understood and lived his priestly role. His teachings reached the men and women who are abbots and abbesses today all over the world. The arrangement of the notes from general to specific shows great respect for his students; his imagination working with the immense variety of Scriptural passages allowed his students to develop not only a way of prayer but a poetic imagination as well. Merton may have said he outgrew a pious earlier self; however, these notes provide a glimpse at how solid the foundation was that supported his later works.

2011 Bibliographic Review
Pointing Fingers at the Calm Eye of the Storm

Joseph Quinn Raab

Introduction

Superstorm Sandy has struck, flooding huge swaths of land, taking lives, destroying homes, and countless folks on the eastern seaboard are still without power as I write this. Like a mantra, Merton's words from Bangkok, "You cannot rely on structures,"[1] keep hammering in my head. Of course, we must rely on each other and to a lesser degree on the structures we create. Yet sometimes forceful events remind us that such reliance is fragile and tentatively placed. Upon what can we rely? What refuge, what ark, what invisible lifeboat keeps hope afloat in such times? Merton was never short of words on these questions, assuring himself and his readers that it was "neither a what nor a thing" upon which we could ultimately rely. Rather, his words were pointing to Christ and His Peace – a peace that the world cannot give. His words were always pointing. As the old Zen saying goes: "all instruction is but a finger pointing and those whose gaze is fixed upon the pointer will never see beyond." It's consoling to discover that those who continue to write about Merton, and those just beginning to, generally portray Merton as a "finger pointing" and help us to follow the trajectory of that pointing. Gladly, few get too fixated on the dirt under the fingernail.

Wading through what seems a flood of materials about Merton published in 2011, I began to think of Merton as analogous to the weather. In his prophetic voice, he was a rage of lightning-flash epiphanies and thundering revelations, bursting in a deluge of baptismal words that could flood out evil and birth new life. In his contemplative voice, words like gentle rains nourished faith and opened petals of promise; the raging storm quieted, leaving only the silent and central Word of that Love that is hidden and shining everywhere. At his best, Merton's literary life was either a raging storm whose calm eye is Christ or a playful, sapiential shower. At his worst, Merton felt his voice could turn petty or defensive or "verbological" and obscure the center – his words pointing too much to himself or to some other distracting triviality. The same can be said of the words written about him. Some of them stingingly convict, clarify

---

1. Thomas Merton, *The Asian Journal*, ed. Naomi Burton Stone, Brother Patrick Hart and James Laughlin (New York: New Directions, 1973) 338.

and reveal, some obfuscate and blur, but still through these words one can glimpse the calm eye shining at Merton's own center, the wisdom at play in the rain of his words – the better ones just make it easier.

Books[2]

John Eudes Bamberger, OCSO once commented on Merton's wide appeal, suggesting that when people read Merton they find him speaking from within themselves, as if Merton were giving voice to their most intimate thoughts. I recalled this comment when reading Fiona Gardner's *Precious Thoughts: Daily Readings from the Correspondence of Thomas Merton* (London: Darton, Longman & Todd, 2011). Here Merton, through Gardner's expert editing, gives voice to some of our deepest longings and most dearly held truths, but he also speaks *to us* with words we need to hear. At times I felt that the jewels that Gardner had lifted from Merton's copious correspondences were really addressed to me. Of course this was her intent and she admirably succeeds in this little book. With Merton, Gardner clearly desires "to gradually lift us toward divinity" and she has selected some precious thoughts that do just that (12).

Kenneth Bragan, in his book *The Making of a Saint: A Psychological Study of the Life of Thomas Merton* (Durham, CT: Strategic Book Group, 2011), is interested in how writing functioned for Merton as a means to becoming a spiritual master. But Bragan's central thesis, that Merton's falling in love with the nurse marked *the pinnacle* of his spiritual journey, is ultimately reductive and not effectively tied to his broader theme of writing as a means to spiritual maturity. Undoubtedly, Merton's affair is a significant piece of his overall story, but to emphasize it to the extent that Bragan does requires a forced reading. Bragan would certainly arrive at a more substantive understanding of Merton's embrace of the *anima* if he were to contextualize that embrace in a theological rather than a Jungian and Freudian paradigm. The latter can be useful to be sure, but if one wants to argue that Merton had become "a saint," one might need to venture into a theological or transcendent horizon, to follow Merton's pointed finger even further.

Several other books appeared during 2011 in which Merton receives significant attention, ranging in topics from art to interreligious dialogue. These include *Profiles in Discipleship: Stories of Faith and Courage* by

---

2. Books that receive individual reviews in this volume of *The Merton Annual* will not be considered in this essay. Likewise, though Monica Weis's *The Environmental Vision of Thomas Merton* (Lexington: University Press of Kentucky) was published in 2011, it was the subject of a review symposium in the previous volume of *The Merton Annual* (24 [2011] 281-323) and so will not be reviewed herein.

Gregory C. Higgins (New York: Paulist Press, 2011); *Peace Be with You: Monastic Wisdom for a Terror-Filled World* by David Carlson (Nashville, TN: Thomas Nelson, 2011); Joseph Masheck's *Texts On (Texts On) Art* (Berkeley, CA: Brooklyn Rail and Black Square Editions, 2011); and *The Third Desert: The Story of Monastic Interreligious Dialogue* by Fabrice Blée (Collegeville, MN: Liturgical Press, 2011). In a chapter called "Strangers" in *Profiles in Discipleship* (57-75), Higgins reflects on Antony of the Desert, Mother Syncletica, John Cassian and Thomas Merton.   Here, Merton is lauded both for his capacity to discuss the spiritual life in compelling and accessible ways and for opening dialogue with other faith traditions on spiritual virtues such as humility and purity of heart.   David Carlson, a former Baptist who through an engagement with monastic sources and the Christian contemplative tradition found his way to Orthodox Christianity, brings us a compelling and thoughtful book of "Monastic Wisdom for a Terror-Filled World" (as the subtitle reads). Much of the book relays interviews Carlson conducted post-9/11 with members of contemplative orders about their reactions to that day and lessons learned in its wake.   Merton, whom Carlson had come to trust as a guide who tells "the uncommon truth," provides a constant hermeneutic lens for Carlson as he interprets the correspondences with contemporary monks and nuns.   I found the chapters on "9/11's Most Taboo Word – Forgiveness" and "The Death of Osama bin Laden and America's Via Dolorosa" challenging and wise. Merton would be delighted, I think, at the use that Carlson makes of Merton's prophetic voice. Joseph Masheck's fascinating book *Texts On (Texts On) Art* covers a lot of ground, astutely commenting on the work of modern artists, architects and theorists such as Matisse, Duchamp, Le Corbusier and Lacan.   Most of the material extends far beyond the realm of my own expertise; however, Merton's friend Ad Reinhardt is featured in two chapters.   One of those chapters explores the friendship of Merton and Reinhardt through the lens of Columbia's influence on both of them.   Mascheck, noted art critic, historian and professor, is himself a fellow Columbia graduate and later a Columbia professor.   This gives Masheck's perspective an unusual and welcome sympathy with both Merton and Reinhardt. Finally, in *The Third Desert*, Blée traces the official level of monastic interreligious dialogue, from its unofficial beginnings in the work of figures such as Merton, Bede Griffiths and Abishiktananda (Henri le Saux) through the official establishment of the Pontifical Council for Interreligious Dialogue, and various other conferences connected to specific monastic orders, in the wake of Vatican II.   In spite of the absence of a serious look at Benedict XVI's promotion of interreligious dialogue (Blée focuses much more on what precedes Benedict XVI), the book is an indispensable resource for scholars of this important area and anyone who wants to consider where Merton fits into the official trajectory of Catholicism's engagement with non-Christian religious traditions.

Articles

Ryan Scruggs pens a challenging and substantial exploration of Merton's theological position and method with respect to interreligious dialogue that avoids the two extremes of an insular and defensive apologetics on the one hand and a facile syncretism on the other. In "Faith Seeking Understanding: Theological Method in Thomas Merton's Interreligious Dialogue" (*Journal of Ecumenical Studies* 46.3 [Summer 2011] 411-26), Scruggs skillfully demonstrates how Merton, through a careful study of Karl Barth's explication of St. Anselm's *Proslogion*, settles on a position for dialogue "that seeks a common ground with the other and a *purpose* for dialogue that, already obscurely apprehending the truth in faith, seeks the joy of faith fully understood" (411).

In "Thomas Merton, Spiritual Identity, and Religious Dialogue: The Walls of New Freedom" (*Perspectives in Religious Studies* 38.2 [2011] 195-213), Bill Leonard travels familiar territory, examining Merton's life and works. Leonard, however, insightfully focuses in on Merton as a bridge between Catholicism and Protestantism, faith and action, peace and justice, and religious pluralism in the American context, both during Merton's own time and for us today. Especially fascinating in this piece is Leonard's look at Merton's assessment of the "genius and disaster" of the *sola fides* principle. Following Merton, Leonard elucidates how *sola fides* can lead to a truncated grasp of conversion, what he calls "conversionism," where the great problem becomes the salvation of the saved – or quoting Merton – "the salvation of those who, being good, think they have no further need to be saved and imagine their task is to make others 'good' like themselves" (208). This "conversionism" opposes a *conversio morum* that is an ongoing struggle for sanctity, a downward path into genuine humility. The culture-bound conversionism which mutes prophecy continues, Leonard suggests, "to haunt American evangelicalism" (208). Leonard concludes his piece with some thoughtful bullet points regarding Merton's lessons for us today.

Dennis Patrick O'Hara's "Thomas Merton and Thomas Berry: Reflections from a Parallel Universe," which was originally published in *The Merton Annual* 13 (2000) 222-34, reappeared in *Religion and Science: Critical Concepts in Religious Studies* edited by Sara Fletcher Harding and Nancy Morvillo (vol. 4 [New York: Routledge, 2011] 362-73). O'Hara's piece examines how the work of Merton and Berry parallel one another, sacralizing the universe and the Earth community through a Christocentrism that admits no divine afterthoughts. That is to say, the Incarnation is not understood as a response to sin, but as eternally willed and linked to creation itself. Therefore, the entire universe is being presently spoken in the Word and, as Merton put it in a letter to Rachel Carson, is "a transparent manifestation of the love of God . . . a paradise of His own wisdom, manifested in all its creatures, down to the tiniest, and in the most wonderful interrelationship between them."[3]

In "Legacies of Reading in the Late Poetry of Thomas Merton" (*Texas Studies in Literature and Language* 53.2 [Summer 2011] 115-37), Dustin Stewart examines two legacies that influenced Merton's reading and writing of poetry, one from Rainer Maria Rilke and the other from Roland Barthes. Rilke's hopeful vision is dialogical in nature, intends a reader, and owns then a responsibility to the reader. The other legacy, according to Stewart, stemming from Barthes' *Writing Degree Zero*,[4] is less concerned, or even hopeful about, an author's ability to write for someone else, or for a writer *to be read*. In this view, the author is solely responsible to the writing, since the reader doesn't read the poet but "just reads writing" and any pretension to ascendency on the part of the poet must be abandoned. This leaves the writer "anti-writing" in Merton's view. While this second legacy is surely helpful as a hermeneutical key to Merton's later poetry, Stewart persuasively concludes that Merton's later work, especially *The Geography of Lograire*, is influenced by both legacies and "invites the sort of appropriation that it also mourns" (127).

Paul Contino offers a powerful presentation of Merton's friendship with Czeslaw Milosz (1911-2004) in "Milosz and Merton at the Metropolis: The Corn of Wheat Bears Fruit in *Second Space*" (*Renascence* 63.3 [Spring 2011] 177-87). In Contino's presentation, Merton and Milosz reflect Dostoevsky's characters Alyosha and Ivan as the latter pair converse in a tavern called the Metropolis in *The Brothers Karamazov*. Through their deeply personal correspondence, Merton plays the Christ-centered Alyosha to Milosz's more cynical Ivan. In Contino's reading of their relationship, Merton may have planted seeds that help Milosz, long after Merton's death, to finally come around to a view much closer to Alyosha's than to Ivan's. Contino finds evidence for this fruition in

---

3. The full quotation O'Hara includes is much longer and is taken from Thomas Merton, *Witness to Freedom: Letters in Times of Crisis*, ed. William H. Shannon (New York: Farrar, Straus, Giroux, 1994) 71.

4. Roland Barthes, *Writing Degree Zero*, trans. Annette Lavers and Colin Smith (London: Jonathan Cape, 1967).

several of Milosz's poems that appear in *Second Space*.[5]

In the Eastertide edition of *The Merton Journal* (18.1 [2011]), we find several gems. "Another Kind of Trifling" (33-40), by former *Merton Journal* editor Gary Hall, explores some of the technological traps that lead us into various degrees of trifling, distracting us from a pure and singular desire. Merton, even early at the dawn of the information age, expressed concern that his own life was being cluttered up by trivialities and "pure trifling" and that these distractions were beginning to cloud his own work (33). Hall, reflecting on the ubiquitous role of screens in our lives, finds consolation and sober clarity in Merton's critique of our trifling, a critique that keeps us critically on guard against the disintegration that inevitably comes when we begin to define ourselves through our purchases and virtual avatars.

Three other pieces in the same issue are tied together by their meditation on the transformative power of silence: Nass Cannon's "Attending to the Presence of God: Thomas Merton and *Le Point Vierge*" (11-17); Fiona Gardner's "Being in the Dark: Explorations in Purification and Renewal" (20-26); and Paul Pearson's "Let Mercy Fall Like Rain: Thomas Merton and the Ox Mountain Parable" (42-49). Drawing from a wide swath of Merton's corpus, Cannon writes beautifully and freshly in a voice close to Merton's own: "Through grace we recover our true self by the work of Christ in us who transforms us by shrouding himself with the wounds of our sins." This transformative process, facilitated by long periods of silence, reveals the hiding place of God in us, "inaccessible to our meddling but realized by . . . the recovery of our innocence before God, [by which] we see through spiritual eyes that paradise is all around, that every point is equidistant to God, that God's light shines through the natural world, and a blazing light like a diamond resides in everyone" (13). In her piece, Fiona Gardner links ascetic discipline with mystical union. Drawing from Merton's poems, letters, journal writings, and even the more theoretical *Ascent to Truth*, she highlights a self-emptying withdrawal, even from *meaning*. This mystic path does not end in melancholic *asymbolia* but is rather an *acedia* opening to divine illumination. With her masterful facility, Gardner compellingly illustrates that "being in the heart of darkness" can awaken consolations and desolations but the "purification of the night" as the Ox Mountain Parable reminds us, "brings renewal with the dawn" (24). In his illuminating article, Paul Pearson, through a detailed study of Merton's life and writings in the late fifties and early sixties, elucidates Merton's changing conception of himself from an innocent to a guilty bystander and finally to a declared

---

5. Czeslaw Milosz, *Second Space: New Poems* (New York: HarperCollins, 2004).

witness to the mercy of God that like the night spirit and the dawn air in Mencius' parable saves us from a persistent *rhinoceritis*, that left alone, would lay waste to the world.

Dr. Pearson also published "Hospitality to the Stranger: Thomas Merton and St. Benedict's Exhortation to Welcome the Stranger as Christ" (*American Benedictine Review* 62.1 [March 2011] 27-41), in which he explores the relevance of this exhortation even for Merton the hermit, and the eremitical life more broadly. Pearson shows how Merton struggles to overcome a *fuga mundi* that would have him turn his back on the world and arrives at a welcoming disposition that allows the strangers of the world to be bearers to him and to us of God's mercy. As he writes in his conclusion: "we learn to do many of the things we were warned about as a child, using knives properly, driving a car, drinking a gin and tonic, but we find it much harder to overcome our fear of strangers and to be open to the gifts they bring us including, as St. Benedict tells us, the mercy of God" (39). This requires, as Pearson notes, the courage to risk having our hearts broken.

In the Advent edition of *The Merton Journal* (18:2 [2011]), John Collins shares a reflection on "Thomas Merton and *Siddhartha*" (32-42). The bulk of the article familiarizes the reader with Hermann Hesse and the influences operative upon him as he told the story of a man on a journey who finally realizes a perfect unity that spills out in compassion. Though Merton finished reading this novel just as he was embarking on his Asian journey to discover the absolute emptiness that is at once compassion, he does not comment on it at all in his journal. Collins, noting the congruencies of the fictional Siddhartha's epiphany and Merton's actual epiphany at Polonnaruwa, is emboldened to conjecture about the former's potential influence on the latter.

Jonathan Martin Ciraulo has given us a thoughtful and balanced analysis of "Thomas Merton's Creative (dis)Obedience" in *Cistercian Studies Quarterly* 46.2 (2011) 189-219. Ciraulo demonstrates how Merton struggled to submit both to his immediate religious superiors and the wider Church but still "developed a thoughtful spirituality of obedience that kept him faithful to his vows" (189-90). Most compelling is Ciraulo's depiction of Merton's growing admiration for the nineteenth-century "saintly Englishman" John Henry Cardinal Newman. By listening to Meriol Trevor's biography of Newman[6] as it was read aloud to the monks dur-

---

6. Ciraulo says the biography was Meriol Trevor's *Newman's Journey*, but that book first appeared in 1974 (St. Anthony Messenger Press); more likely it was Trevor's two-volume work: *Newman: The Pillar of the Cloud*; *Newman: Light in Winter* (London: Macmillan, 1962-63). Also possible, but less likely, is *Newman: A Portrait Restored*, which Trevor wrote

ing their silent meals, Merton drew strength from the theologian. Ciraulo includes this passage from Merton's July 9, 1965 journal entry:[7]

The Life of Newman, which still goes on in the refectory is to me inexhaustibly important and full of meaning. The whole thing is there, existentially not explicit, but there for the grasping. The reality is on his kind of obedience and his kind of refusal. Complete obedience to the Church and complete, albeit humble, refusal of the pride and chicanery of Churchmen. (210)

Through his essay, Ciraulo hopes to lift up Merton as a kind of model for those who struggle with fidelity, and with discerning to whom it is owed, in a Church worthy of our allegiance and yet in need of prophetic refusals of the sham and lies tied up with it.

Reaching a French-speaking audience, Dominique Brulé's "Thomas Merton: Une Biographie Spirituelle (1915-1941)," which appeared in *Collectanea Cisterciensia* 72 (2010) 385-404, employs Kierkegaard's vision of "purity of heart" as "the capacity to will one thing" as a lens to view Merton's route from seemingly aimless wandering to Catholicism, monasticism and then priesthood. Using material from *The Seven Storey Mountain* augmented by materials from Merton's personal journal entries, Brulé recounts the focusing of Merton's multidirectional and contradictory hungers into a singular desire to love Christ.

Christopher Pramuk, in his article "Wisdom, Our Sister: Thomas Merton's Reception of Russian Sophiology" (*Spiritus: A Journal of Christian Spirituality* 11.2 [Fall 2011] 177-99), brilliantly explores how Merton had internalized "a deep thread in the Christian East, namely the Sophia tradition of Russian Orthodoxy" (177). This article serves as a nice summative introduction to Pramuk's 2009 masterful work *Sophia: The Hidden Christ of Thomas Merton* (Collegeville, MN: Liturgical Press, 2009).

Two "dialogue" pieces from doctoral students also deserve mention. First, Joan Braune, a doctoral candidate at the University of Kentucky, published the interesting piece "Erich Fromm and Thomas Merton: Biophilia, Necrophilia, and Messianism" in *Fromm Forum* (English Edition, vol. 15 [Tuebingen: Selbtsverlag, 2011] 43-48).[8] Braune explores Fromm's biophilic messianism as articulated in his 1963 pamphlet *War Within Man* which includes critical responses from Merton and three

---

with A. M. Allchin and John Coulson (New York: Sheed and Ward, 1965).

    7. Thomas Merton, *Dancing in the Water of Life: Seeking Peace in the Hermitage. Journals, vol. 5: 1963-1965*, ed. Robert E. Daggy (San Francisco: HarperCollins, 1997) 266.

    8. Available online at: http://www.erich-fromm.de/biophil/joomla/images/stories/pdf-Dateien?Braune_J_2011.pdf.

others: psychoanalysts Roy Menninger and Jerome Frank and theologian Paul Tillich.[9] In Braune's view, only Merton gives Fromm a fair and favorable hearing and she explores Fromm's concepts of necrophilia and biophilia in light of Fromm's and Merton's long-time correspondence which she considers a model for Marxist-Christian dialogue. Secondly, Stefanie Hugh-Donovan, a doctoral student at Heythrop College, University of London, published "Ecclesial Thought and Life Trajectories: An Ecumenical Dialogue" (*One in Christ* 45.1 [2011] 35-53), in which she examines the parallels that obtain between Thomas Merton and the French Orthodox lay theologian Olivier Clément, who were both born in the Languedoc region of France and "journeyed through atheistic negation to a mature experience of Christian faith" (35). She explores how each was influenced by the Patristic tradition, Orthodoxy and iconography, arriving at "a faithful rootedness in his own ecclesial tradition with a deep respect for the 'other'" (35).

"Thomas Merton, An Artist of the Monastery" (*Benedictines* 63.1 [2010] 14-20) by psychologist and longtime Merton scholar Suzanne Zuercher, OSB, offers a brief and poignant reflection on Merton's perennial struggle against narcissism, his love-hate relationship with his artist self. In Zuercher's reading, Merton exemplifies the universal struggle we share to let God create us, to be the Artist of our lives, rather than "trying to be God in our lives, remaking ourselves into people we judge to be 'satisfactory'" (15). A contemplative discipline serves as a gracious antidote, and for Merton this led over time to increasing simplicity in his art, whereby his sketches and literary and photographic productions began to "speak peacefully and straightforwardly that their very existence is their justification. Just being is good" (20).

In a similar vein, Kick Bras's "Thomas Merton: Word from the Silence" (*Studies in Spirituality* 21 [2011] 261-71) explores Merton's essay "Day of a Stranger" and through his analysis of that piece suggests that "the man of language, the language artist" learned to listen to the silence and to give it expression in a language that does not "betray the experience of unity, that does not cause violence" and faithfully renders an expression of the "one central tonic note . . . *the* Word" (271).

In "Thomas Merton and Confucianism: Why the Contemplative Never Got the Religion Quite Right" (*First Things* [March 2011] 41-46), Confucian scholar Wm. Theodore de Bary considers why Merton's assessment of Confucianism, though generally positive, never rose to the level of appreciation that he had for Buddhism and Daoism, the two other great

9. Erich Fromm, *War Within Man: A Psychological Enquiry into the Roots of Destructiveness* (Philadelphia: American Friends Service Committee, 1963).

traditions that shaped China. Though Merton lauded what he called the "pure" Confucian ideal which was personalistic and humanistic, he was critical of a too worldly tendency within Confucianism, that was concerned with "making a living, raising a family and leaving a good name." On de Bary's reading, this Confucian concern did not jive well with Merton's personal history and his monastic vocation. A second and related reason de Bary finds for Merton not ranking Confucianism with the other two traditions stems from Merton's tendency to preference personal transformation and liberation as prior to social reform, something Confucianism resists, since it emphasizes the social constitution of personal identity. A third critique of Merton's lacking a grasp of Confucianism stems from Merton's less than thorough understanding of China's long history. In this insightful and substantive piece, de Bary also points out the irony of Merton's attraction to the Jesuit missionary Matteo Ricci, someone whom de Bary considers to have gotten Confucianism right, while in de Bary's expert opinion, Merton never quite did.

Another interesting piece is Patrick Henry Reardon's "A Many-Storied Monastic: A Critical Memoir of Thomas Merton at Gethsemani Abbey" (*Touchstone* [September/October 2011] 50-57). Reardon, who is now pastor of All Saints Antiochian Orthodox Church in Chicago, was one of the two monks at Gethsemani who recited the psalms for an hour in front of Merton's casket for the repose of his soul before the funeral Mass. In an honest and loving voice Reardon recalls what it was like learning from Merton and living with him for the last thirteen years of Merton's life. Without taking away from Merton's good name, indeed wanting to safeguard it against what he considers popular misinterpretations, he takes issue with both Edward Rice's and Monica Furlong's portrayals of Merton.[10] According to Reardon, Rice's remembrance led readers to the impression that Merton was becoming Buddhist and leaving Catholicism behind and Furlong unjustly portrayed Dom James Fox as a foil undermining rather than serving Merton's spiritual journey. Personally, however, Reardon was drawn to Merton the scholar of the Patristic period, expositor of Catholic monastic and contemplative tradition; he admittedly never appreciated or perhaps understood Merton's "great interest in non-biblical religions." He also admits that, although he was not in material disagreement with Merton's political activism, he "sort of [wishes] Merton had avoided it" (56).

Somewhat contrasting Reardon's wish, in the same journal we have

---

10. Edward Rice, *The Man in the Sycamore Tree: The Good Times and Hard Life of Thomas Merton* (Garden City, NY: Doubleday, 1970) and Monica Furlong, *Merton: A Biography* (San Francisco: Harper & Row, 1985).

"A Friendship of Letters: On the Correspondence between Thomas Merton and Dorothy Day" by Jim Forest, the peace activist, friend and biographer of both Merton and Dorothy Day (*Touchstone* [September/October 2011] 58-63). This piece is really a three-way conversation because Forest knows his two subjects so intimately and in many ways stands among them. By reviewing letters between these two "icons" of twentieth-century American Catholicism, Forest shows us both Day's iron-clad dedication to unrestricted loving service, and Merton's vacillating temperament, still wondering if he was doing enough, if he was where he ought to be. Day emerges as a trusted confidante with whom Merton can frankly express his vulnerability. There is a refreshing, earthy intimacy in their letters, and Forest helps us feel that we are not strangers to this friendship but somehow belong with them. I should note too that the editors of *U.S. Catholic* also published an "anonymous" interview with Jim Forest about his friendships with both Merton and Day and about the correspondence that is preserved between the latter pair ("Work Hard, Pray Hard," *U.S. Catholic* 76.11 [November 2011] 18-21).

John Dear, SJ stands in communion with the peacefully resistant spirit of Jim Forest, Dorothy Day and Thomas Merton. In many ways he stands on their shoulders. "Thomas Merton and the Wisdom of Non-Violence" (*Benedictines* 64.2 [Fall/Winter 2011] 18-27) is an accessible and profound essay in which Dear shares what he has learned, and what we can learn, from Thomas Merton about non-violence, the Peace of Christ and our duty to become apostles, visionaries and prophets of non-violence. Dear reminds us that if Merton could do so much for peace as a hermit in the woods, on the grounds of a cloistered monastery, those of us on the outside need to do what we can where we are, and Merton is a trustworthy guide for us.

In "Thomas Merton: A Study in Twentieth-Century Ambiguity" (*American Benedictine Review* 62.1 [2011] 103-11), Dominic Milroy, OSB offers a penetrating and honest reflection on the messy contradictions that raged within this creative genius. Milroy's piece was adapted from a talk he presented at a meeting of the Chevetogne Group, an informal group comprised of roughly twenty European monastic superiors, and the topic of the meeting was "fatherhood." Milroy was intrigued by the awkward distrust that characterized Merton's 1961 meeting with Fr. Jean Leclercq, who told Merton he was "a pessimist, too anxious and too negative" (104). From this beginning, Milroy examines a number of ambiguities in Merton's life, and sees them partly rooted in the fact that Merton was first an existentialist orphan, in search of a trustworthy ground, but always suspicious of authority. Milroy suggests that Leclercq's distrust of Merton stemmed from the fact that the former took for granted his whole life the benevolent fatherhood of God and the trustworthiness of superiors who reflected that. Milroy explores many facets here, but the deepest ambiguity he explores that Merton faced was the doubt about whether Merton really was a monk, or whether he was a journalist posing as a monk in order to write about the experiment. This essay shuns no question, and Milroy ends with an insightful comment and an interesting, albeit rhetorical question: "If he had a stronger sense of filial submission and of stability, he might have had fewer problems. But would he have been so creative?" (111).

The final piece to be considered in this essay gives Merton the last word. David M. Odorisio received a Shannon Fellowship in 2008 that provided him the support necessary to do the archival work that stands behind his article, "Thomas Merton's Novitiate Conferences on Philoxenos of Mabbug (April-June 1965): Philoxenos on the Foundations of the Spiritual Life and the Recovery of Simplicity" (*Hugoye: Journal of Syriac Studies* 13.2 [2010] 251-71). There are thirteen recorded conferences that Merton had given on Philoxenos and Odorisio's article publishes selections from four of these. The selections are preceded by an introduction by Odorisio that helps the reader locate the intersection of Merton's interest in Philoxenos and his interest in Zen. Merton's facility with connecting the wisdom of this desert father with the stories of Zen masters comes through in these conferences with humorous levity yet without ever losing a serious centeredness. The reader has the delightful experience of listening to Merton the teacher, of watching him point his finger, and trying to follow the pointing to the target Merton intends. As usual, the target Merton intends is humility, simplicity and an attendant singular focus on the divine Word speaking – the calm eye hidden and shining at the center of our often stormy lives.[11]

11. I wish to thank Melissa Sissen, Research Librarian at Siena Heights University, and Nathan Woods, Student Assistant to the Religious Studies Department, for their cheerful help in acquiring most of the materials reviewed in this essay.

Reviews

WILLIAMS, Rowan, *A Silent Action: Engagements with Thomas Merton*, Preface by Jim Forest, Afterword by Kallistos Ware (Louisville, KY: Fons Vitae, 2011), pp. 96. ISBN 978-189178578-8 (paper) $19.95.

This carefully revised group of essays does an excellent job of examining some of the tensions which Merton experienced as a writer who functioned on so many different levels from the poetic to the political. The gathering – Author's Foreword, five chapters and a poem, with a Preface by Jim Forest and an Afterword by Kallistos Ware – makes a compact collation of nine ways to ponder Merton and monasticism as a "provisional phenomenon," necessary "until the city is truly baptized" (25). It would be possible to argue only someone as well-known as Archbishop Rowan Williams could warrant such a specialized small book, yet in an important way these explorations, done over a period of almost forty years, are immensely valuable.

In the "Author's Foreword" (9-10), Williams focuses immediately on the gift of a writer whose skill was that he could assume so many poses. "Repeatedly, when you are inclined to exasperation at Merton's ability to dramatize himself in yet another set of borrowed clothes, you are brought up by his own clear-eyed acknowledgement that this is what he is doing" (9). The fact is, Williams' five essays and poem accomplish a similar kind of thing. Reading Merton from 1973 to 2011 allows this sophisticated interpreter to assume different roles as he encounters the changing Merton. I myself remember being given a copy of *Raids on the Unspeakable*[1] in December of 1966 and at first not quite knowing what to make of it. Now I perceive its timelessness, having reread that nonclassifiable book many times, because Merton could assume so many different roles there. It is lyrical, magisterial, personal, often surprising. It is a book about what Williams calls our "being-in-Christ" (31).

All of the best work of Merton, Williams wisely sees (early, in the 1948 autobiography, and later throughout the mature journals) is "like [that of so] many great religious poets and autobiographers, [used] to exorcise rather than indulge fantasy" (9). And so whenever one returns to Merton, the writing becomes both his personal record and a record cleansed of the personal. We can see his story as our story. Williams explains that

---

1. Thomas Merton, *Raids on the Unspeakable* (New York: New Directions, 1966).

Merton's gift, "a silent action," is to draw readers into his story so that his seeking of God becomes our story too.

Wisely chosen as authors of the "Preface" (11-13) and "Afterword" (87-89), Jim Forest and Kallistos Ware offer insights about how Merton provides ways of triangulating on big questions about poetry, contemplation and ecumenism by focusing on the particulars of language (11). Forest stresses that Williams, like Merton, regards the Christian life as incomplete "without a contemplative dimension." By looking at aspects of the contemplative life as fundamental ingredients in the Christian life, Merton informed us that "One of the major tasks of the contemplative life is the ongoing search for the actual self, the unmasked self, a self that is not merely the stage clothes and scripted sentences that we assemble and dutifully exhibit each day in the attempt to appear to be someone" (12). Forest alludes to the sacramental life and implies that in Merton we *all* (along with Williams) can possess a friendship. But like all friendship, this requires care and love and attention, and the longer one "knows" a friend the more valuable earlier insights become. Williams' poem, "Thomas Merton: summer 1966" (85), explores a time when Williams was sixteen. Placed at the conclusion of his text, it implies what a reader needs to know (in retrospect) about how each particular journey can be transformed into a universal one:

> . . . You spent my sixteenth birthday
> making a clean(ish) breast of things to the steel smile
> of Abbot James. You staged show after show
> for friends, then cancelled. Not to make sense is
> what most matters.

We therefore learn from this 2002 poem how Merton does keep on teaching.

A similar thing is said in the "Afterword" lovingly presented by Ware. In the words of a tale by Martin Buber, we are reminded that each person needs two pockets "so that he can reach into the one or the other, according to his needs. In his right pocket are to be the words: 'For my sake the world was created,' and in his left: 'I am earth and ashes'" (87). Ware's point, and Williams', is that Merton knew, sang, celebrated, in all kinds of verbal costumes, creation as wonderful mystery. As human beings, above all, we need always to remember both our uniqueness and God's mercy. I had the pleasure of hearing Kallistos Ware speak at an Ecumenical Prayer Gathering in Atlanta in 2010, and his talk about the difficulties of ecumenism and dialogue was united by metaphor about his travel. Williams, so open to traditions beyond his own, and Merton, an ecumenical pioneer, would have enjoyed that striking talk. With laughter, Ware remarked that he was thankful that at a recent Austrian ecumenical meeting heavy study briefcases were given to all the delegates. He held his up high for all to see and said, "We need these. . . . It will be a long journey" as we slowly learn to respect one another's traditions.

Williams and Merton, both intensely respectful of the mystery of God's love, as unfolded in language, know this. It is such wonder about mystery and linguistic accomplishment which is at the core of this group of essays. Williams' middle article, "'New Words for God': Contemplation and Religious Writing" (43-51), is central to the book's organization and to Rowan's insights. I heard this dense piece delivered in 1998 at the Meeting of the Thomas Merton Society of Great Britain and Ireland at Oakham. What strikes me, now, after rereading, it is how compacted it is – in the best sense – and, when I heard it delivered and discussed, how modest and self-deprecating Williams seemed to be. What Williams reminds us of is that poetry was exceedingly important for Merton because it allows the "self" of the artist to escape. Here Williams is celebrating "religious writing" as an activity fundamental to "allow truth, allow God" (47). We "see" God by forgetting about self.

Insights throughout these five essays continually demonstrate how Williams' engagements, open and ecumenical, provide an approach to Merton's monastic commitment to entering into wisdom. Williams is building a wedge to reposition our understanding. His critical acumen serves to move a sometimes opaque theory about contemplativeness (embedded in Merton's life-long fascination with language) into an illuminating tool which can transform our grasp of mysticism.

In Merton the gift for seeking to lose the false self can seem, at times, to be a fragile template for waiting. In other cases, it is a magnifying glass of trust, concentrating the rays of the givenness of this world into glimpses of the unfathomable Mystery of God's entry in humankind's history and consciousness. What Williams does is to celebrate Merton in such a way that we know we are also co-creators in this mystery of the self becoming ever more aware of the hiddenness of God within each person. Williams calls this pattern "the theme of the illusory self" (17).

The "illusory self" is the person we must keep forgetting, but the paradox remains that only through the "concrete and the historical" do we learn this mystery and truth of unknowing. In Williams' words, employing Merton's use of a Hindu writer on the function of poetry, "'to make us aware of . . . dharma,'" the poetic voice makes us aware that "There is no isolated, pure, and independent 'I,' but there is a vast and universal web of 'I's, in which I have a true and right place" (18). Merton's gift, then, is to show us he is learning to know his "real place" (19).

What Merton found of great value in pondering God's presence *via* Islam and thus to

> 'being a son of this instant' – in the phrase Merton adapts from Ibn Abbad – is encountering and entering into that elusive 'there before us' quality of God's action, that active reality – or indeed, to use the scholastic language which was not at all alien to Merton's thinking, that 'pure act' which is both beyond memory and fantasy. (47)

Such presence, too, is what Merton found so significantly examined in the Russian Orthodox theologians who informed his own study in the mid-sixties. Williams' doctoral mentor, and Merton's good friend, Donald Allchin, knew that in all Christian religions (Anglican, Catholic, Protestant, Orthodox) we celebrate the wonder of God's presence. It is so appropriate, therefore, that Allchin and Merton were together on that fateful day of Martin Luther King's assassination (see the interview in *The Merton Annual* 17[2]).

Williams wisely informs us that for Merton, and for all theologians open to mystery, an "attunement to the 'pure act' of God [is what] seems to be fundamental." Thus, to study the article "'Bread in the Wilderness': The Monastic Ideal in Thomas Merton and Paul Evdokimov" is a reward and revelation. Again, much is packed into this study, and Williams was doing this type of work (which grew out of his doctoral dissertation) in the middle 1970s, thirty-five years before Christopher Pramuk's *Sophia*.[3] Williams asserts: "Contemplation is not a religious exercise but an ontological necessity in the intense *personalism* of Christian faith, the encounter of the human person with the Divine Council of Persons" (30-31). The importance of this insight is a key for all of us to learn, and then to refuse to accept labels as well. Williams recognizes, as did Merton, that to see into the wonder and mercy of God one has, to some degree, to forget roles, rules and labels. This was also Merton's basic insight in his references to Karl Barth in *Conjectures*,[4] and thus to Williams' essay about God's pleasure in humankind. "'Not Being Serious': Thomas Merton and Karl Barth" (71-82) is a careful consideration of Merton's

---

2. "'A Very Disciplined Person' from Nelson County: An Interview with Canon A. M. Donald Allchin about Merton," conducted by Victor A. Kramer, edited by Glenn Crider, *The Merton Annual* 17 (2004) 235-55.

3. Christopher Pramuk, *Sophia: The Hidden Christ of Thomas Merton* (Collegeville, MN: Liturgical Press, 2009).

4. Thomas Merton, *Conjectures of a Guilty Bystander* (Garden City, NY: Doubleday, 1966) 3-4, 8-9, 10-11, 303-305, 311, 317-18.

many references to Barth and wisdom.

In these many essays Williams reminds us that for Merton to function well as a monk, in a very real sense he had to refuse "the *role* of 'monk' or 'artist'" (37). Then it begins to be possible to just be.

Perhaps the most insightful piece here is "'The Only Real City': Monasticism and Social Vision" (55-68), given as an address in 2004. Williams does an extended analysis of some related entries from *Turning Toward the World*[5] to demonstrate Merton's engagement with questions about responsibilities of the monk-writer within a world he triangulated upon by reading Hannah Arendt's *The Human Condition*.[6] Here Williams' point is that it is so easy for the monk (or any believer, or professional Christian writer) to forget about what language can do: "the difficulties Merton faces are very like those analysed so unforgettably by Bonheoffer in his prison letters; the words of faith are too well-known to believers for their meaning to be knowable" (65). Ultimately, Williams insists Merton knew he (we) had to be wary of language, yet only through language can we see what is real. Our first responsibility is to authenticity (see also 24-25).

This beautiful book will stimulate much good discussion. It is quite important that one of its motifs is examination of Merton's continuing skepticism about the effectiveness of religious language. It is therefore quite appropriate that the dust cover is a beautiful reproduction of the façade of Canterbury Cathedral "painted by Thomas Merton's father" and now "housed in the archives of the Thomas Merton Center at Bellarmine University" (back cover). What better way to suggest the immense power of art to communicate the strength of God who must remain a mystery we apprehend in silence?

Victor A. Kramer

DEKAR, Paul R., *Thomas Merton: Twentieth-Century Wisdom for Twenty-First-Century Living* (Eugene, OR: Cascade Books, 2011), pp. xviii + 242. ISBN 978-1-60608-970-5 (paper) $29.00.

Although Thomas Merton died decades before the Internet would become a household term, let alone a widespread commodity, before women, men and children would access nearly infinite amounts of information from just about anywhere thanks to "smartphone" technology, and before the

---

5. Thomas Merton, *Turning Toward the World: The Pivotal Years. Journals, vol. 4: 1960-1963*, ed. Victor A. Kramer (San Francisco: HarperCollins, 1996).

6. Hannah Arendt, *The Human Condition* (Chicago: University of Chicago Press, 1958).

truly overwhelming impact of globalization would finally take its inter-
cultural, trans-temporal and rapid toll, interest in the twentieth-century
monk's thought on technology continues to rise today. In recent years
conferences have been dedicated to Merton's thought on this theme and
continued applicability in this age (e.g., "Contemplation in a Technological Era: Thomas Merton's Insight for the Twenty-First Century" at
Bellarmine University in September 2011) and scholarly volumes have
been slated for the same purpose (e.g., *The Merton Annual* 24, based
largely on the Bellarmine conference). Paul Dekar's *Thomas Merton:
Twentieth-Century Wisdom for Twenty-First-Century Living* is among
the recent contributions to the field of Merton studies that take seriously
consideration of Merton's thought for a technologically advanced (and
saturated) world.

Dekar, emeritus professor of evangelism and mission at Memphis Theological Seminary, has written extensively in recent years on the so-called
"new monasticism" movement that has become somewhat popular within
certain Protestant and Catholic circles. Largely focused in urban areas and
centered on concerns of social justice and engaged spirituality, key figures
like Shane Claiborne and Jonathan Wilson-Hartgrove have led the way in
this correlative effort to retrieve the wisdom and model of Christian monastic
living of ages past for contemporary appropriation in entirely new social
settings. Rather than following the millennia-old structures of traditional
monastic communities, which sequester the lives of its members in a stable
cloister, the "new monastics" desire to live in the world (more akin to the
Catholic mendicant orders – Franciscans, Dominicans, Augustinians, etc.),
while also engaging in the spiritual exercises of the ancient monastic traditions (common prayer, liturgical worship, etc.).

One can see why Merton would be a logical resource in this effort.
Never before has a member of a traditional monastic community so widely
and publicly engaged with and influenced the popular culture. Merton's
writings have been and continue to be read by millions of Christians and
non-Christians alike, and his spirituality, worldview and social concern
were all deeply shaped by his own religious vocation and spiritual practices. Dekar recognizes this opportunity for engagement and inspiration,
centering his book on precisely this possibility. What Dekar sets out to
answer is the question that Paul Pearson, author of the volume's foreword,
succinctly presents at the opening of the book: "Merton's choice [to stay
in the monastery in the 1960s] begs the question for his readers of whether
it is possible for a voice from the monastic enclosure to speak to us here
in the new millennium? Can Merton's voice still speak to us?" (x).

The book opens with a presentation of Dekar's own social location and his experience teaching seminary students about monastic traditions (mostly Christian, but also some Buddhist). The captivation and interest that these contemporary, technophile students express about the practices and traditions of monastic living led Dekar to explore in a deeper way the possibility of a more sustained incorporation of these insights into his own life. The project here is one of a deeply personal tenor, expressed as such at the end of his introductory chapter: "Having experienced Merton's writings as a source of growth for myself and for many others, I now write for all persons seeking to enrich their lives, to find their place in the world, and to experience community" (9). In the chapter that follows, Dekar presents a necessarily brief biographical overview of Merton's life. It is, as one might imagine given the limitations of the space and the simple introductory character of the chapter, unavoidably idiosyncratic. Nevertheless (a few minor factual particularities aside) it is a sufficient overview for the uninitiated reader of Merton.

The major body of the book, which begins with chapter three and continues through the final chapter of the text, can be divided into two sections: Merton's thought and writing and Dekar's application of Merton's thought for twenty-first-century use. Chapters three through seven are Dekar's reading and presentation of Merton's thought on several themes: the monastic vocation (chapter three), the simplification of life (chapter four), technology (chapter five), environmental stewardship (chapter six) and violence (chapter seven). Structured in such a way as to ostensibly present the material as objectively as possible, Dekar adds a concluding section titled "Reflections" at the end of each of these chapters. This is not to suggest that Dekar always succeeds in avoiding editorializing in earlier sections of each chapter, but the effort to demarcate these two dimensions of content in a way analogous to some biblical commentaries that offer exegesis and then interpretation is a welcome convention.

Other authors have examined Merton's thought on the monastic vocation, simplicity and nonviolence previously, which leads me to suggest that the most valuable chapters by way of relatively new contributions to Merton scholarship are the two on technology and ecology. Although two recent monographs have also focused on these two themes (Phillip Thompson's *Returning to Reality: Thomas Merton's Wisdom for a Technological World* [1] and Monica Weis's *The Environmental Vision of Thomas Merton* [2]), Dekar's chapters are worthy of close reading.

---

1. Phillip M. Thompson, *Returning to Reality: Thomas Merton's Wisdom for a Technological World* (Eugene, OR: Cascade Books, 2012).
2. Monica Weis, SSJ, *The Environmental Vision of Thomas Merton* (Lexington: University Press of Kentucky, 2011).

In his chapter on technology, Dekar explains that "Merton approached technology as inherently neutral" (96), that, as a tool, the manifold developments in technology could serve humanity for purposes of good or ill. However, the noticeable majority of the chapter is geared toward the myriad ways that Merton's insight might be used to caution against technological advancements or, perhaps more accurately, how his thought warns against obsession with the latest technological advances as ends in themselves. It is difficult to read Dekar's organization of some of Merton's thoughts on technology into "Three Baskets of Concern: Destruction, Distortion, and Distraction" (97-109) without getting the sense that the Trappist monk was a technological iconoclast or at least an embracer of ludditism. True, Merton struggled with technological innovations and the automaticity of modern life, but did so in a way both more nuanced and more abstract than Dekar's presentation can sometimes suggest. Much of Dekar's reflections are insightful and inspiring, but regarding the suggestion that Merton "anticipates the new monastic movement" (113), which appears at the end of the technology chapter, I remain incredulous.

The chapter on ecology, titled "Thomas Merton on Care of Earth" (115-30), both reflects and complements the earlier work of Weis. The two-fold lens through which the reader is invited to consider Merton's views on creation, first as part of an interrelated created order and second as caretaker, is greatly appreciated. The one reservation I have about this particular chapter is the brevity with which the subject is treated. It would have been nice to see some more primary-source material and secondary scholarship on this often overlooked dimension of Merton's thought, indeed truly a source of wisdom for living in our age.

Merton was certainly aware of and in communication with members of several new spiritual movements emerging in his day, as Dekar presents toward the end of chapter eight. It is unclear how much the Shakers, those attracted to Taizé, or the hundreds who have committed themselves to lives of prayerful service and solidarity in the communities of Madonna House or the Catholic Worker anticipate or are related to the "new monasticism" of the 2000s already mentioned. Dekar's grouping of these communities alongside the canonically established tertiary orders of various denominations, such as the Third Order or "Secular" Franciscans, complicates the chapter on twenty-first-century Christian communities. While these are all praiseworthy groups, and communities that could benefit very well from Merton's insight, there are significant distinctions among them that go unacknowledged.

Chapter nine, "Building Communities of Love" (185-204), is perhaps the most constructive chapter of the book. Here Dekar seeks to offer something of a heuristic for communities, of one sort or another, interested in appropriating monastic practices and spirituality into their modern lives. The centerpiece is the building of communities of authentic love, not simply the "'infantile' and 'narcissistic' approaches to love characteristic of popular culture" (187), but an *agapic* love resembling that of the evangelical life.

Among the important highlights of this book are the two appendices Dekar includes. These are transcriptions of Merton's conferences on subjects relating to technology: "The Christian in a Technological World" (June 5, 1966) (205-13) and "Marxism and Technology" (June 26, 1966) (214-23). Dekar has provided Merton scholars and enthusiasts with helpful and previously unpublished primary material on the theme at hand. Additionally, Dekar's lengthy bibliography and lists of source material offer readers a valuable resource. All in all, this book is presented in an accessible style that points its readers to several useful paths along which the modern applicability of Merton's wisdom will be become clear. It will surely be a standard text in the personal and professional libraries of Merton scholarship for decades to come.

Daniel P. Horan, OFM

AGUILAR, Mario I., *Thomas Merton: Contemplation and Political Action* (London: SPCK, 2011), pp. ix + 150. ISBN 978-0-281-06058-0 (paper) $29.99.

In this short book, Mario Aguilar presents a concise biography of Thomas Merton's life as a contemplative monk who was also engaged with the pressing political and moral issues of his day. He traces Merton's life through a series of six phases which begin with Merton's role as instructor of novices at Gethsemani and end with Merton's travels to Asia at the end of his life. Aguilar then adds a brief concluding chapter on the relevance of Merton for today. As such, Aguilar presents a helpful summary of Merton's life, but he does not delve deeply into Merton's contemplative theology. This book is a documentation of Merton's theology, but it is not an exploration. Perhaps a better title would have been, *Thomas Merton: The Life of a Contemplative Political Activist*. This observation, however, is not an overall condemnation of Aguilar's work. Merton scholars have produced numerous texts on Merton's theology, and extensive biographies also exist. For those looking for a brief introduction into Merton, this book would serve as a good starting point from which more extensive study of Merton could be launched.

To this reader, the most intriguing starting point for further investigation is Aguilar's emphasis on Merton's activity as a writer. Two of Aguilar's six phases describe Merton as a writer in their titles, and Merton's letter-writing receives attention throughout the book. In fact, Aguilar focuses on Merton's letters more than the latter's books, articles and addresses. This is in accordance with Merton's description of himself: "It is possible to doubt whether I have become a monk (a doubt I have to live with), but it is not possible to doubt that I am a writer, that I was born one and will most likely die as one."[1] For Aguilar, this is the key for understanding the well-noted tension in Merton's life between his desire to live as a hermit and his concerns about the social-political realities of his time.

For Aguilar, writing, even though it is a solitary activity, is "a public statement of self" (33). As such, despite Merton's desire to lead the life of a hermit, his identity as a writer necessarily engaged others and "challenge[d] other members of society's perception of self, society and God" (33). By putting pen to paper, Merton could not help but engage the world. If Merton was not a writer in the very core of his being, his challenge to the injustices of his day would have been more symbolic than anything else, which is not to diminish such a contribution. As John F. Kavanaugh indicates, "religious have the opportunity to bear unambiguous witness to *faith*, founded in the God who invites."[2] In other words, by rejecting the world's promotion of truncated relationships based on self-interest, men and women religious demonstrate the life based on the love desired by God for human beings. Hermits, then, would stand as symbols to Christians that love of God should stand at the center of their lives. Through his writing, Merton moved beyond being a reminder of the importance of God to someone who is actively engaged in the world.

Likewise, Aguilar's treatment of Merton as a writer sets Merton apart from the view that the spiritual life "fuels" political engagement. Evelyn Underhill, for instance, argues that mystics cannot help but become agents of goodness after intimately encountering God.[3] From this perspective, Christians are so moved by coming to know God that they become involved in the world in a manner that promotes communities based on love rather than selfishness. As with Kavanaugh's explanation

---

1. Thomas Merton, "First and Last Thoughts," in *A Thomas Merton Reader*, ed. Thomas P. McDonnell (New York: Harcourt, Brace, 1962) x; rev. ed. (Garden City, NY: Doubleday Image, 1974) 17.

2. John F. Kavanaugh, *Following Christ in a Consumer Society: The Spirituality of Cultural Resistance*, 25th Anniversary ed. (Maryknoll, NY: Orbis, 2006) 170.

3. Evelyn Underhill, *Mysticism: The Nature and Development of Spiritual Consciousness* (Oxford: Oneworld, 1999) 84.

of the connection between the spiritual life and justice, Merton resists Underhill's understanding. Although he engaged issues such as civil rights and the Vietnam War in his writing, he did not participate in the demonstrations of his time.

I am of the opinion that because Merton does not fit neatly into either category, scholars have mainly noted the tension in Merton's life between his socio-political advocacy and monastic life without explaining its source or its inner dynamics. As such, Aguilar stands to contribute significantly to Merton studies. However, Aguilar does not follow up adequately on his insight about Merton's life as a writer. I believe that his contribution would have been greater if he had explored the nature of the act of writing in greater detail. Though I do not disagree with anything Aguilar writes about Merton as a writer or how that activity provided a means for Merton the mystic to also be Merton the activist, I question whether the two pages (32-33) on the nature of writing is adequate.

In particular, I would like to have seen more investigation of Merton's writing as a conversation with the wider world. For Aguilar, writing is a solitary experience which is directed at the public sphere. However, he does not devote much time to Merton's audience(s). How might this have affected his writing and thus his challenge to society's conceptions of self, society and God? Moreover, public writing is not just communication from the author to audience. It is a conversation. If Aguilar's contention about the challenges inherent in the act of writing is correct, were not Merton's conceptions of self, society and God similarly challenged by his literary conversation partners? Merton underwent considerable development over the course of his life, and his conversations more than likely played a part. Perhaps an interdisciplinary study of Merton that incorporated literary theory could pick up on Aguilar's promising start.

In conclusion, Aguilar's book can serve as a starting point for two lines of further investigation. First, it is a brief and accessible introduction to the life of Thomas Merton. A reader unfamiliar with Merton could use Aguilar's book as a stepping-stone to more in-depth studies of this important spiritual figure. Secondly, I believe that Aguilar's emphasis on Merton as a writer holds great promise for investigating the tension in Merton's life between his eremitic desires and socio-political activism. With further attention paid to the conversational nature of writing for the public sphere, I believe this to hold great potential for further advances in Merton studies.

Ian Bell

WALDRON, Robert, *The Wounded Heart of Thomas Merton* (Mahwah, NJ: Paulist Press, 2011), pp. ix +207. ISBN 978-0-8091-4684-0 (paper) $17.95.

In his poem "Posterity," Philip Larkin gives an acerbic glance at the view of a future mythical biographer who will use his research work on Larkin after the poet's death to further future career prospects: "Just let me put this bastard on the skids"; and asked by a colleague what his research subject (Larkin) is like, the biographer replies: "One of those old-type *natural* fouled-up guys."[1] The poem reminds the reader that the subject is always at the mercy of the biographer and their motives. Whilst in no way suggesting that Waldron has approached the writing of this book with career prospects in mind, the reading of the book does nonetheless raise the question: why write this book? What is Waldron trying to tell us the readers? He writes in the preface that the book is "a Jungian interpretation of the life and the work of the Trappist monk . . . . My only hope is that I will indeed shed some light on Thomas Merton, a very complicated man who deserves the efforts of attentive, close reading" (vii). Does the book shed some light? Well, for this reviewer the answer is "no."

In the preface Waldron explains his lack of credentials for writing the book (he is not a trained psychotherapist or the equivalent, but has read Jung's work), and in Thomas Sheridan's recent spirited and insightful review of this book Waldron's lack of qualifications and flawed perspective are dealt with well. Sheridan also critically and skillfully unpicks some of Waldron's at-times astonishingly wild and highly subjective interpretations of Merton.[2]

In his introduction, Waldron offers us his immediate "diagnosis": Merton's "life-long battle with depression . . . . commenced with his mother's death from cancer when he was six years old" (1). Merton's autobiography is "one of the best modern confessions of a depressive" (2). Straightaway the reader understands that this is no speculative, open-minded psychobiography but rather a delineated pathography. The subject is nailed, or to refer back to Larkin's verse, the biographer has "put the bastard on the skids." It's worth noting that in psychoanalytical training and practice, diagnoses or labels are rarely of interest to the analyst, for people are not diagnoses; rather the interest is always in what lies behind. The process is one of discovering and uncovering, with open and mutual exploration based on

---

1. Philip Larkin, *Collected Poems*, ed. Anthony Thwaite (London: Marvell Press / Faber & Faber, 1988) 170.
2. Thomas Sheridan, "Psyching Out Merton," Review of *The Wounded Heart of Thomas Merton* by Robert Waldron, *The Merton Seasonal* 36.3 (Fall 2011) 26-33.

the psychodynamics of the relationship. Interpretations are offered from associations and interaction. Psychoanalytic (Freudian and post-Freudian) and analytical psychology (Jungian and post-Jungian) theory offer ways of thinking about the inner world, and would not be recommended as a pedantic template to apply to someone's life. In this book Waldron has misunderstood the analytical psychology approach which is often speculative, and misunderstood the way Jung approached and understood his thinking about the human condition that emerged from Jung's deep personal and professional experiences over a lifetime.

The book ploughs through more or less chronologically, with the first four chapters on Merton's childhood and adult life leading to his entering the monastery of Gethsemani. Much emphasis is placed on the child Merton reportedly fathered (indeed this is pursued all the way through). The second half of the book is about Merton's life as a monastic and takes us to his death. There is the inevitable (and it now seems for some recent biographers, obligatory) build-up to and highlighting of the relationship with the student nurse M. as bringing Merton healing. Each chapter draws on Merton's own writings, including his poetry, books and journals, and also on other biographers, and each is jam-packed with Waldron's interpretations as a pretend psychologist and sometimes as a pretend Jungian analyst. I have to mention here Waldron's breathtaking ticking off of Merton for practicing psychoanalysis on the novices: "His motive is pure, but he surely has no business posing even as an amateur psychologist" (62). This has to be one of the more blatant examples of projection by Waldron which litter the book. It's worth noting that as early as 1911 Freud began to publish papers to curb the danger of what he termed "wild" analysis from those he deemed "amateurish" – along the lines of a little knowledge is a dangerous thing.[3] Fortunately Merton, and indeed Jung, can both well survive Waldron's hatchet job, but an unwary reader new to both might get a very strange view of the thinking of Merton, and indeed the practice of Jungian psychology.

From my own perspective as a psychoanalytical psychotherapist and as someone who has had two lengthy and intensive Jungian analyses (the first a training analysis with a woman many years ago, and the second more recently with a male analyst), it is the astonishing way that Waldron interprets Merton's dreams and poetry that is the most destructive. A good psychobiography is not all about finding some childhood origin for adult

---

3. See Sigmund Freud, "'Wild' Psycho-analysis" in *The Standard Edition of the Complete Psychological Works of Sigmund Freud*, ed. James Strachey, 24 vols. (London: Hogarth Press, 1956-74) 11.219-27, and Peter Gay, *Freud: A Life for Our Time* (London: J. M. Dent, 1988) 293-94.

behaviors,[4] but Waldron is determined to hammer home the early maternal loss and the effect on Merton's relationships with women. Translated into Waldron's misunderstanding of Jungian archetypes this means that Merton's "anima problem," "anima dilemma" and "anima projections," to name but a few of the phrases, are endlessly and repetitively flagged up. Sheridan rightly heavily criticizes Waldron's use of revisioned Jungian concepts, especially Waldron's identification of the feminine dimension (anima) with an actual woman or women.

This misunderstanding becomes at times absurd. So, for example, even Waldron is at a loss when he reports a Merton dream from 1966, a dream where there are a number of women. Here is a short extract from Waldron's interpretation:

There is an unflattering woman ("battle-axe type") and a girl who is *not* M. The anima is multifaced, confusing Merton [surely confusing Waldron!]. . . . In the dream, he moves from actual women to symbols of a woman: The woman is a luminous pink rose but discerned through a tangle of dark briars. . . . He must view his pink rose (M.) through the many obstacles (briars like spying monks, Abbot Fox . . .). . . . His mother's face then appears. . . . His student nurse visits him in the monastery. She obviously represents M., and he is brusque and rude. Is it because of the appearance of a negative anima . . . ? (163-64)

A Jungian analysis of dreams assumes that the dream images are all aspects of the dreamer's inner world, and that if there are representations of actual people they are representations of the dreamer's psyche. Each dream that Waldron includes is (one might say) analyzed to death. As Freud once so memorably is reported to have said, "Sometimes a cigar is just a cigar."

Similarly Waldron misunderstands the concept of individuation by his reference to an "individuated person" (52) and to Merton as "the individuated man who survives the dark night of the soul" (151), to give two examples. Individuation is a process, not a state, and certainly in contemporary thinking is seen as somewhat problematic when viewed in this way as an idealized condition or achievement. I'm reminded of my second analyst, who once described a referral meeting at the London-based Society of Analytical Psychology many years ago, where all the top Jungian analysts of the time were present, and a request came from a potential analysand asking to be seen by an "individuated analyst." Here, as for Waldron, was an idealization of the theory with the assumption that an individuated state is indeed achievable. Instead the person had to be told that no one could

---

4. See www.williamtoddschultz.wordpress.com/what-is-psychobiography [accessed 09/07/12].

claim this state, but he could be seen by a qualified analyst instead. This critique of Waldron's usage of the theory brings me to my central reason for seeing this book as obfuscating the life of Merton rather than shedding light. Nowhere does the author seek to explore whether or not it is appropriate for such psychological theories to be applied in this evangelical and somewhat literal way to spiritual development. Instead, Waldron seems to assume that the two are the same. For example, he claims: "It is amazing how accurately Merton's journey correlates with Jung's theory of individuation, particularly his encounter with the anima archetype" (155). My response at this stage of the book is to disagree, for it is not at all amazing given the extraordinary insistence by Waldron to force the two into an artificial fit.

While Jungian theory and practice is most helpful for psychological understanding and development, it comes from a different context, and emphasizes something different from religious and spiritual development. The psychological and the spiritual are not always necessarily the same, though there is clear overlap. A recent essay by Rachel Blass helps to open up reflections on the difference and divide between religious and psychological worldviews. One approach understands the individual in terms of his or her connectedness or lack of connectedness to the spiritual/ ethical nature of reality, and the other, a psychological view, does not necessarily take this reality either into account or as being the primary focus. "Instead the psychological worldview offers a notion of pathology and well-being that rests on psychological criteria alone."[5]

One of the central differences between the spiritual and psychological is the understanding of human suffering and how adverse life experiences can work towards deepening the focus of spiritual connectedness with God rather than the focus as the person's emotional wellbeing and ego-functioning. Jung, who was very interested in religion, tended in his theory to merge religious and psychological understandings to the extent that a religious form of understanding is superseded by the psychological. I think this is indeed what Waldron demonstrates in the text where the psychological and spiritual levels of discourse are seen either as equivalent or where the psychological takes precedence. As Buber put it in his critique of Jung, "Man does not deny a transcendent God; he simply dispenses with Him. . . . In his place he knows the soul, or rather the self."[6] This links with Waldron's repeated references to Jung's work

---

5. Rachel B. Blass, "Sin and Transcendence Versus Psychopathology and Emotional Wellbeing: On the Catholic Church's Problem of Bridging Religious and Therapeutic Views of the Person," *Spiritus* 12.1 (Spring 2012) 24.

6. Martin Buber, *Eclipse of God* (Atlantic Highlands: Humanities Press International,

Modern Man in Search of a Soul as his exemplar.[7]

A further criticism for the purposes of this review is about the writing style. Waldron writes in the present tense, contributing to the breathless and indigestible feel to the text. Prudent editing could have reduced some of the repetitions. For example in chapter 5 we are told three times that Merton did not write a journal between March 1953 and July 1956 (57, 58, 63). There are also inaccuracies: for example, the famous Jungian analyst Marie-Louise von Franz is misnamed Maria von France (154) and she is referenced incorrectly as writing one of Jung's books, which would have surprised both of them (197).

So why reduce the life of Merton and the profound thinking of Jung to force a fit? The answer seems to lie in the author's need to show us, the readers, something new. Waldron says that Merton "deserves the efforts of attentive, close reading" (vii). This implicitly suggests that this has not happened up until now, and that Waldron alone can offer definitive insight where others have failed. Waldron's claim to nail Merton's inner pathology is not only wrong and patronizing, but seems to suggest then closure of all else. The irony is that Merton's very style of writing is the complete reverse. It is about opening things up, by giving space through his observations of – yes, himself – but always in the context of spirituality, and from that into the world and the environment. As David Belcastro notes, "Merton . . . enters into a relationship with his readers and through his writings awakens in us the *yes* that affirms life and the presence of God in our lives."[8] His writing is "autobiographical theology" and is about the human search and response to God.[9]

Merton's writings seem to invite each reader personally to attentive and close reading and so different identifications and subtle resonances and associations become available. One of Merton's attractions is the at-times enigmatic sense that we too understand him and that he somehow is able to reach us. This is not because he is a great saint or a great sinner, a depressive or someone full of cheer; perhaps it is just because he is – like us – "One of those old-type *natural* fouled-up guys" trying to reach out to the "more than ourselves."

Fiona Gardner

1988) 86, quoted by Blass (29).

7. C. G. Jung, *Modern Man in Search of a Soul* (London: Routledge and Kegan Paul, 1961).

8. David Belcastro, "2009 Bibliographic Review: Beneath the Habit of Holiness," *The Merton Annual* 23 (2010) 256.

9. Gary Hall, "The Fiction of Merton," *The Merton Journal* 16.1 (Easter 2009) 10.

NUGENT, Robert, *Silence Speaks: Teilhard de Chardin, Yves Congar, John Courtney Murray, and Thomas Merton* (Mahwah, NJ: Paulist Press, 2011), pp. viii + 144. ISBN 978-0-8091-4649-9 (paper) $14.95.

This book by Robert Nugent is an important contribution to the theme of the most recent ITMS conference and consequently of this volume of *The Merton Annual*. Both conference and journal, in various ways, focus our attention on the relationship between the individual and society. *Silence Speaks* presents the marginalized voices of four Roman Catholics who challenged and eventually changed the Church that sought to silence them. The cover photo of steps half-shaded and half-illuminated provides an apt reminder that humanity's ascent into Truth is challenged by seemingly endless obstacles and yet blessed with unending grace that sheds sufficient light to reveal the path for today. Censorship is the fine line that subtly marks the intersection of shadow and light. To be sure, censorship is a burden to those on whom it is imposed. It may, however, be a necessary prompt for the silence of the human heart to speak with new insights and questions that will guide the pilgrim Church. As they endured the burden of censorship, Teilhard de Chardin, Yves Congar, John Courtney Murray and Thomas Merton would come to exemplify the Christian virtues of Faith, Hope and Love and thereby rise above the misunderstandings, accusations and conflicts that preceded and followed their silencing by the Church they loved and sought to serve. Nugent underscores this at the outset with a quotation from Father Bernard Haring:

> I love the Church because Christ loved it, love it to her utmost extreme. I love it even when I discover painful attitudes and structures, which I do not find in harmony with the Gospel. I love it as it is because Christ also loved me with all my imperfections, with all my shadows and constantly gives me the first fruits of the Kingdom so that my love may correspond to his eternal plan. . . . Christ and the Church with him remind me of all the limitless evidence of love, grace and mercy. In this the Church helps me to form a grateful memory. If we open ourselves to this and gratefully remember all the good, which has flowed to us in the Church, and constantly flows to us, then we can and will all succeed in giving even the suffering from the Church its place in the heart of Jesus. (iii-iv)

Theologian Richard Gaillardetz provides a fine introduction that situates Nugent's book within the history of the Church's censorship of theologians. His brief history points out that the accusations for departing from "the unchangeable doctrine of the church" (1) must be considered in light of a particular ecclesiological framework. Noting the rise of ultramontanism in the nineteenth century, Gaillardetz clarifies that situation in which Teilhard, Congar, Murray and Merton lived and worked, a situation that he critically examines and finds insufficient for and detrimental to the life and work of the Church. His clarification of the work of the theologian and the potentially collaborative relationship of Catholic theologians with the college of bishops eventually unfolds into a proposal for change. The change that Gaillardetz proposes would safeguard the integrity of the apostolic faith (the responsibility of bishops) and the freedom to explore and discover the depths of that faith in the context of changing times that raise new questions and shed new light (the work of theologians).

Nugent organizes his book in four chapters, one chapter for each of the four men: "Teilhard de Chardin and the Holy Office"; "Yves Congar: Apostle of Patience"; "The Censuring of John Courtney Murray"; and "Thomas Merton: The Silenced Monk." While different in various ways, the four men have one thing in common. Each in his own way explored the depths of the Apostolic Faith with every intention to be faithful to the Church and of service to the world. Yet it was that commitment that brought them into conflict with the authorities in Rome. Teilhard de Chardin's effort to harmonize a modern scientific view of the world with the Church's teachings on humankind would lead to the 1962 reprimand by Rome denouncing his works:

> The above-mentioned works abound in such ambiguities and indeed even serious errors, as to offend Catholic doctrine. . . . For this reason, the most eminent and most reverend Fathers of the Holy Office exhort all Ordinaries as well as the superiors of Religious institutes, rectors of seminaries and presidents of universities, effectively to protect the minds, particularly of the youth, against the dangers presented by the works of Fr. Teilhard de Chardin and his followers. (*Warning Considering the Writings of Father Teilhard de Chardin*, Sacred Congregation of the Holy Office, June 30, 1962)

Yves Congar's commitment to the ecumenical movement and in particular his role as a driving force in the French worker-priest movement resulted in the Church disallowing him to teach or publish for two years. John Courtney Murray's interest in religious freedom in the modern state and his re-examination of Catholic doctrines on church/state relations resulted in conflict with Rome and the Vatican's demand in 1954 that he stop publishing. All three men continued to write. Their ideas continue to be discussed. Their efforts to bring the Church into dialogue with the world of the twentieth and now twenty-first centuries were eventually successful and in some cases contributed to the shape of the Second Vatican Council.

Nugent's chapter on Merton provides a detailed account of Merton's relationship with censors. The relationship reaches a breaking point over his writings on peace and justice. He was silenced. And, as is well known, he obediently found a way to continue writing. What are we to make of this contradiction? How did he in good conscience both obey and circumvent the orders of his superiors? Why did Merton feel compelled to be both silent and vocal? Nugent explains, "Merton was . . . deeply concerned about what he called complicity in observing the silencing, and at the same time what effect his disobeying the silence would have on others" (89). Merton's interior struggle with the censors is reflected in his book entitled *Vow of Conversation*:

> silent complicity is presented as a greater good than honest, conscientious protest. This is supposed to be part of my vowed life and this is supposed to give glory to God. Certainly I refuse complicity. My silence itself is a protest and those who know me are aware of the fact. I have at least been able to write enough to define the meaning of my silence. Apparently, I cannot leave here in order to protest, since the meaning of any protest depends on my staying here, or does it? This is a great question.[1]

Merton lived questions – questions that oftentimes emerged from contradictions that existed within him. Perhaps this is one of the most valuable lessons one may find in Merton's life and work. If one is to be both faithful to the Church and true to oneself, one must live the questions and embody the contradictions rather than try to craft all-too-simple answers that are no answers at all, or resolve the contradiction by rejecting one of the two opposing sides. Nugent's chapter on Merton allows us to see and understand how the silence of this monk would eventually speak volumes.

The book ends with an epilogue that integrates the insights that Nugent has gained by comparing and contrasting the lives and work of these four men. This book comes at an important moment in our history. We are deeply indebted to these four men. Their courage, faithfulness and work leave an invaluable legacy. Nugent has reminded us that their legacy is our inheritance. It is now up to us to raise our voices on a whole host of contemporary issues, not out of anger and contempt, but with the same fidelity to Faith, endurance of Hope and redeeming Love that is the hallmark of the Church we serve.

David Joseph Belcastro

---

1. Thomas Merton, *A Vow of Conversation: Journals 1964-1965*, ed. Naomi Burton Stone (New York: Farrar, Straus, Giroux, 1988) 28 [March 3, 1964] (quoted in Nugent 88).

CIORRA, Anthony, *Thomas Merton: A Spiritual Guide for the Twenty-First Century* (Rockville, MD: Now You Know Media, 2011) (4 CDs) $119.95.

GOERGEN, Donald, *A Retreat with Thomas Merton* (Rockville, MD: Now You Know Media, 2011) (2 CDs) $25.95.

It is comforting to see that 45 years after his death, Thomas Merton continues to attract new readers (or, perhaps, consumers of his message, considering the way ideas are now disseminated). NowYouKnowMedia. com, the company which now distributes Merton's classroom lectures delivered at the Abbey of Gethsemani, is also offering sets of lectures *about* Merton distributed on compact disks and MP3 files.

Rev. Anthony Ciorra recorded twelve lectures on four CDs for *Thomas Merton: A Spiritual Guide for the Twenty-First Century*. This would be ideal for those newly introduced to Merton's life and works or those looking for a refresher course. The lectures, offered in a friendly, inviting delivery, provide listeners with enough context to understand Merton's spirituality, the value he found in journaling and solitude, and how seeds planted by his work with Catherine de Hueck Doherty and others came to fruition in his advocacy for social justice and interreligious dialogue. Ciorra effectively builds his case that Merton's reflections on life and faith are as applicable today as they were in the mid-twentieth century. A fifth CD contains a study guide that offers questions for reflection; careful proofreading would have avoided elementary errors like "Carthusaians", "Gethsemance" or Gregory of Nyssa's "epektesis."

If Ciorra's lectures could be categorized as introductory, then Rev. Donald Goergen's set of six conferences would be more suited to those interested in studying Merton on an advanced level. As indicated in his program notes, the two CDs follow "more of a retreat format than a systematic presentation of a particular individual's thought." Goergen's emphatic and enthusiastic delivery examines Merton's philosophy of solitude, his study of Zen, work for peace, his correspondence, and the flash of insight Merton gained at the corner of Fourth and Walnut in Louisville. The third CD contains a study guide that is helpful, but not without glaring errors such as the date of Merton's entrance into Gethsemani, spelling the name of the Abbey two different ways on two consecutive lines, and mangling the title of the second lecture, referring to it erroneously as "New *Scenes* of Contemplation."

This writer hopes to see more of these recorded lectures in the future, making Merton more accessible to busy commuters and others who, because of the pressure to *make* a living, have little leisure time left to actually *live* and read.

Robert Grip

BARRON, Robert, *Catholicism: A Journey to the Heart of Faith* (New York: Image Books, 2011), pp. 291. ISBN 978-0-307-72051-1 (cloth) $27.99. *Catholicism: A Journey to the Heart of Faith* (Skokie, IL: Word on Fire Catholic Ministries, 2011) (DVD – 10 discs) $149.95.

This video series and accompanying book by Robert Barron, priest of the Archdiocese of Chicago, prolific author, director of Word on Fire Ministries, which has a wide-ranging internet presence, and recently-appointed rector of Chicago's Mundelein Seminary, where he has taught for many years, is an impressive example of what has been termed "the new evangelization," an effort to present the Catholic vision of life in contemporary terms and through contemporary means of communication. In ten episodes, ranging in length from about 40 minutes to just under an hour, Fr. Barron guides his viewers across space and time to highlight what he considers to be the central dimensions of Catholic faith. The ten chapters of the book correspond closely in content and in language to the respective video segments, expanding somewhat on the scripts and incorporating numerous photographs (mainly in black and white but including an 8-page color section as well) of artwork and of sites found in the film. Videos and text complement one another, but each stands quite well on its own, sharing the engaging voice of Fr. Barron as speaker and writer.

He begins with a focus on the person of Jesus and on the Incarnation as "*the* great principle of Catholicism" (1), then moves on in the second section to Jesus' teaching, with particular focus on the Beatitudes, the Parable of the Prodigal Son, and the Judgment scene of Matthew 25. The third segment discusses the Catholic understanding of the mystery of God, moving from Anselm's and Aquinas' arguments for the existence of God to the problem of evil to a presentation of the doctrine of the Trinity featuring Augustine's use of the analogy of the human mind with its self-knowledge and self-love. The fourth segment focuses on Mary, first as the embodiment and fulfillment of the hope of Israel, then as Mother of God, Theotokos, as defined by the Council of Ephesus (431), then in the dogmas of the Immaculate Conception (linked with the apparitions at Lourdes) and the Assumption, presented as providing insights not just on Mary but on the central meaning of redemption and resurrection, respectively. Peter and Paul as the two "Indispensable Men" (116) of the early Christian movement are the focus of the fifth segment, citing Hans Urs von Balthasar's presentation of the two figures as the archetypes of the two central dimensions of the Church, its structural authority and its missionary outreach, existing in "tensive harmony" (141) that has provided both coherence and dynamism to the Church through the centuries. The sixth section focuses on the Church itself, looking at its four-fold creedal identity as one, holy, catholic and apostolic, while the following section takes the viewer/reader through the successive sections of the Mass, with a pause at the point of the Consecration to explore the meaning of the Catholic doctrine of the Real Presence of Christ in the Eucharist. Then follows an exploration of the communion of saints through biographical sketches of four modern women saints, Katherine Drexel, Thérèse of Lisieux, Theresa Benedicta of the Cross (Edith Stein) and Mother Teresa of Calcutta, presented as exemplifying respectively the cardinal virtues of justice, prudence, fortitude and temperance, elevated and transfigured by grace. The penultimate section focuses on prayer, moving from the contemporary figure of Thomas Merton back to his great model John of the Cross, and to John's own teacher Teresa of Avila, balancing a focus on contemplative prayer with a consideration of the centrality of the prayer of petition, before returning to Merton to complete the discussion. The final section is appropriately devoted to the "last things," drawing largely on Dante for a Catholic explanation of hell and purgatory, pausing for consideration of the existence of angels and devils, and then moving on to heaven, considered under the images of the beatific vision, the city of God, and new heavens and new earth, with its promise of resurrected bodies and a transfigured cosmos.

Fr. Barron's high regard for Thomas Merton, already evident in his earlier book *And Now I See: A Theology of Transformation* (1998) and in his plenary address at the ITMS Seventh General Meeting in 2001, is apparent in his focus on Merton as a thoroughly modern model of prayer. In the video his discussion of Merton begins in bustling Times Square in the heart of Manhattan, and summarizes the process of Merton's spiritual quest and eventual conversion from alienated skeptic to committed Catholic, including the famous incidents of his first experience of Mass, at Corpus Christi Church, and its aftermath of sitting in a diner and feeling as though he were "in the Elysian Fields" (229); Robert Lax's challenge to his friend as they walked along Sixth Avenue that "You should want to be a saint" (230); and his 1941 Holy Week retreat at the Abbey of Gethsemani that led him to recognize it as "the still point around which the whole country revolves" (231) and to return there at the end of that year to spend the rest of his life as a member of the monastic community. Barron clearly presents Merton as a figure with whom contemporary seekers can identify, and therefore as a potential catalyst for a similar spiritual transformation, as Merton has of course been for so many through his writings. After his portraits of the classical figures of John of the Cross and Teresa of Avila, Barron returns to Merton, and specifically to his epiphany at

Fourth and Walnut, where as a result of his immersion in contemplative prayer, Barron suggests, Merton had a vision of the divine presence in ordinary human beings that was "in some ways as extraordinary as Teresa of Avila's encounter with the angel" (248), an experience in which "it all came together for Merton: metaphysics, creation, incarnation, contemplation, nonviolence, and universal love" (249). In the film, the climactic line "There is no way of telling people that they are all walking around shining like the sun" is aptly accompanied by the blinding sunlight hitting the camera lens and bringing the episode to a conclusion.

While the use of Merton as archetype of prayer is very effective, it is also rather selective. While Fr. Barron does mention in the book (though not in the film) Merton's commitment to nonviolence, and even defends him against accusations of "a surrender to trendiness . . . and an abandonment of the more classically Catholic spirituality he espoused earlier in his life" (248), essentially the Fourth and Walnut episode is presented as the culmination of Merton's contemplative experience rather than as the inauguration of his "turn toward the world," and the final decade of his life is given virtually no attention. (Even the scenes shot at the hermitage precede those of downtown Louisville.) The word "Zen" is never mentioned; the brief listing of his books (232) includes none on eastern religions or social criticism; there is no reference to his Asian pilgrimage, no mention of Polonnaruwa to complement Fourth and Walnut, no allusion to the circumstances of his death, no focus on his more "prophetic" and even "controversial" stances with regard to both American society and the Church in the final years of his life. Many of these omissions, of course, could be justified as not pertinent to the particular focus on prayer in this section, but certainly for Merton and many of his readers, and at least in theory for Fr. Barron as well, Merton's contemplative consciousness was an integral dimension of all his interests, concerns and activities. It is perhaps telling that in specifically mentioning a sampling of Merton's hundreds of correspondents, along with Czeslaw Milosz, Jean Leclercq, Joan Baez (who was in fact only the co-addressee of a single letter) and John XXIII, Barron includes the Swiss theologian Hans Urs von Balthasar; while Merton certainly admired von Balthasar, who in turn arranged for a German translation of some of Merton's poetry, for which he wrote a gracious and admiring preface, his name is probably not among the first that would spring to the minds of most of those familiar with Merton's correspondence. (Five letters to von Balthasar are included in *The School of Charity*). One wonders if Barron includes the name of von Balthasar, whom John Paul II named a cardinal in 1988, as a kind of reassurance to a segment of his audience that Merton is indeed, despite his reputation in some quarters, "safely" orthodox, and thus deserving of his prominent place in *Catholicism*. This treatment of Merton may be considered as characteristic of Fr. Barron's perspective throughout the entire project.

There is certainly much to appreciate and admire in both book and videos. They provide a robust and appealing proclamation and explanation of central tenets of the Catholic faith in a coherent and well-organized sequence. Fr. Barron is a genial and dependable guide in both media. His mastery of his material and fluency of delivery is flawless: in the films, while much of the script is delivered in voice-over, a considerable portion is presented as the narrator walks through an Irish field or down a Ugandan road, or stands in a Roman basilica or atop a Mexican pyramid, and there is never the least hesitation or impression of searching for the right word. He has a gift for explaining abstruse ideas in clear and readily comprehended terms, as when he shows how Anselm's description of God as "that than which nothing greater can be thought" presupposes a God that is not simply a Being among other beings, not even the greatest of beings, since by definition "the God Anselm describes added to the world as we know it is not greater than God alone" (63). He can compress an idea into epigrammatic pithiness, as when he points out that the Trinity is not to be considered as "a one plus one plus one adding up to three, but a one times one times one, equaling one" (87). He forthrightly places nonviolence at the heart of the message of Jesus (48-52) and as the essence of the divine nature and of God's dealings with creation (76-77), visible from the Annunciation (89) through the Cross (45-47), and exemplified by incidents in the lives of Mother Teresa and Desmond Tutu (51), by John Paul II in Poland (51), and at some length by the life and work of Peter Maurin and Dorothy Day (56-59).

The production values of the films are stunning, weaving together narration, music, and visuals both of classic works of art and architecture and of natural and urban scenes in a seamless, integrated whole. In a single episode (that on the Mass) the scene moves from Calcutta to Uganda to New York City to the Philippines to Brazil to Chartres to Athens to Mexico City to Lourdes to Chicago to Rome; other segments include Jerusalem, Ireland, Poland, Asia Minor and elsewhere, vivid testimony to the Church's universality (and to the broad vision – as well as the evidently abundant financial resources – behind the project). Both book and videos are intended to present Catholicism in its best light and so to encourage the faithful and attract the curious, and one may hope for and expect their success in doing so.

At the same time, the project may leave at least some readers and viewers with a sense of an incomplete depiction of the full range of the

Catholic experience. Some of the emphases may seem to be less than comprehensive. While identifying the Incarnation as the core of the Gospel message, Fr. Barron emphasizes the fact of *God* becoming human rather than of God becoming *human*. He repeatedly speaks of Jesus as "Yahweh moving among his people" (15; see also 18, 25, 33, 36), a rather unusual formulation that sounds almost modalist in its apparently straightforward identification of the Son with the one God of Israel. When he quotes the Philippians hymn in chapter 5 as "a pithy encapsulation" of Paul's teaching (133), he points out that in the passage "the divinity of Jesus is clearly affirmed" and that as a consequence of that affirmation "Jesus is the *kyrios* (the Lord)" to whom all allegiance is owed; but he never mentions the *kenosis*, the self-emptying of Christ in assuming full humanity, that is at the heart of the hymn. Of course the human nature of Jesus is affirmed, but the full consequences of that affirmation are not explored in nearly as much depth or detail as is the meaning of Christ's divinity. Likewise more attention to the humble Mary of the Magnificat (only quoted briefly in passing [104]) would have complemented the focus on the Mother of God as "the Queen of all the saints, the Queen of the angels, and the Queen of heaven" (89). As with Jesus, the main focus is more on what differentiates Mary from the rest of humanity ("Our Tainted Nature's Solitary Boast" as the chapter title has it [88]), than on her kinship with all of us. While valid and valuable, this largely traditional perspective, evident throughout the book and the videos, tends to downplay equally significant elements characteristic of much of contemporary theological reflection.

Fr. Barron also seems to be at pains to avoid any topics that might ruffle anyone's ideological feathers – including, in large part, the Second Vatican Council and the contemporary American Church. The current polemical contrast in interpreting the council between a so-called hermeneutic of continuity and a hermeneutic of disruption (in fact a simplistic and reductive distinction) is perhaps responsible for his drawing on the council documents only occasionally, while the present tensions and turmoil in the Church in the United States may have been as potent in determining the paucity of references and scenes in this country as the desire to emphasize the universality of Catholicism. The image of the Church as the People of God, central to the Dogmatic Constitution *Lumen Gentium*, is notably absent, as is any reference to *Gaudium et Spes*, the Pastoral Constitution on the Church in the Modern World. The term charism is used only to refer to apostolic succession and papal infallibility (168, 169). The universal call to holiness is mentioned (150), but aside from Dorothy Day and Peter Maurin and the nineteenth-century Ugandan martyr Charles Lwanga, there is virtually no focus on the laity. The inclusion, for example, of Blessed Franz Jägerstätter, executed for his resistance to the Nazis, or Jean Donovan, murdered in El Salvador with three other American church women, would have enhanced the presentation. There is relatively little attention given to the Church's prophetic dimension, its denunciation of structural injustice and systemic violations of human dignity and human rights, little emphasis on "action on behalf of justice and participation in the transformation of the world" as "a constitutive dimension of the preaching of the Gospel," as the 1971 Synod of Bishops declared. Some attention to such courageous figures as Archbishop Denis Hurley opposing South African apartheid, Dom Helder Camara speaking out against Brazilian dictatorship, Archbishop Oscar Romero of El Salvador giving his life in solidarity with the oppressed poor of his country, or Cardinal Jaime Sin inspiring the Philippine "People Power" movement that ousted dictator Ferdinand Marcos, would have complemented the presentation of Pope John Paul's challenge to Polish communism. While reference is made to the declaration in *Nostra Aetate*, the document on non-Christian religions, that other traditions may reflect a ray of the true light, the implications of that statement are not explored in any detail. In fact, in a telling comment from one of the informal interviews interspersed in the film, Fr. Barron suggests that we need to recover a way to have a good religious argument as an alternative to bland religious tolerance on the one hand and violence prompted by religion on the other, as though this were the only mean between the two extremes. The term "dialogue" is absent from the discussion here and throughout both book and film, and the notion that the Church could or should learn anything from the secular world, or from other spiritual traditions, is given virtually no consideration. Inclusion of the Atlas martyrs, Christian de Chergé and his Cistercian brothers, as models of interreligious dialogue would have provided an excellent example of the Church's outreach to other faiths, even in the face of terrorism. There is even a whiff of triumphalism at the outset of the book (not in the film) in the assertion that Protestants and the Orthodox don't "embrace the doctrine [of the Incarnation] in its fullness ... don't see all the way to the bottom of it or draw out all of its implications" (3) – somewhat ironic in that he has just been referring to the idea of divinization, which for more than a thousand years had been looked on with suspicion in the West and had been preserved principally in the Eastern Church, and also in the fact that he will rely in his discussion of the Incarnation in the following chapter largely on the Anglican layman C. S. Lewis (14, 27) and the Anglican bishop N. T. Wright (15, 30, 31). Fortunately this line of approach is not subsequently developed.

The exposure to great works of art and architecture of the past is exhilarating, but may give the impression that the Church of the future merely needs to recover the riches of the past. There is an interesting comment in the video on Cardinal Newman's notion of the development of doctrine as explaining the fact of change in the Church, which is unaccountably missing in the corresponding place in the book – did some pre-publication reader suggest that any such reference to change be omitted as too controversial? Fr. Barron is frank in acknowledging the sinfulness of Church leaders over the centuries, including the recent sexual abuse scandals, but there is no hint that the problem might run deeper than individual failure, that it might indicate serious flaws in the institutional structure of the Church and the ways authority has been exercised. While the spiritual witness of women is highlighted throughout, there is certainly no suggestion that a system in which half the human race is automatically excluded because of its gender not only from presiding at the Eucharist but from exercising any sort of official ecclesial authority might need to be seriously re-examined.

Of course the central purpose of the project is not to provide a critical evaluation of the institution of the Church but to reveal the riches and the vitality of its teaching and its lived experience. But those Catholics who are quite content with the present state of the Church and the direction it seems to be taking will in the end probably be more comfortable with and comforted by Fr. Barron's overview than those Catholics whose equally deep love for the Church is more conflicted and complicated – perhaps more akin to that of Thomas Merton – than that which is conveyed in book and videos. As admirable, impressive and inspiring as it is, *Catholicism* may be found by some of its audience to fall somewhat short of the full scope of catholicity.

Patrick F. O'Connell

QUENON, Paul, *Afternoons with Emily* (Windsor, ON: Black Moss Press, 2011), pp. 88. ISBN 978-0887534928 (paper) $17.

THURSTON, Bonnie Bowman, *Belonging to Borders: A Sojourn in the Celtic Tradition* (Collegeville, MN: Liturgical Press, 2011), pp. xx + 104. ISBN 978-0814633670 (paper) $14.95.

The inner life, the outer life. Journeys across miles and journeys into the self. Journeys dominate two recent books of verse by two poets whose attention to detail and language heightens the spiritual depth of their work. Poetry has always been about the demarcation of spirit – what it is, who has it, how to get it and how to know when it is slipping away. These two works, one by a Trappist monk and the other by a theologian and former professor, offer graceful journeys across the landscape of spirit.

Kentucky Trappist monk Brother Paul Quenon, in his *Afternoons with Emily*, has interesting companions who haunt his daily routine: Emily Dickinson in the morning, Rilke in the evening, and a character named Mad Monk in, I guess, the midnight hours and beyond. Like Dickinson, Quenon reflects on the coalescence of nature and existence, and, also like Dickinson, produces startling results. In "Day Withholding," Quenon explores the paradox of how the most uneventful days can be the most meaningful:

> Some days the world holds off
> at a distance, neither hot nor cold.
> No promise is on the breeze,
> birds converse elsewhere. (17)

Earth and heaven are just "grey halves / of a closed shell" (17). It is indeed a day that, like the breeze, holds no promise. But Quenon's point, I think, is that most days are like these, and it is through our noticing, our concentration, our willingness to let things go, that any "promise" is found anyway.

Quenon also includes his translations of a number of Rilke's poems, including everyone's favorite, "The Panther." In translation, tone is more important than literalness, and Quenon's tone is distinctive:

> His gaze, from passing bars,
> has worn so blurred, it holds no more
> than bars, a thousand bars.
> Beyond the thousand – a world no more. (39)

Notice the nice resonance of "blurred," "barred" and "world," an almost incremental repetition of variation in the "r" sound. This is what good translation should do – bring us the music of the poem. It is very difficult to pull off, and Quenon has done it earnestly here.

Bonnie Thurston grew up in rural West Virginia, and in *Belonging to Borders: A Sojourn in the Celtic Tradition*, she attempts to trace the Celtic lineage of her family and neighbors who inhabited that area during her youth. In the introduction to her book, titled "The Autobiographical Why," she quotes her friend, Brother Jack, as asking, "When the scholar and poet wrestles within you, who wins?" (xx). Not being a scholar of theology myself, I am glad the poet won, in this case.

In fact, I generally mistrust any book of poetry that purports to be anything more than a book of poetry. To paraphrase Oscar Wilde, art should be as useless as a flower is useless, and if the reader takes away any message other than the sheer enjoyment of the work for enjoyment's sake, the work is either flawed or has been misinterpreted. Therefore, though Thurston does provide contextual essays for each section of the book, I went into Thurston's book looking for good poems, not necessarily interested in any historical or theological context.

And there are good poems indeed in this book. Consider the first two stanzas of "Wind Holds," part of a sequence inspired by the Iona community:

> Only the sharpest wind
> clears away the enveloping fog.
>
> On the blusteriest days
> the wind holds gulls
> suspended on shelves of air. (44)

"Shelves of air" is a brilliant metaphor, perfectly capturing the paradox of stasis created by constant movement of the nothing that is air. The poem ends with the line "storm's clarifying wisdom," an almost Zen-like epiphany underscoring the ability of chaos to help us achieve peace.

The best poems are about the simplest things. In "Poetic Justice: Berrying" Thurston's scratched forearm is a sweet pain, bringing memories of "canes taller than I am / gently dancing around me" (89). The poem ends with a delicious variation on the cliché that nothing ever comes for free, as she playfully asserts that while she got the raspberries, "they also got me."

Both books, then, offer simple pleasures without being simplistic, intelligence without pretention or pedantry, and – ultimately – fine poetry. Delights that end in wisdom abound in both works.

Kevin Griffith

Contributors

David Joseph Belcastro is currently serving as co-editor of *The Merton Annual* and vice president of The International Thomas Merton Society. Presentations and publications on Thomas Merton since 1988 have focused on Albert Camus, Czeslaw Milosz and the Beats. He received a Ph.D. from the University of St. Andrews in Scotland with a dissertation on the biblical hermeneutics of Philo of Alexandria, and is currently Professor of Religious Studies, Assistant Dean of the School of Humanities and Director of General Education at Capital University, Bexley, OH.

Ian Bell graduated from Marquette University in 2005 with a Ph.D. in Religious Studies and is currently Associate Professor of Religious Studies and Humanities Division Chair at Siena Heights University in Adrian, MI, where he teaches courses in biblical and systematic theology.

Nass Cannon is a Clinical Professor of Medicine at the University of Alabama School of Medicine and former Chief of Staff at Cooper Green Mercy Hospital. He has a particular interest in the writings of Thomas Merton on contemplation and the formation of the contemplative with their implications for integrative medicine, and has spoken at numerous Merton conferences in the US and in Great Britain.

John P. Collins received his Ph.D. from Boston College and served on the faculties of the College of the Holy Cross, Worcester State University and the International Education Program Inc. He has contributed articles to: *Cistercian Studies Quarterly*, *The Merton Annual*, *The Merton Seasonal*, *The Merton Journal* and *Religion and the Arts*, as well as a chapter in the book entitled, *Destined for Evil*. For the past ten years, he has written a monthly Thomas Merton column for the *Catholic Free Press*, the Worcester, MA diocesan newspaper and has served for over a decade as director and facilitator of the ITMS Chapter that meets at St. Mary's Parish, Shrewsbury, MA.

Vaughn Fayle, OFM was born in South Africa in 1960 into a musical and literary family: his father was a pipe organ builder, his aunt a concert pianist and his uncle on his mother's side, Denis Brutus, an international poet and activist who was imprisoned with Nelson Mandela. He completed graduate studies in philosophy and theology in Europe and came to the USA in 1990 to direct a department of undergraduate philosophy of religion in Texas. He has taught both religion and philosophy at Our Lady of the Lake University. Through the influence of his uncle, he began studying the poetry of Thomas Merton, and in 2007 was awarded an ITMS Shannon Fellowship for his musical setting of Merton's poetry. Since 1999, he has served as director of philosophy studies and adjunct professor of the philosophy of religion at Catholic Theological Union in Hyde Park, where he has taught courses on Merton's political philosophy. He is a member of the American Composers Forum, the American Guild of Organists and the American Philosophical Association. His settings of four of Merton's "Freedom Songs" received their world premiere at the ITMS Twelfth General Meeting at Loyola University, Chicago in June 2011.

Fiona Gardner is the award leader for the MA in Counselling and Psychotherapy Practice at Bath Spa University, Bath, England. She is a psychoanalytic psychotherapist, a trained spiritual director and author. Her latest book is *Precious Thoughts: Daily Readings from the Correspondence of Thomas Merton* (Darton Longman & Todd, 2011). She is the co-editor of *The Merton Journal* in the UK, ex-chair of the Thomas Merton Society of Great Britain and Ireland (2004-2008), and has given papers at Thomas Merton Society of Great Britain and Ireland and ITMS General Meetings.

Kevin Griffith is the author of four books of poetry, the most recent of which is *101 Kinds of Irony* (Folded Word Press, 2012). He teaches creative writing at Capital University, Bexley, OH.

Robert Grip is a former President of the International Thomas Merton Society and Program Chair of the ITMS Thirteenth General Meeting at Sacred Heart University. He is a television news anchor at WALA-TV in Mobile, Alabama and an instructor at Spring Hill College where he teaches Multimedia Journalism.

Hans Gustafson is currently assistant director of the Jay Phillips Center for Interfaith Learning at Saint John's University (Collegeville, MN) and the University of St. Thomas (St. Paul, MN), where he also teaches as an adjunct professor in the theology department. He holds a Ph.D. in philosophy of religion from Claremont Graduate University. He presented as an emerging scholar at the Twelfth General Meeting of the International Thomas Merton Society at Loyola University Chicago (2011). Recent publications include "Sacramental Mediation between Theology & Spirituality," in *Spirituality in the 21ˢᵗ Century: Explorations* (2013), "Sacramental Spirituality in *The Brothers Karamazov* and Wendell Berry's Port William Characters," *Literature and Theology* (2012) and "Substance Beyond Illusion: The Spirituality of Bede Griffiths," *The Way* (2008).

Joshua Hollmann is a Ph.D. candidate in the Faculty of Religious Studies of McGill University. His doctoral dissertation is on Nicholas of Cusa and Christian-Muslim dialogue. He is also assistant professor of religion at Concordia College-New York and serves as pastor of Christ Lutheran Church in New York City.

Daniel P. Horan, OFM is a Franciscan friar of Holy Name Province (New York), a former Daggy Scholar and a former Shannon Fellow, who currently serves on the ITMS Board of Directors. A former lecturer in the Department of Religious Studies at Siena College and a visiting professor in the Department of Theology at St. Bonaventure University, he is currently a Ph.D. student in systematic theology at Boston College. He is the author of several books, including *Dating God: Live and Love in the Way of St. Francis* (St. Anthony Messenger Press, 2012) and *Francis of Assisi and the Future of Faith: Exploring Franciscan Spirituality and Theology in the Modern World* (Tau Publishing, 2012), as well as more than thirty scholarly and popular articles. He is currently completing two books on Merton: *The Franciscan Heart of Thomas Merton: A New Look at the Spiritual Inspiration of His Life, Thought, and Writing* (Ave Maria Press, 2014) and the edited correspondence between Thomas Merton and Naomi Burton Stone. He writes a blog at: www.DatingGod.org.

Victor A. Kramer was the founding editor of *The Merton Annual* and served as its editor for twenty-two years (1986-2008). He is the author of the Twayne United States Authors Series volume on Thomas Merton, expanded as *Thomas Merton: Monk and Artist* for Cistercian Publications (1987), and edited *Turning Toward the World*, the fourth volume of Merton's complete journals. He has written on a wide range of topics in American Studies and literature, such as James Agee and Walker Percy, as well as on literary theory and religion and literature. He served as Director of The Aquinas Center of Theology at Emory University for four years after teaching for 30 years at Georgia State University in Atlanta. He has completed a Certificate Program in Spiritual Direction at Spring Hill College, Atlanta campus, for which he also teaches. He does spiritual direction and gives retreats on subjects such as Merton, Dorothy Day and Flannery O'Connor.

Hyeokil Kwon is a Ph.D. student in Christian spirituality at the Graduate Theological Union, Berkeley, CA. He is the author of *Flowers of Contemplation: Peace and Social Justice.* His research interests include: poetry and spirituality, contemplation and action, and monasticism and urban life.

Martin E. Marty is the Fairfax M. Cone Distinguished Service Professor of the History of Modern Christianity at the University of Chicago. A long-time editor at *The Christian Century* and an ordained Lutheran minister, he has written sixty-five books. A National Book Award winner and holder of a National Humanities medal, he has been honored with 84 honorary degrees. Academically and intellectually, he has focused chiefly on American Religious History since 1956, and since 1988 has widened his scope to study world religions, especially in their attitudes toward conflict or peace-making. Throughout his career he has participated in Christian ecumenical ventures and keeps Christian devotional interests in mind. It was these activities and concerns that drew him into the orbit of Thomas Merton's influence. After his retirement, the University of Chicago named its Institute for the Advanced Study of Religion "The Martin Marty Center," for which he writes a weekly column, "Sightings" (Divsightings@uchicago.edu). He and his wife Harriet, a musician, live in downtown Chicago, where they are active in musical and charitable activities. His website is: www.memarty.com.

Mary Murray McDonald directs the Writing Center and the Writing across the Curriculum Program at Cleveland State University; her M.A. and Ph.D. are in Rhetoric and Composition from Purdue University. More on the rhetoric of Thomas Merton can be found in her recent book, *It Draws Me: The Art of Contemplation* (Liguori, 2012).

Patrick F. O'Connell, professor of English and theology at Gannon University, Erie, PA, is a founding member and former president of the International Thomas Merton Society and editor of *The Merton Seasonal*. He is co-author (with William H. Shannon and Christine M. Bochen) of the *Thomas Merton Encyclopedia* (2002), and has edited six volumes of Merton's monastic conferences, most recently *The Life of the Vows* (2012). His edition of *The Selected Essays of Thomas Merton* is scheduled for publication in spring 2013.

Malgorzata Poks is an International Advisor of the ITMS for Poland. She teaches courses in American Literature and Culture. Her main interests concern spirituality and modern literature. In 2009 her monograph *Thomas Merton and Latin America: A Consonance of Voices* received the ITMS "Louie" award for outstanding contribution to Merton studies. She is interested in Merton's late poetics.

Christopher Pramuk teaches theology and spirituality at Xavier University in Cincinnati and is a member of the Board of Directors of the International Thomas Merton Society. His essays have appeared in *America* magazine, *Theological Studies*, *Cross Currents*, and the prayer journal *Give Us This Day*. He is the author of four books, including *Hope Sings, So Beautiful: Graced Encounters across the Color Line* (Liturgical Press, 2013) and *Sophia: The Hidden Christ of Thomas Merton* (Liturgical Press, 2009), which received an ITMS "Louie" award in 2011. A lifelong musician and student of African American history and spirituality, his recent work has focused on racial justice and interracial solidarity in society and church.

Joseph Quinn Raab is associate professor of religious studies and director of the Liberal Arts Studies Program at Siena Heights University in Adrian, Michigan. He has presented papers at Thomas Merton Society of Great Britain and Ireland and ITMS General Meetings and has published scholarly articles in *Theology Today*, *The Journal of Religious Education* and *The Merton Annual*, which he currently co-edits with David Belcastro.

Robert Weldon Whalen is the Carolyn G. and Sam H. McMahon Professor of History at Queens University of Charlotte and Visiting Professor of Church History at Union Theological Seminary, in Charlotte, North Carolina.

Index

A

Ace of Freedoms (Kilcourse) 30, 115
acedia 118, 210
Achebe, Chinua 64
Adventures of Ibn Battuta (Dunn) 32, 33, 37, 42, 45
Afternoons with Emily (Quenon) 243-44
Aguilar, Mario I. 225–27
Alexander, Michelle 97, 98
Amazing Grace (Kozol) 97
Ancient Maya, The (Morley) 50
And Now I See (Barron) 77, 238
Angelic Mistakes (Lipsey) 7
"Another Kind of Trifling" (Hall) 210
Anthropologie Structurale (Lévi-Strauss) 59
Anthropology as Cultural Critique (Marcus & Fischer) 56
Apel, William 169
Apocalypse 134
"Aquinas and the Angels" (Kreeft) 76
Arendt, Camus and Modern Rebellion (Isaac) 143
Arendt, Hannah 11, 132–143, 173, 221
Argonauts of the Western Pacific (Malinowski) 53
Art of Thomas Merton, The (Labrie) 7, 30
Asian Journal, The (Merton) 86, 150, 154, 205
asymbolia 210
"Attending to the Presence of God" (Cannon) 10
Augustine, St. 80, 89, 90, 141, 180, 186, 201, 237

B

Bachelard, Gaston 66
Bamberger, John Eudes 145
Barron, Robert 77, 237–43
Barthes, Roland 209
Beckingham, Charles 32
Behavior of Titans, The (Merton) 92
"Being in the Dark" (Gardner) 210

Belcastro, David Joseph 107, 122, 235, 246
Bell, Ian 227, 246
Belonging to Borders (Thurston) 243-44
Bennett, Tom Izod 62, 67
Bessenecker, Scott A. 162
Bhabha, Homi 68
Birmingham 10, 13, 15, 18, 19, 97
Black Elk Speaks (Neihardt) 252
Black Like Me (Griffin) 97
Blée, Fabrice 207
Bochen, Christine M. 30, 146, 178
body 15, 29, 61, 62, 64, 78, 83, 86, 135, 155, 160, 192, 193, 194, 223
Bonhoeffer, Dietrich 77, 139, 140, 160
Bragan, Kenneth 206
Bras, Kick 213
Bread in the Wilderness (Merton) 202, 203, 220
Brennan, Michael 23
Brothers Karamazov, The (Dostoevsky) 209, 247
Brown vs. Board of Education 25
Brulé, Dominique 212
Buber, Martin 78, 218, 231
Buddhism 71, 88, 159, 213
Burton-Christie, Douglas 148

C

Cables to the Ace (Merton) 52, 73
Camus, Albert 11, 57, 104–15, 117-20, 122-23, 143
Cannon, Nass 11, 154, 210, 246
Captive Mind, The (Milosz) 105, 106
Cargo Cult (Lindstrom) 51
Carlson, David 207
Carson, Rachel 105, 209
Cartesianism 77, 78
Casey, Michael 197
Cassian and the Fathers (Merton) 145
Catholicism (Barron) 237-43
Character of Man, The (Mounier) 84
Chasing the Wild Goose (Ferguson) 161

Christian Century, The 27, 249
Christifideles Laici (John Paul II) 185
Chute, La (Camus) 106
Ciorra, Anthony 236
Ciraulo, Jonathan Martin 211
Clément, Olivier 213
Clifford, James 53, 55
Cold War 75, 132, 133, 143, 156
Collected Poems (Larkin) 228
Collected Poems (Merton) 30, 93, 147
Collected Works of St. John of the Cross, The 163
Collins, John P. 11, 113, 120, 121, 122, 211, 246
Commonweal 23
Compassionate Fire (Merton & Doherty) 131
Conjectures of a Guilty Bystander (Merton) 10, 11, 82, 93, 94, 134, 145, 170, 220
Conrad, Joseph 63-65
Contemplation in a World of Action (Merton) 107, 111, 115, 141, 148, 154
contemplative awareness 80, 82, 83, 87, 89
"Contemporary Marital Spirituality" (Sandor) 180
Contino, Paul 209
"Contrapuntal Irony and Theme in Thomas Merton's *The Geography of Lograire*" (Randall) 30
Conversations with Walker Percy (Kramer & Lawson) 118
Cooper, David D. 30, 107, 113, 117
Cosmos and Hearth (Yi-Fu) 7
Courage for Truth, The (Merton) 114, 125
Cru et le Cuit, Le (Lévi-Strauss) 50, 59
Cunningham, Lawrence S. 75, 94, 104, 145, 190, 203

D
Daggy, Robert 52
Dancing in the Water of Life (Merton) 93, 104, 212
Day of a Stranger (Merton) 107, 112, 152, 213
Dear, John 215
Death at an Early Age (Kozol) 97

Death in Venice (Mann) 66, 67
de Bary, Wm. Theodore 213
Dekar, Paul R. 221-22
de Nicolò, Georg 73
Derrida, Jacques 58
Desert Fathers 11, 144–153
dharmakaya 83
Diary in the Strict Sense of the Term (Malinowski) 52, 54, 56, 59, 61, 63, 70
Disputed Questions (Merton) 128, 149, 165
divinization 76, 168, 242
Dr. Zhivago (Pasternak) 125, 129
Documents of Vatican II, The 177
Dostoevsky, Fyodor 209, 247
Du Bois, Cora 51
Dunn, Ross E. 32, 33, 37, 42, 45

E
"Ecclesial Thought and Life Trajectories" (Hugh-Donovan) 213
Eichmann in Jerusalem (Arendt) 133
1870 Ghost Dance, The (Du Bois) 51
Eliade, Mircea 74, 80
Emblems of a Season of Fury (Merton) 97
emptiness 83, 89, 128, 146, 147, 148, 153, 167, 211
enthusiasm 40, 77, 106, 119
Environmental Vision of Thomas Merton, The (Weis) 139, 206, 223
ethnographer 9, 53, 56, 57, 58, 61, 68, 70
ethnography 24, 26, 53, 54, 55, 71, 72
ethno-poesis 71
evil 18, 23, 76, 91, 106, 134, 135, 192, 201, 205, 237

F
Faggen, Robert 8, 104, 113
"Faith Seeking Understanding" (Scruggs) 208
Fanon, Franz 57
Fayle, Vaughn, OFM 23, 24, 246
Ferguson, Ronald 161
"Fiction of Merton, The" (Hall) 232
Finley, James 7, 166
Fisher, Michael M. J. 56
Following Christ in a Consumer Society (Kavanaugh) 226
Forest, Jim 215

Foster, Richard 161
Fourth and Walnut Epiphany 82, 83, 94,
    100, 101, 105, 141, 145, 236, 239
Fox, James 214, 230
Fox, Robert 95
"Fragments: The Spiritual Situation of
    Our Times" (Tracy) 73
Frank, Jerome 213
"A Friendship of Letters, A" (Forest) 215
Fromm, Erich 132, 212-13
Frontiers in American Catholicism (Ong)
    25
fuga mundi 94, 211
Furlong, Monica 214

G

Gaillardetz, Richard 180, 233, 234
Gardner, Fiona 11, 124, 206, 210, 232,
    247
Geertz, Clifford 55, 56, 57, 72, 137
Geography of Lograire, The (Merton) 8,
    30-48, 49, 50, 52, 53, 72, 73, 209
"*Geography of Lograire* as Merton's *Ges-
    tus* – Prolegomena, The" (Poks) 30
"*Geography of Lograire*: Merton's Final
    Prophetic Vision, The" (Pearson) 30
Gibb, H. A. R. 31, 32, 33, 37, 38, 40
A Gift of Love (Linthors) 182
Glimm, James York 30
Goergen, Donald 236
Griffin, John Howard 97, 98
Griffith, Kevin 245, 247
Grip, Robert 236, 247
Guardini, Romano 202
Gustafson, Hans 9, 74, 247

H

Hagia Sophia (Merton) 100, 170, 172,
    175
Hall, Gary 210, 232
Hannah Arendt: Life as Narrative
    (Kristeva) 136
Harris, John P. 11, 124–131
Hasidism, Hasidic 78
Heart of Darkness (Conrad) 63, 64, 65
Heidegger, Martin 133
Heretic Blood (Higgins) 132
Hidden Ground of Love, The (Merton) 49,
    124, 156, 169

Higgins, Gregory 206
Higgins, Michael 132, 136, 143
Hollmann, Joshua 11, 169, 248
homo faber 137, 138
Horan, Daniel P., OFM 12, 149, 177, 225,
    248
"Hospitality to the Stranger" (Pearson)
    211
Hugh-Donovan, Stefanie 213
Human Condition, The (Arendt) 11, 133,
    134, 136, 137, 139, 140, 141, 221
"Human Identity and the Particularity of
    Place" (Sheldrake) 88
Human Journey, The (Padovano) 30
"Hurly-Burly Secrets" (Daggy) 52
hypostatic union 76

I

Ibn Battūta 8, 9, 30–48, 52, 62, 69, 70
"Image of Africa" (Achebe) 64
Inchausti, Robert 132
Inner Experience, The (Merton) 118, 168,
    188
intellectus 116
interior life 11, 82, 111, 112, 120, 163
Interpretation of Cultures, The (Geertz)
    57, 137
Introduction to Christian Mysticism, An
    (Merton) 197
Isaac, Jeffrey C. 143
Ishi in Two Worlds (Kroeber) 51
Ishi Means Man (Merton) 51

J

Jarvie, Ian C. 52
Jeffery, Peter 180
John Paul II 185
*Journey to Mecca: In the Footsteps of Ibn
    Battuta* 32
Julian of Norwich 29

K

Kavanaugh, John F. 226
Kelty, Matthew 113
kenosis 79, 241
Kilcourse, George 30, 115, 116, 121
Kozol, Jonathan 97, 98
Kramer, Victor A. 30, 118, 221, 248
Kreeft, Peter 76
Kristeva, Julia 68, 136

Kroeber, Theodora 51
Kwon, Hyeokil 11, 144, 248

L

Labrie, Ross 7, 30
Lacan, Jacques 66, 207
Lakota 80
Larkin, Philip 228
Laughlin, James 30, 31, 86, 113, 150,
    154, 205
Lawrence, Peter 67
Learning to Love (Merton) 50, 91, 104,
    149
lectio divina 12, 115, 116, 197–204
"Lectio Divina" (Merton) 197-204
Lectio Divina (Pennington) 197
"Legacies of Reading in the Late Poetry
    of Thomas Merton" (Stewart) 209
Legends of Modernity (Milosz) 110
Lentfoehr, Thérèse 30
Leonard, Bill 208
"Let Mercy Fall Like Rain" (Pearson) 210
"Letters to a White Liberal" (Merton) 10,
    23, 96
Lévi-Strauss, Claude 50, 59, 60
Life and Holiness (Merton) 175, 183, 193
Life of the Mind, The (Arendt) 141
Life Together (Bonhoeffer) 160
Linthors, Ann 182
Lipsey, Roger 7
Literary Essays (Merton) 57, 104, 114
Location of Culture, The (Bhabha) 68
logos 66, 79
Lumen Gentium 184, 185, 241

M

Making of a Saint (Bragan) 206
Malinowski, Bronislaw 49-73
Mann, Thomas 66-67
"Many-Storied Monastic, A" (Reardon)
    214
Marcus, George E. 56
Marriage in the Western Church (Reyn-
    olds) 180
Martone, Lawrence 177
Marty, Martin E. 10, 23, 24, 249
Masheck, Joseph 207
Mason, Herbert 169
Massignon, Louis 169, 170, 175

McDonald, Mary Murray 12, 197, 249
McKenna, Thomas 147
McNerney, James R. 145
Mecca 32, 33, 36, 41, 42, 62
Mechtild of Magdeburg 29
Meditations before Mass (Guardini) 202
Men in Dark Times (Arendt) 136
Menninger, Roy 213
"Merton and Camus on Christian Dia-
    logue with a Postmodern World"
    (Belcastro) 107, 122
"Merton and Massignon" (Mason) 169
Merton and Sufism: The Untold Story 169
"Merton and the Desert Experience"
    (McNerney) 145
"Merton's Insights Applied to Marriage"
    (Martone) 177
Merton's Palace of Nowhere (Finley) 7
metaphysics 60, 239
"Milosz and Merton at the Metropolis"
    (Contino) 209
Milosz, Czeslaw 7, 8, 11, 104–112, 113,
    114, 116, 121, 123, 209, 210
Milroy, Dominic 215
Monastic Journey, The (Merton) 146, 155
Monastic Vision for the 21st Century, A
    (Hart, ed.) 157
monasticism 7, 26, 69, 157, 158, 159,
    160, 161, 212, 217, 222, 224, 248
Monk in the World, A (Teasdale) 158
Morley, Sylvanus Griswold 50
Mott, Michael 113, 123
Mounier, Emmanuel 84
Moviegoer, The (Percy) 114, 118, 119,
    120, 121, 122, 123
Mystery of Christian Marriage, The (Jef-
    fery) 180
Mystic Heart, The (Teasdale) 159
Mysticism (Underhill) 226
Mystics and Zen Masters (Merton) 119

N

Nabokov, Peter 51
National Catholic Reporter, The 23
nature 12, 44, 45, 60, 76, 79, 106, 110,
    112, 118, 122, 123, 139, 142, 159,
    167, 180, 189, 191, 192, 209, 227,
    231, 240, 241, 244

Neihardt, John 51
New Friars, The (Bessenecker) 162
New Jim Crow, The (Alexander) 97
New Man, The (Merton) 75, 165, 177
New Monasticism (Wilson-Hartgrove) 11, 154, 159, 160, 161
New Seeds of Contemplation (Merton) 75, 77, 151, 167, 184
New Testament 76
New York Herald Tribune 23
Nicholas of Cusa 169–76, 248
Nietzsche, Friedrich 67
No Man Is an Island (Merton) 177, 184, 190, 195
Nugent, Robert 233

O

O'Connell, Patrick F. 8, 30, 32, 116, 145, 146, 147, 150, 178, 197, 243, 249
Odorisio, David M. 216
Of Grammatology (Derrida) 58
O'Hara, Patrick 208
Ong, Walter J. 25
Opening the Bible (Merton) 202
Orality and Literacy (Ong) 25
Origen 77
Origin and Meaning of Hasidism, The (Buber) 78
Original Child Bomb (Merton) 61
Origins of Totalitarianism, The (Arendt) 133
Other Side of the Mountain, The (Merton) 51, 74, 104

P

Pacem in Terris (John XXIII) 18
Padovano, Anthony T. 30
Pannikar, Raimon 79
Pasternak, Boris 11, 115, 124, 125, 128, 129, 130
Pauline teaching 76, 191
Peace Be with You (Carlson) 207
Pearson, Paul M. 30, 210, 211
Pennington, Basil 197
Pensée Sauvage, La (Lévi-Strauss) 50
Percy, Walker 11, 114-15, 118-23
Phelps, Sr. Jamie 102
Pilgrims in Their Own Land (Marty) 24
Plague, The (Camus) 107

Playing and Reality (Winnicott) 130
"Poetic Rhetoric and Baffling Illogic" (Stull) 30
Poetique de l'Espace, La (Bachelard) 66
point vierge 101
Poks, Malgorzata 8, 9, 30, 49, 50, 249
polis 137, 138, 139, 140, 141, 142, 175
post-structuralist moment 59, 60
Pramuk, Christopher 9, 91, 100, 101, 103, 173, 174, 212, 220, 249
Praying the Psalms (Merton) 202, 203
Precious Thoughts (Merton) 206, 247
Predicament of Culture, The (Clifford) 53
Profiles in Discipleship (Higgins) 206
Protestant 25, 26, 27, 29, 76, 220, 222

Q

Quenon, Paul 243-44

R

Raab, Joseph Quinn 12, 23, 205, 250
Rahner, Karl 29, 102, 184
Raids on the Unspeakable (Merton) 32, 100, 112, 148, 217
Randall, Virginia F. 30
Reardon, Patrick Henry 214
Redeeming the Time (Merton) 192
Retreat with Thomas Merton, A (Goergen) 236
Returning to Reality (Thompson) 223
revelation 39, 134, 137, 141, 142, 171, 173, 175, 199, 220
Revolution in Anthropology, The (Jarvie) 52
Reynolds, Philip Lyndon 180
Rhythm of Being, The (Pannikar) 79
Rice, Edward 214
Rilke, Rainer Maria 209, 244
Road Belong Cargo (Lawrence) 67
Road to Joy, The (Merton) 114
Run to the Mountain (Merton) 93, 104

S

sacrament 77, 160, 177, 178, 181, 186, 187, 188, 189, 190, 192, 194, 195
sacramentality 76, 78, 181
Sacred and the Profane, The (Eliade) 74
Sacred Reading (Casey) 197
Sanctuary of the Soul (Foster) 161
Sandor, Monica 180

Sapientia 116
Savage Inequalities (Kozol) 97
School of Charity, The (Merton) 144
Schweitzer, Albert 29
scientia 116
Scruggs, Ryan 208
Search for Solitude, A (Merton) 94, 104, 145, 190, 203
Second Space: New Poems (Milosz) 111, 210
Seeds of Destruction (Merton) 10, 23, 26, 27, 94
"Seven Essays on Albert Camus" (Merton) 104
Seven Mountains of Thomas Merton, The (Mott) 113
Seven Storey Mountain, The (Merton) 26, 61, 93, 94, 176, 212
Shame of the Nation, The (Kozol) 97
Shannon, William H. 30, 141, 146, 178
Sheldrake, Philip 88
Sign of Jonas, The (Merton) 7, 101, 111, 151, 156
Signs of Peace (Apel) 169
Silence Speaks (Nugent) 233
Silent Action, A (Williams) 217
Silent Life, The (Merton) 155
Silent Spring (Carson) 105
Six Letters (Pasternak/Merton) 125
Smith, Huston 29
Songs in the Key of Life (Wonder) 91
Sophia 169–76, 212
Sophia (Pramuk) 100, 173, 212, 220, 250
soul 67, 76, 110, 163, 166, 183, 214, 230, 231
Space and Place (Yi-Fu) 7
Speech and Phenomena (Derrida) 58
spiritual anthropology 75
spiritual theology 90
spirituality of marriage 177–196
Springs of Contemplation, The (Merton) 152
Stewart, Dustin 209
Stranger, The (Camus) 57, 114, 117, 118, 119
Striving towards Being (Merton/Milosz) 8, 104, 113

"Structure, Sign and Play in the Discourses of the Human Sciences" (Lévi-Strauss) 60
Stull, Brad T. 30
Sutton, Walter 30

T

Teasdale, Wayne 158-59
technology 135, 137, 147, 149, 153, 221, 222, 223, 224, 225
Teilhard de Chardin, Pierre, SJ 77, 233–235
Testament to Freedom, A (Bonhoeffer) 160
Texts On (Texts On) Art (Mashek) 207
thesis 60, 73, 100, 206
Third Desert (Blée) 207
Thomas Aquinas, St. 76, 77, 78, 140, 141, 171, 237, 248
Thomas Merton: A Spiritual Guide for the Twenty-First Century (Ciorra) 236
"Thomas Merton: A Study in Twentieth-Century Ambiguity" (Milroy) 215
"Thomas Merton, An Artist of the Monastery" (Zuercher) 213
Thomas Merton: An Introduction (Shannon) 141
"Thomas Merton and Confucianism" (de Bary) 213
Thomas Merton and Latin America (Poks) 50, 249
"Thomas Merton and Siddhartha" (Collins) 211
"Thomas Merton and the American Epic Tradition: The Last Poems" (Sutton) 30
"Thomas Merton and the Christian East" (Bamberger) 145
Thomas Merton and the Monastic Vision (Cunningham) 75
"Thomas Merton and the Wisdom of Non-Violence" (Dear) 215
"Thomas Merton and Thomas Berry" (O'Hara) 208
Thomas Merton: Contemplation and Political Action (Aguilar) 225-27
Thomas Merton Encyclopedia, The (Shannon, Bochen, O'Connell) 30, 146,

178
Thomas Merton in Alaska (Merton) 118, 167
"Thomas Merton, Spiritual Identity, and Religious Dialogue" (Leonard) 208
Thomas Merton: Twentieth-Century Wisdom for Twenty-First-Century Living (Dekar) 221-22
"Thomas Merton: Une Biographie Spirituelle (1915-1941)" (Brulé) 212
"Thomas Merton: Word from the Silence" (Bras) 213
Thomas Merton's American Prophecy (Inchausti) 132
"Thomas Merton's Anti-Poetry" (de Nicolò) 73
Thomas Merton's Art of Denial (Cooper) 107, 117
"Thomas Merton's Creative (dis)Obedience" (Ciraulo) 211
"Thomas Merton's Last Poem" (Glimm) 30
"Thomas Merton's Novitiate Conferences on Philoxenos of Mabbug" (Odorisio) 216
"Thomas Merton's *The Geography of Lograire*" (Kramer) 30
Thomist 76, 78
Thompson, Philip M. 223
Thoughts in Solitude (Merton) 147
Thurman, Howard 98
Thurston, Bonnie Bowman 84, 157, 243-44
Tillich, Paul 29, 76, 133, 213
"To Elsie" (Williams) 53
Tracy, David 73
transcendence 78, 110
Travels of Ibn Battūta, The 32-49
Tristes Tropiques (Lévi-Strauss) 59
Turning Toward the World (Merton) 104, 139, 221
Two Leggings (Nabokov) 51

U
Underhill, Evelyn 226

V
Varieties of Unbelief (Marty) 23
via negativa 77, 78

"Voice in the Postmodern Wilderness, A" (McKenna) 147
von Balthasar, Hans Urs 29, 237, 239

W
Waldron, Robert 228
War Within Man (Fromm) 212-13
Weis, Monica 139, 206, 223
Whalen, Robert Weldon 11, 132, 250
Why Arendt Matters (Young-Bruehl) 136
Williams, Rowan 217
Williams, William Carlos 53
Wilson-Hartgrove, Jonathan 11, 154, 159, 160, 161
Winnicott, D. W. 130
Wisdom of the Desert, The (Merton) 145
"Wisdom, Our Sister" (Pramuk) 212
Witness to Freedom (Merton) 186, 209
Wonder, Stevie 91
Woods, Shore, Desert (Merton) 82
Words and Silence (Lentfoehr) 30
"Work of Loneliness, The" (Burton-Christie) 148
Works and Lives (Geertz) 57
Wounded Heart of Thomas Merton, The (Waldron) 228
Wretched of the Earth, The (Fanon) 57
Writing and Difference (Derrida) 58
Writing Culture (Clifford) 55
Writing Degree Zero (Barthes) 209

Y
Yi-Fu Tuan 7
Young-Bruehl, Elizabeth 133, 136

Z
Zuercher, Suzanne 213

The Merton Annual:
Index to Volumes 17 (2004)-25 (2012)

The Merton Annual 17 (2004) 286-340 contains a comprehensive index of the contents of the first sixteen volumes of the Annual, compiled by Patricia A. Burton. What follows is a similar index of the next nine volumes, up to and including the present volume. The format is basically that established in the previous index:

- The main list of authors and titles is in alphabetical order.
- Author entries are listed in three categories: articles; reviews; cross-references to works of the author reviewed in the Annual.
- Within the main list are specialized sections: Bibliographic Reviews; Editor's Introductions; Interviews.
- Reviews are divided into three categories: Merton's Works; Works about Merton; Other Works.
- A section on "Subjects, Themes, People" follows the main section and includes a listing of works by Merton that are the main focus of particular articles.

"Abraham Heschel and Thomas Merton: Prophetic Personalities, Prophetic Friendship," by Edward K. Kaplan. 23 (2010) 106-15.

Adams, Daniel J. "Han Yong-Un and Thomas Merton: Brothers in Different Guises." 19 (2006) 311-39.

Aguilar, Mario I. Thomas Merton: Contemplation and Political Action. See Reviews: Works about Merton.

Anderson, Tyson. "What Matters Is Clear." 23 (2010) 67-79.

Apel, William.
"Terrible Days: Merton/Yungblut Letters and MLK Jr.'s Death." 21 (2008) 25-32.
Rev. of Thomas Merton: A Life in Letters – The Essential Collection selected and edited by William H. Shannon and Christine M. Bochen. 23 (2010) 294-97.
Signs of Peace. See Reviews: Works about Merton.

"Art and Worship," by Thomas Merton, edited by Glenn Crider and Victor A. Kramer. 18 (2005) 19-21.

"Art in The Merton Annual, Volumes 1-5: A Bibliographical Note and Compilation," by Glenn Crider and Paul M. Pearson. 18 (2005) 315-17.

Atkinson, Morgan. Soul Searching. See Reviews: Works about Merton.

Atwood, Ron. Rev. of Lent and Easter Wisdom by Thomas Merton, edited by Jonathan Montaldo. 21 (2008) 282-85.

Au, Wilkie and Noreen. The Discerning Heart. See Reviews: Other Works.

"Authentic Identity Is Prayerful Existence," by Thomas Merton. 20 (2007) 16-24.

Bamberger, John Eudes, OCSO.
"Thomas Merton, Monk and Prophet of Peace: The Opening Address at the 2005 International Thomas Merton Society General Meeting." 19 (2006) 18-23.

Rev. of *Monastic Observances: Initiation into the Monastic Tradition 5* by Thomas Merton, edited with an Introduction by Patrick F. O'Connell. 24 (2011) 329-31.

Barron, Robert. *Catholicism: A Journey to the Heart of Faith. See* Reviews: Other Works.

"Be Alone, Together: Religious Individualism, Community and the American Spirit in Emerson, Merton and Heschel," by Shaul Magid. 23 (2010) 116-31.

Beach, Dennis (ed.). "Remarks Following a 2004 Poetry Reading," by Ernesto Cardenal, transcribed and edited by Dennis Beach with an Introduction by Patrick Hart and a Note by Corey Shouse. 18 (2005) 65-71.

Becker, Holly (producer). *Original Child Bomb. See* Reviews: Works about Merton.

Behrens, James. *Portraits of Grace. See* Reviews: Other Works.

Belcastro, David Joseph.
"An Obscure Theology Misread: 2003 Bibliographic Review." 17 (2004) 256-85.
"Thomas Merton's Revelation of Justice & Revolutions of Love: Perspectives from the San Diego Conference." 19 (2006) 39-42.
"Praying the Questions: Merton of Times Square, Last of the Urban Hermits." 20 (2007) 123-50.
"A Vow of Conversation: Past, Present & Past-Present – Thomas Merton Bibliographic Review 2007." 21 (2008) 214-54.
"Introduction: Angular Clouds of Unknowing." 22 (2009) 5-10.
"2009 Bibliographic Review: Beneath the Habit of Holiness." 23 (2010) 240-59.
"2010 Bibliographic Review: Fire Watch When the Web Goes Down." 24 (2011) 256-80.
"Introduction: The Ineffable Desert and the City or What We Call Home." 25 (2012) 7-12.
"Voices from the Desert: Merton, Camus and Milosz." 25 (2012) 104-12.
Rev. of *Silence Speaks: Teilhard de Chardin, Yves Congar, John Courtney Murray, and Thomas Merton* by Robert Nugent. 25 (2012) 233-35.

Bell, Ian. Rev. of *Thomas Merton: Contemplation and Political Action* by Mario I. Aguilar. 25 (2012) 225-27.

Beltrán Llavador, Fernando (ed.). *Seeds of Hope / Semillas de Esperanza. See* Reviews: Works about Merton.

Bibliographic Reviews
2003 "An Obscure Theology Misread: 2003 Bibliographic Review," by David Joseph Belcastro. 17 (2004) 256-85.
2004 "Reading Merton from the (Polish) Margin: 2004 Bibliographic Survey," by Malgorzata Poks. 18 (2005) 318-48.
2005 "Return to Sources, Holy Insecurity and Life in a Tiny House: 2005 Bibliographic Essay," by Gray Matthews. 19 (2006) 369-96.
2006 "Week of a Stranger: Thomas Merton Bibliographic Review 2006," by Donald Grayston. 20 (2007) 299-340.
2007 "A Vow of Conversation: Past, Present & Past-Present – Thomas Merton Bibliographic Review 2007," by David Joseph Belcastro. 21 (2008) 214-54.
2008 "Bibliographic Review: The Mystic's Hope: Thomas Merton's Contemplative Message to a Distracted World," by Gray Matthews. 22 (2009) 227-60.

2009 "2009 Bibliographic Review: Beneath the Habit of Holiness," by David Joseph Belcastro. 23 (2010) 240-59.

2010 "2010 Bibliographic Review: Fire Watch When the Web Goes Down," by David Joseph Belcastro. 24 (2011) 256-80.

2011 "2011 Bibliographic Review: Pointing Fingers at the Calm Eye of the Storm," by Joseph Quinn Raab. 25 (2012) 205-16.

Bilbro, Jeffrey. "From Violence to Silence: The Rhetorical Means and Ends of Thomas Merton's Antipoetry." 22 (2009) 120-49.

Billy, Dennis, CSsR. *With Open Heart. See* Reviews: Other Works.

Bludworth, Patrick. "Desert Fathers and Asian Masters: Thomas Merton's Outlaw Lineage." 17 (2004) 166-94.

Bochen, Christine M.
Rev. of *Between Two Souls: Conversations with Ryokan* by Mary Lou Kownacki. 18 (2005) 355-60.
Rev. of *Echoing Silence: Thomas Merton on the Vocation of Writing* by Thomas Merton, edited by Robert Inchausti. 21 (2008) 274-77.
Rev. of *Beneath the Mask of Holiness: Thomas Merton and the Forbidden Love Affair That Set Him Free* by Mark Shaw. 23 (2010) 306-15.
(ed.) *Cold War Letters* by Thomas Merton. *See* Reviews: Merton's Works.
(ed.) *Thomas Merton: A Life in Letters. See* Reviews: Merton's Works.

Bogert-O'Brien, Daniel. "Thomas Merton and Ivan Illich: Two Mendicant Anti-professionals in the Age of the Simulacra of the Professions and the System." 24 (2011) 233-43.

Borgmann, Albert. "Contemplation in a Technological Era: Learning from Thomas Merton." 24 (2011) 54-66.

Borys, Peter N., Jr. *Transforming Heart and Mind. See* Reviews: Other Works.

Bourgeault, Cynthia.
"Centering Prayer and Attention of the Heart." 20 (2007) 151-63.
Chanting the Psalms. See Reviews: Other Works.

Boykin, Kimberly. Rev. of *Waking Up to What You Do: A Zen Practice for Meeting Every Situation with Intelligence and Compassion* by Diane Eschin Rizzetto. 20 (2007) 394-97.

"A Bricoleur in the Monastery: Merton's Tactics in a Nothing Place," by Fred W. Herron. 19 (2006) 114-27.

Burgdof, Craig. Rev. of *Merton & Buddhism: Wisdom, Emptiness & Everyday Mind* edited by Bonnie Bowman Thurston. 21 (2008) 272-74.

Burridge, Kenelm. "Merton, Cargo Cults and *The Geography of Lograire.*" 17 (2004) 206-15.

Burton, Patricia A.
"Editorial Note Concerning Thomas Merton's *Peace in the Post-Christian Era*, Chapter 15." 17 (2004) 14-15.
"Forbidden Book: Thomas Merton's *Peace in the Post-Christian Era.*" 17 (2004) 27-57.
"Index to *The Merton Annual*, Volumes 1-16." 17 (2004) 286-340.
More Than Silence: A Bibliography of Thomas Merton. See Reviews: Works about Merton.

Cannon, Nassif.
  "Thomas Merton and St. John of the Cross: Lives on Fire." 21 (2008) 205-13.
  "No Mirror, No Light – Just This! Merton's Discovery of Global Wisdom." 23 (2010)
    184-96.
  "Stand on Your Own Feet! Thomas Merton and the Monk without Vows or Walls."
    25 (2012) 154-68.
Cardenal, Ernesto. "Remarks Following a 2004 Poetry Reading," transcribed and edited
  by Dennis Beach with an Introduction by Patrick Hart and a Note by Corey Shouse.
  18 (2005) 65-71.
Carrere, E. Daniel. *Creating a Human World. See* Reviews: Other Works.
Casey, Michael. *Fully Human, Fully Divine. See* Reviews: Other Works.
Casey, Thomas G. *Humble and Awake. See* Reviews: Other Works.
"Centennial Vignettes in Homage to My Father," by John Wu, Jr. 19 (2006) 283-310.
"Centering Prayer and Attention of the Heart," by Cynthia Bourgeault. 20 (2007) 151-63.
Chittister, Joan.
  Called to Question: A Spiritual Memoir. See Reviews: Other Works.
  In the Heart of the Temple. See Reviews: Other Works.
  The Way We Were. See Reviews: Other Works.
"The Christian Exploration of Non-Christian Religions: Merton's Example of Where it
  Might Lead Us," by Roger Corless. 20 (2007) 206-24.
"Christian Perspectives in World Crisis," by Thomas Merton, ed. Patricia A. Burton. 17
  (2004) 16-26.
Ciorra, Anthony. *Thomas Merton: A Spiritual Guide for the Twenty-First Century. See*
  Reviews: Works about Merton.
Collins, John P.
  "From the 'Political Dance of Death' to the 'General Dance': The Cold War Letters of
    Thomas Merton." 19 (2006) 162-77.
  "The Myth of the Fall from Paradise: Thomas Merton and Walker Percy." 21 (2008)
    150-72.
  "Two Antiheroes: Meursault and Binx Bolling Viewed through Thomas Merton's
    Literary Imagination." 25 (2012) 113-23.
  Rev. of *All the Way to Heaven: The Selected Letters of Dorothy Day* edited by Robert
    Ellsberg. 24 (2011) 332-36.
"Complementary Approaches Illuminate Merton's Continuing Relevance for Today's Broken
  World," by Dewey Weiss Kramer. 19 (2006) 17.
"Comrades for Peace: Thomas Merton, The Dalai Lama and the Preferential Option for
  Nonviolence," by Joseph Quinn Raab. 19 (2006) 255-66.
"The Conflict Not Yet Fully Faced: Thomas Merton as Reader in His Journals," by Chris
  Orvin. 18 (2005) 205-36.
Conner, James, OCSO.
  "Thomas Merton – Final Integration through Interreligious Dialogue." 23 (2010) 20-28.
  Rev. of *The Rule of Saint Benedict: Initiation into the Monastic Tradition 4* by Thomas
    Merton, edited with an Introduction by Patrick F. O'Connell. 23 (2010) 286-88.
  The Voice of the Stranger. See Reviews: Works about Merton.

"Contemplation in a Technological Era: Learning from Thomas Merton," by Albert Borgmann. 24 (2011) 54-66.

"Contemporary Architectural Witness to the Lived Cistercian Ideal: The Abbey Churches of Gethsemani and Conyers," by Dewey Weiss Kramer. 18 (2005) 96-108.

"The Context of Thomas Merton's Letter Concerning 'The Jesus Prayer,'" by Thomas Francis Smith. 19 (2006) 15-16.

Cooper, Jeffrey A., CSC.
  "Divining the Inscaped-Landscape: Hopkins, Merton and the Ascent to True Self." 18 (2005) 127-39.
  Rev. of *The Pocket Thomas Merton* edited by Robert Inchausti. 19 (2006) 397-99.

Corless, Roger. "The Christian Exploration of Non-Christian Religions: Merton's Example of Where It Might Lead Us." 20 (2007) 206-24.

Corris, Michael. *Ad Reinhardt. See* Reviews: Other Works.

Crider, Glenn.
  & Paul M. Pearson. "Art in *The Merton Annual*, Volumes 1-5: A Bibliographical Note and Compilation." 18 (2005) 315-17.
  (ed.) "The Monk and Sacred Art" (1956) and "Art and Worship" (1959), by Thomas Merton, edited by Glenn Crider and Victor A. Kramer. 18 (2005) 14-21.
  (ed.) "'Unadorned Ideal': An Interview in Two Parts with Methodius Telnack," conducted and edited with notes by Victor A. Kramer and Glenn Crider. 18 (2005) 77-95.and Paul M. Pearson. "Art in *The Merton Annual*, Volumes 1-5: A Bibliographical Note and Compilation." 18 (2005) 315-17.
  (ed.) "Interview with James Finley: Cultivating a Contemplative Lifestyle." 19 (2006) 355-68.
  (ed.) "An Interview with Fr. Raymond Pedrizetti, O.S.B. – February 12, 2005." 20 (2007) 278-91.
  Rev. of *The Vision of Thomas Merton* edited by Patrick F. O'Connell. 17 (2004) 345-48.
  Rev. of *Writing Your Spiritual Autobiography* by Richard B. Patterson. 18 (2005) 363-64.
  Rev. of *Creating a Human World: A New Psychology and Religious Anthropology in Dialogue with Freud, Heidegger, and Kierkegaard* by E. Daniel Carrere. 20 (2007) 363-67.

Crosby, Catherine.
  Rev. of *Humble and Awake: Coping with Our Comatose Culture* by Thomas G. Casey. 19 (2006) 435-37.
  Rev. of *Contemplation in Action* by Richard Rohr and Friends. 20 (2007) 375-78.

Dadosky, John D. "Merton as Method for Inter-religious Engagement: Examples from Buddhism." 21 (2008) 33-43.

Dannenfelser, Mark A. Rev. of *With Open Heart: Spiritual Direction in the Alphonsian Tradition* by Dennis Billy, CSsR. 19 (2006) 430-34.

Dart, Ron. "Thomas Merton and George Grant: Hawk's Dream, Owl's Insight," 17 (2004) 120-36.

Davis, Robert Leigh. "Sacred Play: Thomas Merton's *Cables to the Ace*." 20 (2007) 243-64.

Dear, John. "The God of Peace is Never Glorified by Human Violence: Keynote Address to the International Thomas Merton Society, June 2005." 19 (2006) 24-38.

Deignan, Kathleen, CND.
"'In the Night of Our Technological Barbarism': Thomas Merton's Light on the Matter." 24 (2011) 112-27.
Review Symposium of *The Environmental Vision of Thomas Merton* by Monica Weis, SSJ. 24 (2011) 289-305.
A Book of Hours. See Reviews: Merton's Works.

Dekar, Paul R.
"What the Machine Produces and What the Machine Destroys: Thomas Merton on Technology." 17 (2004) 216-34.
"*The Spirit of Simplicity*: Thomas Merton on Simplification of Life." 19 (2006) 267-82.
"Thomas Merton, Guide to the Right Use of Technology." 24 (2011) 150-75.
Rev. of *Cold War Letters* by Thomas Merton, edited by William H. Shannon and Christine M. Bochen. 20 (2007) 341-43.
Rev. of *Signs of Peace: The Interfaith Letters of Thomas Merton* by William Apel. 20 (2007) 344-46.
Creating the Beloved Community. See Reviews: Other Works.
Thomas Merton: Twentieth-Century Wisdom for Twenty-First-Century Living. See Reviews: Works about Merton.

DelCogliano, Mark.
Rev. of *Cassian and the Fathers: Initiation into the Monastic Tradition* by Thomas Merton, edited with an Introduction by Patrick F. O'Connell. 19 (2006) 400-407.
Rev. of *Pre-Benedictine Monasticism: Initiation into the Monastic Tradition 2* by Thomas Merton, edited with an Introduction by Patrick F. O'Connell. 20 (2007) 346-53.

De Pillis, Mario, Sr. Rev. of *A Meeting of Angels: The Correspondence of Thomas Merton with Edward Deming and Faith Andrews* edited by Paul M. Pearson. 23 (2010) 290-94.

Derkse, Wil. *The Rule of Benedict for Beginners. See* Reviews: Other Works.

"Desert Fathers and Asian Masters: Thomas Merton's Outlaw Lineage," by Patrick Bludworth. 17 (2004) 166-94.

de Waal, Esther. *Lost in Wonder: Rediscovering the Spiritual Art of Attentiveness. See* Reviews: Other Works.

"Digital Natives and the Digital Self: The Wisdom of Thomas Merton for Millennial Spirituality and Self-Understanding," by Daniel P. Horan, OFM. 24 (2011) 83-111.

"A Discovery: Thomas Merton's Poetry As Art Song; Compositions by Bryan Beaumont Hays, OSB: A Bibliographical Note," by Anthony Feuerstein. 18 (2005) 72-76.

"Divining the Inscaped-Landscape: Hopkins, Merton and the Ascent to True Self," by Jeffrey A. Cooper. 18 (2005) 127-39.

"Do I Want a Small Painting? The Correspondence of Thomas Merton and Ad Reinhardt: An Introduction and Commentary," by Roger Lipsey. 18 (2005) 260-314.

Driscoll, Jeremy. *A Monk's Alphabet. See* Reviews: Other Works.

Durken, Daniel, Eric Hollas and Stefanie Weisgram. "Three Comments about Benedictine Monastic Community Reading." 18 (2005) 59-64.

"Early Reflections in a 'Nothing Place': Three Gethsemani Poems," by Deborah P. Kehoe. 17 (2004) 61-75.

"Editorial Note Concerning Thomas Merton's *Peace in the Post-Christian Era*, Chapter 15," by Patricia A. Burton. 17 (2004) 14-15.

Editors' Introductions

2004 "Introduction: A Simplicity of Wonder: Merton's Honor for the Particular Extending Outward," by Victor A. Kramer. 17 (2004) 7-13.

2005 "Introduction: Monastic Awareness, Liturgy and Art: The Benedictine Tradition in Relation to Merton's Growing Artistic Interests," by Victor A. Kramer. 18 (2005) 7-10.

2006 "The Continuing Tradition of Prayer and Continuing Social Awareness Sustain the Vision of Thomas Merton," by Victor A. Kramer. 19 (2006) 7-12.

2007 "Introduction: To Pray Contemplatively Is to Work Mysteriously toward the Center," by Victor A. Kramer 20 (2007) 7-15.

2008 "Introduction: Wide Open to Marveling, Fearing, Burning and Enduring," by Gray Matthews. 21 (2008) 7-12.

2009 "Introduction: Angular Clouds of Unknowing," by David Joseph Belcastro. 22 (2009) 5-10.

2010 "Introduction: Facing the Astonishing," by Gray Matthews. 23 (2010) 7-12.

2011 "Introduction: Upon Hearing an Aeolian Harp," by Gray Matthews. 24 (2011) 7-14.

2012 "Introduction: The Ineffable Desert and the City or What We Call Home," by David Joseph Belcastro. 25 (2012) 7-12.

Egan, Keith J. "Thomas Merton's Approach to St. John of the Cross." 20 (2007) 62-78.

Ellsberg, Robert.
"Thomas Merton, Henri Nouwen, and the Living Gospel." 19 (2006) 340-54.
All the Way to Heaven. See Reviews: Other Works.

"Encounter in a Secret Country: Thomas Merton and Jorge Carrera Andrade," by Malgorzata Poks. 18 (2005) 140-66.

"The Ends of Anxiety in Merton and Heschel," by Martin Kavka. 23 (2010) 132-48.

Farge, Emile J. "Thomas Merton and Paramahansa Yogananda: Two Prayerful Mergings of Cult and Culture." 20 (2007) 164-84.

Fayle, Vaughn, OFM. "An Interview about Thomas Merton" with Martin E. Marty, edited by Joseph Quinn Raab. 25 (2012) 23-29.

Ferry, W. H. "The Technophiliacs." 24 (2011) 29-38.

Feuerstein, Anthony.
"A Discovery: Thomas Merton's Poetry As Art Song; Compositions by Bryan Beaumont Hays, OSB: A Bibliographical Note." 18 (2005) 72-76.
Rev. of *The Benedictine Handbook* by Anthony Marett-Crosby and *Prayer in All Things: A Saint Benedict's St. John's Prayer Book* edited by Kate E. Riger and Michael Kwatera, OSB. 17 (2004) 357-59.
Rev. of *Benedictine Daily Prayer: A Short Breviary* compiled and edited by Maxwell E. Johnson. 19 (2006) 440-43.
Rev. of *Angelic Mistakes: The Art of Thomas Merton* by Roger Lipsey. 20 (2007) 360-63.

"Firewatch in the Belly of the Whale: Imagery of Fire, Water, and Place in *The Sign of Jonas,*" by David Leigh, SJ. 17 (2004) 153-65.

"Forbidden Book: Thomas Merton's *Peace in the Post-Christian Era,*" by Patricia A. Burton. 17 (2004) 27-57.

Foreman, Mary, OSB. Rev. of *Seeking Paradise: The Spirit of the Shakers* by Thomas Merton, edited by Paul M. Pearson. 17 (2004) 343-45.

Forest, Jim. *Living with Wisdom.* See Reviews: Works about Merton.

"Four Unpublished Poems," by Thomas Merton. 22 (2009) 210-19.

"Frank Kacmarcik and the Cistercian Architectural Tradition," by R. Kevin Seasoltz. 18 (2005) 22-32.

Frazier, Julie. Rev. of *Gandhi on Non-Violence: Selected Texts from Gandhi's Non-Violence in Peace and War* by Thomas Merton. 21 (2008) 269-72.

"From the 'Political Dance of Death' to the 'General Dance': The Cold War Letters of Thomas Merton," by John P. Collins. 19 (2006) 162-77.

"From Thomas Merton's 'Contemplation' to Ignatius of Loyola's 'Contemplation to Obtain Love': A Personal Prayer Journey," by Richard J. Hauser. 20 (2007) 93-108.

"From Violence to Silence: The Rhetorical Means and Ends of Thomas Merton's Anti-poetry," by Jeffrey Bilbro. 22 (2009) 120-49.

Gardner, Fiona.
"A Kind of Arduous and Unthanked Pioneering." 23 (2010) 59-66.
"You Are You: That Is the Most Important Thing – Everything Is in It Somewhere: An Analysis of the Correspondence from Thomas Merton to John Harris." 25 (2012) 124-31.
Rev. of *The Wounded Heart of Thomas Merton* by Robert Waldron. 25 (2012) 228-32.

"*The Geography of Lograire* as Merton's *Gestus* – Prolegomena," by Malgorzata Poks. 22 (2009) 150-69.

"The Geography of Solitude: Inner Space and the Sense of Place," by Angus F. Stuart. 17 (2004) 76-87.

Giacalone, Arthur. Rev. of *Soul Searching: The Journey of Thomas Merton,* a film by Morgan Atkinson. 21 (2008) 277-81.

"The God of Peace is Never Glorified by Human Violence: Keynote Address to the International Thomas Merton Society, June 2005," by John Dear. 19 (2006) 24-38.

Goergen, Donald, OP. *A Retreat with Thomas Merton.* See Reviews: Works about Merton.

Golemboski, David. "What Kind of World-Lover? Thomas Merton on Dietrich Bonhoeffer and Death-of-God Theology." 23 (2010) 197-211.

Grayston, Donald.
"Week of a Stranger: Thomas Merton Bibliographic Review 2006." 20 (2007) 299-340.
Rev. of *Thomas Merton: An Introduction* by William H. Shannon. 19 (2006) 410-13.
Rev. of *In My Own Words* by Thomas Merton, edited by Jonathan Montaldo. 21 (2008) 281-82.
Rev. of *Professional Morality and Guilty Bystanding: Merton's Conjectures and the Value of Work* by Barry L. Padgett. 23 (2010) 300-303.

Review Symposium of *The Environmental Vision of Thomas Merton* by Monica Weis, SSJ. 24 (2011) 305-13.

Greene, Dana.
Rev. of *Grace through Simplicity: The Practical Spirituality of Evelyn Underhill* by John Kirvan. 18 (2005) 362-63.
Rev. of *Transforming Heart and Mind: Learning from the Mystics* by Peter N. Borys, Jr. 20 (2007) 383-84.

Griffith, Kevin.
Rev. of *Pax Intrantibus: A Meditation on the Poetry of Thomas Merton* by Frederick Smock. 21 (2008) 261-63.
Rev. of *Afternoons with Emily* by Paul Quenon and *Belonging to Borders: A Sojourn in the Celtic Tradition* by Bonnie Thurston. 25 (2012) 243-45.

Griffith, Michael. "Thomas Merton on William Blake: 'To Look through Matter into Eternity.'" 18 (2005) 109-26.

Grip, Robert. Rev. of *Thomas Merton: A Spiritual Guide for the Twenty-First Century* [CDs] by Anthony Ciorra & *A Retreat with Thomas Merton* [CDs] by Donald Goergen, OP. 25 (2012) 236.

Gross, Martha. Rev. of *Great Mystics & Social Justice: Walking on the Two Feet of Love* by Susan Rakoczy. 20 (2007) 378-82.

Gustafson, Hans. "Place, Spiritual Anthropology and Sacramentality in Thomas Merton's Later Years." 25 (2012) 74-90.

Hall, Gary. "Openness, Availability, Capacity for Gift." 24 (2011) 176-87.

"Han Yong-Un and Thomas Merton: Brothers in Different Guises," by Daniel J. Adams. 19 (2006) 311-39.

Harford, James.
"Lax, Merton and Rice on War and Peace." 19 (2006) 234-54.
Merton and Friends. *See* Reviews: Works about Merton.

Harmless, William, SJ. *Mystics*. *See* Reviews: Other Works.

Harpur, James. *Love Burning in the Soul*. *See* Reviews: Other Works.

Hart, Patrick. Introduction to "Remarks Following a 2004 Poetry Reading," by Ernesto Cardenal. 18 (2005) 65-66.

Hauser, Richard J. "From Thomas Merton's 'Contemplation' to Ignatius of Loyola's 'Contemplation to Obtain Love': A Personal Prayer Journey." 20 (2007) 93-108.

"The Heart Is the Common Ground: Thomas Merton and Chögyam Trungpa in Dialogue," by Judith Simmer-Brown. 23 (2010) 47-58.

"The Heart of the Fire: Technology, Commotion and Contemplation," by Gray Matthews. 24 (2011) 128-49.

Herron, Fred W.
"A Bricoleur in the Monastery: Merton's Tactics in a Nothing Place." 19 (2006) 114-27.
"'Our Transformation in Christ': Thomas Merton and Transformative Learning." 21 (2008) 186-204.

Higgins, Michael W. "The Priestly Imagination: Thomas Merton and the Poetics of Critique." 22 (2009) 11-23.

Hinkle, Harry L. *Thomas Merton's Gethsemani. See* Reviews: Works about Merton.

Hinson, E. Glenn. "Ignatian and Puritan Prayer: Surprising Similarities; A Comparison of Ignatius Loyola and Richard Baxter on Meditation." 20 (2007) 79-92.

Hizer, Cynthia Ann. Rev. of *Thomas Merton's Gethsemani: Landscapes of Paradise* by Monica Weis, photographs by Harry L. Hinkle. 19 (2006) 417-19.

Hoffman, Kathy. "Praying the Psalms: A Layperson's Path to Contemplation." 20 (2007) 38-61.

Holder, Arthur. *Christian Spirituality: The Classics. See* Reviews: Other Works.

Hollas, Eric, Daniel Durken and Stefanie Weisgram. "Three Comments about Benedictine Monastic Community Reading." 18 (2005) 59-64.

Hollmann, Joshua. "Searching for *Sophia*: Nicholas of Cusa and Thomas Merton." 25 (2012) 169-76.

Horan, Daniel P., OFM.
    "'Those Going Among the Saracens and Other Nonbelievers': Thomas Merton and Franciscan Interreligious Dialogue." 21 (2008) 44-66.
    "Striving toward Authenticity: Merton's 'True Self' and the Millennial Generation's Search for Identity." 23 (2010) 80-89.
    "Digital Natives and the Digital Self: The Wisdom of Thomas Merton for Millennial Spirituality and Self-Understanding." 24 (2011) 83-111.
    "No Spouse Is an Island: Thomas Merton's Contribution toward a Contemporary Spirituality of Marriage." 25 (2012) 177-96.
    Rev. of *Living with Wisdom: A Life of Thomas Merton* by Jim Forest, rev. ed. 22 (2009) 273-76.
    Review Symposium of *Sophia: The Hidden Christ of Thomas Merton* by Christopher Pramuk. 23 (2010) 260-65.
    Rev. of *Thomas Merton: Twentieth-Century Wisdom for Twenty-First-Century Living* by Paul R. Dekar. 25 (2012) 221-25.

"'A Humanly Impoverished Thirst for Light': Thomas Merton's Receptivity to the Feminine, to Judaism, and to Religious Pluralism," by Edward K. Kaplan. 17 (2004) 137-52.

Hunter, Judith. "No Solution in Withdrawal – No Solution in Conforming: Merton, Teilhard, Kung and Curran." 19 (2006) 43-90.

"Ignatian and Puritan Prayer: Surprising Similarities; A Comparison of Ignatius Loyola and Richard Baxter on Meditation," by E. Glenn Hinson. 20 (2007) 79-92.

"In Memoriam: 'We Are Life, Its Shining Gift' – Roger Jonathan Corless (26 June 1938-12 January 2007)," by Harry Wells. 20 (2007) 203-205.

"'In the Dark before Dawn': Thomas Merton's Mystical Poetics," by Lynn R. Szabo. 22 (2009) 24-40.

"'In the Night of Our Technological Barbarism': Thomas Merton's Light on the Matter," by Kathleen Deignan, CND. 24 (2011) 112-27.

"In the Zen Garden of the Lord: Thomas Merton's Stone Garden," by Roger Lipsey. 21 (2008) 91-105.

Inchausti, Robert
    (ed.). *The Pocket Thomas Merton. See* Reviews: Merton's Works.

(ed.). *Echoing Silence. See* Reviews: Merton's Works.

"Index to *The Merton Annual*, Volumes 1-16," compiled by Patricia A. Burton. 17 (2004) 286-340.

"Insights from the Inter-Contemplative Dialogue: Merton's Three Meanings of 'God' and Religious Pluralism," by Joseph Quinn Raab. 23 (2010) 90-105.

Interviews
  Allchin, Canon A. M. "'A Very Disciplined Person'. . . from Nelson County: An Interview with Canon A. M. Allchin about Merton." Interview by Victor A. Kramer. 17 (2004) 235-55.

  Conner, James, OCSO. "'A Dedication to Prayer and a Dedication to Humanity': An Interview about Thomas Merton with James Conner, OCSO," conducted and edited by Paul M. Pearson. 23 (2010) 212-39.

  Ferlinghetti, Lawrence. "Interview with Lawrence Ferlinghetti," conducted by Paul Wilkes and edited by Gray Matthews. 22 (2009) 220-26.

  Ferry, W. H. "An Interview with W. H. (Ping) Ferry about Thomas Merton," conducted by Paul Wilkes, transcribed and edited by Paul M. Pearson. 24 (2011) 39-53.

  Finley, James. "Interview with James Finley: Cultivating a Contemplative Lifestyle," conducted and edited by Glenn Crider. 19 (2006) 355-68.

  Kramer, Victor A. "'Living and Learning with Merton for Decades': An Interview with Victor A. Kramer, Editor," conducted and edited by Glenn Crider. 20 (2007) 292-98.

  Marty, Martin E. "An Interview about Thomas Merton," conducted by Vaughn Fayle, OFM and edited by Joseph Quinn Raab. 25 (2012) 23-29.

  McDonnell, Kilian. "An Interview with Fr. Kilian McDonnell, O.S.B. – February 11, 2005," conducted and edited by Victor A. Kramer. 20 (2007) 265-77.

  Pedrizetti, Raymond. "An Interview with Fr. Raymond Pedrizetti, O.S.B. – February 12, 2005," conducted and edited by Victor A. Kramer. 20 (2007) 278-91.

  Telnack, Methodius. "'Unadorned Ideal': An Interview in Two Parts with Methodius Telnack," conducted and edited with notes by Victor A. Kramer and Glenn Crider. 18 (2005) 77-95.

"Is Desert Spirituality Viable in the Twenty-First-Century City? The Legacy of the Desert Fathers in Thomas Merton," by Hyeokil Kwon. 25 (2012) 144-53.

"Islands in the Stream: Thomas Merton's Poetry of the Early 1950s," by Patrick F. O'Connell. 22 (2009) 61-105.

"Jewels upon His Forehead: Spiritual Vision in the Poetry and Photography of Thomas Merton," by Marilyn Sunderman. 18 (2005) 167-88.

Johnson, Maxwell E. (ed.) *Benedictine Daily Prayer. See* Reviews: Other Works.

Kaplan, Edward K.
  "'A Humanly Impoverished Thirst for Light': Thomas Merton's Receptivity to the Feminine, to Judaism, and to Religious Pluralism." 17 (2004) 137-52.

  "Abraham Heschel and Thomas Merton: Prophetic Personalities, Prophetic Friendship." 23 (2010) 106-15.

  Review Symposium of *Sophia: The Hidden Christ of Thomas Merton* by Christopher Pramuk. 23 (2010) 265-69.

Kardong, Terrence G. "'Simply Go In and Pray!': St. Benedict's Oratory In RB 52." 20 (2007) 25-37.

Kavka, Martin. "The Ends of Anxiety in Merton and Heschel." 23 (2010) 132-48.

Keating, Ross. "Wisdom, Sapiential Poetry, and Personalism: Exploring Some of Thomas Merton's Ideas for Values Education." 18 (2005) 189-204.

Kehoe, Deborah P.
"Early Reflections in a 'Nothing Place': Three Gethsemani Poems." 17 (2004) 61-75.
"Thomas Merton's Ecopoetry: Bearing Witness to the Unity of Creation." 22 (2009) 170-88.

Kiernan, Jeffrey T. "Technology, Freedom and the Human Person: Some Teen Insights into Merton and Benedict XVI." 24 (2011) 244-55.

"A Kind of Arduous and Unthanked Pioneering," by Fiona Gardner. 23 (2010) 59-66.

"Kindred Spirits in Revelation and Revolution: Rachel Carson and Thomas Merton," by Monica Weis. 19 (2006) 128-41.

King, David. Rev. of *Original Child Bomb* produced by Holly Becker and directed by Carey Schonegevel. 19 (2006) 407-10.

King, John. Rev. of *More Than Silence: A Bibliography of Thomas Merton* by Patricia A. Burton. 22 (2009) 265-69.

King, Robert H. Rev. of *We Walk the Path Together: Learning from Thich Nhat Hanh & Meister Eckhart* by Brian J. Pierce. 20 (2007) 372-75.

Kirvan, John. *Grace through Simplicity: The Practical Spirituality of Evelyn Underhill.* *See* Reviews: Other Works.

Kramer, Dewey Weiss.
"Contemporary Architectural Witness to the Lived Cistercian Ideal: The Abbey Churches of Gethsemani and Conyers." 18 (2005) 96-108.
"Complementary Approaches Illuminate Merton's Continuing Relevance for Today's Broken World." 19 (2006) 17.
& Victor A. Kramer. "Standing to the Side and Watching: An Introduction and Remembrance about Interviewing Walker Percy." 21 (2008) 173-75.
"An Interview with Walker Percy about Thomas Merton," conducted by Victor A. Kramer and Dewey Weis Kramer, edited by Paul M. Pearson. 21 (2008) 176-85.
Rev. of *The Rule of Benedict for Beginners: Spirituality for Daily Life* by Wil Derkse and *Lost in Wonder: Rediscovering the Spiritual Art of Attentiveness* by Esther de Waal. 17 (2004) 355-57.
Rev. of *Engaging Benedict: What the Rule Can Teach Us Today* by Laura Swan. 19 (2006) 437-40.
Rev. of *Chanting the Psalms: A Practical Guide* by Cynthia Bourgeault. 20 (2007) 384-90.
Rev. of *Hidden in the Same Mystery: Thomas Merton and Loretto* edited by Bonnie Thurston. 24 (2011) 324-28.

Kramer, Victor A.
"Introduction: A Simplicity of Wonder: Merton's Honor for the Particular Extending Outward." 17 (2004) 7-13.
"'A Very Disciplined Person' . . . from Nelson County: An Interview with Canon A. M. Allchin about Merton." 17 (2004) 235-55.
"Introduction: Monastic Awareness, Liturgy and Art: The Benedictine Tradition in Relation to Merton's Growing Artistic Interests." 18 (2005) 7-10.

(ed.) "The Monk and Sacred Art" (1956) and "Art and Worship" (1959), by Thomas Merton, edited by Glenn Crider and Victor A. Kramer. 18 (2005) 14-21.

(ed.) "'Unadorned Ideal': An Interview in Two Parts with Methodius Telnack," conducted and edited with notes by Victor A. Kramer and Glenn Crider. 18 (2005) 77-95.

"The Continuing Tradition of Prayer and Continuing Social Awareness Sustain the Vision of Thomas Merton." 19 (2006) 7-12.

"Introduction: To Pray Contemplatively Is to Work Mysteriously toward the Center." 20 (2007) 7-15.

(ed.) "An Interview with Fr. Kilian McDonnell, O.S.B. – February 11, 2005." 20 (2007) 265-77.

(ed.) "An Interview with Fr. Raymond Pedrizetti, O.S.B. – February 12, 2005." 20 (2007) 278-91.

& Dewey Weiss Kramer. "Standing to the Side and Watching: An Introduction and Remembrance about Interviewing Walker Percy." 21 (2008) 173-75.

"An Interview with Walker Percy about Thomas Merton," conducted by Victor A. Kramer and Dewey Weis Kramer, edited by Paul M. Pearson. 21 (2008) 176-85.

Rev. of *In the Dark Before Dawn: New Selected Poems of Thomas Merton* edited by Lynn R. Szabo. 18 (2005) 349-52.

Rev. of *A Silent Action: Engagements with Thomas Merton* by Rowan Williams. 25 (2012) 217-21.

Kownacki, Mary Lou. *Between Two Souls. See* Reviews: Other Works.

Kwatera, Michael, OSB, and Kate E. Riger (eds.). *Prayer in All Things. See* Reviews: Other Works.

Kwon, Hyeokil. "Is Desert Spirituality Viable in the Twenty-First-Century City? The Legacy of the Desert Fathers in Thomas Merton." 25 (2012) 144-53.

Labrie, Ross.
"Wholeness in Thomas Merton's Poetry." 22 (2009) 41-60.
Rev. of *Thomas Merton: Hermit at the Heart of Things* by J. S. Porter. 21 (2008) 263-65.

"Landscapes of Disaster: The War Poems of Thomas Merton," by Patrick F. O'Connell. 19 (2006) 178-233.

"Lax, Merton and Rice on War and Peace," by James Harford. 19 (2006) 234-54.

Leigh, David, SJ. "Firewatch in the Belly of the Whale: Imagery of Fire, Water, and Place in *The Sign of Jonas.*" 17 (2004) 153-65.

Lipsey, Roger.
"Do I Want a Small Painting? The Correspondence of Thomas Merton and Ad Reinhardt: An Introduction and Commentary." 18 (2005) 260-314.
"In the Zen Garden of the Lord: Thomas Merton's Stone Garden." 21 (2008) 91-105.
Rev. of *Ad Reinhardt* by Michael Corris. 21 (2008) 255-57.
The Art of Thomas Merton. See Reviews: Works about Merton.

"Machine Culture and the Lone Zone: Discussing Technology and Contemplation at the 1964 Peacemaker Retreat," by Gordon Oyer. 24 (2011) 188-232.

"*Madhyamika* and *Dharmakaya*: Some Notes on Thomas Merton's Epiphany at Polonnaruwa," by Joseph Quinn Raab. 17 (2004) 195-205.

Magid, Shaul. "Be Alone, Together: Religious Individualism, Community and the American Spirit in Emerson, Merton and Heschel." 23 (2010) 116-31.

Marett-Crosby, Anthony. *The Benedictine Handbook. See* Reviews: Other Works.

Matthews, Gray.
"Reality as Sacred Place: The Parallel Insights of Thomas Merton and Henry Bugbee." 17 (2004) 88-119.
"Return to Sources, Holy Insecurity and Life in a Tiny House: 2005 Bibliographic Essay." 19 (2006) 369-96.
"Introduction: Wide Open to Marveling, Fearing, Burning and Enduring." 21 (2008) 7-12.
(ed.) "Interview with Lawrence Ferlinghetti," conducted by Paul Wilkes. 22 (2009) 220-26.
"Bibliographic Review: The Mystic's Hope: Thomas Merton's Contemplative Message to a Distracted World." 22 (2009) 227-60.
"Introduction: Facing the Astonishing." 23 (2010) 7-12.
"Introduction: Upon Hearing an Aeolian Harp." 24 (2011) 7-14.
"The Heart of the Fire: Technology, Commotion and Contemplation." 24 (2011) 128-49.
Rev. of *The Promise of Paradox: A Celebration of Contradictions in the Christian Life* by Parker J. Palmer. 21 (2008) 265-68.
Rev. of *An Introduction to Christian Mysticism: Initiation into the Monastic Tradition 3* by Thomas Merton, edited with an Introduction by Patrick F. O'Connell. 22 (2009) 261-65.
Rev. of *Seeds of Hope: Thomas Merton's Contemplative Message / Semillas de Esperanza: El Mensaje Contemplativo de Thomas Merton* edited by Fernando Beltrán Llavador and Paul M. Pearson. 22 (2009) 270-73.

McCaslin, Susan. "Pivoting toward Peace: The Engaged Poetics of Thomas Merton and Denise Levertov." 22 (2009) 189-203.

McDermott, Rachel Fell. "Why Zen Buddhism and Not Hinduism? The Asias of Thomas Merton's Voyages East." 23 (2010) 29-46.

McDonald, Mary Murray. "The Soul-Rich Monk/Priest: Thomas Merton on *Lectio Divina*." 25 (2012) 197-204.

Meade, Mark C. Rev. of *Compassionate Fire: The Letters of Thomas Merton and Catherine de Hueck Doherty* edited by Robert A. Wild. 23 (2010) 288-90.

"The Meeting of Strangers: Thomas Merton's Engagement with Latin America," by Malgorzata Poks. 20 (2007) 225-42.

Merton, Thomas.
"Christian Perspectives in World Crisis," edited Patricia A. Burton. 17 (2004) 16-26.
"'Three Prayers' Written for Frank Kacmarcik." 18 (2005) 11-14.
"The Monk and Sacred Art" (1956) and "Art and Worship" (1959), edited by Glenn Crider and Victor A. Kramer. 18 (2005) 14-21.
"To Father Thomas Fidelis (Francis) Smith, O.C.S.O." 19 (2006) 13-14.
"Authentic Identity Is Prayerful Existence." 20 (2007) 16-24.
"Four Unpublished Poems." 22 (2009) 210-19.
"Preface to Dom Denys Rutledge's *In Search of a Yogi*." 23 (2010) 13-19.
"The Wild Places," edited by Patrick F. O'Connell. 24 (2011) 15-28.
"Some Points from the Birmingham Non-Violence Movement." 25 (2012) 13-22.

"Merton as Method for Inter-religious Engagement: Examples from Buddhism," by John D. Dadosky. 21 (2008) 33-43.

"Merton, Cargo Cults and *The Geography of Lograire*," by Kenelm Burridge. 17 (2004) 206-15.

"A Merton Connection: Frank Kacmarcik, OblSB, Monk and Artist. (1920-2004)," by Charlotte Anne Zalot. 18 (2005) 33-58.

"Merton's Reflections on the Christian Artist: Art as Doorway into Eternity," by Pamela Proietti. 21 (2008) 106-16.

Miller, Lucien. "The Thomas Merton – John C. H. Wu Letters: The Lord as Postman." 19 (2006) 142-61.

Minderman, Patrick. Rev. of *The Spiritual Landscape of Mark* by Bonnie B. Thurston. 22 (2009) 280-83.

"The Monk and Sacred Art," by Thomas Merton, edited by Glenn Crider and Victor A. Kramer. 18 (2005) 15-18.

"A Monk with the Spiritual Equipment of an Artist: The Art of Thomas Merton," by Paul M. Pearson. 18 (2005) 237-59.

Montaldo, Jonathan.
(ed.) *In My Own Words. See* Reviews: Merton's Works.
(ed.) *Lent and Easter Wisdom. See* Reviews: Merton's Works.

Montello, Paul A. Rev. of *Merton and Friends: A Joint Biography of Thomas Merton, Robert Lax, and Edward Rice* by James Harford. 20 (2007) 353-60.

Morneau, Robert. *Poetry as Prayer: Jessica Powers. See* Reviews: Other Works.

"The Myth of the Fall from Paradise: Thomas Merton and Walker Percy," by John P. Collins. 21 (2008) 150-72.

"No Mirror, No Light – Just This! Merton's Discovery of Global Wisdom," by Nassif Cannon. 23 (2010) 184-96.

"No Solution in Withdrawal – No Solution in Conforming: Merton, Teilhard, Kung and Curran," by Judith Hunter. 19 (2006) 43-90.

"No Spouse Is an Island: Thomas Merton's Contribution toward a Contemporary Spirituality of Marriage," by Daniel P. Horan, OFM. 25 (2012) 177-96.

"A (Not So) Secret Son of Francis: Thomas Merton's Franciscan Lens for Seeing Heaven and Earth," by Timothy Shaffer. 21 (2008) 67-90.

Nouwen, Henri J. M.
Eternal Seasons: A Liturgical Journey with Henry J. M. Nouwen. See Reviews: Other Works.
Three Meditations on the Christian Life. See Reviews: Other Works.

Nugent, Robert. *Silence Speaks. See* Reviews: Works about Merton.

"Nurture by Nature: Emblems of Stillness in a Season of Fury," by Patrick F. O'Connell. 21 (2008) 117-49.

O'Connell, Patrick F.
"Landscapes of Disaster: The War Poems of Thomas Merton." 19 (2006) 178-233.
"Nurture by Nature: Emblems of Stillness in a Season of Fury." 21 (2008) 117-49.
"Islands in the Stream: Thomas Merton's Poetry of the Early 1950s." 22 (2009) 61-105.

"'A Son of This Instant': Thomas Merton and Ibn 'Abbād of Ronda." 23 (2010) 149-83.

(ed.) "The Wild Places," by Thomas Merton. 24 (2011) 15-28.

"Pilgrimage, the Prophet, Persecutions and Perfume: East with Ibn Battūta and Thomas Merton." 25 (2012) 30-48.

Rev. of *Seek the Silences with Thomas Merton: Reflections on Identity, Community and Transformative Action* by Charles R. Ringma. 17 (2004) 348-52.

Rev. of *A Year With Thomas Merton: Daily Meditations From His Journals* selected and edited by Jonathan Montaldo. 18 (2005) 352-55.

Rev. of *Love Burning in the Soul: The Story of the Christian Mystics, from St. Paul to Thomas Merton* by James Harpur. 19 (2006) 413-17.

Rev. of *Spirituality and Mysticism: A Global View* by James Wiseman. 20 (2007) 367-72.

Rev. of *Thomas Merton and Latin America: A Consonance of Voices* by Malgorzata Poks. 21 (2008) 257-61.

Rev. of *Mystics* by William Harmless, SJ. 22 (2009) 276-80.

Rev. of *Hidden Holiness* by Michael Plekon. 23 (2010) 315-18.

Rev. of *Christian Spirituality: The Classics* edited by Arthur Holder. 24 (2011) 336-42.

Rev. of *Catholicism: A Journey to the Heart of Faith* [book and DVDs] by Robert Barron. 25 (2012) 237-43.

(ed.) *Cassian and the Fathers. See* Reviews: Merton's Works.

(ed.) *An Introduction to Christian Mysticism. See* Reviews: Merton's Works.

(ed.) *Monastic Observances. See* Reviews: Merton's Works.

(ed.) *Pre-Benedictine Monasticism. See* Reviews: Merton's Works.

(ed.) *The Rule of Saint Benedict. See* Reviews: Merton's Works.

(ed.) *The Vision of Thomas Merton. See* Reviews: Works about Merton.

O'Malley, John W. *Four Cultures of the West. See* Reviews: Other Works.

"Openness, Availability, Capacity for Gift," by Gary Hall. 24 (2011) 176-87.

Orvin, Chris. "The Conflict Not Yet Fully Faced: Thomas Merton as Reader in His Journals." 18 (2005) 205-36.

"'Our Transformation in Christ': Thomas Merton and Transformative Learning," by Fred W. Herron. 21 (2008) 186-204.

Oyer, Gordon. "Machine Culture and the Lone Zone: Discussing Technology and Contemplation at the 1964 Peacemaker Retreat." 24 (2011) 188-232.

Padgett, Barry L. *Professional Morality and Guilty Bystanding. See* Reviews: Works about Merton.

Palmer, Parker J. *The Promise of Paradox. See* Reviews: Other Works.

Parry, Richard D. Rev. of *Creating the Beloved Community* by Paul R. Dekar. 19 (2006) 422-24.

Patterson, Richard B. *Writing Your Spiritual Autobiography. See* Reviews: Other Works.

Pearson, Paul M.

"A Monk with the Spiritual Equipment of an Artist: The Art of Thomas Merton." 18 (2005) 237-59.

& Glenn Crider. "Art in *The Merton Annual*, Volumes 1-5: A Bibliographical Note and Compilation." 18 (2005) 315-17.

(ed.) "An Interview with Walker Percy about Thomas Merton," conducted by Victor A. Kramer and Dewey Weis Kramer. 21 (2008) 176-85.

(ed.) "'A Dedication to Prayer and a Dedication to Humanity': An Interview about Thomas Merton with James Conner, OCSO" conducted and edited by Paul M. Pearson. 23 (2010) 212-39.

(ed.) "An Interview with W. H. (Ping) Ferry about Thomas Merton," conducted by Paul Wilkes. 24 (2011) 39-53.

(ed.) *A Meeting of Angels. See* Reviews: Merton's Works.

(ed.). *Seeds of Hope / Semillas de Esperanza. See* Reviews: Works about Merton.

(ed.) *Seeking Paradise: The Spirit of the Shakers. See* Reviews: Merton's Works.

Pierce, Brian J. *We Walk the Path Together. See* Reviews: Other Works.

"Pilgrimage, the Prophet, Persecutions and Perfume: East with Ibn Battūta and Thomas Merton," by Patrick F. O'Connell. 25 (2012) 30-48.

"Pivoting toward Peace: The Engaged Poetics of Thomas Merton and Denise Levertov," by Susan McCaslin. 22 (2009) 189-203.

"Place, Spiritual Anthropology and Sacramentality in Thomas Merton's Later Years," by Hans Gustafson. 25 (2012) 74-90.

Plaiss, Mark. *The Inner Room: A Journey into Lay Monasticism. See* Reviews: Other Works.

Plekon, Michael. *Hidden Holiness. See* Reviews: Other Works.

Poks, Malgorzata.
"Encounter in a Secret Country: Thomas Merton and Jorge Carrera Andrade." 18 (2005) 140-66.
"Reading Merton from the (Polish) Margin: 2004 Bibliographic Survey." 18 (2005) 318-48.
"The Meeting of Strangers: Thomas Merton's Engagement with Latin America." 20 (2007) 225-42.
"*The Geography of Lograire* as Merton's *Gestus* – Prolegomena." 22 (2009) 150-69.
"With Malinowski in the Postmodern Desert: Merton, Anthropology and the Ethnopoetics of *The Geography of Lograire*." 25 (2012) 49-73.
Thomas Merton and Latin America. See Reviews: Works about Merton.

Porter, J. S. *Thomas Merton: Hermit at the Heart of Things. See* Reviews: Works about Merton.

Pramuk, Christopher.
"'The Street Is for Celebration': Racial Consciousness and the Eclipse of Childhood in America's Cities." 25 (2012) 91-103.
"Author's Response to Review Symposium of *Sophia: The Hidden Christ of Thomas Merton*." 23 (2010) 274-85.
Rev. of *The Voice of the Stranger: Three Papers and a Homily from the Seventh General Meeting and Conference of the Thomas Merton Society of Great Britain and Ireland* by Bonnie Thurston, David Scott and James Conner, OCSO. 23 (2010) 303-306.
Sophia: The Hidden Christ of Thomas Merton. See Reviews: Works about Merton.

"Prayer in a High Tech World," by Phillip Thompson. 20 (2007) 185-202.

"Praying the Questions: Merton of Times Square, Last of the Urban Hermits," by David Joseph Belcastro. 20 (2007) 123-50.

"Praying the Psalms: A Layperson's Path to Contemplation," by Kathy Hoffmann. 20 (2007) 38-61.

"Preface to Dom Denys Rutledge's *In Search of a Yogi*," by Thomas Merton. 23 (2010) 13-19.

"The Priestly Imagination: Thomas Merton and the Poetics of Critique," by Michael W. Higgins. 22 (2009) 11-23.

Proietti, Pamela. "Merton's Reflections on the Christian Artist: Art as Doorway into Eternity." 21 (2008) 106-16.

"The Psychology of Hatred and the Role of Early Relationships in Discovering Our True Self," by Michael Sobocinski. 19 (2006) 91-113.

Quenon, Paul, OCSO.
 Rev. of *A Monk's Alphabet: Moments of Stillness in a Turning World* by Jeremy Driscoll. 20 (2007) 390-91.
 Afternoons with Emily. See Reviews: Other Works.

"Questioning the Goal of Biological Immortality: Mertonian Reflections on Living Eternally," by Phillip Thompson. 24 (2011) 67-82.

Raab, Joseph Quinn.
 "*Madhyamika* and *Dharmakaya*: Some Notes on Thomas Merton's Epiphany at Polonnaruwa." 17 (2004) 195-205.
 "Comrades for Peace: Thomas Merton, The Dalai Lama and the Preferential Option for Nonviolence." 19 (2006) 255-66.
 "Insights from the Inter-Contemplative Dialogue: Merton's Three Meanings of 'God' and Religious Pluralism." 23 (2010) 90-105.
 (ed.) "An Interview about Thomas Merton" with Martin E. Marty, conducted by Vaughn Fayle, OFM. 23-29.
 "2011 Bibliographic Review: Pointing Fingers at the Calm Eye of the Storm." 25 (2012) 205-16.

Raboteau, Albert. "Thomas Merton and Racial Reconciliation." 21 (2008) 13-24.

Rakoczy, Susan. *Great Mystics & Social Justice. See* Reviews: Other Works.

"'A Ray of That Truth Which Enlightens All': Thomas Merton, Poetic Language and Inter-religious Dialogue," by Bonnie B. Thurston. 22 (2009) 106-19.

"Reality as Sacred Place: The Parallel Insights of Thomas Merton and Henry Bugbee," by Gray Matthews. 17 (2004) 88-119.

"Remarks Following a 2004 Poetry Reading," by Ernesto Cardenal, transcribed and edited by Dennis Beach with an Introduction by Patrick Hart and a Note by Corey Shouse. 18 (2005) 65-71.

Reviews: Merton's Works
 A Book of Hours edited by Kathleen Deignan. Review by Matthew Emile Vaughan. 23 (2010) 297-300.
 Cassian and the Fathers: Initiation into the Monastic Tradition edited with an Introduction by Patrick F. O'Connell. Review by Mark DelCogliano. 19 (2006) 400-407.
 Cold War Letters edited by William H. Shannon and Christine M. Bochen. Review by Paul R. Dekar. 20 (2007) 341-43.
 Compassionate Fire: The Letters of Thomas Merton and Catherine de Hueck Doherty edited by Robert A. Wild. Review by Mark C. Meade. 23 (2010) 288-90.

Echoing Silence: Thomas Merton on the Vocation of Writing edited by Robert Inchausti. Review by Christine Bochen. 21 (2008) 274-77.

Gandhi on Non-Violence: Selected Texts from Gandhi's Non-Violence in Peace and War. Review by Julie Frazier. 21 (2008) 269-72.

In My Own Words edited by Jonathan Montaldo. Review by Donald Grayston. 21 (2008) 281-82.

In the Dark Before Dawn: New Selected Poems of Thomas Merton edited by Lynn R. Szabo. Review by Victor A. Kramer. 18 (2005) 349-52.

The Inner Experience: Notes on Contemplation edited by William H. Shannon. Review by Jens Söring. 17 (2004) 341-43.

An Introduction to Christian Mysticism: Initiation into the Monastic Tradition 3 edited with an Introduction by Patrick F. O'Connell. Review by Gray Matthews. 22 (2009) 261-65.

Lent and Easter Wisdom edited by Jonathan Montaldo. Review by Ron Atwood. 21 (2008) 282-85.

A Meeting of Angels: The Correspondence of Thomas Merton with Edward Deming and Faith Andrews edited by Paul M. Pearson. Review by Mario De Pillis, Sr. 23 (2010) 290-94.

Monastic Observances: Initiation into the Monastic Tradition 5 edited with and Introduction by Patrick F. O'Connell. Review by John Eudes Bamberger. 24 (2011) 329-31.

The Pocket Thomas Merton edited by Robert Inchausti. Review by Jeff Cooper, CSC. 19 (2006) 397-99.

Pre-Benedictine Monasticism: Initiation into the Monastic Tradition 2 edited with an Introduction by Patrick F. O'Connell. Review by Mark DelCogliano. 20 (2007) 346-53.

The Rule of Saint Benedict: Initiation into the Monastic Tradition 4 edited with an Introduction by Patrick F. O'Connell. Review by James Conner, OCSO. 23 (2010) 286-88.

Seeking Paradise: The Spirit of the Shakers edited by Paul M. Pearson. Review by Mary Foreman, OSB. 17 (2004) 343-45.

Thomas Merton: A Life in Letters – The Essential Collection selected and edited by William H. Shannon and Christine M. Bochen. Review by William Apel. 23 (2010) 294-97.

A Year With Thomas Merton: Daily Meditations From His Journals selected and edited by Jonathan Montaldo. Review by Patrick F. O'Connell. 18 (2005) 352-55.

Reviews: Works about Merton

Angelic Mistakes: The Art of Thomas Merton by Roger Lipsey. Review by Anthony Feuerstein. 20 (2007) 360-63.

Beneath the Mask of Holiness: Thomas Merton and the Forbidden Love Affair That Set Him Free by Mark Shaw. Review by Christine M. Bochen. 23 (2010) 306-15.

The Environmental Vision of Thomas Merton by Monica Weis, SSJ. Review Symposium by Donald P. St. John. 24 (2011) 281-85; Bonnie Thurston 285-89; Kathleen Deignan, CND 289-305; Donald Grayston 305-13; author response by Monica Weis, SSJ 313-23.

Hidden in the Same Mystery: Thomas Merton and Loretto edited by Bonnie Thurston. Review by Dewey Weiss Kramer. 24 (2011) 324-28.

Living with Wisdom: A Life of Thomas Merton by Jim Forest, rev. ed. Review by Daniel P. Horan, OFM. 22 (2009) 273-76.

Merton & Buddhism: Wisdom, Emptiness & Everyday Mind edited by Bonnie Bowman Thurston. Review by Craig Burgdof. 21 (2008) 272-74.

Merton and Friends: A Joint Biography of Thomas Merton, Robert Lax, and Edward Rice by James Harford. Review by Paul A. Montello. 20 (2007) 353-60.

More Than Silence: A Bibliography of Thomas Merton by Patricia A. Burton. Review by John King. 22 (2009) 265-69.

Original Child Bomb produced by Holly Becker and directed by Carey Schonegevel. Review by David King. 19 (2006) 407-10.

Pax Intrantibus: A Meditation on the Poetry of Thomas Merton by Frederick Smock. Review by Kevin Griffith. 21 (2008) 261-63.

Professional Morality and Guilty Bystanding: Merton's Conjectures and the Value of Work by Barry L. Padgett. Review by Donald Grayston. 23 (2010) 300-303.

A Retreat with Thomas Merton [CDs] by Donald Goergen, OP. Review by Robert Grip. 25 (2012) 236.

Seeds of Hope: Thomas Merton's Contemplative Message / Semillas de Esperanza: El Mensaje Contemplativo de Thomas Merton edited by Fernando Beltrán Llavador and Paul M. Pearson. Review by Gray Matthews. 22 (2009) 270-73.

Seek the Silences with Thomas Merton: Reflections on Identity, Community and Transformative Action by Charles R. Ringma. Review by Patrick F. O'Connell. 17 (2004) 348-52.

Signs of Peace: The Interfaith Letters of Thomas Merton by William Apel. Review by Paul R. Dekar. 20 (2007) 344-46.

Silence Speaks: Teilhard de Chardin, Yves Congar, John Courtney Murray, and Thomas Merton by Robert Nugent. Review by David Joseph Belcastro. 25 (2012) 233-35.

A Silent Action: Engagements with Thomas Merton by Rowan Williams. Review by Victor A. Kramer. 25 (2012) 217-21.

Sophia: The Hidden Christ of Thomas Merton by Christopher Pramuk. Review Symposium by Daniel P. Horan, OFM. 23 (2010) 260-65; Edward K. Kaplan 265-69; Lynn R. Szabo 269-74; Author's Response by Christopher Pramuk 274-85.

Soul Searching: The Journey of Thomas Merton, a film by Morgan Atkinson. Review by Arthur Giacalone. 21 (2008) 277-81.

Thomas Merton: A Spiritual Guide for the Twenty-First Century [CDs] by Anthony Ciorra. Review by Robert Grip. 25 (2012) 236.

Thomas Merton: An Introduction by William H. Shannon. Review by Donald Grayston. 19 (2006) 410-13.

Thomas Merton and Latin America: A Consonance of Voices by Malgorzata Poks. Review by Patrick F. O'Connell. 21 (2008) 257-61.

Thomas Merton: Contemplation and Political Action by Mario I. Aguilar. Review by Ian Bell. 25 (2012) 225-27.

Thomas Merton: Hermit at the Heart of Things by J. S. Porter. Review by Ross Labrie. 21 (2008) 263-65.

Thomas Merton: Master of Attention by Robert Waldron. Review by Monica Weis. 21 (2008) 285-88.

Thomas Merton: Twentieth-Century Wisdom for Twenty-First-Century Living by Paul R. Dekar. Review by Daniel P. Horan, OFM. 25 (2012) 221-25.

Thomas Merton's Gethsemani: Landscapes of Paradise by Monica Weis, photographs by Harry L. Hinkle. Review by Cynthia Ann Hizer. 19 (2006) 417-19.

The Vision of Thomas Merton edited by Patrick F. O'Connell. Review by Glenn Crider. 17 (2004) 345-48.

The Voice of the Stranger: Three Papers and a Homily from the Seventh General Meeting and Conference of the Thomas Merton Society of Great Britain and Ireland by Bonnie Thurston, David Scott and James Conner, OCSO. Review by Christopher Pramuk. 23 (2010) 303-306.

The Wounded Heart of Thomas Merton by Robert Waldron. Review by Fiona Gardner. 25 (2012) 228-32.

Reviews: Other Works

Ad Reinhardt by Michael Corris. Review by Roger Lipsey. 21 (2008) 255-57.

Afternoons with Emily by Paul Quenon. Review by Kevin Griffith. 25 (2012) 243-44.

All the Way to Heaven: The Selected Letters of Dorothy Day edited by Robert Ellsberg. Review by John P. Collins. 24 (2011) 332-36.

Belonging to Borders: A Sojourn in the Celtic Tradition by Bonnie Thurston. Review by Kevin Griffith. 25 (2012) 244-45.

Benedictine Daily Prayer: A Short Breviary compiled and edited by Maxwell E. Johnson. Review by Anthony Feuerstein. 19 (2006) 440-43.

The Benedictine Handbook by Anthony Marett-Crosby. Review by Anthony Feuerstein. 17 (2004) 357-59.

Between Two Souls: Conversations with Ryokan by Mary Lou Kownacki. Review by Christine M. Bochen. 18 (2005) 355-60.

Called to Question: A Spiritual Memoir by Joan Chittister. Review by Joy A. Schroeder. 18 (2005) 360-62.

Catholicism: A Journey to the Heart of Faith [book and DVDs] by Robert Barron. Review by Patrick F. O'Connell. 25 (2012) 237-43.

Chanting the Psalms: A Practical Guide by Cynthia Bourgeault. Review by Dewey Weiss Kramer. 20 (2007) 384-90.

Christian Spirituality: The Classics edited by Arthur Holder. Review by Patrick F. O'Connell. 24 (2011) 336-42.

Contemplation in Action by Richard Rohr and Friends. Review by Catherine Crosby. 20 (2007) 375-78.

Creating a Human World: A New Psychology and Religious Anthropology in Dialogue with Freud, Heidegger, and Kierkegaard by E. Daniel Carrere. Review by Glenn Crider. 20 (2007) 363-67.

Creating the Beloved Community by Paul R. Dekar. Review by Richard D. Parry, 19 (2006) 422-24.

The Discerning Heart: Exploring the Christian Path by Wilkie Au and Noreen Cannon Au. Review by Wendy M. Wright. 20 (2007) 391-94.

Engaging Benedict: What the Rule Can Teach Us Today by Laura Swan. Review by Dewey Weiss Kramer. 19 (2006) 437-40.

Eternal Seasons: A Liturgical Journey with Henry J. M. Nouwen edited by Michael Ford. Review by Angus F. Stuart. 18 (2005) 364-66.

Four Cultures of the West by John W. O'Malley. Review by William H. Shannon. 18 (2005) 367-70.

Fully Human, Fully Divine: An Interactive Christology by Michael Casey. Review by John W. Smith. 19 (2006) 420.

Grace through Simplicity: The Practical Spirituality of Evelyn Underhill by John Kirvan. Review by Dana Greene. 18 (2005) 362-63.

Great Mystics & Social Justice: Walking on the Two Feet of Love by Susan Rakoczy. Review by Martha Gross. 20 (2007) 378-82.

Hidden Holiness by Michael Plekon. Review by Patrick F. O'Connell. 23 (2010) 315-18.

Humble and Awake: Coping with Our Comatose Culture by Thomas G. Casey. Review by Cathy Crosby. 19 (2006) 435-37.

In the Heart of the Temple: My Spiritual Vision for Today's World by Joan Chittister, and *The Way We Were: A Story of Conversion and Hope* by Joan Chittister. Review by Theresa Schumacher, OSB. 19 (2006) 420-22.

The Inner Room: A Journey into Lay Monasticism by Mark Plaiss. Review by Harry Wells. 19 (2006) 425-30.

*Lost in Wonder: Rediscovering the Spiritual Art of Atten*tiveness by Esther de Waal. Review by Dewey Weiss Kramer. 17 (2004) 355-57.

Love Burning in the Soul: The Story of the Christian Mystics, from St. Paul to Thomas Merton by James Harpur. Review by Patrick F. O'Connell. 19 (2006) 413-17.

A Monk's Alphabet: Moments of Stillness in a Turning World by Jeremy Driscoll. Review by Paul Quenon. 20 (2007) 390-91.

Mystics by William Harmless, SJ. Review by Patrick F. O'Connell. 22 (2009) 276-80.

Out of Solitude: Three Meditations on the Christian Life by Henri Nouwen. Review by Angus F. Stuart. 18 (2005) 364-66.

Poetry as Prayer: Jessica Powers by Robert Morneau. Review by Catherine Senne Wallace, OSB. 17 (2004) 352-53.

Portraits of Grace: Images and Words from the Monastery of the Holy Spirit by James Behrens. Review by Louis Scribbelarious. 20 (2007) 397-98.

Prayer in All Things: A Saint Benedict's St. John's Prayer Book edited by Kate E. Riger and Michael Kwatera, OSB. Review by Anthony Feuerstein. 17 (2004) 357-59.

The Promise of Paradox: A Celebration of Contradictions in the Christian Life by Parker J. Palmer. Review by Gray Matthews. 21 (2008) 265-68.

The Rule of Benedict for Beginners: Spirituality for Daily Life by Wil Derkse. Review by Dewey Weiss Kramer. 17 (2004) 355-57.

The Spiritual Landscape of Mark by Bonnie B. Thurston. Review by Patrick Minderman. 22 (2009) 280-83.

Spirituality and Mysticism: A Global View by James Wiseman. Review by Patrick F. O'Connell. 20 (2007) 367-72.

Transforming Heart and Mind: Learning from the Mystics by Peter N. Borys, Jr. Review by Dana Greene. 20 (2007) 383-84.

Waking Up to What You Do: A Zen Practice for Meeting Every Situation with Intelligence and Compassion by Diane Eschin Rizzetto. Review by Kimberly Boykin. 20 (2007) 394-97.

The Way of the Prisoner: Breaking the Chains of Self through Centering Prayer and Centering Practice by Jens Söring. Review by Stefanie Weisgram, OSB. 17 (2004) 353-55.

We Walk the Path Together: Learning from Thich Nhat Hanh & Meister Eckhart by Brian J. Pierce. Review by Robert H. King. 20 (2007) 372-75.

With Open Heart: Spiritual Direction in the Alphonsian Tradition by Dennis Billy, CSsR. Review by Mark A. Dannenfelser. 19 (2006) 430-34.

Writing Your Spiritual Autobiography by Richard B. Patterson. Review by Glenn Crider. 18 (2005) 363-64.

Riger, Kate E., and Michael Kwatera, OSB (eds.). *Prayer in All Things: A Saint Benedict's St. John's Prayer Book. See* Reviews: Other Works.

Ringma, Charles R. *Seek the Silences with Thomas Merton. See* Reviews: Works about Merton.

"'Rising Up Out of the Center': Thomas Merton on Prayer," by Bonnie Thurston. 20 (2007) 109-22.

Rizzetto, Diane Eschin. *Waking Up to What You Do. See* Reviews: Other Works.

Rohr, Richard. *Contemplation in Action. See* Reviews: Other Works.

"Sacred Play: Thomas Merton's *Cables to the Ace,*" by Robert Leigh Davis. 20 (2007) 243-64.

St. John, Donald P. Review Symposium of *The Environmental Vision of Thomas Merton* by Monica Weis, SSJ. 24 (2011) 281-85.

Schonegevel, Carey (director). *Original Child Bomb. See* Reviews: Works about Merton.

Schroeder, Joy A. Rev. of *Called to Question: A Spiritual Memoir* by Joan Chittister. 18 (2005) 360-62.

Schumacher, Theresa, OSB. Rev. of *In the Heart of the Temple: My Spiritual Vision for Today's World* by Joan Chittister, and *The Way We Were: A Story of Conversion and Hope* by Joan Chittister. 19 (2006) 420-22.

Scott, David. *The Voice of the Stranger. See* Reviews: Works about Merton.

Scribbelarious, Louis. Rev. of *Portraits of Grace: Images and Words from the Monastery of the Holy Spirit* by James Behrens. 20 (2007) 397-98.

"Searching for *Sophia*: Nicholas of Cusa and Thomas Merton," by Joshua Hollmann. 25 (2012) 169-76.

Seasoltz, R. Kevin. "Frank Kacmarcik and the Cistercian Architectural Tradition." 18 (2005) 22-32.

"Shadows and Pathways: Four Unpublished Poems by Thomas Merton," by Lynn Szabo. 22 (2009) 204-209.

Shaffer, Timothy. "A (Not So) Secret Son of Francis: Thomas Merton's Franciscan Lens for Seeing Heaven and Earth." 21 (2008) 67-90.

Shannon, William H.

Rev. of *Four Cultures of the West* by John W. O'Malley. 18 (2005) 367-70.

(ed.) *The Inner Experience: Notes on Contemplation* by Thomas Merton. *See* Reviews: Merton's Works.

Thomas Merton: An Introduction. See Reviews: Works about Merton.

(ed.) *Cold War Letters* by Thomas Merton. *See* Reviews: Merton's Works.

(ed.) *Thomas Merton: A Life in Letters. See* Reviews: Merton's Works.

Shaw, Mark. *Beneath the Mask of Holiness. See* Reviews: Works about Merton.

Shouse, Corey. Note to "Remarks Following a 2004 Poetry Reading," by Ernesto Cardenal. 18 (2005) 66-67.

Simmer-Brown, Judith. "The Heart Is the Common Ground: Thomas Merton and Chögyam Trungpa in Dialogue." 23 (2010) 47-58.

"'Simply Go In and Pray!': St. Benedict's Oratory In RB 52," by Terrence G. Kardong. 20 (2007) 25-37.

Smith, John W. Rev. of *Fully Human, Fully Divine: An Interactive Christology* by Michael Casey. 19 (2006) 420.

Smith, Thomas Francis. "The Context of Thomas Merton's Letter Concerning 'The Jesus Prayer.'" 19 (2006) 15-16.

Smock, Frederick. *Pax Intrantibus. See* Reviews: Works about Merton.

Sobocinski, Michael. "The Psychology of Hatred and the Role of Early Relationships in Discovering Our True Self." 19 (2006) 91-113.

"Some Points from the Birmingham Non-Violence Movement," by Thomas Merton. 25 (2012) 13-22.

"'A Son of This Instant': Thomas Merton and Ibn 'Abbād of Ronda," by Patrick F. O'Connell. 23 (2010) 149-83.

Söring, Jens.
    Rev. of *The Inner Experience: Notes on Contemplation* by Thomas Merton. 17 (2004) 341-43.
    The Way of the Prisoner. See Reviews: Other Works.

"The Soul-Rich Monk/Priest: Thomas Merton on *Lectio Divina*," by Mary Murray McDonald. 25 (2012) 197-204.

"*The Spirit of Simplicity*: Thomas Merton on Simplification of Life," by Paul R. Dekar. 19 (2006) 267-82.

"Stand on Your Own Feet! Thomas Merton and the Monk without Vows or Walls," by Nass Cannon. 25 (2012) 154-68.

"Standing to the Side and Watching: An Introduction and Remembrance about Interviewing Walker Percy," by Victor A. Kramer and Dewey Weis Kramer. 21 (2008) 173-75.

"'The Street Is for Celebration': Racial Consciousness and the Eclipse of Childhood in America's Cities," by Christopher Pramuk. 25 (2012) 91-103.

"Striving toward Authenticity: Merton's 'True Self' and the Millennial Generation's Search for Identity," by Daniel P. Horan, OFM. 23 (2010) 80-89.

Stuart, Angus F.
    "The Geography of Solitude: Inner Space and the Sense of Place." 17 (2004) 76-87.
    Rev. of *Out of Solitude: Three Meditations on the Christian Life* by Henri Nouwen and *Eternal Seasons: A Liturgical Journey with Henry J. M. Nouwen* edited by Michael Ford. 18 (2005) 364-66.

Sunderman, Marilyn. "Jewels upon His Forehead: Spiritual Vision in the Poetry and Photography of Thomas Merton." 18 (2005) 167-88.

Swan, Laura. *Engaging Benedict. See* Reviews: Other Works.

Szabo, Lynn R.
  "Thomas Merton's Sacred Landscapes: Perspectives from the Vancouver Conference."
  17 (2004) 58-60.
  "'In the Dark before Dawn': Thomas Merton's Mystical Poetics." 22 (2009) 24-40.
  "Shadows and Pathways: Four Unpublished Poems by Thomas Merton." 22 (2009)
  204-209.
  Review Symposium of *Sophia: The Hidden Christ of Thomas Merton* by Christopher
  Pramuk. 23 (2010) 269-74.

"Technology, Freedom and the Human Person: Some Teen Insights into Merton and Benedict
  XVI," by Jeffrey T. Kiernan. 24 (2011) 244-55.

"The Technophiliacs," by W. H. Ferry. 24 (2011) 29-38.

"Terrible Days: Merton/Yungblut Letters and MLK Jr.'s Death," by William Apel. 21
  (2008) 25-32.

"Thomas Merton and George Grant: Hawk's Dream, Owl's Insight," by Ron Dart. 17
  (2004) 120-36.

"Thomas Merton and Hannah Arendt: Desert and City in Cold-War Culture," by Robert
  Weldon Whalen. 25 (2012) 132-43.

"Thomas Merton and Ivan Illich: Two Mendicant Anti-professionals in the Age of the Simulacra
  of the Professions and the System," by Daniel Bogert-O'Brien. 24 (2011) 233-43.

"Thomas Merton and Paramahansa Yogananda: Two Prayerful Mergings of Cult and
  Culture," by Emile J. Farge. 20 (2007) 164-84.

"Thomas Merton and Racial Reconciliation," by Albert Raboteau. 21 (2008) 13-24.

"Thomas Merton and St. John of the Cross: Lives on Fire," by Nass Cannon. 21 (2008)
  205-13.

"Thomas Merton – Final Integration through Interreligious Dialogue," by James Conner,
  OCSO. 23 (2010) 20-28.

"Thomas Merton, Guide to the Right Use of Technology," by Paul R. Dekar. 24 (2011)
  150-75.

"Thomas Merton, Henri Nouwen, and the Living Gospel," by Robert Ellsberg. 19 (2006)
  340-54.

"The Thomas Merton – John C. H. Wu Letters: The Lord as Postman," by Lucien Miller.
  19 (2006) 142-61.

"Thomas Merton, Monk and Prophet of Peace: The Opening Address at the 2005 International Thomas Merton Society General Meeting," by John Eudes Bamberger. 19
  (2006) 18-23.

"Thomas Merton on William Blake: 'To Look through Matter into Eternity,'" by Michael
  Griffith. 18 (2005) 109-26.

"Thomas Merton's Approach to St. John of the Cross," by Keith J. Egan. 20 (2007)
  62-78.

"Thomas Merton's Ecopoetry: Bearing Witness to the Unity of Creation," by Deborah
  P. Kehoe. 22 (2009) 170-88.

"Thomas Merton's Revelation of Justice & Revolutions of Love: Perspectives from the
  San Diego Conference," by David Belcastro. 19 (2006) 39-42.

"Thomas Merton's Sacred Landscapes: Perspectives from the Vancouver Conference," by Lynn R. Szabo. 17 (2004) 58-60.

Thompson, Phillip.
"Prayer in a High Tech World." 20 (2007) 185-202.
"Questioning the Goal of Biological Immortality: Mertonian Reflections on Living Eternally." 24 (2011) 67-82.

"'Those Going Among the Saracens and Other Nonbelievers': Thomas Merton and Franciscan Interreligious Dialogue," by Daniel P. Horan, OFM. 21 (2008) 44-66.

"Three Comments about Benedictine Monastic Community Reading," by Eric Hollas, Daniel Durken and Stefanie Weisgram. 18 (2005) 59-64.

"'Three Prayers' Written for Frank Kacmarcik," by Thomas Merton. 18 (2005) 11-14.

Thurston, Bonnie.
"'Rising Up Out of the Center': Thomas Merton on Prayer." 20 (2007) 109-22.
"'A Ray of That Truth Which Enlightens All': Thomas Merton, Poetic Language and Inter-religious Dialogue." 22 (2009) 106-19.
Review Symposium of *The Environmental Vision of Thomas Merton* by Monica Weis, SSJ. 24 (2011) 285-89.
Belonging to Borders. See Reviews: Other Works.
(ed.) *Hidden in the Same Mystery. See* Reviews: Works about Merton.
(ed.) *Merton & Buddhism. See* Reviews: Works about Merton.
The Spiritual Landscape of Mark. See Reviews: Other Works.
The Voice of the Stranger. See Reviews: Works about Merton.

"To Father Thomas Fidelis (Francis) Smith, O.C.S.O," by Thomas Merton. 19 (2006) 13-14.

"Two Antiheroes: Meursault and Binx Bolling Viewed through Thomas Merton's Literary Imagination," by John P. Collins. 25 (2012) 113-23.

Vaughan, Matthew Emile. Rev. of *A Book of Hours* by Thomas Merton, edited by Kathleen Deignan. 23 (2010) 297-300.

"Voices from the Desert: Merton, Camus and Milosz," by David Joseph Belcastro. 25 (2012) 104-12.

Waldron, Robert.
Thomas Merton: Master of Attention. See Reviews: Works about Merton.
The Wounded Heart of Thomas Merton. See Reviews: Works about Merton.

Wallace, Catherine Senne, OSB. Rev. of *Poetry as Prayer: Jessica Powers* by Robert Morneau. 17 (2004) 352-53.

Weis, Monica, SSJ.
"Kindred Spirits in Revelation and Revolution: Rachel Carson and Thomas Merton." 19 (2006) 128-41.
Rev. of *Thomas Merton: Master of Attention* by Robert Waldron. 21 (2008) 285-88.
"Author Response to Review Symposium of *The Environmental Vision of Thomas Merton*." 24 (2011) 313-23.
The Environmental Vision of Thomas Merton. See Reviews: Works about Merton.
Thomas Merton's Gethsemani. See Reviews: Works about Merton.

Weisgram, Stefanie, OSB.

with Eric Hollas and Daniel Durkin. "Three Comments about Benedictine Monastic Community Reading." 18 (2005) 59-64.

Rev. of *The Way of the Prisoner: Breaking the Chains of Self through Centering Prayer and Centering Practice* by Jens Söring. 17 (2004) 353-55.

Wells, Harry.
"In Memoriam: 'We Are Life, Its Shining Gift' – Roger Jonathan Corless (26 June 1938-12 January 2007)." 20 (2007) 203-205.

Rev. of *The Inner Room: A Journey into Lay Monasticism* by Mark Plaiss. 19 (2006) 425-30.

Whalen, Robert Weldon. "Thomas Merton and Hannah Arendt: Desert and City in Cold-War Culture." 25 (2012) 132-43.

"What Kind of World-Lover? Thomas Merton on Dietrich Bonhoeffer and Death-of-God Theology," by David Golemboski. 23 (2010) 197-211.

"What Matters Is Clear," by Tyson Anderson. 23 (2010) 67-79.

"What the Machine Produces and What the Machine Destroys: Thomas Merton on Technology," by Paul R. Dekar. 17 (2004) 216-34.

"Wholeness in Thomas Merton's Poetry," by Ross Labrie. 22 (2009) 41-60.

"Why Zen Buddhism and Not Hinduism? The Asias of Thomas Merton's Voyages East," by Rachel Fell McDermott. 23 (2010) 29-46.

"The Wild Places," by Thomas Merton, edited by Patrick F. O'Connell. 24 (2011) 15-28.

Wild, Robert A. *Compassionate Fire. See* Reviews: Merton's Works.

Wilkes, Paul.
"Interview with Lawrence Ferlinghetti," conducted by Paul Wilkes and edited by Gray Matthews. 22 (2009) 220-26.

"An Interview with W. H. (Ping) Ferry about Thomas Merton," conducted by Paul Wilkes, transcribed and edited by Paul M. Pearson. 24 (2011) 39-53.

Williams, Rowan. *A Silent Action. See* Reviews: Works about Merton.

"Wisdom, Sapiential Poetry, and Personalism: Exploring Some of Thomas Merton's Ideas for Values Education," by Ross Keating. 18 (2005) 189-204.

Wiseman, James. *Spirituality and Mysticism. See* Reviews: Other Works.

"With Malinowski in the Postmodern Desert: Merton, Anthropology and the Ethnopoetics of *The Geography of Lograire*," by Malgorzata Poks. 25 (2012) 49-73.

Wright, Wendy M. Rev. of *The Discerning Heart: Exploring the Christian Path* by Wilkie Au and Noreen Cannon Au. 20 (2007) 391-94.

Wu, John, Jr. "Centennial Vignettes in Homage to My Father." 19 (2006) 283-310.

"You Are You: That Is the Most Important Thing – Everything Is in It Somewhere: An Analysis of the Correspondence from Thomas Merton to John Harris," by Fiona Gardner. 25 (2012) 124-31.

Zalot, Charlotte Anne. "A Merton Connection: Frank Kacmarcik, OblSB, Monk and Artist. (1920-2004)." 18 (2005) 33-58.

* * * * * * *

AMERICA
"Be Alone, Together: Religious Individualism, Community and the American Spirit in Emerson, Merton and Heschel," by Shaul Magid. 23 (2010) 116-31.

ANDRADE, JORGE CARRERA
"Encounter in a Secret Country: Thomas Merton and Jorge Carrera Andrade," by Malgorzata Poks. 18 (2005) 140-66.

ARCHITECTURE
"Contemporary Architectural Witness to the Lived Cistercian Ideal: The Abbey Churches of Gethsemani and Conyers," by Dewey Weiss Kramer. 18 (2005) 96-108.
"Frank Kacmarcik and the Cistercian Architectural Tradition," by R. Kevin Seasoltz. 18 (2005) 22-32.

ARENDT, HANNAH
"Thomas Merton and Hannah Arendt: Desert and City in Cold-War Culture," by Robert Weldon Whalen. 25 (2012) 132-43.

ART
"Art and Worship," by Thomas Merton, edited by Glenn Crider and Victor A. Kramer. 18 (2005) 19-21.
"Merton's Reflections on the Christian Artist: Art as Doorway into Eternity," by Pamela Proietti. 21 (2008) 106-16.
"The Monk and Sacred Art," by Thomas Merton, edited by Glenn Crider and Victor A. Kramer. 18 (2005) 15-18.
"A Monk with the Spiritual Equipment of an Artist: The Art of Thomas Merton," by Paul M. Pearson. 18 (2005) 237-59.

ASIAN JOURNEY
"*Madhyamika* and *Dharmakaya*: Some Notes on Thomas Merton's Epiphany at Polonnaruwa," by Joseph Quinn Raab. 17 (2004) 195-205.
"What Matters Is Clear," by Tyson Anderson. 23 (2010) 67-79.
"Why Zen Buddhism and Not Hinduism? The Asias of Thomas Merton's Voyages East," by Rachel Fell McDermott. 23 (2010) 29-46.

BAXTER, RICHARD
"Ignatian and Puritan Prayer: Surprising Similarities; A Comparison of Ignatius Loyola and Richard Baxter on Meditation," by E. Glenn Hinson. 20 (2007) 79-92.

BENEDICT XVI, POPE
"Technology, Freedom and the Human Person: Some Teen Insights into Merton and Benedict XVI," by Jeffrey T. Kiernan. 24 (2011) 244-55.

BLAKE, WILLIAM
"Thomas Merton on William Blake: 'To Look through Matter into Eternity,'" by Michael Griffith. 18 (2005) 109-26.

BONHOEFFER, DIETRICH
"What Kind of World-Lover? Thomas Merton on Dietrich Bonhoeffer and Death-of-God Theology," by David Golemboski. 23 (2010) 197-211.

BUDDHISM
"The Heart Is the Common Ground: Thomas Merton and Chögyam Trungpa in Dialogue," by Judith Simmer-Brown. 23 (2010) 47-58.
"Merton as Method for Inter-religious Engagement: Examples from Buddhism," by John D. Dadosky. 21 (2008) 33-43.

BUGBEE, HENRY
"Reality as Sacred Place: The Parallel Insights of Thomas Merton and Henry Bugbee," by Gray Matthews. 17 (2004) 88-119.

CAMUS, ALBERT
"Two Antiheroes: Meursault and Binx Bolling Viewed through Thomas Merton's Literary Imagination," by John P. Collins. 25 (2012) 113-23.
"Voices from the Desert: Merton, Milosz and Camus," by David Joseph Belcastro. 25 (2012) 104-12.

CARSON, RACHEL
"Kindred Spirits in Revelation and Revolution: Rachel Carson and Thomas Merton," by Monica Weis. 19 (2006) 128-41.

CENTERING PRAYER
"Centering Prayer and Attention of the Heart," by Cynthia Bourgeault. 20 (2007) 151-63.

CHÖGYAM TRUNGPA
"The Heart Is the Common Ground: Thomas Merton and Chögyam Trungpa in Dialogue," by Judith Simmer-Brown. 23 (2010) 47-58.

CORLESS, ROGER
"In Memoriam: 'We Are Life, Its Shining Gift' – Roger Jonathan Corless (26 June 1938-12 January 2007)," by Harry Wells. 20 (2007) 203-205.

CURRAN, CHARLES
"No Solution in Withdrawal – No Solution in Conforming: Merton, Teilhard, Kung and Curran," by Judith Hunter. 19 (2006) 43-90.

DALAI LAMA
"Comrades for Peace: Thomas Merton, The Dalai Lama and the Preferential Option for Nonviolence," by Joseph Quinn Raab. 19 (2006) 255-66.

DESERT FATHERS
"Desert Fathers and Asian Masters: Thomas Merton's Outlaw Lineage," by Patrick Bludworth. 17 (2004) 166-94.
"Is Desert Spirituality Viable in the Twenty-First-Century City? The Legacy of the Desert Fathers in Thomas Merton," by Hyeokil Kwon. 25 (2012) 144-53.

ECOLOGY
"Thomas Merton's Ecopoetry: Bearing Witness to the Unity of Creation," by Deborah P. Kehoe. 22 (2009) 170-88.
"The Wild Places," by Thomas Merton, edited by Patrick F. O'Connell. 24 (2011) 15-28.

EDUCATION
"'Our Transformation in Christ': Thomas Merton and Transformative Learning," by Fred W. Herron. 21 (2008) 186-204.
"Wisdom, Sapiential Poetry, and Personalism: Exploring Some of Thomas Merton's Ideas for Values Education," by Ross Keating. 18 (2005) 189-204.

EMERSON, RALPH WALDO
"Be Alone, Together: Religious Individualism, Community and the American Spirit in Emerson, Merton and Heschel," by Shaul Magid. 23 (2010) 116-31.

FEMININE
"'A Humanly Impoverished Thirst for Light': Thomas Merton's Receptivity to the

Feminine, to Judaism, and to Religious Pluralism," by Edward K. Kaplan. 17 (2004) 137-52.

FRANCIS OF ASSISI, ST.
"A (Not So) Secret Son of Francis: Thomas Merton's Franciscan Lens for Seeing Heaven and Earth," by Timothy Shaffer. 21 (2008) 67-90.
"'Those Going Among the Saracens and Other Nonbelievers': Thomas Merton and Franciscan Interreligious Dialogue," by Daniel P. Horan, OFM. 21 (2008) 44-66.

GRANT, GEORGE
"Thomas Merton and George Grant: Hawk's Dream, Owl's Insight," by Ron Dart. 17 (2004) 120-36.

HARRIS, JOHN
"You Are You: That Is the Most Important Thing – Everything Is in It Somewhere: An Analysis of the Correspondence from Thomas Merton to John Harris," by Fiona Gardner. 25 (2012) 124-31.

HESCHEL, ABRAHAM JOSHUA
"Abraham Heschel and Thomas Merton: Prophetic Personalities, Prophetic Friendship," by Edward K. Kaplan. 23 (2010) 106-15.
"Be Alone, Together: Religious Individualism, Community and the American Spirit in Emerson, Merton and Heschel," by Shaul Magid. 23 (2010) 116-31.
"The Ends of Anxiety in Merton and Heschel," by Martin Kavka. 23 (2010) 132-48.

HINDUISM
"Why Zen Buddhism and Not Hinduism? The Asias of Thomas Merton's Voyages East," by Rachel Fell McDermott. 23 (2010) 29-46.

HOPKINS, GERARD MANLEY
"Divining the Inscaped-Landscape: Hopkins, Merton and the Ascent to True Self," by Jeffrey A. Cooper. 18 (2005) 127-39.

IBN 'ABBĀD OF RONDA
"'A Son of This Instant': Thomas Merton and Ibn 'Abbād of Ronda," by Patrick F. O'Connell. 23 (2010) 149-83.

IGNATIUS OF LOYOLA, ST.
"From Thomas Merton's 'Contemplation' to Ignatius of Loyola's 'Contemplation to Obtain Love': A Personal Prayer Journey," by Richard J. Hauser. 20 (2007) 93-108.
"Ignatian and Puritan Prayer: Surprising Similarities; A Comparison of Ignatius Loyola and Richard Baxter on Meditation," by E. Glenn Hinson. 20 (2007) 79-92.

ILLICH, IVAN
"Thomas Merton and Ivan Illich: Two Mendicant Anti-professionals in the Age of the Simulacra of the Professions and the System," by Daniel Bogert-O'Brien. 24 (2011) 233-43.

INDIVIDUALISM
"Be Alone, Together: Religious Individualism, Community and the American Spirit in Emerson, Merton and Heschel," by Shaul Magid. 23 (2010) 116-31.

INTERRELIGIOUS DIALOGUE
"The Christian Exploration of Non-Christian Religions: Merton's Example of Where it Might Lead Us," by Roger Corless. 20 (2007) 206-24.

"The Heart Is the Common Ground: Thomas Merton and Chögyam Trungpa in Dialogue," by Judith Simmer-Brown. 23 (2010) 47-58.

"'A Humanly Impoverished Thirst for Light': Thomas Merton's Receptivity to the Feminine, to Judaism, and to Religious Pluralism," by Edward K. Kaplan. 17 (2004) 137-52.

"Insights from the Inter-Contemplative Dialogue: Merton's Three Meanings of 'God' and Religious Pluralism," by Joseph Quinn Raab. 23 (2010) 90-105.

"Merton as Method for Inter-religious Engagement: Examples from Buddhism," by John D. Dadosky. 21 (2008) 33-43.

"No Mirror, No Light – Just This! Merton's Discovery of Global Wisdom," by Nassif Cannon. 23 (2010) 184-96.

"'A Ray of That Truth Which Enlightens All': Thomas Merton, Poetic Language and Inter-religious Dialogue," by Bonnie B. Thurston. 22 (2009) 106-19.

"Thomas Merton – Final Integration through Interreligious Dialogue," by James Conner, OCSO. 23 (2010) 20-28.

"'Those Going Among the Saracens and Other Nonbelievers': Thomas Merton and Franciscan Interreligious Dialogue," by Daniel P. Horan, OFM. 21 (2008) 44-66.

ISLAM

"Pilgrimage, the Prophet, Persecutions and Perfume: East with Ibn Battūta and Thomas Merton," by Patrick F. O'Connell. 25 (2012) 30-48.

"Searching for *Sophia*: Nicholas of Cusa and Thomas Merton," by Joshua Hollmann. 25 (2012) 169-76.

"'A Son of This Instant': Thomas Merton and Ibn 'Abbād of Ronda," by Patrick F. O'Connell. 23 (2010) 149-83.

JOHN OF THE CROSS, ST.

"Thomas Merton and St. John of the Cross: Lives on Fire," by Nass Cannon. 21 (2008) 205-13.

"Thomas Merton's Approach to St. John of the Cross," by Keith J. Egan. 20 (2007) 62-78.

JUDAISM

"'A Humanly Impoverished Thirst for Light': Thomas Merton's Receptivity to the Feminine, to Judaism, and to Religious Pluralism," by Edward K. Kaplan. 17 (2004) 137-52.

KACMARCIK, FRANK

"Frank Kacmarcik and the Cistercian Architectural Tradition," by R. Kevin Seasoltz. 18 (2005) 22-32.

"A Merton Connection: Frank Kacmarcik, OblSB, Monk and Artist. (1920-2004)," Charlotte Anne Zalot. 18 (2005) 33-58.

KING, MARTIN LUTHER, JR.

"Terrible Days: Merton/Yungblut Letters and MLK Jr.'s Death," by William Apel. 21 (2008) 25-32.

KUNG, HANS

"No Solution in Withdrawal – No Solution in Conforming: Merton, Teilhard, Kung and Curran," by Judith Hunter. 19 (2006) 43-90.

LATIN AMERICA

"The Meeting of Strangers: Thomas Merton's Engagement with Latin America," by Malgorzata Poks. 20 (2007) 225-42.

LAX, ROBERT
"Lax, Merton and Rice on War and Peace," by James Harford. 19 (2006) 234-54.

LECTIO DIVINA
"The Soul-Rich Monk/Priest: Thomas Merton on *Lectio Divina*," by Mary Murray McDonald. 25 (2012) 197-204.

LEVERTOV, DENISE
"Pivoting toward Peace: The Engaged Poetics of Thomas Merton and Denise Levertov," by Susan McCaslin. 22 (2009) 189-203.

MARRIAGE
"No Spouse Is an Island: Thomas Merton's Contribution toward a Contemporary Spirituality of Marriage," by Daniel P. Horan, OFM. 25 (2012) 177-96.

MERTON'S WORKS
CABLES TO THE ACE
"Sacred Play: Thomas Merton's *Cables to the Ace*," by Robert Leigh Davis. 20 (2007) 243-64.

THE GEOGRAPHY OF LOGRAIRE
"*The Geography of Lograire* as Merton's *Gestus* – Prolegomena," by Malgorzata Poks. 22 (2009) 150-69.
"Merton, Cargo Cults and *The Geography of Lograire*," by Kenelm Burridge. 17 (2004) 206-15.
"Pilgrimage, the Prophet, Persecutions and Perfume: East with Ibn Battūta and Thomas Merton," by Patrick F. O'Connell. 25 (2012) 30-48.
"With Malinowski in the Postmodern Desert: Merton, Anthropology and the Ethnopoetics of *The Geography of Lograire*," by Malgorzata Poks. 25 (2012) 49-73.

JOURNALS
"The Conflict Not Yet Fully Faced: Thomas Merton as Reader in His Journals," by Chris Orvin. 18 (2005) 205-36.

LETTERS
"From the 'Political Dance of Death' to the 'General Dance': The Cold War Letters of Thomas Merton," by John P. Collins. 19 (2006) 162-77.
"The Context of Thomas Merton's Letter Concerning 'The Jesus Prayer,'" by Thomas Francis Smith. 19 (2006) 15-16.
"You Are You: That Is the Most Important Thing – Everything Is in It Somewhere: An Analysis of the Correspondence from Thomas Merton to John Harris," by Fiona Gardner. 25 (2012) 124-31.

PEACE IN THE POST-CHRISTIAN ERA
"Editorial Note Concerning Thomas Merton's *Peace in the Post-Christian Era*, Chapter 15," by Patricia A. Burton. 17 (2004) 14-15.
"Forbidden Book: Thomas Merton's *Peace in the Post-Christian Era*," by Patricia A. Burton. 17 (2004) 27-57.

POETRY
"A Discovery: Thomas Merton's Poetry As Art Song; Compositions by Bryan Beaumont Hays, OSB: A Bibliographical Note," by Anthony Feuerstein. 18 (2005) 72-76.
"Early Reflections in a 'Nothing Place': Three Gethsemani Poems" ["After the Night Office – Gethsemani Abbey"; "The Trappist Cemetery – Gethsemani"; "Spring: Monastery Farm"] by Deborah P. Kehoe. 17 (2004) 61-75.

"From Violence to Silence: The Rhetorical Means and Ends of Thomas Merton's Anti-poetry," by Jeffrey Bilbro. 22 (2009) 120-49.

"'In the Dark before Dawn': Thomas Merton's Mystical Poetics," by Lynn R. Szabo. 22 (2009) 24-40.

"Islands in the Stream: Thomas Merton's Poetry of the Early 1950s" ["A Prelude: For the Feast of St. Agnes"; "Early Mass"; "The Annunciation"; "Elegy for the Monastery Barn";"The Guns of Fort Knox"; "Stranger"] by Patrick F. O'Connell. 22 (2009) 61-105.

"Jewels upon His Forehead: Spiritual Vision in the Poetry and Photography of Thomas Merton," by Marilyn Sunderman. 18 (2005) 167-88.

"Landscapes of Disaster: The War Poems of Thomas Merton" ["Poem 1939";"The Dark Morning"; "Iphigenia: Politics"; "The Night Train"; "Dirge for a Town in France"; "Poem: Light plays like a radio . . ."; "The Pride of the Dead"; "The Bombarded City"; "Lent in a Year of War"] by Patrick F. O'Connell. 19 (2006) 178-233.

"Nurture by Nature: Emblems of Stillness in a Season of Fury" ["Love Winter When the Plant Says Nothing"; "Song for Nobody"; "O Sweet Irrational Worship";"Night-Flowering Cactus"], by Patrick F. O'Connell. 21 (2008) 117-49.

"Pivoting toward Peace: The Engaged Poetics of Thomas Merton and Denise Levertov," by Susan McCaslin. 22 (2009) 189-203.

"The Priestly Imagination: Thomas Merton and the Poetics of Critique," by Michael W. Higgins. 22 (2009) 11-23.

"Thomas Merton's Ecopoetry: Bearing Witness to the Unity of Creation," by Deborah P. Kehoe. 22 (2009) 170-88.

"Wholeness in Thomas Merton's Poetry," by Ross Labrie. 22 (2009) 41-60.

"Wisdom, Sapiential Poetry, and Personalism: Exploring Some of Thomas Merton's Ideas for Values Education," by Ross Keating. 18 (2005) 189-204.

THE SIGN OF JONAS

"Firewatch in the Belly of the Whale: Imagery of Fire, Water, and Place in *The Sign of Jonas*," by David Leigh, SJ. 17 (2004) 153-65.

THE SPIRIT OF SIMPLICITY

"*The Spirit of Simplicity*: Thomas Merton on Simplification of Life," by Paul R. Dekar. 19 (2006) 267-82.

"THE STREET IS FOR CELEBRATION"

"'The Street Is for Celebration': Racial Consciousness and the Eclipse of Childhood in America's Cities," by Christopher Pramuk. 25 (2012) 91-103.

MILOSZ, CZESLAW

"Voices from the Desert: Merton, Milosz and Camus," by David Joseph Belcastro. 25 (2012) 104-12.

MONASTICISM

"Stand on Your Own Feet! Thomas Merton and the Monk without Vows or Walls," by Nass Cannon. 25 (2012) 154-68.

NICHOLAS OF CUSA

"Searching for *Sophia*: Nicholas of Cusa and Thomas Merton," by Joshua Hollmann. 25 (2012) 169-76.

NONVIOLENCE

"Comrades for Peace: Thomas Merton, The Dalai Lama and the Preferential Option for Nonviolence," by Joseph Quinn Raab. 19 (2006) 255-66.

"The God of Peace is Never Glorified by Human Violence: Keynote Address to the International Thomas Merton Society, June 2005," by John Dear. 19 (2006) 24-38.

"Lax, Merton and Rice on War and Peace," by James Harford. 19 (2006) 234-54.

"Machine Culture and the Lone Zone: Discussing Technology and Contemplation at the 1964 Peacemaker Retreat," by Gordon Oyer. 24 (2011) 188-232.

NOUWEN, HENRI

"Thomas Merton, Henri Nouwen, and the Living Gospel," by Robert Ellsberg. 19 (2006) 340-54.

PARADISE

"The Myth of the Fall from Paradise: Thomas Merton and Walker Percy," by John P. Collins. 21 (2008) 150-72.

PARAMAHANSA YOGANANDA

"Thomas Merton and Paramahansa Yogananda: Two Prayerful Mergings of Cult and Culture," by Emile J. Farge. 20 (2007) 164-84.

PEACE

"Christian Perspectives in World Crisis," by Thomas Merton, ed. Patricia A. Burton. 17 (2004) 16-26.

"Thomas Merton, Monk and Prophet of Peace: The Opening Address at the 2005 International Thomas Merton Society General Meeting," by John Eudes Bamberger. 19 (2006) 18-23.

PERCY, WALKER

"The Myth of the Fall from Paradise: Thomas Merton and Walker Percy," by John P. Collins. 21 (2008) 150-72.

"Standing to the Side and Watching: An Introduction and Remembrance about Interviewing Walker Percy," by Victor A. Kramer and Dewey Weis Kramer. 21 (2008) 173-75.

"Two Antiheroes: Meursault and Binx Bolling Viewed through Thomas Merton's Literary Imagination," by John P. Collins. 25 (2012) 113-23.

PHOTOGRAPHY

"Jewels upon His Forehead: Spiritual Vision in the Poetry and Photography of Thomas Merton," by Marilyn Sunderman. 18 (2005) 167-88.

PLACE

"A Bricoleur in the Monastery: Merton's Tactics in a Nothing Place," by Fred W. Herron, 19 (2006) 114-27.

"The Geography of Solitude: Inner Space and the Sense of Place," by Angus F. Stuart. 17 (2004) 76-87.

"Place, Spiritual Anthropology and Sacramentality in Thomas Merton's Later Years," by Hans Gustafson. 25 (2012) 74-90.

"Reality as Sacred Place: The Parallel Insights of Thomas Merton and Henry Bugbee," by Gray Matthews. 17 (2004) 88-119.

PRAYER

"Authentic Identity Is Prayerful Existence," by Thomas Merton. 20 (2007) 16-24.

"Prayer in a High Tech World," by Phillip Thompson. 20 (2007) 185-202.

"Praying the Questions: Merton of Times Square, Last of the Urban Hermits," by David Joseph Belcastro. 20 (2007) 123-50.

"Praying the Psalms: A Layperson's Path to Contemplation," by Kathy Hoffmann. 20 (2007) 38-61.

"'Rising Up Out of the Center': Thomas Merton on Prayer," by Bonnie Thurston. 20 (2007) 109-22.

"'Simply Go In and Pray!': St. Benedict's Oratory In RB 52," by Terrence G. Kardong. 20 (2007) 25-37.

PROPHECY

"Abraham Heschel and Thomas Merton: Prophetic Personalities, Prophetic Friendship," by Edward K. Kaplan. 23 (2010) 106-15.

PSYCHOLOGY

"The Psychology of Hatred and the Role of Early Relationships in Discovering Our True Self," by Michael Sobocinski. 19 (2006) 91-113.

RACE

"Some Points from the Birmingham Non-Violence Movement," by Thomas Merton. 25 (2012) 13-22.

"'The Street Is for Celebration': Racial Consciousness and the Eclipse of Childhood in America's Cities," by Christopher Pramuk. 25 (2012) 91-103.

"Thomas Merton and Racial Reconciliation," by Albert Raboteau. 21 (2008) 13-24.

REINHARDT, AD

"Do I Want a Small Painting? The Correspondence of Thomas Merton and Ad Reinhardt: An Introduction and Commentary," by Roger Lipsey. 18 (2005) 260-314.

RICE, EDWARD

"Lax, Merton and Rice on War and Peace," by James Harford. 19 (2006) 234-54.

SOLITUDE

"The Geography of Solitude: Inner Space and the Sense of Place," by Angus F. Stuart. 17 (2004) 76-87.

TECHNOLOGY

"Contemplation in a Technological Era: Learning from Thomas Merton," by Albert Borgmann. 24 (2011) 54-66.

"Digital Natives and the Digital Self: The Wisdom of Thomas Merton for Millennial Spirituality and Self-Understanding," by Daniel P. Horan, OFM. 24 (2011) 83-111.

"The Heart of the Fire: Technology, Commotion and Contemplation," by Gray Matthews. 24 (2011) 128-49.

"'In the Night of Our Technological Barbarism': Thomas Merton's Light on the Matter," by Kathleen Deignan, CND. 24 (2011) 112-27.

"Machine Culture and the Lone Zone: Discussing Technology and Contemplation at the 1964 Peacemaker Retreat," by Gordon Oyer. 24 (2011) 188-232.

"Questioning the Goal of Biological Immortality: Mertonian Reflections on Living Eternally," Phillip Thompson. 24 (2011) 67-82.

"Technology, Freedom and the Human Person: Some Teen Insights into Merton and Benedict XVI," by Jeffrey T. Kiernan. 24 (2011) 244-55.

"The Technophiliacs," by W. H. Ferry. 24 (2011) 29-38.

"Thomas Merton, Guide to the Right Use of Technology," by Paul R. Dekar. 24 (2011) 150-75.

"What the Machine Produces and What the Machine Destroys: Thomas Merton on Technology," by Paul R. Dekar. 17 (2004) 216-34.

TEILHARD DE CHARDIN, PIERRE
"No Solution in Withdrawal – No Solution in Conforming: Merton, Teilhard, Kung and Curran," by Judith Hunter. 19 (2006) 43-90.

TRUE SELF
"Divining the Inscaped-Landscape: Hopkins, Merton and the Ascent to True Self," by Jeffrey A. Cooper. 18 (2005) 127-39.
"The Psychology of Hatred and the Role of Early Relationships in Discovering Our True Self," by Michael Sobocinski. 19 (2006) 91-113.
"Striving toward Authenticity: Merton's 'True Self' and the Millennial Generation's Search for Identity," by Daniel P. Horan, OFM. 23 (2010) 80-89.

WU, JOHN
"Centennial Vignettes in Homage to My Father," by John Wu, Jr. 19 (2006) 283-310.
"The Thomas Merton – John C. H. Wu Letters: The Lord as Postman," by Lucien Miller. 19 (2006) 142-61.

YUNGBLUT, JUNE
"Terrible Days: Merton/Yungblut Letters and MLK Jr.'s Death," by William Apel. 21 (2008) 25-32.

ZEN
"In the Zen Garden of the Lord: Thomas Merton's Stone Garden," by Roger Lipsey. 21 (2008) 91-105.

The International Thomas Merton Society

The ITMS came into being in 1987 to promote a greater knowledge of the life and writings of Thomas Merton, one of the most influential religious figures of our time. The Society sponsors a biennial conference devoted to Merton and his work and supports the writing of general-interest and scholarly books and articles about Merton. In addition, the ITMS regularly awards grants to researchers and scholarships to young people. It encourages a variety of activities such as Merton retreats. Local Chapters of the ITMS throughout the world reflect a wide range of personal interest and approaches to Thomas Merton.

> *Finding the ITMS has been among the most enriching experiences of my life as a student and teacher of Thomas Merton. None who have been fed by Merton should deny themselves the banquet of the ITMS. None should refuse the Society the fruits of their Merton insights.*
>
> *Walt Chura*
> *Albany, NY*

ITMS Members Benefits

Members of the ITMS receive information on a regular basis about events connected with Thomas Merton at international, national, regional, and local levels. Members receive *The Merton Seasonal* quarterly (which includes the ITMS *Newsletter* twice a year).

An enhanced membership package also includes *The Merton Annual* at a reduced rate. Both publications contain articles and updated bibliographies giving members access to the most recent thinking about Merton. Members are entitled to reduced rates for General Meetings and have access to the rich collection of Merton manuscripts, photographs, drawings, and memorabilia at the Thomas Merton Center at Bellarmine University in Louisville, Kentucky.

ITMS Conferences

The ITMS holds a General Meeting every other year. These forums produce lively exchanges, spiritual renewal and new scholarly Merton research on an international scale.

ITMS Fellowships and Scholaships

Shannon Fellowships

. . . Are awarded annually to enable qualified researchers to visit the Thomas Merton Center archives at Bellarmine University in Louisville, Kentucky, or other repositories of Merton materials, such as Columbia University, Harvard University and St. Bonaventure University. The awards are named in honor of William H. Shannon, founding President of the International Thomas Merton Society.

The ITMS has played an essential role in my studies of Thomas Merton's works, beginning with the Shannon Fellowship which launched my research at the archives in Louisville. Since then, I have met a host of fascinating colleagues who work together to further Merton studies and many friends who share in the causes of peace and spiritual hospitality promoted by the ITMS.

> *Lynn Szabo*
> *Langley, British Columbia*
> *Shannon Fellow*

Daggy Youth/Student Scholarships

. . . Enable young people (ages 14-29) to participate in an ITMS General Meeting, thereby inspiring the next generation of Merton readers and scholars. These scholarships honor the late Robert E. Daggy, founding member and second president of the ITMS.

A fascinating experience to be surrounded by such deep minds and wise souls. Merton is serving as a marvelous vehicle for bringing people of intellect and spirit together to share knowledge, stories, and life. Not least among these were the Daggy scholars, who simply astounded me with their abilities and their concern for our world. No more intriguing and inspiring group of young people have I been a part of.

> *David W. Golemboski*
> *Louisville, Kentucky*
> *Daggy Scholar*

It was a great spiritual blessing for me to have shared this faith affirming experience with such a diverse crowd, people also interested in what Merton was so successful at doing in his own life: transforming the deep silence of faith into real, audible, and tangible action.

> *Rob Peach*
> *Philadelphia, Pennsylvania*
> *Daggy Scholar*

2021